The Writer's Audience

The Writer's Audience
A Reader for Composition

Nancy G. Anderson
Auburn University at Montgomery

Holt, Rinehart and Winston, Inc.
Fort Worth   Chicago   San Francisco   Philadelphia
Montreal   Toronto   London   Sydney   Tokyo

Publisher Ted Buchholz
Acquisitions Editor Michael A. Rosenberg
Developmental Editor Stacy Schoolfield
Project Editor Vicki Young
Production Manager Kathleen Ferguson
Art & Design Supervisor John C. Ritland
Text Designer Ritter & Ritter, Inc.

Library of Congress Cataloging-in-Publication Data

Anderson, Nancy G., 1940–
   The writer's audience: a reader for composition/Nancy G. Anderson.
   ISBN 0-03-028773-1
   1. College readers.   2. English language—Rhetoric.   I. Title.
PE1417.A53   1991   90-42036
808'.0427—dc20

Address editorial correspondence to: 301 Commerce Street, Suite 3700, Forth Worth, TX 76102
Address orders to: 6277 Sea Harbor Drive, Orlando, FL 32887
1-800-782-4479 or 1-800-433-0001 (in Florida)

Printed in the United States of America

1 2 3 4   0 9 0   9 8 7 6 5 4 3 2 1

Holt, Rinehart and Winston, Inc.
The Dryden Press
Saunders College Publishing

Acknowledgments begin on page 316.

*Dedicated to
my students in Advanced Expository Writing.*

PREFACE

Inherent in the definition of *writing*, as a means of communication, is the importance of the reader, the audience. F. L. Lucas, in "What Is Style?," argues that "respect for the reader" is one of the "cornerstones of style." That attentive awareness of audience is not only a matter of style, but also the foundation of effective writing. Writers with this respect for their audiences must select the organization, level of diction, and tone that will, in combination with subject, achieve their purpose. The results will be works that entertain, works that explain or inform, works that challenge, works that persuade. Therefore, writers must ask themselves: what do I want my audience to know? how can I organize the material effectively for my readers? what language will communicate my purpose to my audience? what tone is most appropriate for my intention and audience?

When writing in a diary (or a journal) for ourselves or writing a letter to a close friend, we find that content, organization, language, and tone come together rather automatically because we know our audience intimately. Since the questions writers must ask themselves are easily answered, the writing is easier. But as the audience becomes more remote, less personal, the writing becomes more difficult; we do not know the readers well enough to answer the questions so precisely. Still, an awareness of that unknown audience—professional and lay, young and old, present and future, sympathetic and skeptical—should guide us as writers toward the goal of communication with some, if not all, of that readership.

Students in elementary and secondary grades work on fundamental writing skills—grammar, punctuation, sentence structure, paragraph development, coherence, essay structure. By the time they enter college, they are refining these skills in general types of essays such as comparison and contrast, process, definition, description. All along, they have been discussing the process of writing and the role of the audience. Then as they enter more advanced courses, instructors assume mastery of certain writing skills and make precise assignments: keep a journal of your observations during lab experiments, write an essay explaining . . . , write an essay persuading me about . . . , write a review of . . . , write an annotated bibliography on the subject of . . . , write a research paper about. . . . Students must now apply these writing skills to assignments required by their major professors for a more specialized audience.

These assignments are categories, or forms, of writing that also appear in both scholarly and popular publications.

The authors of the selections in this anthology have used these forms of writing to communicate information to their respective audiences. These authors may have been writing for themselves or for the thousands (or millions) of readers who buy newspapers or popular magazines, or for a more select group of readers interested in scholarly journals or books of personal memoirs. The resultant essays can be classified into the following subgenres, depending on their audience and purpose: autobiographical narratives, expository essays, persuasive essays, reviews, and research studies. Professionals in the fields of art, business, education, law, mass communication, medicine, and the sciences (natural, physical, and social) routinely use these forms of writing to inform or persuade their audiences. Even though technical vocabulary may vary from field to field, the principles of good writing remain constant as writers fulfill the readers' expectations of each type of writing.

Readers of this anthology will find examples of all these specialized forms of writing: autobiography, including diaries, journals, and formal autobiographical essays; exposition; persuasion; a variety of reviews of everything from murder mysteries to art exhibitions and piano recitals; and research essays. There are also selections that can blur the boundary lines between forms: autobiography that is also exposition of an era; exposition that hints of argument in its selection of facts; persuasion that relies on exposition for argument; review that is also autobiography; research that is strong persuasion or exposition. But writers are simply using all the tools available to them to communicate with their intended audiences and achieve their purposes.

The twentieth-century authors of these essays have carefully approached their various subjects, ranging from random thoughts about themselves to analytical studies of controversial scientific theories, and selected the forms, organization, diction, and tone appropriate for their audiences, audiences that range from the most personal to the professional scientific community. The subjects of the essays cover a broad spectrum. Many of the writers have grappled with the subjects or controversies of their day and inform, or persuade, their readers about art and architecture, business ethics, education, evolutionist theory, euthanasia, abortion, censorship, literary canon, murder mysteries, medicine, and mythology. A number of the authors also write about writing, as a subject in itself or within the context of other, seemingly unrelated topics. Through their subjects, drawn from a variety of fields, and the ways in which they are presented, these selections generate discussion about both substance and form.

Within each chapter the essays, on many different subjects of interest to contemporary students of writing, are arranged alphabetically by authors or, if anonymous, by title (with the exception of the multiple reviews of a single work grouped together in Chapter 4). The emphasis on form shows that effective writers in all fields must select the organization, diction, and tone appropriate for their respective audiences. Each selection is independent of others in the same chapter, but reading several works in each section will introduce students to characteristics of each form. In these selections students see how professional writers have fulfilled the expectations—or demands—of a variety of audiences. The authors of works included in this anthology have the requisite "respect for the reader."

This textbook is designed for experienced instructors who want to develop their own courses and for writing students who, building on past writing experience, want to develop their skills by applying them to specific forms used in many fields of study. Thus, the philosophic foundation of this textbook reflects its unifying theme of "respect for the reader."

The following reviewers offered valuable comments throughout the development of the text: Larry Andrews, Kent State University; Ernest Lee, Wingate College; Bruce Appleby, Southern Illinois University; Cynthia Bates, University of California at Davis; Patricia E. Connors, Memphis State University; Margaret Tebo-Messino, Winthrop College; Harriet Williams, College of Applied Professional Sciences; Priscilla Tate, Texas Christian University; John Ruszkiewicz, University of Texas at Austin.

CONTENTS

Chapter One
AUTOBIOGRAPHY   1

Maya Angelou, *I Know Why the Caged Bird Sings*   3
Russell Baker, *Growing Up*   14
James Baldwin, *Notes of a Native Son*   20
Anatole Broyard, *Moving Day*   24
Freeman Dyson, *A Scientific Apprenticeship*   29
Etty Hillesum, *An Interrupted Life*   38
Richard Marius, *The Home That Lies Always in Memory*   41
Tom Paulk, *Thoughts on Myself That I'm Willing to Share*   50
Scottie Fitzgerald Smith, *Foreword*   51
John Edgar Wideman, *To Robby*   55

Chapter Questions   56

Chapter Two
EXPOSITION   58

James Agee, *At the Forks*   61
Susan Dentzer with Maggie Malone, *M.B.A.'s Learn a Human
      Touch*   65
Ron Fimrite, *When the World Series Became "A Modest Little Sporting
      Event"*   69
Garrison Keillor, *How It Was in America a Week Ago Tuesday*   73
Konrad Z. Lorenz, *The Language of Animals*   79
Richard Marius, *How I Write*   88
John McPhee, *The Headmaster*   96
Money Majors   105
Much About Wallace Has Changed As He Campaigns for Nomination
      109
Saul Pett, *JFK Slaying "Cut the Heart of a Nation"*   111
John Stone, *Cadence of the Heart* and *The Wolf Inside*   115
James Thurber, *How To Tell A Fine Old Wine*   121

Chapter Questions   124

Chapter Three
PERSUASION   125

Pearl S. Buck, *America's Medieval Women*   127
Gerald Clarke, *The Need for New Myths*   137
Robert Coles, *Gatsby at the B School*   141
Susan Dudley, *Abortion Issues Affect Real Women in Real World*   147
Henry Louis Gates, Jr., *Whose Canon Is It, Anyway?*   150
F. L. Lucas, *What Is Style?*   157
Judith H. Paterson, *Let the Dying Die Gracefully*   165
Reynolds Price, *The Heroes of Our Times*   167
William Raspberry, *The Money Chase*   171
William Safire, *Euphemism*   173
R. Z. Sheppard, reported by John M. Scott and Janice C. Simpson, *The Decline of Editing*   176
Daphne Simpkins, *Don't They Know Education Takes Evil Out of Evolution?*   182
James Thurber, *Which*   185
Frank Lloyd Wright, *Organic Architecture*   187
Fareed Zakaria, *Ethics for Greedheads*   191

Chapter Questions   195

Chapter Four
REVIEW   196

Reviews of *The Panda's Thumb* by Stephen Jay Gould   199
  Books Fit for Rooftop Delivery,   200
  H. Jack Geiger, *Turning Nature's Sprawl Into Literature*   200
  Ashley Montagu, *More Variations on a Biological Theme*   203
Reviews of *A Taste for Death* by P. D. James   205
  James Campbell, *Looking into the Murky and Murderous*   206
  Carl E. Ericson, in *Theology Today*   208
  Christopher Lehmann-Haupt, Books of *the Times*   211
  J. D. Reed, *Crime's Le Carré*   213
The Editors of *Time, Disney's Cinesymphony*   214
Ada Louise Huxtable, *A Major Chicago Firm at Its Centennial*   218
Kenneth Langbell, *A Humid Recital Stirs Bangkok*   221
Melvin Maddocks, *Babel Builders*   223
H. L. Mencken, *Gamalielese*   225
Judith H. Paterson, *The Modern Way of Dying*   228
John Russell, *England Rediscovers Its Age of Chivalry*   230
Zelda Sayre [Fitzgerald], *The Beautiful and Damned:* Friend Husband's Latest   233
Daphne Simpkins, *Book Won't Mystify*   236

Chapter Questions   237

Chapter Five
RESEARCH 238

Bob Coleman, *Science Writing* 241

Paul Fussell, *Killing, in Verse and Prose* 247

Stephen Jay Gould, *Women's Brains* 257

Randi Hacker and Jackie Kaufman, *The Sisters Brontë and The Sisters Collins* 263

Edward B. Jenkinson, *The New Age of Schoolbook Protest* 267

Dumas Malone, *At the College, 1760–1762* 274

Horace Miner, *Body Ritual Among the Nacirema* 285

James L. Muyskens, *Acting Alone* 290

Eugenie C. Scott and Henry P. Cole, *The Elusive Scientific Basis of Creation "Science"* 294

Perry A. Zirkel, *Narrowing the Spectrum of Student Expression* 309

Chapter Questions 313

Author Index 314

Selection Index 315

Acknowledgments 316

THEMATIC CONTENTS

ART AND MUSIC

Editors of *Time, Disney's Cinesymphony*   214
Huxtable, Ada Louise, *A Major Chicago Firm at Its Centennial*
   218
Langbell, Kenneth, *A Humid Recital Stirs Bangkok*   221
Russell, John, *England Rediscovers Its Age of Chivalry*   230
Wright, Frank Lloyd, *Organic Architecture*   187

CULTURE

Agee, James, *At the Forks*   61
Angelou, Maya, *I Know Why the Caged Bird Sings*   3
Baker, Russell, *Growing Up*   14
Baldwin, James, *Notes of a Native Son*   20
Broyard, Anatole, *Moving Day*   24
Gates, Henry Lewis, Jr., *Whose Canon Is It, Anyway?*   150
Hacker, Randi and Jackie Kaufman, *The Sisters Brontë and The
   Sisters Collins*   263
Paulk, Tom, *Thoughts on Myself That I'm Willing to Share*   50
Smith, Scottie Fitzgerald, *Foreword*   51
Wideman, John Edgar, *To Robby*   55
Wright, Frank Lloyd, *Organic Architecture*   187

EDUCATION

Coles, Robert, *Gatsby at the B School*   141
Dentzer, Susan with Maggie Malone, *M.B.A.'s Learn a Human
   Touch*   65
Gates, Henry Lewis, Jr., *Whose Canon Is It, Anyway?*   150
Jenkinson, Edward B., *The New Age of Schoolbook Protest*   267
Maddocks, Melvin, *Babel Builders*   223
McPhee, John, *The Headmaster*   96
Money Majors   105
Raspberry, William, *The Money Chase*   171

Simpkins, Daphne, *Don't They Know Education Takes Evil Out of Evolution?* 182
Wright, Frank Lloyd, *Organic Architecture* 187
Zakaria, Fareed, *Ethics for Greedheads* 191
Zirkel, Perry A., *Narrowing the Spectrum of Student Expression* 309

FAMILY AND RELATIONSHIPS

Angelou, Maya, *I Know Why the Caged Bird Sings* 3
Baker, Russell, *Growing Up* 14
Baldwin, James, *Notes of a Native Son* 20
Buck, Pearl S., *America's Medieval Women* 127
Marius, Richard, *The Home That Lies Always in Memory* 41
Paterson, Judith H., *The Modern Way of Dying* 228
Smith, Scottie Fitzgerald, *Foreword* 51
Wideman, John Edgar, *To Robby* 55

GROWING UP

Angelou, Maya, *I Know Why the Caged Bird Sings* 3
Baker, Russell, *Growing Up* 14
Baldwin, James, *Notes of a Native Son* 20
Marius, Richard, *The Home that Lies Always in Memory* 41

HISTORY AND SOCIAL COMMENT

Agee, James, *At the Forks* 61
Buck, Pearl S. *America's Medieval Women* 127
Clarke, Gerald, *The Need for New Myths* 137
Dudley, Susan, *Abortion Issues Affect Real Women in Real World* 147
Fimrite, Ron, *When the World Series Became a "Modest Little Sporting Event"* 69
Hillesum, Etty, *An Interrupted Life* 38
Keillor, Garrison, *How It Was in America a Week Ago Tuesday* 73
Malone, Dumas, *At the College, 1760–1762* 274
McPhee, John, *The Headmaster* 96
Mencken, H. L., *Gamalielese* 225
Much About Wallace Has Changed As He Campaigns for Nomination 109
Paterson, Judith H., *Let the Dying Die Gracefully* 165
Pett, Saul, *JFK Slaying "Cut the Heart of a Nation"* 111
Price, Reynolds, *The Heroes of Our Times* 167
Raspberry, William, *The Money Chase* 171
Zakaria, Fareed, *Ethics for Greedheads* 191
Zirkel, Perry A., *Narrowing the Spectrum of Student Expression* 309

SATIRE

Hacker, Randi and Jackie Kaufman, *The Sisters Brontë and The Sisters Collins*   263
Langbell, Kenneth, *A Humid Recital Stirs Bangkok*   221
Mencken, H. L., *Gamalielese*   225
Miner, Horace, *Body Ritual Among the Nacirema*   285
Thurber, James, *How to Tell a Fine Old Wine*   121
Thurber, James, *Which*   185

SCIENCE

Coleman, Bob, *Science Writing*   241
Dyson, Freeman, *A Scientific Apprenticeship*   29
Gould, Stephen Jay, *Women's Brains*   257
Lorenz, Konrad Z., *The Language of Animals*   79
Miner, Horace, *Body Ritual Among the Nacirema*   285
Muyskens, James L., *Acting Alone*   290
Paterson, Judith H., *Let the Dying Die Gracefully*   165
Paterson, Judith H., *The Modern Way of Dying*   228
Reviews of *The Panda's Thumb* by Stephen J. Gould   199
Scott, Eugenie C. and Henry P. Cole, *The Elusive Scientific Basis of Creation "Science"*   294
Stone, John, *Cadence of the Heart* and *The Wolf Inside*   115

WOMEN

Angelou, Maya, *I Know Why the Caged Bird Sings*   3
Buck, Pearl S., *America's Medieval Women*   127
Dudley, Susan, *Abortion Issues Affect Real Women in Real World*   147
Gould, Stephen Jay, *Women's Brains*   257
Hacker, Randi and Jackie Kaufman, *The Sisters Brontë and The Sisters Collins*   263
Hillesum, Etty, *An Interrupted Life*   38

WRITING AND READING

Baldwin, James, *Notes of a Native Son*   20
Broyard, Anatole, *Moving Day*   24
Clarke, Gerald, *The Need for New Myths*   137
Coles, Robert, *Gatsby at the B School*   141
Coleman, Bob, *Science Writing*   241
Editors of *Time*, *Disney's Cinesymphony*   214
Fussell, Paul, *Killing, in Verse and Prose*   247
Gates, Henry Lewis, J., *Whose Canon It Is, Anyway*   150

Hacker, Randi and Jackie Kaufman, *The Sisters Brontë and the Sisters Collins*   263

Hillesum, Etty, *An Interrupted Life*   38

Lucas, F. L., *What Is Style?*   157

Marius, Richard, *How I Write*   88

Reviews of *The Panda's Thumb* by Stephen J. Gould   199

Reviews of *A Taste For Death* by P. D. James   205

Safire, William, *Euphemism*   173

Sayre [Fitzgerald], Zelda, *The Beautiful and Damned:* Friend Husband's Latest   233

Sheppard, R. Z., reported by John M. Scott and Janice C. Simpson *The Decline of Editing*   176

Simpkins, Daphne, *Book Won't Mystify*   236

Stone, John, *The Wolf Inside*   115

Thurber, James, *Which*   185

Chapter One
AUTOBIOGRAPHY

R eaders are basically curious about the lives of others, especially when people tell their own stories. In recent years autobiographies by Shirley MacLaine, Elizabeth Taylor, Bill Cosby, Margaret Mead, Russell Baker, and Elie Wiesel have been widely read. James Herriot's memoirs are a best-selling book series and a popular television show. Even Garfield the Cat has debated writing a book about his life but concluded "there are already too many autobiographies out there."

Despite our interest in others' autobiographies, and our interest in ourselves, we balk at *writing* autobiographies. Why would anyone want to read about my dull (monotonous, mundane, trivial—whatever) life? But on occasion we must tell our own story, or some part of it. To write an effective autobiography, we must set aside this reluctance and consider our readers: what do they *need* to know about me? what do they *want* to know? what about my life might inform or enlighten my readers? what can they learn from my story, my life, my world?

Autobiography is essentially exposition, the recording of one's own story for an audience, whether for only one's self, the general reading public, an admissions committee, or a personnel director. But there is, oftentimes, an undercurrent of persuasion (understand me, like me, appreciate my family or my world, select me).

In addition to telling the author's life, an autobiography may capture the author's environment—home, family, possessions, town, state, and national or international events as they affect individuals. Thus, in personal narratives readers not only read about sensational, humorous, ordinary, exciting, or tragic lives but also, from them, learn about history, politics, sociology, professions, customs, dress, or important people. Diaries and journals are often excellent sources for details about local, national, and international events (where were you when you learned of John F. Kennedy's assassination or the Challenger disaster?), or at least for personal perceptions of these events. An entry in a used-book catalogue summarizes some of the added benefits of an autobiography: ". . . not only the autobiography of a rural physician with the trials and tribulations (and joys) of a rural medical practice, it is also a local history of Pickens County [Alabama] with page after page of anecdotes, stories and folklore about local citizens and institutions." (The price of this "almost unknown book" was $135.) John Chancellor described Russell Baker's *Growing*

Up as "an American memoir," praising Baker for capturing American life in the twentieth century through personal narrative.

An autobiography can be anything from personal thoughts recorded in a diary to a chronological narrative written on an application, an introspective essay about an event in one's life, or a public account written for an audience eager to know more about public figures. The selections in this anthology include private thoughts in a diary, family narratives, school memories, and even a protest against pragmatic autobiographical writing for job applications. Several of these works capture details of twentieth-century life, from funny to horrible. These varied purposes emphasize equally varied audiences. Etty Hillesum initially wrote for herself and, in so doing, recorded details of the Holocaust. In contrast, Scottie Fitzgerald Smith wrote for fans of her famous parents, the present and future readers of the works by Scott and Zelda Fitzgerald. In addition to setting down her own memories, prompted by treasures in her attic, she quotes from her mother's writing to provide yet another autobiographical perspective on "the paradise years" of the Jazz Age. Thus, she fulfills the expectations of her audience both by reminiscing about her parents and by giving readers her mother's reflections on the same period.

In the "Author's Preface" to *Disturbing the Universe*, Freeman Dyson tells a story that comments upon the relationship between author and audience of autobiography: "The physicist Leo Szilard once announced to his friend Hans Bethe that he was thinking of keeping a diary: 'I don't intend to publish it; I am merely going to record the facts for the information of God.' 'Don't you think God knows the facts?' Bethe asked. 'Yes,' said Szilard. 'He knows the facts, but He does not know *this version of the facts.*' "

Autobiography is *our* version of the facts, recorded for *our* audience, whether that audience be ourselves, our families, selection committees, or the general reading public.

I Know Why the Caged Bird Sings

MAYA ANGELOU

The dedication in Maya Angelou's autobiography identifies a special audience for her book: ". . . all the strong black birds of promise who defy the odds and gods and sing their songs." Her story of growing up in the segregated south is an account of one who has succeeded in her defiance.

The opening sentence of Chapter 1 (there is a brief narrative preceding this chapter), "When I was three . . . ," is a variation on the stereotypical "I was born" introduction. From there her organization is essentially chronological, but the book is much more than a recital of what happened when. In Chapters 1–4, she introduces her readers to herself, her family, life in her town, education, religion, and most significantly, the line dividing blacks and whites.

Original publication: *I Know Why the Caged Bird Sings*. New York: Random House, 1970.

1

WHEN I was three and Bailey four, we had arrived in the musty little town, wearing tags on our wrists which instructed—"To Whom It May Concern"— that we were Marguerite and Bailey Johnson Jr., from Long Beach, California, en route to Stamps, Arkansas, c/o Mrs. Annie Henderson.

Our parents had decided to put an end to their calamitous marriage, and Father shipped us home to his mother. A porter had been charged with our welfare—he got off the train the next day in Arizona—and our tickets were pinned to my brother's inside coat pocket.

I don't remember much of the trip, but after we reached the segregated southern part of the journey, things must have looked up. Negro passengers, who always traveled with loaded lunch boxes, felt sorry for "the poor little motherless darlings" and plied us with cold fried chicken and potato salad.

Years later I discovered that the United States had been crossed thousands of times by frightened Black children traveling alone to their newly affluent parents in Northern cities, or back to grandmothers in Southern towns when the urban North reneged on its economic promises.

The town reacted to us as its inhabitants had reacted to all things new before our coming. It regarded us a while without curiosity but with caution, and after we were seen to be harmless (and children) it closed in around us, as a real mother embraces a stranger's child. Warmly, but not too familiarly.

We lived with our grandmother and uncle in the rear of the Store (it was always spoken of with a capital *s*), which she had owned some twenty-five years.

Early in the century, Momma (we soon stopped calling her Grandmother) sold lunches to the sawmen in the lumberyard (east Stamps) and the seedmen at the cotton gin (west Stamps). Her crisp meat pies and cool lemonade, when joined to her miraculous ability to be in two places at the same time, assured her business success. From being a mobile lunch counter, she set up a stand between the two points of fiscal interest and supplied the workers' needs for a few years. Then she had the Store built in the heart of the Negro area. Over the years it became the lay center of activities in town. On Saturdays, barbers sat their customers in the shade on the porch of the Store, and troubadours on their ceaseless crawlings through the South leaned across its benches and sang their sad songs of The Brazos while they played juice harps and cigar-box guitars.

The formal name of the store was the Wm. Johnson General Merchandise Store. Customers could find food staples, a good variety of colored thread, mash for hogs, corn for chickens, coal oil for lamps, light bulbs for the wealthy, shoestrings, hair dressing, balloons, and flower seeds. Anything not visible had only to be ordered.

Until we became familiar enough to belong to the Store and it to us, we were locked up in a Fun House of Things where the attendant had gone home for life.

Each year I watched the field across from the Store turn caterpillar green, then gradually frosty white. I knew exactly how long it would be before the big wagons would pull into the front yard and load on the cotton pickers at daybreak to carry them to the remains of slavery's plantations.

During the picking season my grandmother would get out of bed at four o'clock (she never used an alarm clock) and creak down to her knees and chant in a sleep-filled voice, "Our Father, thank you for letting me see this New Day. Thank you that you didn't allow the bed I lay on last night to be my cooling board, nor my blanket my winding sheet. Guide my feet this day along the straight and narrow, and help me to put a bridle on my tongue. Bless this house, and everybody in it. Thank you, in the name of your Son, Jesus Christ, Amen."

Before she had quite arisen, she called our names and issued orders, and pushed her large feet into homemade slippers and across the bare lye-washed wooden floor to light the coal-oil lamp.

The lamplight in the Store gave a soft make-believe feeling to our world which made me want to whisper and walk about on tiptoe. The odors of onions and oranges and kerosene had been mixing all night and wouldn't be disturbed until the wooded slat was removed from the door and the early morning air forced its way in with the bodies of people who had walked miles to reach the pickup place.

"Sister, I'll have two cans of sardines."

"I'm gonna work so fast today I'm gonna make you look like you standing still."

"Lemme have a hunk uh cheese and some sody crackers."

"Just gimme a coupla them fat peanut paddies." That would be from a picker who was taking his lunch. The greasy brown paper sack was stuck behind the bib of his overalls. He'd use the candy as a snack before the noon sun called the workers to rest.

In those tender mornings the Store was full of laughing, joking, boasting and bragging. One man was going to pick two hundred pounds of cotton, and another three hundred. Even the children were promising to bring home fo' bits and six bits.

The champion picker of the day before was the hero of the dawn. If he prophesied that the cotton in today's field was going to be sparse and stick to the bolls like glue, every listener would grunt a hearty agreement.

The sound of the empty cotton sacks dragging over the floor and the murmurs of waking people were sliced by the cash register as we rang up the five-cent sales.

If the morning sounds and smells were touched with the supernatural, the late afternoon had all the features of the normal Arkansas life. In the dying sunlight the people dragged, rather than their empty cotton sacks.

Brought back to the Store, the pickers would step out of the backs of trucks and fold down, dirt-disappointed, to the ground. No matter how much they had picked, it wasn't enough. Their wages wouldn't even get them out of debt to my grandmother, not to mention the staggering bill that waited on them at the white commissary downtown.

The sounds of the new morning had been replaced with grumbles about cheating houses, weighted scales, snakes, skimpy cotton and dusty rows. In later years I was to confront the stereotyped picture of gay song-singing cotton pickers with such inordinate rage that I was told even by fellow Blacks that my paranoia was embarrassing. But I had seen the fingers cut by the mean little cotton bolls, and I had witnessed the backs and shoulders and arms and legs resisting any further demands.

Some of the workers would leave their sacks at the Store to be picked up the following morning, but a few had to take them home for repairs. I winced to picture them sewing the coarse material under a coal-oil lamp with fingers stiffening from the day's work. In too few hours they would have to walk back to Sister Henderson's Store, get vittles and load, again, onto the trucks. Then they would face another day of trying to earn enough for the whole year with the heavy knowledge that they were going to end the season as they started it. Without the money or credit necessary to sustain a family for three months. In cotton-picking time the late afternoons revealed the harshness of Black Southern life, which in the early morning had been softened by nature's blessing of grogginess, forgetfulness and the soft lamplight.

2

WHEN Bailey was six and I a year younger, we used to rattle off the times tables with the speed I was later to see Chinese children in San Francisco employ on their abacuses. Our summer-gray pot-bellied stove bloomed rosy red during winter, and became a severe disciplinarian threat if we were so foolish as to indulge in making mistakes.

Uncle Willie used to sit, like a giant black Z (he had been crippled as a child), and hear us testify to the Lafayette County Training Schools' abilities. His face pulled down on the left side, as if a pulley had been attached to his lower teeth, and his left hand was only a mite bigger than Bailey's, but on the second mistake or on the third hesitation his big overgrown right hand would catch one of us behind the collar, and in the same moment would thrust the culprit toward the dull red heater, which throbbed like a devil's toothache. We were never burned, although once I might have been when I was so terrified I tried to jump onto the stove to remove the possibility of its remaining a threat. Like most children, I thought if I could face the worst danger voluntarily, and *triumph*, I would forever have power over it. But in my case of sacrificial effort I was thwarted. Uncle Willie held tight to my dress and I only got close enough to smell the clean dry scent of hot iron. We learned the times tables without understanding their grand principle, simply because we had the capacity and no alternative.

The tragedy of lameness seems so unfair to children that they are embarrassed in its presence. And they, most recently off nature's mold, sense that they have only narrowly missed being another of her jokes. In relief at the narrow escape, they vent their emotions in impatience and criticism of the unlucky cripple.

Momma related times without end, and without any show of emotion, how Uncle Willie had been dropped when he was three years old by a woman who was minding him. She seemed to hold no rancor against the baby-sitter, nor for her just God who allowed the accident. She felt it necessary to explain over and over again to those who knew the story by heart that he wasn't "born that way."

In our society, where two-legged, two-armed strong Black men were able at best to eke out only the necessities of life, Uncle Willie, with his starched shirts, shined shoes and shelves full of food, was the whipping boy and butt of jokes of the underemployed and underpaid. Fate not only disabled him but laid a double-tiered barrier in his path. He was also proud and sensitive. Therefore he couldn't pretend that he wasn't crippled, nor could he deceive himself that people were not repelled by his defect.

Only once in all the years of trying not to watch him, I saw him pretend to himself and others that he wasn't lame.

Coming home from school one day, I saw a dark car in our front yard. I rushed in to find a strange man and woman (Uncle Willie said later they were schoolteachers from Little Rock) drinking Dr. Pepper in the cool of the Store. I sensed a wrongness around me, like an alarm clock that had gone off without being set.

I knew it couldn't be the strangers. Not frequently, but often enough, travelers pulled off the main road to buy tobacco or soft drinks in the only Negro store in Stamps. When I looked at Uncle Willie, I knew what was pulling my mind's coattails. He was standing erect behind the counter, not leaning forward or resting on the small shelf that had been built for him. Erect. His eyes seemed to hold me with a mixture of threats and appeal.

I dutifully greeted the strangers and roamed my eyes around for his walking stick. It was nowhere to be seen. He said, "Uh . . . this this . . . this . . . uh, my niece. She's . . . uh . . . just come from school." Then to the couple—"You know . . . how, uh, children are . . . th-th-these days . . . they play all d-d-day at school and c-c-can't wait to get home and pl-play some more."

The people smiled, very friendly.

He added, "Go on out and pl-play, Sister."

The lady laughed in a soft Arkansas voice and said, "Well, you know, Mr. Johnson, they say, you're only a child once. Have you children of your own?"

Uncle Willie looked at me with an impatience I hadn't seen in his face even when he took thirty minutes to loop the laces over his high-topped shoes. "I . . . I thought I told you to go . . . go outside and play."

Before I left I saw him lean back on the shelves of Garret Snuff, Prince Albert and Spark Plug chewing tobacco.

"No, ma'am . . . no ch-children and no wife." He tried a laugh. "I have an old m-m-mother and my brother's t-two children to l-look after."

I didn't mind his using us to make himself look good. In fact, I would have pretended to be his daughter if he wanted me to. Not only did I not feel any loyalty to my own father, I figured that if I had been Uncle Willie's child I would have received much better treatment.

The couple left after a few minutes, and from the back of the house I watched the red car scare chickens, raise dust and disappear toward Magnolia.

Uncle Willie was making his way down the long shadowed aisle between the shelves and the counter—hand over hand, like a man climbing out of a dream. I stayed quiet and watched him lurch from one side, bumping to the other, until he reached the coal-oil tank. He put his hand behind that dark recess and took his cane in the strong fist and shifted his weight on the wooden support. He thought he had pulled it off.

I'll never know why it was important to him that the couple (he said later that he'd never seen them before) would take a picture of a whole Mr. Johnson back to Little Rock.

He must have tired of being crippled, as prisoners tire of penitentiary bars and the guilty tire of blame. The high-topped shoes and the cane, his uncontrollable muscles and thick tongue, and the looks he suffered of either contempt or pity had simply worn him out, and for one afternoon, one part of an afternoon, he wanted no part of them.

I understood and felt closer to him at that moment than ever before or since.

During these years in Stamps, I met and fell in love with William Shakespeare. He was my first white love. Although I enjoyed and respected Kipling, Poe, Butler, Thackeray and Henley, I saved my young and loyal passion for Paul Lawrence Dunbar, Langston Hughes, James Weldon Johnson and W.E.B. Du Bois' "Litany at Atlanta." But it was Shakespeare who said, "When in disgrace with fortune and men's eyes." It was a state with which I felt myself most familiar. I pacified myself about his whiteness by saying that after all he had been dead so long it couldn't matter to anyone any more.

Bailey and I decided to memorize a scene from *The Merchant of Venice*, but we realized that Momma would question us about the author and that we'd have to tell her that Shakespeare was white, and it wouldn't matter to her whether he was dead or not. So we chose "The Creation" by James Weldon Johnson instead.

3

WEIGHING the half-pounds of flour, excluding the scoop, and depositing them dust-free into the thin paper sacks held a simple kind of adventure for me. I developed an eye for measuring how full a silver-looping ladle of flour, mash, meal, sugar or corn had to be to push the scale indicator over to eight ounces or one pound. When I was absolutely accurate our appreciative customers used to admire: "Sister Henderson sure got some smart grandchildrens." If I was off in the Store's favor, the eagle-eyed women would say, "Put some more in that sack, child. Don't you try to make your profit offa me."

Then I would quietly but persistently punish myself. For every bad judgment, the fine was no silver-wrapped Kisses, the sweet chocolate drops that I loved more than anything in the world, except Bailey. And maybe canned pineapples. My obsession with pineapples nearly drove me mad. I dreamt of the days when I would be grown and able to buy a whole carton for myself alone.

Although the syrupy golden rings sat in their exotic cans on our shelves year round, we only tasted them during Christmas. Momma used the juice to make almost-black fruit cakes. Then she lined heavy soot-encrusted iron skillets with the pineapple rings for rich upside-down cakes. Bailey and I received one slice each, and I carried mine around for hours, shredding off the fruit until nothing was left except the perfume on my fingers. I'd like to think that my desire for pineapples was so sacred that I wouldn't allow myself to steal a can (which was possible) and eat it alone out in the garden, but I'm certain that I must have weighed the possibility of the scent exposing me and didn't have the nerve to attempt it.

Until I was thirteen and left Arkansas for good, the Store was my favorite place to be. Alone and empty in the mornings, it looked like an unopened present from a stranger. Opening the front doors was pulling the ribbon off the unexpected gift. The light would come in softly (we faced north), easing itself over the shelves of mackerel, salmon, tobacco, thread. It fell flat on the big vat of lard and by noontime during the summer the grease had softened to a thick soup. Whenever I walked into the Store in the afternoon, I sensed that it was tired. I alone could hear the slow pulse of its job half done. But just before bedtime, after numerous people had walked in and out, had argued over their bills, or joked about their neighbors, or just dropped in "to give Sister Henderson a 'Hi y'all,' " the promise of magic mornings returned to the Store and spread itself over the family in washed life waves.

Momma opened boxes of crispy crackers and we sat around the meat block at the rear of the Store. I sliced onions, and Bailey opened two or even three cans of sardines and allowed their juice of oil and fishing boats to ooze down and around the sides. That was supper. In the evening, when we were alone like that, Uncle Willie didn't stutter or shake or give any indication that he had an "affliction." It seemed that the peace of a day's ending was an assurance that the covenant God made with children, Negroes and the crippled was still in effect.

Throwing scoops of corn to the chickens and mixing sour dry mash with leftover food and oily dish water for the hogs were among our evening chores. Bailey and I sloshed down twilight trails to the pig pens, and standing on the first fence rungs we poured down the unappealing concoctions to our grateful hogs. They mashed their tender pink snouts down into the slop, and rooted and grunted their satisfaction. We always grunted a reply only half in jest. We were also grateful that we had concluded the dirtiest of chores and had only gotten the evil-smelling swill on our shoes, stockings, feet and hands.

Late one day, as we were attending to the pigs, I heard a horse in the front yard (it really should have been called a driveway, except that there was nothing to drive into it), and ran to find out who had come riding up on a Thursday evening when even Mr. Steward, the quiet, bitter man who owned a riding horse, would be resting by his warm fire until the morning called him out to turn over his field.

The used-to-be sheriff sat rakishly astraddle his horse. His nonchalance was meant to convey his authority and power over even dumb animals. How much more capable he would be with Negroes. It went without saying.

His twang jogged in the brittle air. From the side of the Store, Bailey and I heard him say to Momma, "Annie, tell Willie he better lay low tonight. A crazy nigger messed with a white lady today. Some of the boys'll be coming over here later." Even after the slow drag of years, I remember the sense of fear which filled my mouth with hot, dry air, and made my body light.

The "boys"? Those cement faces and eyes of hate that burned the clothes off you if they happened to see you lounging on the main street downtown on Saturday. Boys? It seemed that youth had never happened to them. Boys? No, rather men who were covered with graves' dust and age without beauty or learning. The ugliness and rottenness of old abominations.

If on Judgment Day I were summoned by St. Peter to give testimony to the used-to-be sheriff's act of kindness, I would be unable to say anything in his behalf. His confidence that my uncle and every other Black man who heard of the Klan's coming ride would scurry under their houses to hide in chicken droppings was too humiliating to hear. Without waiting for Momma's thanks, he rode out of the yard, sure that things were as they should be and that he was a gentle squire, saving those deserving serfs from the laws of the land, which he condoned.

Immediately, while his horse's hoofs were still loudly thudding the ground, Momma blew out the coal-oil lamps. She had a quiet, hard talk with Uncle Willie and called Bailey and me into the Store.

We were told to take the potatoes and onions out of their bins and knock out the dividing walls that kept them apart. Then with a tedious and fearful slowness Uncle Willie gave me his rubber-tipped cane and bent down to get into the now-enlarged empty bin. It took forever before he lay down flat, and then we covered him with potatoes and onions, layer upon layer, like a casserole. Grandmother knelt praying in the darkened Store.

It was fortunate that the "boys" didn't ride into our yard that evening and insist that Momma open the Store. They would have surely found Uncle Willie and just as surely lynched him. He moaned the whole night through as if he had, in fact, been guilty of some heinous crime. The heavy sounds pushed their way up out of the blanket of vegetables and I pictured his mouth pulling down on the right side and his saliva flowing into the eyes of new potatoes and waiting there like dew drops for the warmth of morning.

4

WHAT sets one Southern town apart from another, or from a Northern town or hamlet, or city high-rise? The answer must be the experience shared between the unknowing majority (it) and the knowing minority (you). All of childhood's unanswered questions must finally be passed back to the town and answered there. Heroes and bogey men, values and dislikes, are first encountered and labeled in that early environment. In later years they change faces, places and maybe races, tactics, intensities and goals, but beneath those penetrable masks they wear forever the stocking-capped faces of childhood.

Mr. McElroy, who lived in the big rambling house next to the Store, was very tall and broad, and although the years had eaten away the flesh from his shoulders, they had not, at the time of my knowing him, gotten to his high stomach, or his hands or feet.

He was the only Negro I knew, except for the school principal and the visiting teachers, who wore matching pants and jackets. When I learned that men's clothes were sold like that and called suits, I remember thinking that somebody had been very bright, for it made men look less manly, less threatening and a little more like women.

Mr. McElroy never laughed, and seldom smiled, and to his credit was the fact that he liked to talk to Uncle Willie. He never went to church, which Bailey and I thought also proved he was a very courageous person. How great it would be to grow up like that, to be able to stare religion down, especially living next door to a woman like Momma.

I watched him with the excitement of expecting him to do anything at any time. I never tired of this, or became disappointed or disenchanted with him, although from the perch of age, I see him now as a very simple and uninteresting man who sold patent medicine and tonics to the less sophisticated people in towns (villages) surrounding the metropolis of Stamps.

There seemed to be an understanding between Mr. McElroy and Grandmother. This was obvious to us because he never chased us off his land. In summer's late sunshine I often sat under the chinaberry tree in his yard, surrounded by the bitter aroma of its fruit and lulled by the drone of flies that fed on the berries. He sat in a slotted swing on his porch, rocking in his brown three-piece, his wide Panama nodding in time with the whir of insects.

One greeting a day was all that could be expected from Mr. McElroy. After his "Good morning, child," or "Good afternoon, child," he never said a word, even if I met him again on the road in front of his house or down by the well, or ran into him behind the house escaping in a game of hide-and-seek.

He remained a mystery in my childhood. A man who owned his land and the big many-windowed house with a porch that clung to its sides all around the house. An independent Black man. A near anachronism in Stamps.

Bailey was the greatest person in my world. And the fact that he was my brother, my only brother, and I had no sisters to share him with, was such good fortune that it made me want to live a Christian life just to show God that I was grateful. Where I was big, elbowy and grating, he was small, graceful and smooth. When I was described by our playmates as being shit color, he was lauded for his velvet-black skin. His hair fell down in black curls, and my head was covered with black steel wool. And yet he loved me.

When our elders said unkind things about my features (my family was handsome to a point of pain for me), Bailey would wink at me from across the room, and I knew that it was a matter of time before he would take revenge. He would allow the old ladies to finish wondering how on earth I came about, then he would ask, in a voice like cooling bacon grease, "Oh Mizeriz Coleman, how is your son? I saw him the other day, and he looked sick enough to die."

Aghast, the ladies would ask, "Die? From what? He ain't sick."

And in a voice oilier than the one before, he'd answer with a straight face, "From the Uglies."

I would hold my laugh, bite my tongue, grit my teeth and very seriously erase even the touch of a smile from my face. Later, behind the house by the black-walnut tree, we'd laugh and laugh and howl.

Bailey could count on very few punishments for his consistently outrageous behavior, for he was the pride of the Henderson/Johnson family.

His movements, as he was later to describe those of an acquaintance, were activated with oiled precision. He was also able to find more hours in the day than I thought existed. He finished chores, homework, read more books than I and played the group games on the side of the hill with the best of them. He could even pray out loud in church, and was apt at stealing pickles from the barrel that sat under the fruit counter and Uncle Willie's nose.

Once when the Store was full of lunchtime customers, he dipped the strainer, which we also used to sift weevils from meal and flour, into the barrel and fished for two fat pickles. He caught them and hooked the strainer onto the side of the barrel where they dripped until he was ready for them. When the last school bell rang, he picked the nearly dry pickles out of the strainer, jammed them into his pockets and threw the strainer behind the oranges. We ran out of the Store. It was summer and his pants were short, so the pickle juice made clean streams down his ashy legs, and he jumped with his pockets full of loot and his eyes laughing a "How about that?" He smelled like a vinegar barrel or a sour angel.

After our early chores were done, while Uncle Willie or Momma minded the Store, we were free to play the children's games as long as we stayed within yelling distance. Playing hide-and-seek, his voice was easily identified, singing, "Last night, night before, twenty-four robbers at my door. Who all is hid? Ask me to let them in, hit 'em in the head with a rolling pin. Who all is hid?" In follow the leader, naturally he was the one who created the most daring and interesting things to do. And when he was on the tail of the pop the whip, he would twirl off the end like a top, spinning, falling, laughing, finally stopping just before my heart beat its last, and then he was back in the game, still laughing.

Of all the needs (there are none imaginary) a lonely child has, the one that must be satisfied, if there is going to be hope and a hope of wholeness, is the unshaking need for an unshakable God. My pretty Black brother was my Kingdom Come.

In Stamps the custom was to can everything that could possibly be preserved. During the killing season, after the first frost, all neighbors helped each other to slaughter hogs and even the quiet, big-eyed cows if they had stopped giving milk.

The missionary ladies of the Christian Methodist Episcopal Church helped Momma prepare the pork for sausage. They squeezed their fat arms elbow deep in the ground meat, mixed it with gray nose-opening sage, pepper and salt, and made tasty little samples for all obedient children who brought wood for the slick black stove. The men chopped off the larger pieces of meat and laid them in the smokehouse to begin the curing process. They opened the knuckle of the hams with their deadly-looking knives, took out a certain round harmless bone ("it could make the meat go bad") and rubbed salt, coarse brown salt that looked like fine gravel, into the flesh, and the blood popped to the surface.

Throughout the year, until the next frost, we took our meals from the smokehouse, the little garden that lay cousin-close to the Store and from the shelves of canned foods. There were choices on the shelves that could set a hungry child's mouth to watering. Green beans, snapped always the right length, collards, cabbage, juicy red tomato preserves that came into their own on steaming buttered biscuits, and sausage, beets, berries and every fruit grown in Arkansas.

But at least twice yearly Momma would feel that as children we should have fresh meat included in our diets. We were then given money—pennies, nickels, and dimes entrusted to Bailey—and sent to town to buy liver. Since the whites had refrigerators, their butchers bought the meat from commercial slaughter-houses in Texarkana and sold it to the wealthy even in the peak of summer.

Crossing the Black area of Stamps which in childhood's narrow measure seemed a whole world, we were obliged by custom to stop and speak to every person we met, and Bailey felt constrained to spend a few minutes playing with each friend. There was a joy in going to town with money in our pockets (Bailey's pockets were as good as my own) and time on our hands. But the pleasure fled when we reached the white part of town. After we left Mr. Willie Williams' Do Drop Inn, the last stop before whitefolksville, we had to cross the pond and adventure the railroad tracks. We were explorers walking without weapons into man-eating animals' territory.

In Stamps the segregation was so complete that most Black children didn't really, absolutely know what whites looked like. Other than that they were different, to be dreaded, and in that dread was included the hostility of the powerless against the powerful, the poor against the rich, the worker against the worked for and the ragged against the well dressed.

I remember never believing that whites were really real.

Many women who worked in their kitchens traded at our Store, and when they carried their finished laundry back to town they often set the big baskets down on our front porch to pull a singular piece from the starched collection and show either how graceful was their ironing hand or how rich and opulent was the property of their employers.

I looked at the items that weren't on display. I knew, for instance, that white men wore shorts, as Uncle Willie did, and that they had an opening for taking out their "things" and peeing, and that white women's breasts weren't built into their dresses, as some people said, because I saw their brassieres in the baskets. But I couldn't force myself to think of them as people. People were Mrs. LaGrone, Mrs. Hendricks, Momma, Reverend Sneed, Lillie B, and Louise and Rex. Whitefolks couldn't be people because their feet were too small, their skin too white and see-throughy, and they didn't walk on the balls of their feet the way people did—they walked on their heels like horses.

People were those who lived on my side of town. I didn't like them all, or, in fact, any of them very much, but they were people. These others, the strange pale creatures that lived in their alien un-life, weren't considered folks. They were whitefolks.

Growing Up

RUSSELL BAKER

Russell Baker devotes the opening and closing chapters of his autobiography to his elderly mother, emphasizing her importance in his life and career. Inside the frame of those two chapters, he narrates the chronology of his life and education, beginning with the origins of his journalism career—selling copies of the *Saturday Evening Post* during the Depression. In addition to learning about Baker and members of his family, readers learn something of the history and culture of America between World War I and World War II.

Original publication: *Growing Up*. New York: Congdon & Weed, 1982.

I began working in journalism when I was eight years old. It was my mother's idea. She wanted me to "make something" of myself and, after a levelheaded appraisal of my strengths, decided I had better start young if I was to have any chance of keeping up with the competition.

The flaw in my character which she had already spotted was lack of "gumption." My idea of a perfect afternoon was lying in front of the radio rereading my favorite Big Little Book, *Dick Tracy Meets Stooge Viller*. My mother despised inactivity. Seeing me having a good time in repose, she was powerless to hide her disgust. "You've got no more gumption than a bump on a log," she said. "Get out in the kitchen and help Doris do those dirty dishes."

My sister Doris, though two years younger than I, had enough gumption for a dozen people. She positively enjoyed washing dishes, making beds, and cleaning the house. When she was only seven she could carry a piece of short-weighted cheese back to the A&P, threaten the manager with legal action, and come back triumphantly with the full quarter-pound we'd paid for and a few ounces extra thrown in for forgiveness. Doris could have made something of herself if she hadn't been a girl. Because of this defect, however, the best she could hope for was a career as a nurse or schoolteacher, the only work that capable females were considered up to in those days.

This must have saddened my mother, this twist of fate that had allocated all the gumption to the daughter and left her with a son who was content with Dick Tracy and Stooge Viller. If disappointed, though, she wasted no energy on self-pity. She would make me make something of myself whether I wanted to or not. "The Lord helps those who help themselves," she said. That was the way her mind worked.

She was realistic about the difficulty. Having sized up the material the Lord had given her to mold, she didn't overestimate what she could do with it. She didn't insist that I grow up to be President of the United States.

Fifty years ago parents still asked boys if they wanted to grow up to be President, and asked it not jokingly but seriously. Many parents who were hardly more than paupers still believed their sons could do it. Abraham Lincoln had done it. We were only sixty-five years from Lincoln. Many a grandfather who walked among us could remember Lincoln's time. Men of grandfatherly age were the worst for asking if you wanted to grow up to be President. A surprising number of little boys said yes and meant it.

I was asked many times myself. No, I would say, I didn't want to grow up to be President. My mother was present during one of these interrogations. An elderly uncle, having posed the usual question and exposed my lack of interest in the Presidency, asked, "Well, what *do* you want to be when you grow up?"

I loved to pick through trash piles and collect empty bottles, tin cans with pretty labels, and discarded magazines. The most desirable job on earth sprang instantly to mind. "I want to be a garbage man," I said.

My uncle smiled, but my mother had seen the first distressing evidence of a bump budding on a log. "Have a little gumption, Russell," she said. Her calling me Russell was a signal of unhappiness. When she approved of me I was always "Buddy."

When I turned eight years old she decided that the job of starting me on the road toward making something of myself could no longer be safely delayed. "Buddy," she said one day, "I want you to come home right after school this afternoon. Somebody's coming and I want you to meet him."

When I burst in that afternoon she was in conference in the parlor with an executive of the Curtis Publishing Company. She introduced me. He bent low from the waist and shook my hand. Was it true as my mother had told him, he asked, that I longed for the opportunity to conquer the world of business?

My mother replied that I was blessed with a rare determination to make something of myself.

"That's right," I whispered.

"But have you got the grit, the character, the never-say-quit spirit it takes to succeed in business?"

My mother said I certainly did.

"That's right," I said.

He eyed me silently for a long pause, as though weighing whether I could be trusted to keep his confidence, then spoke man-to-man. Before taking a crucial step, he said, he wanted to advise me that working for the Curtis Publishing Company placed enormous responsibility on a young man. It was one of the great companies of America. Perhaps the greatest publishing house in the world. I had heard, no doubt, of the *Saturday Evening Post?*

Heard of it? My mother said that everyone in our house had heard of the *Saturday Post* and that I, in fact, read it with religious devotion.

Then doubtless, he said, we were also familiar with those two monthly pillars of the magazine world, the *Ladies Home Journal* and the *Country Gentleman.*

Indeed we were familiar with them, said my mother.

Representing the *Saturday Evening Post* was one of the weightiest honors that could be bestowed in the world of business, he said. He was personally proud of being a part of that great corporation.

My mother said he had every right to be.

Again he studied me as though debating whether I was worthy of a knighthood. Finally: "Are you trustworthy?"

My mother said I was the soul of honesty.

"That's right," I said.

The caller smiled for the first time. He told me I was a lucky young man. He admired my spunk. Too many young men thought life was all play. Those young men would not go far in this world. Only a young man willing to work and save and keep his face washed and his hair neatly combed could hope to come out on top in a world such as ours. Did I truly and sincerely believe that I was such a young man?

"He certainly does," said my mother.

"That's right," I said.

He said he had been so impressed by what he had seen of me that he was going to make me a representative of the Curtis Publishing Company. On the following Tuesday, he said, thirty freshly printed copies of the *Saturday Evening Post* would be delivered at our door. I would place these magazines, still damp with the ink of the presses, in a handsome canvas bag, sling it over my shoulder, and set forth through the streets to bring the best in journalism, fiction, and cartoons to the American public.

He had brought the canvas bag with him. He presented it with reverence fit for a chasuble. He showed me how to drape the sling over my left shoulder and across the chest so that the pouch lay easily accessible to my right hand, allowing the best in journalism, fiction, and cartoons to be swiftly extracted and sold to a citizenry whose happiness and security depended upon us soldiers of the free press.

The following Tuesday I raced home from school, put the canvas bag over my shoulder, dumped the magazines in, and, tilting to the left to balance their weight on my right hip, embarked on the highway of journalism.

We lived in Belleville, New Jersey, a commuter town at the northern fringe of Newark. It was 1932, the bleakest year of the Depression. My father had died two years before, leaving us with a few pieces of Sears, Roebuck furniture and not much else, and my mother had taken Doris and me to live with one of her younger brothers. This was my Uncle Allen. Uncle Allen had made something of himself by 1932. A salesman for a soft-drink bottler in Newark, he had an income of $30 a week; wore pearl-gray spats, detachable collars, and a three-piece suit; was happily married; and took in threadbare relatives.

With my load of magazines I headed toward Belleville Avenue. That's where the people were. There were two filling stations at the intersection with Union Avenue, as well as an A&P, a fruit stand, a bakery, a barber shop, Zuccarelli's drugstore, and a diner shaped like a railroad car. For several hours I made myself highly visible, shifting position now and then from corner to corner, from shop window to shop window, to make sure everyone could see the heavy black lettering on the canvas bag that said THE SATURDAY EVENING POST. When the angle of the light indicated it was suppertime, I walked back to the house.

"How many did you sell, Buddy?" my mother asked.

"None."

"Where did you go?"

"The corner of Belleville and Union Avenues."

"What did you do?"

"Stood on the corner waiting for somebody to buy a *Saturday Evening Post*."

"You just stood there?"

"Didn't sell a single one."

"For God's sake, Russell!"

Uncle Allen intervened. "I've been thinking about it for some time," he said, "and I've about decided to take the *Post* regularly. Put me down as a regular customer." I handed him a magazine and he paid me a nickel. It was the first nickel I earned.

Afterwards my mother instructed me in salesmanship. I would have to ring doorbells, address adults with charming self-confidence, and break down resistance with a sales talk pointing out that no one, no matter how poor, could afford to be without the *Saturday Evening Post* in the home.

I told my mother I'd changed my mind about wanting to succeed in the magazine business.

"If you think I'm going to raise a good-for-nothing," she replied, "you've got another think coming." She told me to hit the streets with the canvas bag and start ringing doorbells the instant school was out next day. When I objected that I didn't feel any aptitude for salesmanship, she asked how I'd like to lend her my leather belt so she could whack some sense into me. I bowed to superior will and entered journalism with a heavy heart.

My mother and I had fought this battle almost as long as I could remember. It probably started even before memory began, when I was a country child in northern Virginia and my mother, dissatisfied with my father's plain workman's life, determined that I would not grow up like him and his people, with calluses on their hands, overalls on their backs, and fourth-grade educations in their heads. She had fancier ideas of life's possibilities. Introducing me to the *Saturday Evening Post*, she was trying to wean me as early as possible from my father's world where men left with their lunch pails at sunup, worked with their hands until the grime ate into the pores, and died with a few sticks of mail-order furniture as their legacy. In my mother's vision of the better life there were desks and white collars, well-pressed suits, evenings of reading and lively talk, and perhaps—if a man were very, very lucky and hit the jackpot, really made something important of himself—perhaps there might be a fantastic salary of $5,000 a year to support a big house and a Buick with a rumble seat and a vacation in Atlantic City.

And so I set forth with my sack of magazines. I was afraid of the dogs that snarled behind the doors of potential buyers. I was timid about ringing the doorbells of strangers, relieved when no one came to the door, and scared when someone did. Despite my mother's instructions, I could not deliver an engaging sales pitch. When a door opened I simply asked, "Want to buy a *Saturday Evening Post?*" In Belleville few persons did. It was a town of 30,000 people, and most weeks I rang a fair majority of its doorbells. But I rarely sold my thirty copies. Some weeks I canvassed the entire town for six days and still had four or five unsold magazines on Monday evening; then I dreaded the coming of Tuesday morning, when a batch of thirty fresh *Saturday Evening Posts* was due at the front door.

"Better get out there and sell the rest of those magazines tonight," my mother would say.

I usually posted myself than at a busy intersection where a traffic light controlled commuter flow from Newark. When the light turned red I stood on the curb and shouted my sales pitch at the motorists.

"Want to buy a *Saturday Evening Post?*"

One rainy night when car windows were sealed against me I came back soaked and with not a single sale to report. My mother beckoned to Doris.

"Go back down there with Buddy and show him how to sell these magazines," she said.

Brimming with zest, Doris, who was then seven years old, returned with me to the corner. She took a magazine from the bag, and when the light turned red she strode to the nearest car and banged her small fist against the closed window. The driver, probably startled at what he took to be a midget assaulting his car, lowered the window to stare, and Doris thrust a *Saturday Evening Post* at him.

"You need this magazine," she piped, "and it only costs a nickel."

Her salesmanship was irresistible. Before the light changed half a dozen times she disposed of the entire batch. I didn't feel humiliated. To the contrary, I was so happy I decided to give her a treat. Leading her to the vegetable store on Belleville Avenue, I bought three apples, which cost a nickel, and gave her one.

"You shouldn't waste money," she said.

"Eat your apple." I bit into mine.

"You shouldn't eat before supper," she said. "It'll spoil your appetite."

Back at the house that evening, she dutifully reported me for wasting a nickel. Instead of a scolding, I was rewarded with a pat on the back for having the good sense to buy fruit insteady of candy. My mother reached into her bottomless supply of maxims and told Doris, "An apple a day keeps the doctor away."

By the time I was ten I had learned all my mother's maxims by heart. Asking to stay up past normal bedtime, I knew that a refusal would be explained with, "Early to bed and early to rise, makes a man healthy, wealthy, and wise." If I whimpered about having to get up early in the morning, I could depend on her to say, "The early bird gets the worm."

The one I most despised was, "If at first you don't succeed, try, try again." This was the battle cry with which she constantly sent me back into the hopeless struggle whenever I moaned that I had rung every doorbell in town and knew there wasn't a single potential buyer left in Belleville that week. After listening to my explanation, she handed me the canvas bag and said, "If at first you don't succeed . . ."

Three years in that job, which I would gladly have quit after the first day except for her insistence, produced at least one valuable result. My mother finally concluded that I would never make something of myself by pursuing a life in business and started considering careers that demanded less competitive zeal.

One evening when I was eleven I brought home a short "composition" on my summer vacation which the teacher had graded with an A. Reading it with her own schoolteacher's eye, my mother agreed that it was top-drawer seventh grade prose and complimented me. Nothing more was said about it immediately, but a new idea had taken life in her mind. Halfway through supper she suddenly interrupted the conversation.

"Buddy," she said, "maybe you could be a writer."

I clasped the idea to my heart. I had never met a writer, had shown no previous urge to write, and hadn't a notion how to become a writer, but I loved stories and thought that making up stories must surely be almost as much fun as reading them. Best of all, though, and what really gladdened my heart, was the ease of the writer's life. Writers did not have to trudge through the town peddling from canvas bags, defending themselves against angry dogs, being rejected by surly strangers. Writers did not have to ring doorbells. So far as I could make out, what writers did couldn't even be classified as work.

I was enchanted. Writers didn't have to have any gumption at all. I did not dare tell anybody for fear of being laughed at in the schoolyard, but secretly I decided that what I'd like to be when I grew up was a writer.

Notes of a Native Son

JAMES BALDWIN

James Baldwin's death, late in 1987, has renewed interest in his life and his works. Though this excerpt begins with the traditional "I was born . . . ," it quickly takes its audience into Baldwin's family to learn about his background, his values, his motivations.

Original publication: *Notes of a Native Son*. Boston: Beacon Press, 1965.

I was born in Harlem thirty-one years ago. I began plotting novels at about the time I learned to read. The story of my childhood is the usual bleak fantasy, and we can dismiss it with the restrained observation that I certainly would not consider living it again. In those days my mother was given to the exasperating and mysterious habit of having babies. As they were born, I took them over with one hand and held a book with the other. The children probably suffered, though they have since been kind enough to deny it, and in this way I read *Uncle Tom's Cabin* and *A Tale of Two Cities* over and over and over again; in this way, in fact, I read just about everything I could get my hands on—except the Bible, probably because it was the only book I was encouraged to read. I must also confess that I wrote—a great deal—and my first professional triumph, in any case, the first effort of mine to be seen in print, occurred at the age of twelve or thereabouts, when a short story I had written about the Spanish revolution won some sort of prize in an extremely short-lived church newspaper. I remember the story was censored by the lady editor, though I don't remember why, and I was outraged.

Also wrote plays, and songs, for one of which I received a letter of congratulations from Mayor La Guardia, and poetry, about which the less said, the better. My mother was delighted by all these goings-on, but my father wasn't, he wanted me to be a preacher. When I was fourteen I became a preacher, and when I was seventeen I stopped. Very shortly thereafter I left home. For God knows how long I struggled with the world of commerce and industry—I guess they would say they struggled with *me*—and when I was about twenty-one I had enough done of a novel to get a Saxton Fellowship. When I was twenty-two the fellowship was over, the novel turned out to be unsalable, and I started waiting on tables in a Village restaurant and writing book reviews—mostly, as it turned out, about the Negro problem, concerning which the color of my skin made me automatically an expert. Did another book, in company with photographer Theodore Pelatowski, about the store-front churches in Harlem. This book met exactly the same fate as my first—fellowship, but no sale. (It was a Rosenwald Fellowship.) By the time I was twenty-four I had decided to stop reviewing books about the Negro problem—which, by this time, was only slightly less horrible in print than it was in life—and I packed my bags and went to France, where I finished, God knows how, *Go Tell It on the Mountain*.

Any writer, I suppose, feels that the world into which he was born is nothing less than a conspiracy against the cultivation of his talent—which attitude certainly has a great deal to support it. On the other hand, it is only because the world looks on his talent with such a frightening indifference that the artist is compelled to make his talent important. So that any writer, looking back over even so short a span of time as I am here forced to assess, finds that the things which hurt him and the things which helped him cannot be divorced from each other; he could be helped in a certain way only because he was hurt in a certain way; and his help is simply to be enabled to move from one conundrum to the next—one is tempted to say that he moves from one disaster to the next. When one begins looking for influences one finds them by the score. I haven't thought much about my own, not enough anyway; I hazard that the King James Bible, the rhetoric of the store-front church, something ironic and violent and perpetually understated in Negro speech—and something of Dickens' love for bravura—have something to do with me today; but I wouldn't stake my life on it. Likewise, innumerable people have helped me in many ways; but finally, I suppose, the most difficult (and most rewarding) thing in my life has been the fact that I was born a Negro and was forced, therefore, to effect some kind of truce with this reality. (Truce, by the way, is the best one can hope for.)

One of the difficulties about being a Negro writer (and this is not special pleading, since I don't mean to suggest that he has it worse than anybody else) is that the Negro problem is written about so widely. The bookshelves groan under the weight of information, and everyone therefore considers himself informed. And this information, furthermore, operates usually (generally, popularly) to reinforce traditional attitudes. Of traditional attitudes there are only two—For or Against—and I, personally, find it difficult to say which attitude has caused me the most pain. I am speaking as a writer; from a social point of view I am perfectly aware that the change from ill-will to good-will, however motivated, however imperfect, however expressed, is better than no change at all.

But it is part of the business of the writer—as I see it—to examine attitudes, to go beneath the surface, to tap the source. From this point of view the Negro problem is nearly inaccessible. It is not only written about so widely; it is written about so badly. It is quite possible to say that the price a Negro pays for becoming articulate is to find himself, at length, with nothing to be articulate about. ("You taught me language," says Caliban to Prospero, "and my profit on't is I know how to curse.") Consider: the tremendous social activity that this problem generates imposes on whites and Negroes alike the necessity of looking forward, of working to bring about a better day. This is fine, it keeps the waters troubled; it is all, indeed, that has made possible the Negro's progress. Nevertheless, social affairs are not generally speaking the writer's prime concern, whether they ought to be or not; it is absolutely necessary that he establish between himself and these affairs a distance which will allow, at least, for clarity, so that before he can look forward in any meaningful sense, he must first be allowed to take a long look back. In the context of the Negro problem neither whites nor blacks, for excellent reasons of their own, have the faintest desire to look back; but I think that the past is all that makes the present coherent, and further, that the past will remain horrible for exactly as long as we refuse to assess it honestly.

I know, in any case, that the most crucial time in my own development came when I was forced to recognize that I was a kind of bastard of the West; when I followed the line of my past I did not find myself in Europe but in Africa. And this meant that in some subtle way, in a really profound way, I brought to Shakespeare, Bach, Rembrandt, to the stones of Paris, to the cathedral at Chartres and to the Empire State Building, a special attitude. These were not really my creations, they did not contain my history; I might search in them in vain forever for any reflection of myself. I was an interloper; this was not my heritage. At the same time I had no other heritage which I could possibly hope to use—I had certainly been unfitted for the jungle or the tribe. I would have to appropriate these white centuries, I would have to make them mine—I would have to accept my special attitude, my special place in this scheme—otherwise I would have no place in *any* scheme. What was the most difficult was the fact that I was forced to admit something I had always hidden from myself, which the American Negro has had to hide from himself as the price of his public progress; that I hated and feared white people. This did not mean that

I loved black people; on the contrary, I despised them, possibly because they failed to produce Rembrandt. In effect, I hated and feared the world. And this meant, not only that I thus gave the world an altogether murderous power over me, but also that in such a self-destroying limbo I could never hope to write.

One writes out of one thing only—one's own experience. Everything depends on how relentlessly one forces from this experience the last drop, sweet or bitter, it can possibly give. This is the only real concern of the artist, to recreate out of the disorder of life that order which is art. The difficulty then, for me, of being a Negro writer was the fact that I was, in effect, prohibited from examining my own experience too closely by the tremendous demands and the very real dangers of my social situation.

I don't think the dilemma outlined above is uncommon. I do think, since writers work in the disastrously explicit medium of language, that it goes a little way towards explaining why, out of the enormous resources of Negro speech and life, and despite the example of Negro music, prose written by Negroes has been generally speaking so pallid and so harsh. I have not written about being a Negro at such length because I expect that to be my only subject, but only because it was the gate I had to unlock before I could hope to write about anything else. I don't think that the Negro problem in America can be even discussed coherently without bearing in mind its context; its context being the history, traditions, customs, the moral assumptions and preoccupations of the country; in short, the general social fabric. Appearances to the contrary, no one in America escapes its effects and everyone in America bears some responsibility for it. I believe this the more firmly because it is the overwhelming tendency to speak of this problem as though it were a thing apart. But in the work of Faulkner, in the general attitude and certain specific passages in Robert Penn Warren, and, most significantly, in the advent of Ralph Ellison, one sees the beginnings—at least—of a more genuinely penetrating search. Mr. Ellison, by the way, is the first Negro novelist I have ever read to utilize in language, and brilliantly, some of the ambiguity and irony of Negro life.

About my interests: I don't know if I have any, unless the morbid desire to own a sixteen-millimeter camera and make experimental movies can be so classified. Otherwise, I love to eat and drink—it's my melancholy conviction that I've scarcely ever had enough to eat (this is because it's *impossible* to eat enough if you're worried about the next meal)—and I love to argue with people who do not disagree with me too profoundly, and I love to laugh. I do *not* like bohemia, or bohemians, I do not like people whose principal aim is pleasure, and I do not like people who are *earnest* about anything. I don't like people who like me because I'm a Negro; neither do I like people who find in the same accident grounds for contempt. I love America more than any other country in the world, and, exactly for this reason, I insist on the right to criticize her perpetually. I think all theories are suspect, that the finest principles may have to be modified, or may even be pulverized by the demands of life, and that one must find, therefore, one's own moral center and move through the world hoping that this center will guide one aright. I consider that I have many responsibilities, but none greater than this: to last, as Hemingway says, and get my work done.

I want to be an honest man and a good writer.

Moving Day

The Books I Left Behind

ANATOLE BROYARD

Anatole Broyard has turned from reviewing books to teaching writing. As he makes the move, he turns to his bookshelves for an account of his life, using the contents of those shelves as the source of autobiography. In this article, written for a general audience, he sees his life through the books he has bought or sold, discarded or kept. These possessions also stimulate his thoughts on philosophy, cultural changes, and literary fads, as well as changes in his personal tastes.

Original publication: *The New York Times Book Review*, November 19, 1989.

I have always thought of books not so much as something to read but as something to live with. Anthony Powell has a novel called "Books Do Furnish a Room," and for me they have furnished a life. They are not bound volumes of pages but companions. In my first apartment, a tenement in Greenwich Village, books were all the furniture I had, except for a bed and a table.

One morning I woke up in that apartment with 13 cents in my pocket and no immediate prospect of anything more. My friends were just as poor as I was and to ask my parents was unthinkable, so I began looking around my apartment for liquid assets. I didn't even have a wristwatch to pawn. Eventually my eye fell on my bookcase, which was the most conspicuous thing in the room, and I felt a thrill of protest rising like a cry to my lips.

Could one pawn a book? No, and I certainly could not sell one. It would be like selling one of my nerves or a ligament. My books held me together. I was at that age when a young man is a fragile structure.

I took down a book, as if to reassure the author personally. It was an out-of-print edition of "The Poet in New York" by Lorca that I knew for a fact would bring $7.50 at the Gotham Book Mart. This was in 1949, when $7.50 would feed me, with careful management, for four days. But of course I could never sell my Lorca—for you see, it was my Lorca, my friend Lorca.

I opened the book at random and read a few lines to demonstrate the inconceivability of parting with it. I can still quote those lines from memory:

A cast-off suit weighs so heavily on the shoulders
That heaven often groups them in angry droves.

I read the lines again, then I turned the pages and browsed here and there. There were lots of lines like that. I did not recognize this Lorca and I felt that I had never really read this book. Or perhaps I had read it as a "swoon reader," to use I. A. Richards' phrase. I had read it idly, never under pressure. A good book should have grace under pressure.

I felt deceived by Lorca, as if he had entered my apartment under false pretenses. Perhaps, I thought, it's the translation—but it is too easy to blame faults on the translation. (There's a new, highly touted translation now that reads just as badly, or worse.)

An awful realization rose like a snake in my mind: I *could* sell this book. I could live without it, or at least I was willing to try. Still, when I went to the Gotham Book Mart and handed it over to Frances Steloff and pocketed the $7.50 I felt that I had crossed a divide. It was as if I had taken a step whose consequences would not be fully comprehended for years.

Yet this was only an isolated incident, brought on by hunger, like a hallucination. Before long, I fell under the spell of books again and looked upon them as tenderly as ever. The bookcase was in my bedroom and every night before turning out the light I took comfort in it. Each time I moved—and I moved often, for each tenement was awful and I hoped for a better one—each time I moved, I boxed my books carefully and carried them in my arms down the stairs of one top-floor apartment and up the stairs of another. You don't really know a book until you have carried it in a box with 20 or 30 others.

Must have built half a dozen different bookcases, each one larger than the last, until, 30 years later, there were bookshelves in most of the rooms of my house. It was insulated with books. When I became a daily book critic for The New York Times, books flowed into my house like illegal immigrants crossing the border.

It didn't matter—by then I was living in Connecticut where there is always room for books. This swollen condition lasted for years, for I took on books as people put on weight. Then it all came to an end last August when I moved to Cambridge, Mass. This is a much smaller house, a city house, and beyond that it is peculiarly inhospitable to books.

The house is Victorian, with all sorts of nooks and crannies, a witty, whimsical house that would not welcome large multicolored oblongs along its walls. Besides, now that I thought about it, I didn't like the idea of books in every room. It was like giving authors too much influence—which, of course, was just what they wanted.

For example, I don't think books belong in a dining room. There is something indigestible or dyspeptic about such an arrangement. I need to eat in peace. For that matter, I don't really care for books in a living room either. A living room is for—well, for living, relaxing, entertaining, and books are severe witnesses in these circumstances. Perhaps only people who can ignore books put them in their dining rooms and living rooms. When I was younger, as I said, I liked books in my bedroom, but my relation to them was sexier then.

Well, it was no use philosophizing. Some of my books, perhaps as many as a third, would have to go. Unless of course, I put them in boxes in the basement. But what good is a book in a box? Does anyone ever go down to the basement to take a book out of a box? No, I would go through my books volume by volume and examine my reasons for keeping them. An unexamined library is not worth keeping. I realized for the first time that a book can be a false consolation.

There were books on my shelves that I had never read. I had carried them from place to place because I liked the idea of them, what they promised—yet the circumstances had never been right for me to open them. In a way we stood in an ideal relation—so I would hold on to them.

In eliminating books, I planned to go by categories, and my first category was occasional novels. An occasional novel is one in which the occasion is apparent only to the novelist. He is driven by a necessity that to anyone else seems quixotic, determined to define what does not need defining. Like an occasional chair, it is something you take only when nothing else is available. James Gould Cozzens' "By Love Possessed" is an occasional novel. I'm tempted to plunge and say that most novels are occasional, but I wouldn't get anywhere thinking that way.

Some of the occasional novels on my shelves were by friends or acquaintances and I wondered whether that was a reason for keeping them. In some cases, in most cases, it's like holding a grudge against someone.

I had held on to many of these books because I imagined I might need them someday to serve as an illustration, a mote of evidence, for a beautiful generalization. I was always saving things up for a great generalization—my house and my head were filled with such material. I had one novel, for example, called "Burning Questions," by Alix Kates Shulman, in which a young woman who has been housekeeping for an ungrateful lover asks a heart-rending question: "For who would putter gratis," she says, "for someone who doesn't love you?" That "putter gratis" was a mistake of such purity that I was sure I could build an indictment of contemporary fiction around it.

The question, though, was whether I would ever make that generalization for which this line would be a starting point. It was getting late in the day. Generalizations were like infatuations—you don't go in for them so much as you get older.

I found that I had a surprising number of mildly amusing books and I thought these could go. I never want to be mildly amused again, even by Malcolm Bradbury. Should experimental novels go? As a friend of mine said, "An experimental novel is one in which the experiment fails." Yet I was uneasy about giving them up. They were like scars that reminded you of old escapades.

Phrases of historical indignation: there's a class of books I could do without. A book like Erich Fromm's "Escape From Freedom" could no longer be considered pertinent when we had already escaped into freedom. Rollo May's "Love and Will," a good effort in its time, could go, too. In fact, I could get rid of all books about love or will, or the failure of will or love or nerve. As for psychology, I would jettison any volume that attempted to explain human nature or behavior in anything but extravagant metaphors. Books about education—especially those by Ivan Illich—could go.

Should I keep philosophies of literature, all those Kenneth Burkes and René Welleks? What is a philosophy of literature, anyway? Does literature need, should it have, a philosophy? Still, there was something wonderful about Kenneth Burke. He reminded me of that old rhyme: "I shot an arrow into the air. / It fell to earth I know not where."

For a wild, intoxicating moment, I considered giving away all my French novels, with the possible exception of Proust and Céline. I have never believed in Gide or Malraux, and "Madam Bovary" has petrified, for me at least, into a monument. Balzac has the same effect on me as a bad meal in a cheap restaurant in Paris. As you can see, once I started thinking about getting rid of books, a kind of delirium came over me. At times, I wanted to do away with them all. Because of the demands they make, books excite this kind of ambivalence. Once you willingly suspend your disbelief about giving them up, anything can happen. To be pious about books is just another kind of bigotry.

Books of art criticism are a grim kind of fun. They are like cocktail party chatter raised to the level of desperation, a life-or-death cocktail party. It's as if each critic showed us the limits of his shamefulness, how far he's prepared to go. Art criticism is like the sweat of culture, in armpit and crotch—I ought to keep it, if only for the funkiness.

What is there about anthologies that makes me so reluctant to read them? Is it a case of too many cooks spoiling the broth? There is a feeling of contention in anthologies, as if each author were determined to outdo or contradict the others, like a panel discussion. And since each collection allegedly represents the best, one reads them with a sinking feeling: is this it, all there is? To my mind, the arbitrary grouping overwhelms the originality and when I look back, for example, on the "Best Short Stories of the Year" collections I find that the stories no longer exist separately; they adhere to one another, like badly cooked rice.

Poetry anthologies read better for some reason. Poems rattle together rather pleasantly in a collection—the effect is like maracas. Anyway, I would never give up my poetry—it's almost the only instance in modern art in which a perfect narcissism has been wedded to a perfect disinterestedness. Besides, I have a recurrent fantasy—like a threat—that at some time in the future I'll read nothing but poetry.

It was in the 20th-century novel that I faced my hardest choices. Naturally I would keep "Ulysses" and "Parade's End" and "To the Lighthouse"—they are no longer just books, but part of my environment. To have them on my shelves is like looking out of the window and seeing mountains in the distance. They are as close as I am likely to come to a religion. But what about the others? Would I ever read Faulkner again? Of course he was great, but why did I have to crank myself up each time to read him? Had I held my final *corrida* with Hemingway? As with Norman Mailer, I always felt that Hemingway was too much with us and the problem was to escape from him, as Eliot thought poets had to escape from Milton.

Fitzgerald's sadness is like flat champagne now, through no fault of his own. Anyway, how many times can you read a book—even a great book? In my own experience I have found that the fourth reading is almost always disillusioning. I don't know why this should be—it's the same book. Yet I found myself getting tired of Tietjens in "Parade's End" and taking sides with Sylvia against him. Even in a great 19th-century novel like "Middlemarch," only Casaubon remained interesting on the fourth reading.

I discovered that I owned all the books of Saul Bellow, John Updike and Philip Roth. Why was I being so faithful? It was like some kind of club whose origins were obscure. I knew I would never read some of them—or most of them—again and my favorites I knew almost by heart. While in one sense it would seem absurd not to have them, there was no practical reason for keeping them.

Yet they were like family portraits. Though I am not Jewish, I thought of Saul Bellow as my wise Jewish uncle. Most of my friends are Jewish, and I need a Jewish uncle to help me to understand them, to deal with them. Also, he was still teaching me to make metaphysics out of my disillusionments, to make my complaints more spacious.

I like to have John Updike around just in case anything goes wrong with American writing. He is so well equipped, a combination doctor, lawyer, plumber, electrician and carpenter. He's like those L.L. Bean jackets that have a pocket for everything. Also, he is one of the few serious writers who say yes to American life. I ought to have at least one yes in my library.

When I looked at my shelf of Philip Roths, I felt that I had nursed him—or he had nursed me—through the long illness of our literature. He was my cynical big brother and my crazy little brother, too. When he made a mistake—and he made a few—it was I who blushed. Like so many American readers, I felt that I had got gloriously drunk with Philip Roth, we had gone skinny-dipping together, had suffered with the same kind of women. I knew too much about him—and he knew too much about me—for me to give up his books.

These are just a few of the thoughts I had, the questions I asked. Many of my decisions were automatic, frivolous, unconscious or simply inexplicable. At some point I remember condemning my set of the Encyclopedia Britannica to make room. In the end, I gave away 61 boxes of books, good-sized boxes that hold four stacks side by side. My local library in Connecticut was pathetically grateful to get them, and in one of the most convoluted ironies in the world I will receive a tax deduction in return.

As I looked at the volumes still on my shelves, I felt that it was I, not they, who was the survivor. And I asked myself whether after the inquisition, the murders and the burning, I was any nearer to the truth, or to God. I won't know until I build my next bookcases.

A *Scientific Apprenticeship*
from Disturbing the Universe
FREEMAN DYSON

Freeman Dyson dedicates *Disturbing the Universe* to undergraduates at universities where he has spoken. These students "asked the questions which this book tries to answer." Dyson, professor of physics at the Institute for Advanced Study at Princeton, assumes an intelligent audience with some knowledge of physics, but he explains more complex principles of physics and provides necessary historical contexts. Through the publication of his autobiography, his audience has expanded from students to include an interested public.

The questions motivating "A Scientific Apprenticeship" must have been about Dyson's education and significant influences on his life and career. This account of his graduate work tells stories about leaders in atomic research. Thus, this autobiography presents history through personal experiences.

Original publication: *Disturbing the Universe*. New York: Harper & Row, 1979.

In September 1947 I enrolled as a graduate student in the physics department of Cornell University at Ithaca. I went there to learn how to do research in physics under the guidance of Hans Bethe. Bethe is not only a great physicist but also an outstanding trainer of students. When I arrived at Cornell and introduced myself to the great man, two things about him immediately impressed me. First, there was a lot of mud on his shoes. Second, the other students called him Hans. I had never seen anything like that in England. In England, professors were treated with respect and wore clean shoes.

Within a few days Hans found me a good problem to work on. He had an amazing ability to choose good problems, not too hard and not too easy, for students of widely varying skills and interests. He had eight or ten students doing research problems and never seemed to find it a strain to keep us busy and happy. He ate lunch with us at the cafeteria almost every day. After a few hours of conversation, he could judge accurately what each student was capable of doing. It had been arranged that I would only be at Cornell for nine months, and so he gave me a problem that he knew I could finish within that time. It worked out exactly as he said it would.

I was lucky to arrive at Cornell at that particular moment. Nineteen forty-seven was the year of the postwar flowering of physics, when new ideas and new experiments were sprouting everywhere from seeds that had lain dormant through the war. The scientists who had spent the war years at places like Bomber Command headquarters and Los Alamos came back to the universities impatient to get started again in pure science. They were in a hurry to make up for the years they had lost, and they went to work with energy and enthusiasm. Pure science in 1947 was starting to hum. And right in the middle of the renascence of pure physics was Hans Bethe.

At that time there was a single central unsolved problem that absorbed the attention of a large fraction of physicists. We called it the quantum electrodynamics problem. The problem was simply that there existed no accurate theory to describe the everyday behavior of atoms and electrons emitting and absorbing light. Quantum electrodynamics was the name of the missing theory. It was called quantum because it had to take into account the quantum nature of light, electro because it had to deal with electrons, and dynamics because it had to describe forces and motions. We had inherited from the prewar generation of physicists, Einstein and Bohr and Heisenberg and Dirac, the basic ideas for such a theory. But the basic ideas were not enough. The basic ideas could tell you roughly how an atom would behave. But we wanted to be able to calculate the behavior exactly. Of course it often happens in science that things are too complicated to be calculated exactly, so that one has to be content with a rough qualitative understanding. The strange thing in 1947 was that even the simplest and most elementary objects, hydrogen atoms and light quanta, could not be accurately understood. Hans Bethe was convinced that a correct and exact theory would emerge if we could figure out how to calculate consistently using the old prewar ideas. He stood like Moses on the mountain showing us the promised land. It was for us students to move in and make ourselves at home there.

A few months before I arrived at Cornell, two important things had happened. First, there were some experiments at Columbia University in New York which measured the behavior of an electron a thousand times more accurately than it had been measured before. This made the problem of creating an accurate theory far more urgent and gave the theorists some accurate numbers which they had to try to explain. Second, Hans Bethe himself did the first theoretical calculation that went substantially beyond what had been done before the war. He calculated the energy of an electron in an atom of hydrogen and found an answer agreeing fairly well with the Columbia measurement. This showed that he was on the right track. But his calculation was still a pastiche of old ideas held together by physical intuition. It had no firm mathematical basis. And it was not even consistent with Einstein's principle of relativity. That was how things stood in September when I joined Han's group of students.

The problem that Hans gave me was to repeat his calculation of the electron energy with the minimum changes that were needed to make it consistent with Einstein. It was an ideal problem for somebody like me, who had a good mathematical background and little knowledge of physics. I plunged in and filled hundreds of pages with calculations, learning the physics as I went along. After a few months I had an answer, again agreeing near enough with Columbia. My calculation was still a pastiche. I had not improved on Hans's calculation in any fundamental sense. I came no closer than Hans had come to a basic understanding of the electron. But those winter months of calculation had given me skill and confidence. I had mastered the tools of my trade. I was now ready to start thinking.

As a relaxation from quantum electrodynamics, I was encouraged to spend a few hours a week in the student laboratory doing experiments. These were not real research experiments. We were just going through the motions, repeating famous old experiments, knowing beforehand what the answers ought to be. The other students grumbled at having to waste their time doing Mickey Mouse experiments. But I found the experiments fascinating. In all my time in England I had never been let loose in a laboratory. All these strange objects that I had read about, crystals and magnets and prisms and spectroscopes, were actually there and could be touched and handled. It seemed like a miracle when I measured the electric voltage produced by light of various colors falling on a metal surface and found that Einstein's law of the photoelectric effect is really true. Unfortunately I came to grief on the Millikan oil drop experiment. Millikan was a great physicist at the University of Chicago who first measured the electric charge of individual electrons. He made a mist of tiny drops of oil and watched them float around under his microscope while he pulled and pushed them with strong electric fields. The drops were so small that some of them carried a net electric charge of only one or two electrons. I had my oil drops floating nicely, and then I grabbed hold of the wrong knob to adjust the electric field. They found me stretched out on the floor, and that finished my career as an experimenter.

I never regretted my brief and almost fatal exposure to experiments. This experience brought home to me as nothing else could the truth of Einstein's remark, "One may say the eternal mystery of the world is its comprehensibility." Here was I, sitting at my desk for weeks on end, doing the most elaborate and sophisticated calculations to figure out how an electron should behave. And here was the electron on my little oil drop, knowing quite well how to behave without waiting for the result of my calculation. How could one seriously believe that the electron really cared about my calculation, one way or the other? And yet the experiments at Columbia showed that it did care. Somehow or other, all this complicated mathematics that I was scribbling established rules that the electron on the oil drop was bound to follow. We know that this is so. Why it is so, why the electron pays attention to our mathematics, is a mystery that even Einstein could not fathom.

At our daily lunches with Hans we talked endlessly about physics, about the technical details and about the deep philosophical mysteries. On the whole, Hans was more interested in details than in philosophy. When I raised philosophical questions he would often say, "You ought to go and talk to Oppy about that." Oppy was Robert Oppenheimer, then newly appointed as director of the Institute for Advanced Study at Princeton. Sometime during the winter, Hans spoke with Oppy about me and they agreed that after my year at Cornell I should go for a year to Princeton. I looked forward to working with Oppy but I was also a bit scared. Oppy was already a legendary figure. He had been the originator and leader of the bomb project at Los Alamos. Hans had worked there under him as head of the Theoretical Division. Hans had enormous respect for Oppy. But he warned me not to expect an easy life at Princeton. He said Oppy did not suffer fools gladly and was sometimes hasty in deciding who was a fool.

One of our group of students at Cornell was Rossi Lomanitz, a rugged character from Oklahoma who lived in a dilapidated farmhouse outside Ithaca and was rumored to be a Communist. Lomanitz was never at Los Alamos, but he had worked with Oppy on the bomb project in California before Los Alamos was started. Being a Communist was not such a serious crime in 1947 as it became later. Seven years later, when Oppy was declared to be a Security Risk, one of the charges against him was that he had tried to stop the army from drafting Lomanitz. Mr. Robb, the prosecuting attorney at the trial, imputed sinister motives in Oppy's concern for Lomanitz. Oppy replied to Robb, "The relations between me and my students were not that I stood at the head of a class and lectured." That remark summed up exactly what made both Hans and Oppy great teachers. In 1947 security hearings and witch hunts were far from our thoughts. Rossi Lomanitz was a student just like the rest of us. And Oppy was the great national hero whose face could be seen ornamenting the covers of *Time* and *Life* magazines.

I knew before I came to Cornell that Hans had been at Los Alamos. I had not known beforehand that I would find a large fraction of the entire Los Alamos gang, with the exception of Oppy, reassembled at Cornell. Hans had been at Cornell before the war, and when he returned he found jobs for as many as possible of the bright young people he had worked with at Los Alamos. So we had at Cornell Robert Wilson, who had been head of experimental physics at Los Alamos, Philip Morrison, who had gone to the Mariana Islands to take care of the bombs that were used at Hiroshima and Nagasaki, Dick Feynman, who had been in charge of the computing center, and many others. I was amazed to see how quickly and easily I fitted in with this bunch of weaponeers whose experience of the war had been so utterly different from my own. There was endless talk about the Los Alamos days. Through all the talk shone a glow of pride and nostalgia. For every one of these people, the Los Alamos days had been a great experience, a time of hard work and comradeship and deep happiness. I had the impression that the main reason they were happy to be at Cornell was that the Cornell physics department still retained something of the Los Alamos atmosphere. I, too, could feel the vivid presence of this atmosphere. It was youth, it was exuberance, it was informality, it was a shared ambition to do great things together in science without any personal jealousies or squabbles over credit. Hans Bethe and Dick Feynman did, many years later, receive well-earned Nobel Prizes, but nobody at Cornell was grabbing for prizes or for personal glory.

The Los Alamos people did not speak in public about the technical details of bombs. It was surprisingly easy to talk around that subject without getting onto dangerous ground. Only once I embarrassed everybody at the lunch table by remarking in all innocence, "It's lucky that Eddington proved it's impossible to make a bomb out of hydrogen." There was an awkward silence and the subject of conversation was abruptly changed. In those days the existence of any thoughts about hydrogen bombs was a deadly secret. After lunch one of the students took me aside and told me in confidence that unfortunately Eddington was wrong, that a lot of work on hydrogen bombs had been done at Los Alamos, and would I please never refer to the subject again. I was pleased that they trusted me enough to let me in on the secret. After that I felt I was really one of the gang.

Many of the Los Alamos veterans were involved in political activities aimed at educating the public about the nuclear facts of life. The main thrust of their message was that the American monopoly of nuclear weapons could not last, and that in the long run the only hope of survival would lie in a complete surrender of all nuclear activities to a strong international authority. Philip Morrison was especially eloquent in spreading this message. Oppy had been saying the same thing more quietly to his friends inside the government. But by 1948 it was clear that the chance of establishing an effective international authority on the basis of the wartime Soviet-American alliance had been missed. The nuclear arms race had begun, and the idea of international control could at best be a long-range dream.

Our lunchtime conversations with Hans were often centered on Los Alamos and on the moral questions surrounding the development and use of the bomb. Hans was troubled by these questions. But few of the other Los Alamos people were troubled. It seemed that hardly anybody had been troubled until after Hiroshima. While the work was going on, they were absorbed in scientific details and totally dedicated to the technical success of the project. They were far too busy with their work to worry about the consequences. In June 1945 Oppy had been a member of the group appointed by Henry Stimson to advise him about the use of the bombs. Oppy had supported Stimson's decision to use them as they were used. But Oppy did not at that time discuss the matter with any of his colleagues at Los Alamos. Not even with Hans. That responsibility he bore alone.

In February 1948 *Time* magazine published an interview with Oppy in which appeared his famous confession, "In some sort of crude sense, which no vulgarity, no humor, no overstatement can quite extinguish, the physicists have known sin; and this is a knowledge which they cannot lose." Most of the Los Alamos people at Cornell repudiated Oppy's remark indignantly. They felt no sense of sin. They had done a difficult and necessary job to help win the war. They felt it was unfair of Oppy to weep in public over their guilt when anybody who built any kind of lethal weapons for use in war was equally guilty. I understood the anger of the Los Alamos people, but I agreed with Oppy. The sin of the physicists at Los Alamos did not lie in their having built a lethal weapon. To have built the bomb, when their country was engaged in a desperate war against Hitler's Germany, was morally justifiable. But they did not just build the bomb. They enjoyed building it. They had the best time of their lives while building it. That, I believe, is what Oppy had in mind when he said they had sinned. And he was right.

After a few months I was able to identify the quality that I found strange and attractive in the American students. They lacked the tragic sense of life which was deeply ingrained in every European of my generation. They had never lived with tragedy and had no feeling for it. Having no sense of tragedy, they also had no sense of guilt. They seemed very young and innocent although most of them were older than I was. They had come through the war without scars. Los Alamos had been for them a great lark. It left their innocence untouched. That was why they were unable to accept Oppy's statement as expressing a truth about themselves.

For Europeans the great turning point of history was the First World War, not the Second. The first war had created that tragic mood which was a part of the air we breathed long before the second war started. Oppy had grown up immersed in European culture and had acquired the tragic sense. Hans, being a European, had it too. The younger native-born Americans, with the exception of Dick Feynman, still lived in a world without shadows. Things are very different now, thirty years later. The Vietnam war produced in American life the same fundamental change of mood that the First World War produced in Europe. The young Americans of today are closer in spirit to the Europeans than to the Americans of thirty years ago. The age of innocence is now over for all of us.

Dick Feynman was in this respect, as in almost every other respect, an exception. He was a young native American who had lived with tragedy. He had loved and married a brilliant, artistic girl who was dying of TB. They knew she was dying when they married. When Dick went to work at Los Alamos, Oppy arranged for his wife to stay at a sanitarium in Albuquerque so that they could be together as much as possible. She died there, a few weeks before the war ended.

As soon as I arrived at Cornell, I became aware of Dick as the liveliest personality in our department. In many ways he reminded me of Frank Thompson. Dick was no poet and certainly no Communist. But he was like Frank in his loud voice, his quick mind, his intense interest in all kinds of things and people, his crazy jokes, and his disrespect for authority. I had a room in a student dormitory and sometimes around two o'clock in the morning I would wake up to the sound of a strange rhythm pulsating over the silent campus. That was Dick playing his bongo drums.

Dick was also a profoundly original scientist. He refused to take anybody's word for anything. This meant that he was forced to rediscover or reinvent for himself almost the whole of physics. It took him five years of concentrated work to reinvent quantum mechanics. He said that he couldn't understand the official version of quantum mechanics that was taught in textbooks, and so he had to begin afresh from the beginning. This was a heroic enterprise. He worked harder during those years than anybody else I ever knew. At the end he had a version of quantum mechanics that he could understand. He then went on to calculate with his version of quantum mechanics how an electron should behave. He was able to reproduce the result that Hans had calculated using orthodox theories a little earlier. But Dick could go much further. He calculated with his own theory fine details of the electron's behavior that Hans's method could not touch. Dick could calculate these things far more accurately, and far more easily, than anybody else could. The calculation that I did for Hans, using the orthodox theory, took me several months of work and several hundred sheets of paper. Dick could get the same answer, calculating on a blackboard, in half an hour.

So this was the situation which I found at Cornell. Hans was using the old cookbook quantum mechanics that Dick couldn't understand. Dick was using his own private quantum mechanics that nobody else could understand. They were getting the same answers whenever they calculated the same problems. And Dick could calculate a whole lot of things that Hans couldn't. It was obvious to me that Dick's theory must be fundamentally right. I decided that my main job, after I finished the calculation for Hans, must be to understand Dick and explain his ideas in a language that the rest of the world could understand.

In the spring of 1948, Hans and Dick went to a select meeting of experts arranged by Oppy at a lodge in the Pocono Mountains to discuss the quantum electrodynamics problem. I was not invited because I was not yet an expert. The Columbia experimenters were there, and Niels Bohr, and various other important physicists. The main event of the meeting was an eight-hour talk by Julian Schwinger, a young professor at Harvard who had been a student of Oppy's. Julian, it seemed, had solved the main problems. He had a new theory of quantum electrodynamics which explained all the Columbia experiments. His theory was built on orthodox principles and was a masterpiece of mathematical technique. His calculations were extremely complicated, and few in the audience stayed with him all the way through the eight-hour exposition. But Oppy understood and approved everything. After Julian had finished, it was Dick's turn. Dick tried to tell the exhausted listeners how he could explain the same experiments much more simply using his own unorthodox methods. Nobody understood a word that Dick said. At the end Oppy made some scathing comments and that was that. Dick came home from the meeting very depressed.

During the last months of my time at Cornell I made an effort to see as much of Dick as possible. The beautiful thing about Dick was that you did not have to be afraid you were wasting his time. Most scientists when you come to talk with them are very polite and let you sit down, and only after a while you notice from their bored expressions or their fidgety fingers that they are wishing you would go away. Dick was not like that. When I came to his room and he didn't want to talk he would just shout, "Go away, I'm busy," without even turning his head. So I would go away. And next time when I came and he let me sit down, I knew he was not just being polite. We talked for many hours about his private version of physics and I began finally to get the hang of it.

The reason Dick's physics was so hard for ordinary people to grasp was that he did not use equations. The usual way theoretical physics was done since the time of Newton was to begin by writing down some equations and then to work hard calculating solutions of the equations. This was the way Hans and Oppy and Julian Schwinger did physics. Dick just wrote down the solutions out of his head without ever writing down the equations. He had a physical picture of the way things happen, and the picture gave him the solutions directly with a minimum of calculation. It was no wonder that people who had spent their lives solving equations were baffled by him. Their minds were analytical; his was pictorial. My own training, since the far-off days when I struggled with Piaggio's differential equations, had been analytical. But as I listened to Dick and stared at the strange diagrams that he drew on the blackboard, I gradually absorbed some of his pictorial imagination and began to feel at home in his version of the universe.

The essence of Dick's version was a loosening of all constraints. In orthodox physics you say, Suppose an electron is in this state at a certain time, then you calculate what it will do next by solving a certain differential equation, and from the solution of the equation you calculate what it will be doing at some later time. Instead of this, Dick said simply, the electron does whatever it likes. The electron goes all over space and time in all possible ways. It can even go backward in time whenever it chooses. If you start with an electron in this state at a certain time and you want to see whether it will be in some other state at another time, you just add together contributions from all the possible histories of the electron that take it from this state to the other. A history of the electron is any possible path in space and time, including paths zigzagging forward and back in time. The behavior of the electron is just the result of adding together all the histories according to some simple rules that Dick worked out. And the same trick works with minor changes not only for electrons but for everything else—atoms, baseballs, elephants and so on. Only for baseballs and elephants the rules are more complicated.

This sum-over-histories way of looking at things is not really so mysterious, once you get used to it. Like other profoundly original ideas, it has become slowly absorbed into the fabric of physics, so that now after thirty years it is difficult to remember why we found it at the beginning so hard to grasp. I had the enormous luck to be there at Cornell in 1948 when the idea was newborn, and to be for a short time Dick's sounding board. I witnessed the concluding stages of the five-year-long intellectual struggle by which Dick fought his way through to his unifying vision. What I saw of Dick reminded me of what I heard Keynes say of Newton six years earlier: "His peculiar gift was the power of holding continuously in his mind a purely mental problem until he had seen straight through it. I fancy his pre-eminence is due to his muscles of intuition being the strongest and most enduring with which a man has ever been gifted."

In that spring of 1948 there was another memorable event. Hans received a small package from Japan containing the first two issues of a new physics journal, *Progress of Theoretical Physics*, published in Kyoto. The two issues were printed in English on brownish paper of poor quality. They contained a total of six short articles. The first article in issue No. 2 was called "On a Relativistically Invariant Formulation of the Quantum Theory of Wave Fields," by S. Tomonaga of Tokyo University. Underneath it was a footnote saying, "Translated from the paper . . . (1943) appeared originally in Japanese." Hans gave me the article to read. It contained, set out simply and lucidly without any mathematical elaboration, the central idea of Julian Schwinger's theory. The implications of this were astonishing. Somehow or other, amid the ruin and turmoil of the war, totally isolated from the rest of the world, Tomonaga had maintained in Japan a school of research in theoretical physics that was in some respects ahead of anything existing anywhere else at that time. He had pushed on alone and laid the foundations of the new quantum electrodynamics, five years before Schwinger and without any help from the Columbia experiments. He had not, in 1943, completed the theory and developed it as a practical tool. To Schwinger rightly belongs the credit for making the theory into a coherent mathematical structure. But Tomonaga had taken the first essential step. There he was, in the spring of 1948, sitting amid the ashes and rubble of Tokyo and sending us that pathetic little package. It came to us as a voice out of the deep.

A few weeks later, Oppy received a personal letter from Tomonaga describing the more recent work of the Japanese physicists. They had been moving ahead fast in the same direction as Schwinger. Regular communications were soon established. Oppy invited Tomonaga to visit Princeton, and a succession of Tomonaga's students later came to work with us at Princeton and at Cornell. When I met Tomonaga for the first time, a letter to my parents recorded my immediate impression of him: "He is more able than either Schwinger or Feynman to talk about ideas other than his own. And he has enough of his own too. He is an exceptionally unselfish person." On his table among the physics journals was a copy of the New Testament.

An Interrupted Life

The Diaries of Etty Hillesum 1941–43
ETTY HILLESUM

Etty Hillesum gave her diaries to a friend in hopes that they might
survive World War II. In these random thoughts she has captured
the hope and the fear and the horror of the early years of the war.
The excerpts reprinted here all comment on the importance of
writing as she faces the chaos and destruction around her, but she
also writes about many other subjects: art, love, psychology,
psychochirology ("the study and classification of palm prints"),
music, family, friends, politics, religion.

The initials Hillesum used for peoples' names emphasize the
private nature of these diaries; she wrote for herself. But the fact
that she preserved the exercise books in which she recorded her
thoughts and that she gave them to a friend with instructions
indicates that at some point she began to think of an audience
beyond herself.

Etty Hillesum died on November 30, 1943, in Auschwitz. Her
diaries were published in 1981.

Original publication: *An Interrupted Life[:] The Diaries of Etty Hillesum 1941–43*. New
York: Jonathan Cape Ltd., 1983.

SUNDAY, 9 MARCH [1941]. Here goes, then. This is a painful and
well-nigh insuperable step for me: yielding up so much that has been suppressed
to a blank sheet of lined paper. The thoughts in my head are sometimes so clear
and so sharp and my feelings so deep, but writing about them comes hard. The
main difficulty, I think, is a sense of shame. So many inhibitions, so much fear
of letting go, of allowing things to pour out of me, and yet that is what I must
do if I am ever to give my life a reasonable and satisfactory purpose. It is like
the final, liberating scream that always sticks bashfully in your throat when you
make love. I am accomplished in bed, just about seasoned enough I should think
to be counted among the better lovers, and love does indeed suit me to
perfection, and yet it remains a mere trifle, set apart from what is truly essential,
and deep inside me something is still locked away. The rest of me is like that,
too. I am blessed enough intellectually to be able to fathom most subjects, to
express myself clearly on most things; I seem to be a match for most of life's
problems, and yet deep down something like a tightly-wound ball of twine

binds me relentlessly and at times I am nothing more or less than a miserable, frightened creature, despite the clarity with which I can express myself.

[MONTHS LATER]

SATURDAY MORNING. I hope for, and at the same time I dread, the day that I shall be completely alone with myself and with a blank sheet of paper. Then I shall do nothing but write. I haven't dared do it yet. I don't know why. When I was at the concert with S. on Wednesday, indeed whenever I see a lot of people together, I want to write a novel. During the interval I felt compelled to get hold of a piece of paper and to jot something down. I didn't know what. To spin out a few ideas. Instead, S. dictated something about a patient. Interesting enough. And bizarre as well. But it meant that I had to ignore my own promptings, my desire to give an account of myself. I have this ever-present need to write but not yet the courage to get on with it. I think I tend to ignore my own inner needs. I sometimes get the feeling that my personality is growing stronger, but all I demonstrate to others is unwavering amiability and concern and benevolence even when it means effacing myself. The theory is that we should all put a good face on things, be sociable and not bother others with our moods. In fact, when I suppress so much I become all the more antisocial: I don't want to see or speak to anyone for days.

There is a sort of lamentation and loving-kindness as well as a little wisdom somewhere inside me that cry to be let out. Sometimes several different dialogues run through me at the same time, images and figures, moods, a sudden flash of something that must be my very own truth. Love for human beings that must be hard fought for. Not through politics or a party, but in myself. Still a lot of false shame to get rid of. And there is God. The girl who could not kneel but learned to do so on the rough coconut matting in an untidy bathroom. Such things are often more intimate even than sex. The story of the girl who gradually learned to kneel is something I would love to write in the fullest possible way.

I protest too much. I have all the time in the world to write. More time than anyone else, probably. But there is that inner vacillation. Why, I wonder? Because I think I must come out with nothing but brilliant ideas? Because I haven't yet worked it all out? But that can only come with practice. 'Above all be true to yourself.'

22 APRIL. WEDNESDAY . . . 11:00 P.M. Something else: at times I think that I will be able to write one day, to describe things, but then I suddenly grow tired and say to myself, 'Why all these words?' I want every word I write to be born, truly born, none to be artificial, every one to be essential. For otherwise there is no point to it at all. And that is why I shall never be able to make a living by writing, why I must always have a job to earn my keep. Every word born of an inner necessity—writing must never be anything else.

24 APRIL, FRIDAY MORNING 9:30. . . . I was reminded all at once of a time when, at about the age of 15, I was sitting in my father's small study, untidy and impersonal as were all the rooms in all the different houses in which we ever lived—I sat there and suddenly needed to write. And I still remember what I wrote: 'red, green, black. Through the leaves of the green tree I see a girl in a bright red dress.' Etcetera. That was the only way in which I could express all the vehement feelings inside me.

Later, too, on the train to Paris. Excited by the rhythm of the train, by the many impressions—there I sat with a miserable little notepad clutched in my fingers, and again needed to write. And I wrote something like: 'grey, dark, black, but inside it was bright orange and crimson.' And then, in that hurtling train, I also wrote: 'It is certain that the world dies a separate death for each one of us, and yet the world still exists.' How odd. I remember that I thought this sentence immensely impressive and that, for a time, it relaxed me from my inner constriction.

I still need to write things down. I should like, as it were, to caress the paper with just the right word—I should like to write about yellow daffodils, tiny yellow marsh-marigolds, my chestnut twigs, that have stopped blooming now, their many small hands stretched out as gracefully as a dancer's and at the same time raised so defensively towards the sky. And so on. Many unconnected thoughts. But there is one good thing at least: my old asperity has gone. I could list a host of clever formulations overflowing with wit that I used to think up, but nowadays I've grown tired of all that. Indeed, I sometimes wonder whether I haven't been living too much on my 'soul' of late—treating ideas with too much disdain. Sometimes I have a fleeting urge to express this or that in elegant words, but I kill the urge straightaway, finding all that now much too contrived. It will all balance out in the end. Have patience. Slowly, steadily, patiently.

Yesterday I woke up at 6 o'clock and the first thing that struck me was that I'll have to study Dutch all over again and fashion myself an instrument out of that language. I probably place too much trust in the belief that the words will come by themselves when the time is ripe. Perhaps that is my great mistake. I am nothing and I know nothing.

When it comes to portraying character or atmosphere I think I should get stuck at the first attempt. S. said to me one day, 'You still savour your talent.' I sometimes wonder if it is a talent at all. Perhaps I am really squandering everything I've got. No doubt I should be more energetic in concentrating my mind at this desk, my true hub. Sweep together all the scattered pieces from every corner and mould them into a whole. Perhaps I allow myself to be blown too easily with the wind. But I really don't know where to begin. Perhaps one day there will be a beginning, and then I shall know how to go on. But what of that beginning? Above all: be steadfast. Don't let the days crumble away between your clever fingers. Time passes so quickly. It's past 10 o'clock already.

[A MONTH OR TWO LATER]

FRIDAY EVENING, 7:30. Looked at Japanese prints with Glassner this afternoon. That's how I want to write. With that much space round a few words. They should simply emphasise the silence. Just like that print with the sprig of blossom in the lower corner. A few delicate brush strokes—but with what attention to the smallest detail—and all around it space, not empty but inspired. The few great things that matter in life can be said in a few words. If I should ever write—but what?—I would like to brush in a few words against a wordless background. To describe the silence and the stillness and to inspire them. What matters is the right relationship between words and wordlessness, the wordlessness in which much more happens than in all the words one can string together. And the wordless background of each short story—or whatever it may be—must have a distinct hue and a discrete content, just like those Japanese prints. It is not some vague and incomprehensible silence, for silence too must have contours and form. All that words should do is to lend the silence form and contours. Each word is like a small milestone, a slight rise in the ground beside a flat, endless road across sweeping plains. It really is quite laughable: I can write whole chapters on how I would like to write, and it is quite possible that apart from these words of wisdom I shall never put pen to paper. But those Japanese prints suddenly showed me most graphically how I would really like to write. And one day I would love to walk through Japanese landscapes. In fact, I am sure that one day I shall go to the East.

The Home That Lies Always in Memory

RICHARD MARIUS

Richard Marius, Director of Expository Writing at Harvard University and author of biographies, novels, and writing texts, stresses *home* in this autobiographical essay. The article was commissioned by *Touchstone*, the magazine of the Tennessee Humanities Council, for an issue devoted to the question "Can we go home again?" Since the audience of such a publication is regional, Marius wants Tennesseans to see—or remember—the rural Tennessee he knew in his childhood. Thus, readers follow the story of the author and his family as an account of life earlier in the twentieth century, before "the cancerous and unplanned urban sprawl of Knoxville."

Original publication: *Touchstone*, Spring 1986.

Home for me will always be the farm where I was born and where I lived until I was twenty-one. It lay—and lies still—at Dixie Lee Junction some twenty miles west of Knoxville.

My father was first chemist, then superintendent, and finally manager of the Lenoir Car Works, a small subsidiary of Southern Railway making iron wheels and other parts for boxcars at the nearby town of Lenoir City. My older brother is afflicted with Down's Syndrome. Just before I was born in 1933, the family settled on the farm. My mother and father could not bear to put him in an institution, and the isolation of what was then a remote and rural place seemed to offer everyone freedom and safety.

And it was isolation—though now with the cancerous and unplanned urban sprawl of Knoxville eating almost to the edge of our farm and with good roads and the habit of commuting, the isolation I so vividly recall seems dreamlike and unreal.

I remember the sense of tremendous space—the windows of the room where I slept as a child opening onto the mysterious woods, the silence of nights broken by the occasional grumble of a truck shifting gears to pull the hill on Highway 11, or the eerie shriek of a southbound freight pounding through the dark at Martel some four miles away, its wildcat whistle howling like a great exuberant spirit set loose on the world.

After years and years I can remember the fall of morning light against the green leaves of the oaks and maples on the west side of the house in the spring. And I remember the unique smell of fresh-cut hay in the summer and the working smell of farmers that was compounded of sweat, chewing tobacco, hay, and dirt. I remember the smell of cool rain on hot grass. I remember the myriad singing of insects in the woods at night, the fireflies drifting in the hot summer evenings, the morning sound of church bells rung down from the Midway Baptist Church on the hill next to what we have always called our "upper field."

We were Methodists in my early childhood and attended the Martel Methodist Church until a young preacher fresh out of Emory University told my mother that Jesus had made some mistakes. Then we started to the Midway Baptist Church—midway between Muddy Creek and Hickory Creek. The Baptists did not allow preachers to say Jesus had made mistakes. Besides, we could walk to Midway through the woods.

The church bell ringing out over Sunday morning called our community together. It seemed to gong rhythmically in a great calm, and the sound carried for miles. Some people drove to church. But many walked, and I remember the irregular processional down country roads, men and women and children in their Sunday best, coming to worship a God who in His majesty and terror seemed close to life as we knew it.

We lived intimately with nature, but this intimacy did not breed in us any sentimentality about the natural world. We knew the beauties, but we knew the terrors, too. My life on the farm fixed in me the abiding conviction that nature is not benign.

We were always running into snakes in unexpected places. One of my most vivid childhood recollections is of walking, at age four or five, in the furrow behind a neighborhood boy who was plowing our upper field with a horse. The plow ripped a thick blacksnake out of the moist earth. I can recall that writhing body erupting suddenly out of the clean soil, twisting and striking. I fled in panic. I remember a king snake in a bird's nest, its body lumpy with the baby birds it had swallowed and all the adult birds around screaming ineffectually at its looped coils. One of my recurring dreams is of coming on snakes unexpectedly. Sometimes I have to get up and walk around the house, arousing myself to full wakefulness, to convince myself that the nightmare is only that—a nightmare.

The weather had its terrors, too. Once when I was very small, I was in the loft of our barn alone, playing in the hay when a sudden lightning storm blew up. I stood in the big hay window of the barn, shrieking in terror as the rain roared down on the galvanized tin roof and as the lightning crashed down with its burden of thunder out of a black sky. Once when we had a terrible storm at the country consolidated school called Farragut when I was in the first grade, I jumped up screaming from my little chair and ran all over the grammar school building while the principal and two teachers ran after me and finally subdued me by throwing themselves on top of me.

Rural people adapt themselves to the terror and the beauty and live with them both from day to day. We made pets of chickens, ducks, and calves—and then killed and ate them. We hunted and ate what we killed. We accepted some things that seem brutal in retrospect. We did not raise pigs because my mother thought they were too much trouble. But I recall watching pigs slaughtered at the farms of neighbors. Pig-killing time came in late November when the chill air kept the fresh meat from spoiling. The pigs were pierced in the hind legs with hooks and hauled alive up to a beam. Then someone with a long, sharp knife cut their throats one by one. The pigs squealed in shrieking terror and pain when they knew what was happening to them. The squealing went on and on until they died, and the gush of blood came in a flood, draining the carcass and making it easier to work with. But in the aftermath of slaughter, there was the sweetness of plenty. My mother exercised a strange sort of matriarchy over our neighborhood. (I never heard anyone outside the family call her anything but "Mrs. Marius.") At killing time, people sent us packages of fresh meat, and we ate well.

I disliked many things about farm life. The worst was the tedium of its routines. I milked for several years until my mother was kind enough to get rid of our last milch cow when I was a sophomore in high school. Being rid of the cows meant that I could participate in after-school activities.

The routines of milking are implacable—6:30 in the morning and 6:30 at night, seven days a week, fifty-two weeks in the year. You cannot take cows on a vacation, and all the time I was growing up my family never took a holiday together. In winter it was a cold, dark walk to the barn. In summer the cow's switching tail was a flail across the back of my neck.

Cows—and most other farm animals—are more than a nuisance. They are dangerous. I still have the caved-in place on my chest where a Jersey cow kicked me when I was ten, apparently breaking one or two of my ribs back from my breast bone. She objected to fingernails that I had carelessly let grow long. When I was in the first grade, the father of one of my friends was gored to death by a bull. A little later one of the boys in my room was kicked in the head by a mule and reduced to imbecility. I remember him tramping around the country as an adult and preaching ecstatically at primitive churches and tent revivals where people heard his repetitious babbling as a direct inspiration from God. My first-grade class picture reposes on my desk at Harvard. He looks out at me from the time before the mule kicked him—a somber child's face under a blond shock of hair, a face pensive and uneasy at the camera. I never look at him without feeling a pang of grief.

Some of the isolation and the poverty seemed like fun at the time. I remember how leisurely people were with each other at night and on summer Sunday afternoons. We had almost nothing to do then but be together.

The Midway Baptist Church had occasional "socials." Somehow calling them "parties" seemed wicked to some of the deacons; so we called them "socials." We had them in fields and in front of barns and scheduled them by the phases of the moon. We sat around big fires and roasted hot dogs, and then we played wildly active games under the moonlight—red rover, drop the handkerchief, and my favorite, flying Dutchman. Sometimes to this day at a dull party or at a Harvard faculty meeting I feel the urge to clap my hands and shout, "All right, everybody! Out in the yard for a round of flying Dutchman."

When someone died, the neighborhood turned out. The night before the funeral people brought food to the house of the deceased. The corpse was usually laid out in a coffin propped up in the living room. In the old days, I was told, people were supposed to keep watch during the night to see if the corpse took a breath. People had a horror of being buried alive. At every watching of the dead I ever attended, the story circulated about a corpse—sometimes male, sometimes female—that had been exhumed for some reason or another, and the body was found with hair in its hands. The person had waked up in the grave and had torn his hair out before death finally came.

By my time, corpses were being embalmed. There was a macabre sort of comfort in the assurance that if you were not actually dead when people thought you were, the undertaker would kill you with his formaldehyde.

These watchings were social events. Neighbors drifted into the kitchen or out into the yard in summer and drank strong coffee and talked away the night. Some young people courted—though this practice was frowned upon by the upright. But then death was an excuse for young men and women to stay up after ten o'clock. Despite the presence of death, you could hear the gentle murmur of laughter when people told funny stories, sometimes about the deceased. And sometimes theological discussions went on in a desultory flailing of Bible verses and speculative argument. Is it true that what is to be will be? When was Jesus coming again?

The graveyard of the Midway Baptist Church was the final repository of the community. It has always seemed a comfortable place to me. I used to know the graves by heart and the stories that went with them. Here with little Nanny May Foute whose picture was stamped on the tombstone by some photographic process that I never understood. She had jumped rope some five hundred times on a dare about 1927 and dropped dead of a hemorrhage of the brain. There she was and is, looking out forever young across the green quiet of our cemetery.

Lucy Lowe and Bobbie Harbin went for ice cream and a ride one night in August 1941 with a couple of boys in a new car. On a country road that ran down to the Tennessee river, the driver got confused by the moonlight on the water and thought it was the road stretching ahead. He drove at full speed into the ferry landing, and Lucy and Bobbie drowned. They were sixteen. Lucy had blond hair and laughed much. She used to let me sit on her lap on the schoolbus where there were never enough seats. Bobbie was chubby and used to come to sew with my sister.

They lie close to each other in our cemetery. Bobbie's mother planted a flower garden on her grave. For years and years you could go up there and see Mrs. Harbin sitting by her daughter in the twilight. Now Mrs. Harbin is buried next to the girl she lost.

More than anything else I remember the stories. My mother's people told the first stories I heard. They had all been born at a farm called Rattlesnake Springs which my great-grandfather James Curry bought from the Cherokee Indians when they were herded west in 1838 on the infamous Trail of Tears.

I don't know what James Curry paid for the farm. The Cherokees were not in a position to bargain. But get it he did, and named it because he had to kill rattlesnakes by the hundred in the marshy basin where the spring water gushed out of the ground. The Indians were collected on his place to be driven West. One family tale was of a Cherokee man with a feverish wife who knocked at the door one night seeking help. My great-grandmother nursed the woman, and when they departed, the man left a necklace of copper beads which, my mother recalled, was a green relic in the house when her family moved away around 1901. She did not know what happened to it.

Like many East Tennesseans, James Curry and his sons went north to fight for the blue and union in 1861. My mother, born in 1891, and her sisters and brothers could sit together in our big yard on summer nights and tell stories of what it had been for their mother and the other women in the family to endure the War down there in Bradley County where most people espoused the Rebel cause. I can still tell many of those stories—though my own sons, urban and perennially occupied as they are, have never been interested in them.

Anyway, our community at Dixie Lee Junction had its own treasury of old tales. I got from a neighbor named Agnes Ginn the story of how a man about to be hanged in the county back in the nineteenth century stood under the noose and predicted rain during a horrible drought and how the rain came in a whooping storm that nearly tore the county apart the next day. Years after Mrs. Ginn died I adapted that story into my first novel, *The Coming of Rain*.

Molly Montgomery Hand, now buried in our graveyard, told me once that her father had fought for the Union and her father's brother had fought for the Confederacy. There was bad blood between them all their lives afterwards. "Each one of them knew that the other one would have killed him if he'd had the chance," she said.

We suppress the bad memories, but they are there. My family was not poor, but we lived side by side with people who were. Most people I knew had a hard time. The miracle is that most of them made it. When I went to Farragut School, many of the children were off subsistence farms. Many were sharecropper children. Sometime in grade school we started getting a federally assisted lunch program. A hot plate lunch cost eleven cents. Some families got the only cash they had from their tobacco allotment, and that was only a few hundred dollars a year. If they had two or three children, they could not afford eleven cents a day for a hot meal for each of them. Some of the children who brought their lunches wrapped in greasy paper probably ate better than the rest of us. One of the staples of the plate lunch at Farragut was corn pudding, a thick, greasy mess. The memory of corn pudding turns my stomach to this day.

But not long ago I talked to an old friend who is now a truck driver. He recalled that his mother used to fix him country ham with biscuits to take as his lunch to school. He was so ashamed to have to take his lunch while other children were buying theirs that he went out behind the school to wolf down his biscuits and then go back to pretend that he had eaten at the cafeteria. I recalled the corn pudding and told him that he had the better part. But the hurt was still in his face when he remembered.

At Farragut I went to school with children whose powers of survival in retrospect seem remarkable. I remember the boy whose father shot him with a shotgun, whether on purpose or by accident I do not recall. But I remember that child's bad eye and how ready he was to fight with all of us, and how our first grade teacher Miss Elsie Llewellyn took him to Knoxville one Saturday and bought him a red-and-blue striped T-shirt that he then wore every day until it rotted off of his little body. I remember children coming barefoot to school long after the ground was cold, and I remember illness.

It seemed that people were sick all the time. When I think of Farragut School, I remember rooms filled with children coughing. The school was heated with soft coal, and I recall with great affection Mr. Thompson, our janitor, who labored with the great old furnace and kept our rooms hot and always spoke gently to us. I suppose that some children came to school when they were sick because they knew they could be warmer there than at home.

A little girl named Maudie May was, we thought, unusually dirty and misshapen. Poor children, fighting so hard for survival, are not generous with underdogs. To mock one or another of the boys, we would shout that this frail little creature was the unlucky boy's sweetheart. The accused boy would deny it at the top of his lungs, sometimes with tears. These cruel jokes came to an end after the night Maudie May's throat swelled up and she coughed herself to death.

Not many children could get to town to see movies. We had "educational films" every Monday afternoon, and I always looked forward to them. They were about the war or about the Good Neighbor Policy or about how to do safe home canning. They were about exciting places and other worlds. Farragut provided feature films for us about once a month. For fifteen cents we got to sit enthralled and silent in the school auditorium with the heavy shades pulled and watch the romance and the happy endings that movies gave us then. When the principal pulled the shades down, we knew the glory was about to begin.

Many children could not afford the fifteen cents. And so they were herded into some of the large classrooms and put to doing something else while the rest of us trooped into the magic precincts of the glorious auditorium. The fiction was that you could choose to see the movies or choose to stay in a classroom. The reality was that children with fifteen cents chose to see the movies, and those with no money chose to stay away.

What I remember most was how uncomplaining these poor children were at being excluded. I saw then how poverty confers on its victims a certain set of expectations or perhaps a certain absence of expectations. This was the way life was. Some children went to movies, and some children did not. The poor are natural predestinarians. What is to be will be, and much of it will be bad.

One of these boys was Charley Stooksbury who used to wait for me outside the basement cafeteria at Farragut at lunch. My father gave me sixteen cents for lunch, and with the extra nickel I bought a Brown Cow—vanilla ice cream dipped in chocolate and frozen onto a stick. Charley would descend on me and shout, "Gimme ducks," and draw his dirty fingernail across a place about one third from the bottom of my Brown Cow. I could eat down to the fingernail line. Then I had to surrender the rest to Charley, or he would beat me up.

After the movies, which Charley could not afford to see, he would fall on me to get me to tell him the story. So I played David Copperfield to his Steerforth, telling him the stories while he listened rapt with pleasure, sometimes nodding in puzzlement and asking a question, sometimes filling in the parts as though he had seen the picture himself, sometimes running back over what I had said to be sure he had got it right, as if the movie had been some oracle and he had to get it right to make life work. He was a lovely, bright and witty child, always happy—especially when he was eating the last of my ice cream—and I don't know whatever happened to him.

We were an unruly lot, and some of our teachers ruled by the paddle. I recall with special detestation one of my third-grade teachers (we had three that year) who used to snatch us up from our desks for the slightest offense and beat us on the backside or on the hands with a ruler. I think she enjoyed hitting us. Years afterwards I ran into her in a Knoxville cafeteria and realized that time had not dimmed my loathing for her. I imagined picking up her fruit Jell-O and rubbing it into her snow-white hair. But of course I only smiled and told her it was nice to see her and fled as quickly as I could. Who could know? She may have carried a ruler still in her purse in case she met some old student like me.

But most of our teachers at Farragut were wonderful. I went to visit Miss Elsie Llewellyn as long as she lived and by the bye got caught up on which of my former classmates was in Brushy Mountain State Penitentiary where her brother Mr. Frank was warden. When she died in December 1967, old and full of years as the Bible says, I was one of the five or six people who stood by her open grave to bury her. Her picture is on my desk with the members of my first-grade class, and I look at her and still think she was beautiful.

Mrs. Reynolds in the high school used to direct plays in the auditorium. I suppose they were not great plays, but they took us out of an ordinary world of routine and gave us a wonderful world of fantasy in its place. She mobilized students and grown-ups, and suddenly there was our bus driver, Clayton Brown, being a handy man on stage and saying very funny things, and there was the high school math teacher Mr. Crowder being a country father in search of his son who had run off to the evil city, and there was Gene Gibson, the high school agriculture teacher, playing a street bully, and it was all grand.

Somebody had given the school a backdrop for outdoor scenes. It pulled down from the top at the back of the stage like a great shade, and there was a beautiful garden with three painted marble steps leading up to a walkway that led in a slant off to the right into a magical woods. The perspective made it breathtakingly real to little children. No matter what the play, that was the backdrop with its walkway and the great woods for all the outdoor scenes, and when we had PTA programs and speeches, somebody pulled the backdrop down because it was better than the naked stage. I loved that backdrop. In my mind I ran down that walkway into the woods a thousand times and came into a wonderland where everything was soft and gentle and bathed in endless spring light.

Miss Grace Boring was my fourth-grade teacher, and she had a beautiful singing voice. Once, standing in front of the enchantment of the backdrop, she did a solo version of a popular song called "Juanita," and as she sang, her voice filling the auditorium, I could see the whole story unfolding before my mind—the Mexican woman choosing to leave her lover because of her family or something. His pleas that she remain. I don't remember what. Maybe I made it all up. But it was sweet and sad, and when Miss Grace sang, I felt like crying from the beauty of it all—though of course I did not.

Nita, Juanita,
Ask thy soul if we should part
Nita, Juanita,
Lean thou on my heart.
In thy dark eyes' splendor
Softly shines the southern moon;
Through the eastern window,
Comes the day too soon.

Everything has changed now. The monstrous ugliness of West Knoxville has eaten up the green land. The Midway Baptist Church has changed its name to the Dixie Lee Baptist Church and installed saccharine electronic chimes that ooze cloying hymns all over the neighborhood on Sunday mornings—a neighborhood going suburban and not going to church. Miss Elsie's house surrounded by its huge oaks is gone, and a garish shopping mall sprawls on the spot. Old Farragut School is falling into ruin on the silent hill across the highway from a new Farragut School that is huge and sleek and marvelously modern.

Things are better of course. And I would not wish back days that had so much poverty, so much illness, so much tedium, and so much toil. Still I feel a pang of memory when I go home and see the changes, and I miss the things that are gone. All the elders are dead. All the dirt roads have been paved, and people do not know the family that lives two houses away except by name and sometimes not even that.

One warm afternoon last June, driving from the farm to Knoxville I turned off the crowded highway and drove up onto the hill where the brick buildings of old Farragut School stand broken and abandoned. A soft breeze whispered in the branches of the huge elms. I walked around to the crumbling gymnasium where my third-grade class danced a Virginia reel to dedicate the building when it was new. I went into the basement cafeteria. And I went into the auditorium.

The interior of the auditorium was a wreck. All the windows were broken. The black shades had been torn down and lay in heaps on the floor amid shards of splintered glass. The seats had been pulled out of the floor and lay all hugger-mugger in a general litter of discarded paraphernalia. The backdrop with the long walk and the magical woods was gone. I walked up onto the stage and looked out on the desolation. And suddenly on impulse, I stepped forward and began to sing what I could remember of "Juanita."

I must have presented a mad spectacle. A certain foretaste of embarrassment crossed my mind as I stood there singing to the emptiness, wondering in the upper room of thought how on earth I would explain myself to some passerby who might be drawn inside by the sound of a voice coming from such a place at such a time. But then I told myself that the home that lies always in our memories requires no explanation. I thought of all those children who had once sat there, all those teachers, all our faces expectantly upturned waiting for *something*, all the life and fantasy embraced within those once-proud walls, all the years of childhood.

And I sang on to the end.

Thoughts on Myself That I'm Willing To Share

TOM PAULK

Tom Paulk, a businessman, has relied on his sense of humor in an autobiography written in a simulated interview. He had twenty minutes to tell the interviewer what he wanted her to know about him. She was his only audience, and this narrative was the only information that would be available to her for the interview. He makes fun of the "art" of writing autobiography as he provides some details about himself.

Previously unpublished

My primary sources of motivation are responsibility to my family, pride in myself, recognition by others, duty to humanity, and a desire for other people to see in me a few of the attributes that I find appealing in other people. Some of these attributes are truthfulness, honesty, and a sense of humor that has little—yet some—respect for propriety, intelligence, articulateness and eloquence, compassion for others, and physical attractiveness accented by mildly lascivious behavior.

Some things I like include political events, the Bill of Rights, literature, fishing, flying, pornography, filet mignon, crabapples, going back to college, little children (no connection to the pornography, thank you), debates (as participant or observer), space exploration (as observer only), and a job well done. There are also things I dislike, but I dislike discussing them.

My hopes for the future are: that my children will grow up to be healthy, happy doctors, lawyers, research scientists, astronauts, or healthy, happy combinations thereof; that liberals will increasingly dominate U.S. politics; that world leaders will come to their senses and do away with nuclear weapons forever; that the Christians will be proved right about the existence of Heaven; that the atheists will be proved right about the existence of hell; that I will eventually do, create, build, say, or write something that many will believe is a lasting contribution to humanity; and that I never have to write another autobiography.

"Foreword"

from Bits of Paradise
SCOTTIE FITZGERALD SMITH

As "the daughter of a Famous Author," Scottie Fitzgerald Smith knew that the audience of *Bits of Paradise* would be fans of her father and mother, Scott and Zelda Sayre Fitzgerald. Thus, she turned to her memories of her parents to provide some new insights into their lives and works. In addition to her own recollections of the Jazz Age, Scottie Fitzgerald Smith quotes from her mother's writing—a passage in which Zelda Fitzgerald recalls the Twenties in Europe. The autobiographical narratives of mother and daughter provide background for the new collection of stories that Smith describes as "the last book which will ever be published devoted to previously uncollected writings of my parents."

Smith's awareness of her audience and of their interests in her parents has resulted in autobiography with an appropriate emphasis, her memories of life with her parents.

Original publication: *Bits of Paradise[:] 22 Uncollected Stories by F. Scott and Zelda Fitzgerald.* Selected by Matthew J. Bruccoli with the assistance of Scottie Fitzgerald Smith. New York: Scribners, 1974.

Though it was Professor Bruccoli who conceived, delivered, and nursed this volume—he loves 'his' authors so much I do believe if he found all their grocery bills he'd put them out in an annotated edition—it is I who claim the credit for the title. It's a bit corny, but then so are some of the things in these stories, which have some mighty unbelievable heroes and heroines. The only way you'll get through them all, I think, is to imagine my father and mother as two bright meteors streaking across a starry sky back in the days when wars and moons seemed equally far away, and then these stories as a sort of fall-out. For they all have one thing in common: a sense of breathlessness, as if even their authors still were gasping at the wonders glimpsed as they flew past Heaven.

The title has two even more personal meanings for me, however. First, it brings to mind my mother's description of my father in her novel, *Save Me The Waltz*, which tells the story of their romance better than anything else which has been written: 'There seemed to be some heavenly support beneath his shoulder blades that lifted his feet from the ground in ecstatic suspension, as if he secretly enjoyed the ability to fly but was walking as a compromise to convention.'

Secondly, this is the last book which will ever be published devoted to previously uncollected writings of my parents. It's the end of an era, really, marked by the monumental scholarship of Professor Bruccoli and many others, which began about twenty-five years ago and has brought my father from relative obscurity as an artifact of the Jazz Age to his present secure nook in literature. Now everything that's fit to print—and even some that's border-line!—is out on the table for all to see, for the thesis writers to deduce from, and the moralists to point to, and the women's libbers to be shocked by. This is the last addition to the Scott and Zelda story as told by those who lived it, and for this reason I find it a little sad, like an attic which has been emptied of all its secret treasures.

It was in this mood of sentimental leave-taking that I went up to my real-life attic to see what I could find in the way of tangible mementoes still lurking about among the camp trunks and the children's bird cages. Despite a friend's remark that I am the luckiest person she knows because whenever my fortunes take a turn for the worse, I can always try to write myself another batch of undiscovered letters from my father, the fact is that everything of literary interest—the scrapbooks, the photograph albums, the ledgers and notebooks which my father so meticulously kept—has gradually been turned over to the Princeton University Library. The attic is now mostly populated with such unfamiliar titles as *Kultahattu* (Helsinki, 1959): '. . . ja Gatsby riensi sisään pukeutuneena valkoiseen flanellipukuun ja hopeanhohtoiseen paitaan . . .' and *Lepi I Prokleti* (Belgrade, 1969): '. . . jer je Glorija zamahnula rukom brzo ispusti i ona pade na pod. . . .'

But there are a few things which are special, bits and pieces of the child's paradise which my parents created for me, and which is far more vivid to me than any of our later worlds in Alabama, Maryland, or Hollywood.

Item: The paper dolls on which my mother lavished so much time. Some of them represented the three of us. Once upon a time these dolls had wardrobes of which Rumpelstiltskin could be proud. My mother and I had dresses of pleated wallpaper, and one party frock of mine had ruffles of real lace cut from a Belgian handkerchief. More durable were the ball dresses of Mesdames de Maintenon and Pompadour and the coats-of-mail of Galahad and Launcelot, for these were lavishly painted in the most minute detail in water color so thick that it has scarcely faded. Perfectly preserved are the proud members of the courts of both Louis XIV and King Arthur (figures of haughty mien and aristocratic bearing), a jaunty Goldilocks, an *insouciante* Red Riding Hood, an Errol Flynn-like D'Artagnan, and other personages familiar to all little well-instructed boys and girls of that time. It is characteristic of my mother that these exquisite dolls, each one requiring hours of artistry, should have been created for the delectation of a six-year-old; at the time she died, she was working on a series of Bible illustrations for her oldest grandchild, then eighteen months.

Item: A stamp collection with about a third of its spaces filled in, and in the same box two disconsolate toy soldiers in uniforms of the Wars of the Roses . . . all that's left of the armies from Hannibal's to Napoleon's which used to be put through their battle paces on the dining-room table. These Daddy bought at the *Nain Bleu* in Paris in the vain hope, I suppose, that I would become as fascinated by military history as he was. Very little of my extra-curricular education took—some of it backfired, in fact, for I was made to recite so much Keats and Shelley that I came to look upon them as personal enemies—but I do have some occasionally useful bits of information learned at the parental knee, such as what King Solomon said. 'Solomon said,' Daddy loved to declaim very seriously, 'that all men are liars. Therefore, Solomon was a liar. Therefore what Solomon said was not true. Therefore all men are not liars. Therefore Solomon was not a liar. Therefore what Solomon said was true. Therefore all men are liars. Therefore . . .' You can imagine how frequently I have been reminded of King Solomon during the political events of the past two years.

I'm happy to report, by the way, that insofar as my father was a political creature in any way (as he wrote in 1931, 'It was characteristic of the Jazz Age that it had no interest in politics at all.'), he was a Franklin D. Roosevelt Democrat. His dismissal of the idea that Roosevelt was 'a traitor to his class' as pure nonsense was his single most influential legacy to me, and I expect to go to my grave, as he did to his, with the rare distinction of never having voted for a Republican candidate for President.

Item: A handful of Christmas ornaments, peeling here and there but still in use, along with the tiny skaters who were brought out every year to glide across my mother's pocket-mirrors under the tree. They were carried everywhere with us like talismans, for Christmas was a major production with the Fitzgeralds: railroad tracks would be laid down, mountains would be built out of papier mâché, towns would be constructed to look like medieval villages. My mother described her feeling best in one of the letters which I copied before they, too, were sent to Princeton:

'The tree [in Rome] was cooled with silver bells which rang hauntedly through the night by themselves . . . and we had a tree in Paris covered with mushrooms and with snowy houses which was fun. There were myriad birds of paradise on the tree with spun glass tails, and Nanny kept busily admonishing us about the French customs: how they did not give gifts at Christmas but at New Year's . . . then we had a tree on the Avenue McMahon which Nanny and I decorated between sips of champagne until neither we nor the tree could hold any more of fantaisie or decor. We kept our decorations for years in painted toy boxes and when the last of the tails wilted and the last house grew lopsided, it was almost a bereavement.'

That was a slight exaggeration; three of the birds, tails as sleek as ever, still perch on my own family's tree every Christmas. But Nanny—If only Nanny, our symbol of order and respectability, would come back into my life, I could recapture the past as well as Proust! I don't know her married name, or where she lives now; perhaps she will read these musings and phone. 'You and Nanny,' my mother wrote, 'had so much paraphernalia and were such an official entourage that going some place was always an auspicious pilgrimage.

By the time we had been on a boat half an hour she had the staff up to the chief officers running errands and finding all those so comfortable items which give life a completely mastered and domestic flavor in the British Isles.'

There is a blue ostrich feather fan with most of the feathers missing, and there are some postcards addressed to me from all over, usually just signed 'The man with the three noses' in my father's handwriting. This was one of his favorite jokes and I don't remember thinking it particularly funny, though it was better than the ones in which I had to play an active role. For company, I would inevitably be placed on his knee, where the following dialogue would ensue:

> FSF: Do you know the story of three holes in the ground?
> ME (gravely): No, I don't. What is it?
> FSF (triumphantly): Well, well, well!

or—and this one usually went over a little better:

> FSF: Do you know the story of the three eggs?
> ME (gravely): No, I don't. What is it?
> FSF (in mock sorrow): Too bad!

and finally, as the grand climax to his performance:

> FSF: Do you know the story of the dirty shirt?
> ME (gravely): No, I don't. What is it?
> FSF (tossing me off his knee): That's one on you-oo!

He told me why the chicken crossed the road and what's black and white and red all over, and showed me how to make a handkerchief disappear up your sleeve and how to make rabbit ears with your fingers against the light; he loved games and false faces and make-believe and his favorite children's story was *The Rose and The Ring*. That's what *I* remember about the paradise years, but here's a version from my mother, written after I got back from a trip to Europe just before World War II:

'I suppose that few people have seen more varied aspects of life at first hand than we did; known more different kinds of people or participated in more compelling destinies. The truncate wails of the nightingale echoing melancholily through those first years on a deserted Riviera; Paris in the roseate glow of early street lights with violets being sold over the Cafe Weber and dyed roses about the foot of the Madeleine; the blatant prerogative of taxi horns and hotels full of new people all freed from weary sequences of life somewhere else. Do you, by any chance, remember the sparrows at the Cafe Dauphine and how you fed them bread crumbs on those gala mornings?

'Then, too, we saw Rome before the new gilt of Fascism had begun to fade and sipped aperitifs in the eternal glooms of the Piazza Cologna and swept like wraiths through the dim passageways to obscure hotels. We went to London to see a fog and saw Tallulah Bankhead which was, perhaps, about the same effect. Then the fog blew up and we reconstituted Arnold Bennett's *Pretty Lady* and the works of Compton McKenzie which Daddy loved so, and we had a curious nocturnal bottle of champagne with members of the British polo team. We dined with Galsworthy and lunched with Lady Randolph Churchill and had tea in the mellow remembrances of Shane Leslie's house, who later took us to see the pickpockets pick in Wopping. They did.

'I don't know how many other things we saw; we saw Venice and visited the Murphys at Salzburg in the dwarf-haunted fastnesses of inky black lakes and fir-fragrant lanes and we stayed in the royal suite at Munich . . . courtesy of the proprietors. Your generation is the last to bear witness of the grace and gala of those days of the doctrine of free will. I am so glad that you saw where the premium lay and savoured its properties before the end.'

Some of these stories may come as a disappointment to lovers of *Tender Is The Night*, 'The Rich Boy,' or even some of the devastatingly self-revealing articles in *Esquire*. But if one thinks of them less as literature than as reports from another, more romantic world, one will find bits in them that evoke the best of both Fitzgeralds . . . they will at least lay to rest what is in my opinion a popular misconception about their relationship: the notion that they plagiarized from one another in a tense, sometimes hostile, spirit of competition. As can be seen in this collection, their styles, attitudes, and modes of story-telling were so completely different that the only thing they have in common is the material from which they were molded: in 'Southern Girl,' for instance, you find the same theme—Alabama girl feels intimidated and ill at ease in Yankee territory—the well-known FSF story, *The Ice Palace*. To be sure, when it came to drawing upon their experiences in Europe, a serious conflict of interest arose between the characters in *Tender Is The Night* and those in my mother's novel, *Save Me The Waltz*. But that is another story, and the one told in this book is of the brighter side of their personal paradise, a mutually complementary sense of humor and zest for living.

To Robby

JOHN EDGAR WIDEMAN

John Edgar Wideman dedicates *Homewood Trilogy* to his brother, who is in prison convicted of murder. His dedication, in the form of a letter, provides an interpretation of the works in the trilogy through the image of stories as "letters." This letter to Robby, also an open letter to the readers of his fiction, provides everyone with some insight into his life and the meaning of racial barriers.

Original publication: *Homewood Trilogy*. New York: Avon, 1985.

Stories are letters. Letters sent to anybody or everybody. But the best kind are meant to be read by a specific somebody. When you read that kind you know you are eavesdropping. You know a real person somewhere will read the same words you are reading and the story is that person's business and you are a ghost listening in.

Remember. I think it was Geral I first heard call a watermelon a letter from home. After all these years I understand a little better what she meant. She was saying the melon is a letter addressed to us. A story for us from down home. Down Home being everywhere we've never been, the rural South, the old days, slavery, Africa. That juicy, striped message with red meat and seeds, which always looked like roaches to me, was blackness as cross and celebration, a history we could taste and chew. And it was meant for us. Addressed to us. We were meant to slit it open and take care of business.

Consider all these stories as letters from home. I never liked watermelon as a kid. I think I remember you did. You weren't afraid of becoming instant nigger, of sitting barefoot and goggle-eyed and Day-Glo black and drippy-lipped on massa's fence if you took one bit of the forbidden fruit. I was too scared to enjoy watermelon. Too self-conscious. I let people rob me of a simple pleasure. Watermelon's still tainted for me. But I know better now. I can play with the idea even if I can't get down and have a natural ball eating a real one.

Anyway . . . these stories are letters. Long overdue letters from me to you. I wish they could tear down the walls. I wish they could snatch you away from where you are.

•   •   •

Chapter Questions

1. Select one essay from this chapter and characterize the audience for whom the author is writing. What details in the essay lead you to this characterization? How does the audience differ from the audiences of other selections in this chapter?
2. Which essays make specific demands on readers in their use of language or organization?
3. Does race or sex of the authors of these selections affect readers' interpretations?
4. Etty Hillesum's diary entries should be the most private or personal writing in this chapter. Compare this selection with Wideman's public letter to his brother, or the passage from Zelda Sayre Fitzgerald's letter, quoted by her daughter Scottie Smith. What characteristics do all of these more personal writings share?

5. Place the essays in this chapter on a spectrum from most personal to most impersonal in approach to intended audience. Explain your placements.
6. Which one of these autobiographical essays has the strongest suggestion of persuasion?
7. With what expectations did you begin reading the selections in this chapter? Were your expectations fulfilled?

Chapter Two
EXPOSITION

A s readers, we routinely consult dictionaries, encyclopedias, cookbooks, telephone directories, newspapers, or road maps to obtain basic, factual information—"Just the facts, ma'am." We want details that are correct, clear, readable, and above all, objective. This kind of straightforward writing, often found in reference books, is called exposition. However, there may be an undercurrent of argumentation or persuasion in the information we find in these reference books: the details you read here are accurate; follow these instructions to make a *good* pie; call this number and reach the correct party; follow the road signs and reach your destination. But we the readers are imposing the persuasion.

Exposition, especially objective description, can also be a fundamental element in many other, more complex writing genres—autobiography and biography, fiction and nonfiction, persuasion, reviews, and research. Whether exposition is an end in itself or a component of another type of writing, the fundamental information conveyed must be clearly and precisely worded.

As simple as the definitions of *exposition* might be, writing pure exposition is difficult. Expository writing is frequently divided into types or categories. James L. Kinneavy, in *A Theory of Discourse*, for example, discusses three types of expository writing: scientific, informative, and exploratory. Standard rhetoric books, on the other hand, classify expository writing by certain patterns of development: description, process, definition, classification, comparison/contrast, analogy, cause-effect. Frequently, an essay will incorporate a variety of these approaches. For example, a *scientific* essay may use detailed, technical *descriptions* to provide basic information about the *causes and effects* of chemical experiments, thereby enabling researchers to *classify* the data. Although selection of a pattern of development may help us focus on an overall framework for creating expository prose, the actual writing process is more difficult. Achieving true objectivity requires an appreciation of the biases both writers and readers bring to a particular piece of prose.

One serious obstacle to objectivity is diction. Language is highly connotative. As F. L. Lucas says in "What Is Style?" (see Chapter 3), "Words can be more powerful, and more treacherous, than we sometimes suspect; communication more difficult than we may think." As authors, unless we select our words carefully, with attention to audience and expository purpose, they may be loaded, emotional, persuasive. Does an encyclopedia describe a man as a "patriot" or a "traitor"? The choice of words may depend on the nationality of the writer. Do we describe someone as "friend" or "cohort"? The choice depends on our relationship with the person, but we must remember that unspoken in the word "cohort," but understood in its use, is the rest of the phrase, ". . . in crime." The mere juxtaposition of descriptive details may also invite judgment, argument, persuasion. What must a reader conclude from the description of George Wallace's banner, "Trust the People," hanging on the front of an "armored lectern"? Does a biographer describe Robert Falcon Scott as "heroic" or "foolish" because of losses on his expedition to the South Pole?

Readers bring their own emotions, biases, and prejudices to any piece of writing, thus making the task of writing exposition even more difficult. If we can read something into words or organization, we will. For example, as I reread Saul Pett's recounting of the events surrounding the assassination of John F. Kennedy (reprinted in this chapter), I struggled with my own memories of that November weekend in 1963; I reacted emotionally. But as I watched my class of college readers, too young to remember much of those four days—if they had even been born—I saw them react very differently. They argued about the classification of the essay as exposition, yet exhibited little or no emotion about the details in the article. They had no personal memories of the event with which to infuse emotion into their reading.

Most of the essays collected in this chapter first appeared in magazines or newspapers. Thus the authors had to write with a general readership in mind and select organization and diction accordingly. They could not know what emotions, prejudices, biases, desires, or hopes their audience would bring to the piece. Regardless, they have communicated their ideas to these unknown readers. James Agee, in his introduction to *Let Us Now Praise Famous Men*, writes directly to his readers and challenges them "to participate in the subject. . . ." We as readers should meet his challenge and "participate" in what we read if we wish to appreciate a work to its fullest. But we must acknowledge that the act of "participating" may alter exposition.

Whatever approaches the authors have chosen for these expository essays, description remains the predominant characteristic, whether capturing a few hours, a day, or a weekend in a life, a medical instrument, a person, or animals' speech.

•   •   •

At the Forks

from
Let Us Now Praise Famous Men
JAMES AGEE

During the summer of 1936, James Agee and Walker Evans set out
on a job. As Agee described it in the preface to the book, they were
"to prepare, for a New York magazine, an article on cotton tenantry
in the United States in the form of a photographic and verbal record
of the daily living and environment of an average white family of
tenant farmers." They selected three families and ultimately wrote a
book, after the magazine did not publish the original piece. The
book has become a classic. There has been some controversy over it
in recent years as the children of the three families have grown up
and expressed their reactions to what some of them view as
exploitation of the plights of their families.

Agee's preface discusses, in some detail, the purposes of his and
Evans' work. One of his points stresses the expository nature of his
approach: ". . . it is intended that this record and analysis be
exhaustive, with no detail, however trivial it may seem, left
untouched, no relevancy avoided, which lies within the power of
remembrance to maintain, of the intelligence to perceive, and of the
spirit to persist in."

He also emphasizes the role of the reader: ". . . it [the book] is an
effort in human actuality, in which the reader is no less centrally
involved than the authors and those of whom they tell. Those who
wish actively to participate in the subject, in whatever degree of
understanding, friendship, or hostility, are invited to address the
authors in care of the publishers."

Furthermore, Agee seeks to engage the reader directly by stating
that, "The text was written with reading aloud in mind. That cannot
be recommended; but it is suggested that the reader attend with his
ear to what he takes off the page: for variations of tone, pace, shape,
and dynamics are here particularly unavailable to the eye alone, and
with their loss, a good deal of meaning escapes." Since many writers
of fiction urge their readers to read aloud, Agee's suggestion
emphasizes the common qualities of fiction and nonfiction.

Original publication: *Let Us Now Praise Famous Men*. Boston: Houghton Mifflin, 1941.

On a road between the flying shadows of loose woods toward the middle of an afternoon, far enough thrust forward between towns that we had lost intuition of our balance between them, we came to a fork where the sunlight opened a little more widely, but not on cultivated land, and stopped a minute to decide.

Marion would lie some miles over beyond the road on our left; some other county seat, Centerville most likely, out beyond the road on our right; but on which the road the woods might give way to any extension of farm country there was no deducing: for we were somewhere toward the middle of one of the wider of the gaps on the road map, and had seen nothing but woods, and infrequent woods farms, for a good while now.

Just a little behind us on our left and close on the road was a house, the first we had passed in several miles, and we decided to ask directions of the people on the porch, whom, in the car mirror, I could see still watching us. We backed slowly, stopping the car a little short of the house, and I got slowly out and walked back toward them, watching them quietly and carefully, and preparing my demeanors and my words for the two hundredth time.

There were three on the porch, watching me, and they must not have spoken twice in an hour while they watched beyond the rarely traveled road the changes of daylight along the recessions of the woods, and while, in the short field that sank behind their house, their two crops died silently in the sun: a young man, a young woman, and an older man; and the two younger, their chins drawn inward and their heads tall against the grained wall of the house, watched me steadily and sternly as if from beneath the brows of helmets, in the candor of young warriors or of children.

They were of a kind not safely to be described in an account claiming to be unimaginative or trustworthy, for they had too much and too outlandish beauty not to be legendary. Since, however, they existed quite irrelevant to myth, it will be necessary to tell a little of them.

The young man's eyes had the opal lightings of dark oil and, though he was watching me in a way that relaxed me to cold weakness of ignobility, they fed too strongly inward to draw to a focus: whereas those of the young woman had each the splendor of a monstrance, and were brass. Her body also was brass or bitter gold, strong to stridency beneath the unbleached clayed cotton dress, and her arms and bare legs were sharp with metal down. The blenched hair drew her face tight to her skull as a tied mask; her features were baltic. The young man's face was deeply shaded with soft short beard, and luminous with death. He had the scornfully ornate nostrils and lips of an aegean exquisite. The fine wood body was ill strung, and sick even as he sat there to look at, and the bone hands roped with vein; they rose, then sank, and lay palms upward in his groins. There was in their eyes so quiet and ultimate a quality of hatred, and contempt, and anger, toward every creature in existence beyond themselves, and toward the damages they sustained, as shone scarcely short of a state of beatitude; nor did this at any time modify itself.

These two sat as if formally, or as if sculptured, one in wood and one in metal, or as if enthroned, about three feet apart in straight chairs tilted to the wall, and constantly watched me, all the while communicating thoroughly with each other by no outward sign of word or glance or turning, but by emanation.

The other man might have been fifty by appearance, yet, through a particular kind of delicateness upon his hands, and hair, and skin—they were almost infantine—I was sure he was still young, hardly out of his twenties, though again the face was seamed and short as a fetus. This man, small-built and heavy jointed, and wandering in his motions like a little child, had the thorny beard of a cartoon bolshevik, but suggested rather a hopelessly deranged and weeping prophet, a D. H. Lawrence whom male nurses have just managed to subdue into a straitjacket. A broken felt hat struck through with grass hair was banged on flat above his furious and leaky eyes, and from beneath its rascally brim as if from ambush he pored at me walleyed while, clenching himself back against the wall, he sank along it trembling and slowly to a squat, and watched up at me.

None of them relieved me for an instant of their eyes; at the intersection of those three tones of force I was transfixed as between spearheads as I talked. As I asked my questions, and told my purposes, and what I was looking for, it seemed to me they relaxed a little toward me, and at length a good deal more, almost as if into trust and liking; yet even at its best this remained so suspended, so conditional, that in any save the most hopeful and rationalized sense it was non-existent. The qualities of their eyes did not in the least alter, nor anything visible or audible about them, and their speaking was as if I was almost certainly a spy sent to betray them through trust, whom they would show they had neither trust nor fear of.

They were clients of Rehabilitation. They had been given a young sick steer to do their plowing with; the land was woods-clearing, but had been used as long as the house (whose wood was ragged and light as pith); no seed or fertilizer had been given them until the end of May. Nothing they had planted was up better than a few inches, and that was now withering faster than it grew. They now owed the Government on the seed and fertilizer, the land, the tools, the house, and probably before long on the steer as well, who was now so weak he could hardly stand. They had from the start given notice of the weakness and youth of the steer, of the nearly total sterility of the soil, and of the later and later withholding of the seed and fertilizer; and this had had a great deal to do with why the seed was given them so late, and they had been let know it in so many words.

The older man came up suddenly behind me, jamming my elbow with his concave chest and saying fiercely *Awnk, awnk*, while he glared at me with enraged and terrified eyes. Caught so abruptly off balance, my reflexes went silly and I turned toward him questioning 'politely' with my face, as if he wanted to say something, and could, which I had not quite heard. He did want urgently to say something, but all that came out was this blasting of *Awnk*, *awnk*, and a thick roil of saliva that hung like semen in his beard. I nodded, smiling at him, and he grinned gratefully with an expression of extreme wickedness and tugged hard at my sleeve, nodding violently in time to his voice and rooting out over and over this loud vociferation of a frog. The woman spoke to him sharply though not unkindly (the young man's eyes remained serene), as if he were a dog masturbating on a caller, and he withdrew against a post of the porch and sank along it to the floor with his knees up sharp and wide apart and the fingers of his left hand jammed as deep as they would go down his gnashing mouth, while he stayed his bright eyes on me. She got up abruptly without speaking and went indoors and came back out with a piece of stony cornbread and gave it to him, and took her place again in her chair. He took the bread in both hands and struck his face into it like the blow of a hatchet, grappling with his jaws and slowly cradling his head like a piece of heavy machinery, while grinding, passionate noises ran in his throat, and we continued to talk, the young woman doing most of the talking, corroborative and protective of the young man, yet always respectful toward him.

The young man had the asthma so badly the fits of it nearly killed him. He could never tell when he was going to be any good for work, and he was no good for it even at the best, it was his wife did the work; and him—the third—they did not even nod nor shift their eyes toward him; he was just a mouth. These things were said in the voice not of complaint but of statement, quietly stiff with hatred for the world and for living: nor was there any touch of pride, shame, resentment, or any discord among them.

Some niggers a couple of miles down a back road let them have some corn and some peas. Without those niggers there was no saying what they'd be doing by now. Only the niggers hadn't had a bit too much for themselves in the first place and were running very short now; it had been what was left over from the year before, and not much new corn, nor much peas, was coming through the drought. It was—

The older man came honking up at my elbow, holding out a rolled farm magazine. In my effort to give him whatever form of attention could most gratify him I was stupid again; the idea there was something he wanted me to read; and looked at him half-questioning this, and not yet taking what he offered me. The woman, in a voice that somehow, though contemptuous (it implied, You are more stupid than he is), yielded me for the first time her friendship and that of her husband, so that happiness burst open inside me like a flooding of sweet water, said, he wants to give it to you. I took it and thanked him very much, looking and smiling into his earnest eyes, and he stayed at my side like a child, watching me affectionately while I talked to them.

They had told me there was farm country down the road on the right a piece: the whole hoarded silence and quiet of a lonesome and archaic American valley it was to become, full of heavy sunflowers and mediocre cotton, where the women wore sunbonnets without shyness before us and all whom we spoke to were gracious and melancholy, and where we did not find what we sought. Now after a little while I thanked them here on the porch and told them good-bye. I had not the heart at all to say, Better luck to you, but then if I remember rightly I did say it, and, saying it or not, and unable to communicate to them at all what my feelings were, I walked back the little distance to the car with my shoulders and the back of my neck more scalded-feeling than if the sun were on them. As we started, I looked back and held up my hand. The older man was on the dirt on his hands and knees coughing like a gorilla and looking at the dirt between his hands. Neither of the other two raised a hand. The young man lowered his head slowly and seriously, and raised it. The young woman smiled, sternly beneath her virulent eyes, for the first time. As we swung into the right fork of the road, I looked back again. The young man, looking across once more into the woods, had reached his hand beneath the bib of his overalls and was clawing at his lower belly. The woman, her eyes watching us past her shoulder, was walking to the door. Just as I glanced back, and whether through seeing that I saw her I cannot be sure, she turned her head to the front, and disappeared into the house.

M.B.A.'s Learn a Human Touch

Tempering the Money Culture with Shakespeare

SUSAN DENTZER with MAGGIE MALONE

Since Susan Dentzer, with Maggie Malone, wrote this article for the popular weekly news magazine, *Newsweek*, they had to keep a general readership in mind. Of course, they could assume that readers with an interest in education in general, and more specifically, a business education, would choose to read the article as they flipped through the magazine.

They present some common concerns about the education provided students in business schools. Even though they discuss some solutions to these problems, their approach is essentially expository rather than persuasive. The solutions show the positive effects of this "human touch" added to a business education, but they do not argue for one over another.

Original publication: *Newsweek*, June 16, 1986.

When Robert Bies wants his business students to understand the nature of power, he sends many of them off on a real-life case study—to visit the homeless. It's no "gut" course: in suburban Evanston, Ill., not far from Northwestern University's J. L. Kellogg Graduate School of Management where Bies teaches, the problems of homeless people are a complex, highly politicized issue. Bies's organizational-behavior students confront it head-on: they study how local government, business and citizens' groups have tossed the problem around like a football; how sound financial decisions—such as tearing down transient hotels to build high-rises—have had the unintended social effect of displacing people. Bies's primary goal is to draw parallels to the many trade-offs of corporate life—but student Bill Anderson, 27, got so involved that he even volunteered to work at a shelter one night a month. "They begin to see that being a manager means more than numbers," Bies says.

For many of the estimated 70,000 M.B.A. students graduating this year, the "numbers" are still the bottom line. Subjects like finance, marketing and economics remain the core of the M.B.A. curriculum, and proficiency in them is the ticket to fat salaries in hot fields like investment banking and consulting. But alarmed by the narrow focus and dubious ethics of many recent B-school graduates, such as those involved in recent insider-trading scandals, many schools are trying to broaden and "humanize" their course offerings. Courses in ethics are popping up at many institutions, while others are emphasizing study of foreign cultures and languages to prepare students for the challenges of global competition. And even the classics are enjoying a renaissance, on the theory that Shakespeare's plays can shed more light on management problems than the grittiest corporate case study.

'Self-centered': It's all part of a growing belief that "the science of business is a myth . . . and the human challenges [of management] are gargantuan," says John Kotter, professor of organizational behavior at the Harvard Business School. As people rise in the corporate hierarchy, concurs Burton Malkiel, dean of the Yale School of Organization and Management (SOM), "it's less important that they have all the technical details"—and crucial that they have the capacity "to deal with and motivate people." But with the growing competition among M.B.A.'s for jobs, most management schools have usually emphasized hard-core technical training at the expense of "softer" areas like human resources. In a world marked by declining loyalties between individuals and institutions, "you get students who come out very hard and self-centered," says Abraham Zaleznick, a psychoanalyst and professor of leadership at Harvard.

The goal for business schools, Zaleznick thinks, is to mint qualified managers while also "getting them to be better [people]." Some schools are trying to rise to the occasion. At institutions like Yale, Stanford and the University of Pennsylvania's Joseph H. Lauder Institute of Management and International Studies, a few recent graduates are even undertaking unexpected acts of altruism before the paychecks start rolling in. While the move to broaden B-school graduates is still building, moreover, it's already affecting technically oriented, "digit-head" institutions like the University of Chicago's Graduate School of Business. Concentrating on the input side of the equation, the school is attempting to recruit more liberal-arts graduates who might not otherwise consider getting an M.B.A. In a program launched last year, it's offering 40 juniors from 20 colleges—selected on the basis of the students' general talents and leadership abilities—the chance to spend several weeks at the school this summer; the students can return for the full M.B.A. program up to two years after they graduate.

At many institutions, humanizing the curriculum is taking the form of renewed emphasis on old B-school standbys like organizational-behavior courses. At Harvard, where the wheels of change grind slowly, "Human Resource Management" was added in 1981—the first new required course in 20 years. Not surprisingly, there is debate within academia over the merits of many of these courses. "The way it's often put is, 'Why do we need this touchy-feely [baloney]?' " says Malkiel of Yale, which offers students a master's degree in public and private management and places heavy emphasis on "softer" courses like "Personality and Leadership" and "Managing Organizational Systems." But both schools say there's strong evidence that these subjects are in demand. Executives and alumni attending management programs at Yale and Harvard last week said their biggest problems were usually "human" ones— such as fostering leadership or dealing with subordinates.

Some schools increasingly see international industrial competitiveness as a preeminent issue for business education. As countries like Japan and South Korea grow in economic prominence, the Graduate School of Business Administration at the University of California at Berkeley has struck a "joint venture" with the university's East Asian Studies department to encourage a deeper look at Asian issues. The three-year-old Lauder Institute, meanwhile, admits 50 students each year for a combined M.B.A. from the Wharton School and a master's degree from the University of Pennsylvania. Among other requirements, students must become proficient in one foreign language and spend a summer working abroad; a primary aim, says institute director Jerry Wind, is to inculcate in students a "renaissance perspective" and mastery of the subtleties of doing business overseas. After hammering out some hitches in its curriculum, the institute graduated its first class last month. Many students are heading for international units of U.S. firms, but graduate Josh Brown says his Lauder experience helped persuade him to turn down an "excellent" job at American Express to explore U.S. product-and-marketing strategies for a Peruvian unit of the South American conglomerate Bunge & Born.

Other B-schools are taking the "renaissance" approach literally. Literary classics are being used as a tool for management education; this week, for example, retiring Yale president and literature professor A. Bartlett Giamatti will lecture managers at Yale on Machiavelli's "The Prince." "Most people have never read it [and] think it's a handbook for monsters," says Giamatti; in reality, he argues, it's an invaluable "esthetic" rather than moral approach to managing any "polity"—whether renaissance Florence or R. J. Reynolds. And for more than a decade, the University of Kansas has offered undergraduate business majors courses like "On Being Human," which include readings from books such as Joseph Conrad's "Heart of Darkness"; the classes stress the complexities of social and organizational responsibility and moral reasoning.

Similarly, John Clemens, a management professor at Hartwick College in Oneonta, N.Y., and director of The Hartwick Humanities in Management Institute, uses the classics to spark discussion about managing and leadership among his undergraduate students and corporate groups (including salesmen at Computer Solutions, a unit of NYNEX Corp.). Some Shakespearean scholars might cringe; the institute more or less implies that King Lear ended up as one of literature's most tragic figures in part because he was a poor delegator. But Clemens insists that works like "King Lear," "Plutarch's Lives" and Homer's "Iliad" speak profoundly to complex problems like management succession and style. "They're classics because they stimulate argument and raise more questions than answers," he says. "Not even a Harvard Business School case study gets a group that stimulated about big ideas."

A little humanity: All this is still a little too soft for some tastes—and so the American Assembly of Collegiate Schools of Business, an accrediting group, is developing tests to measure student aptitude in 16 "noncognitive" skills, including leadership, creativity and behavior flexibility. But there is some evidence that the broader approach may be achieving results. Students at Yale's SOM, for example, raise money each year for a fund to subsidize classmates who take low-paying or volunteer summer jobs in the public or nonprofit sectors. Last April California B-school students met at Stanford for an annual sports relay to raise money for charity. In a way, it's the same message that Bies, who holds a Ph.D. from Stanford, tries to get across when he shows his students the film classic "It's a Wonderful Life." Like the protagonist and beleaguered banker George Bailey, he tells students, their role in business "can be as simple as maintaining a certain level of humanity"—for the payoff of a lifetime.

When the World Series Became "A Modest Little Sporting Event"

RON FIMRITE

Ron Fimrite is uniquely qualified to be the author of this article for *Sports Illustrated:* he is a senior writer with the magazine, he has lived in the Bay Area for a long time, and he was in the booth at Candlestick Park when the earthquake hit San Francisco on October 17, 1989. He draws on those qualifications to record the events of that night for those who were not in the area. He uses that familiar opening we have all used in connection with memorable or traumatic events: "Where were you when . . . ?" (Read Saul Pett's description of where he was when he heard about the death of JFK.)

Original publication: *Sports Illustrated*, October 30, 1989.

Years from now, when someone asks me where I was when The Earthquake hit at 5:04 p.m. on Oct. 17, 1989, I'll be able to say, certainly without needing to refresh my memory, that I was in Candlestick Park, awaiting the start of the third game of the World Series between the Oakland Athletics and the San Francisco Giants. I realize, of course, that some 60,000 other people can truthfully say the same thing and that, as time passes, at least that many more will lie about being there, since that's the way it is with big events. People want to be where the action is.

But to tell the truth, Candlestick wasn't where the action was at all. And thank God for that. The maligned old bowl was jolted to its foundations, but when the quake had finished its dirty work, the Stick was still standing, which, tragically, is more than can be said for a section of the Bay Bridge, a mile-long stretch of the Nimitz Freeway in Oakland and 60 buildings in San Francisco's Marina district.

There was, in fact, something wholly unreal about being in the ballpark at that terrible moment. Before the quake struck, I was talking to a colleague in the upper-deck press seats about what another fine October day we were having in San Francisco and how television viewers, seeing all that sunshine, would surely never believe any more stories about Candlestick's being baseball's equivalent of a polar ice cap. I would once more have to explain to doubting visitors that unlike July and August, October in this city is generally warm, dry and still. Then, suddenly, it wasn't still anymore.

The entire stadium was reeling, and I watched as the television sets mounted on stands above the press tables swayed like giant cobras. "We're having a quake," I said with the studied nonchalance of a Bay Area native. When the rumbling finally ceased, some reporters, apparently regarding me as the resident disaster expert, asked what I thought this one would measure on the Richter scale. "Oh, maybe 5.4," I said, arriving at a figure which would indicate a tremor that was significant, but hardly, as it were, earthshaking. "Five-four, max."

That guess, I was soon to learn, was every bit as accurate as estimating Ty Cobb's career batting average at .225. This quake had hit 6.9 and was the largest in San Francisco since the 8.3 of 1906. But Candlestick fans couldn't have known that at the time, and when the shaking stopped, they let out an enormous cheer—in part, I'm sure, to demonstrate to outsiders their grace under pressure, and in part because they were just glad to be intact. Some even shouted, "Play ball!" But the scoreboard and the loudspeakers were off in Candlestick, and when police appeared on the field, the fans began to head for the exits in a manner both cheerful and orderly.

It was an odd moment. Here we all were in this huge concrete bowl, some of us perched nearly a hundred feet above the ground, after being rocked by one of this country's biggest earthquakes on record, and we were acting as if we had been through nothing more extraordinary than a grammar school fire drill. As we left the stadium, a friend of mine said, "I've seen bigger crushes when someone at my house shouts, 'Let's eat!' at a family dinner." But none of us had any idea then how serious this thing was. By the time I was outside the stadium, the scare stories had already started: The bridges were all down, downtown was in ruins, thousands were dead, looting and rioting were widespread, the stadium was about to tumble down.

Even with all the wild rumors, I was convinced that conditions were not nearly as bad as they were being made out to be. I had been through enough earthquakes—even slept through a bunch of them—to know that they are invariably described, particularly by novices, as being much worse than they are. Earthquakes, for those who don't experience them regularly, are apparently the most frightening of all natural calamities, possibly because, unlike hurricanes, tornadoes and blizzards, they arrive with no advance warning. But from where I stood, behind Candlestick's centerfield stands, this one seemed no worse than the others. Five-four, max.

When we finally boarded a press bus to take us downtown, the driver told us we would be avoiding the Bayshore Freeway because of possible damage there and taking Third Street. Nothing unusual about that. A lot of experienced Giants fans routinely take Third Street to avoid traffic. But the driver advised us that because of the looting, bottle-throwing and even some shooting that had erupted in the mostly poor neighborhood, we should keep our heads below window level; I was beginning to believe the crazy talk was not so crazy. While our trip along Third was without violent incident, it was more than a little eerie, and even frightening, because all the lights were out. Downtown was even stranger, in an almost impenetrable darkness, recalling for me the blackouts of World War II during which, as a boy, I would peer excitedly from under the window shades in search of Japanese bombers. As we drove along, I could make out shards of glass coating the sidewalks. Entire blocks were cordoned off, and I could see fallen masonry in the street. Pedestrians—some not knowing where to go, others with no means of getting anywhere—huddled on street corners. Our driver, a true samaritan, dropped his passengers off at hotels all over town and even took me within a block of my own candlelit apartment.

Inside, my wife, her nephew and some friends were watching news reports on a battery-powered television set. For the first time in hours, I could separate speculation from fact and see for myself the deadly power of the quake. It was like watching one of those dreadful disaster movies. The Marina, a middle- to upper-class neighborhood built largely on landfill, was by far the hardest hit part of San Francisco. There were films of the collapse of a section of the upper deck of the Bay Bridge that showed one car disappearing into a gaping hole. And reporters were then estimating that 250 people had been trapped in their cars and probably crushed to death when the Cypress Street Viaduct of the Nimitz Freeway fell apart.

It was a section of freeway I had driven countless times. My son, who works in the East Bay, travels it five times a week. My daughter, who lives in Berkeley, uses it to drive to school. Both called that night. Both were safe. We had all been lucky. My own apartment had suffered no more than a crack in the wall and some broken crystal. But I went to bed that night feeling a terrible queasiness, which not even a shot of brandy could cure.

Over the next two days, I drove around town the best I could, stopping in at various hangouts to see how friends were making out. In fact, they were, for the most part, doing just fine. The atmosphere in many parts of San Francisco was almost festive. There was lusty cheering—and free champagne—at the Washington Square Bar & Grill when the lights finally came on again. In the heart of the Marina, Bob Mulhern was barbecuing hamburgers on the sidewalk outside his restaurant. There were, predictably, earthquake T-shirts. Herb Caen of the *San Francisco Chronicle* wrote of one shirt that read: THANK YOU FOR NOT SHARING WHERE YOU WERE WHEN THE QUAKE STRUCK.

There was even some talk about the World Series. That Wednesday morning, in a candelabra-bedecked press conference in the still-dark St. Francis Hotel, baseball commissioner Fay Vincent quickly put matters into perspective. Calling the Series "our modest little sporting event" and deferring to the more important, immediate needs of the community, Vincent postponed Game 3 until the time was "appropriate." Nobody I talked to had a quarrel with that decision.

It is often said that there is nothing like a disaster to bring citizens of a community closer together. To me, that now seemed more true than ever. I liked my town, I told myself; it was so damned resilient, so full of humor in the face of things gone wrong. We'll celebrate anything. And I told this to any number of mostly disbelieving out-of-town radio interviewers who called me at odd hours throughout the day in search of gloomy reports from the scene.

The mood was not nearly so happy on Friday when I walked to the Marina, which is not far from where I live, and spent the morning among people suddenly displaced from their damaged and destroyed homes. There was one gray apartment building that was leaning drunkenly over the street, its hours obviously numbered. Persons carrying red slips openly wept, because those meant your building was unsafe and would have to come down. Property damage in San Francisco alone was estimated to be in the billions of dollars.

And yet, the bad news was tempered. By week's end it became apparent that the death toll in the immediate Bay Area was not in the hundreds but in the scores, for there were fewer cars under the fallen overpass on the Nimitz than was at first believed. Under normal rush-hour conditions, that freeway would have had bumper-to-bumper traffic, but on Oct. 17 many commuters left their jobs early, either to drive to Candlestick or to head home to watch Game 3 on television. The World Series, it was suggested, had actually saved lives.

And on Saturday morning, almost four days after the freeway collapsed, a man was pulled from his flattened auto, alive. The skyscrapers downtown were virtually unaffected by the quake, which says something for modern engineering. And the Ferry Building at the foot of Market Street, which had survived the 1906 quake, appeared largely unharmed, except for a flagpole that was slightly askew.

But it will be a long time before life resumes a normal course here. Traffic, an enormous problem even before the quake, will be a mess for months. And the cleaning up will go on and on. Maybe the resumption of the World Series, now scheduled for Friday, will prove, as many have contended, therapeutic. But the scale of relative importance has shifted significantly. Before the earthquake the city was embroiled in heated debate over Proposition P, the Nov. 7 ballot measure that would permit construction of a new, $115 million downtown stadium for the Giants, to replace the oft-ridiculed Candlestick. Would the fact that the Stick had sturdily survived the quake cast its future into a new light? Will a people confronted by damage in the billions be willing to authorize expenditures for a new ballpark? Maybe, maybe not. But in the wake of the disaster, no one was even asking.

How It Was in America a Week Ago Tuesday

GARRISON KEILLOR

Though most audiences know Garrison Keillor as the soft-spoken humorist on popular radio shows, an unknowing reader might think he is a sociologist or a statistician from reading this essay. And some readers might argue that this exposition of details moves into the realm of satire, to make fun of sociology and statistics. But he exposes facts, details, descriptions.

Many of Keillor's fans are disappointed when they read his narratives printed on the page. They lament the loss of Keillor's "voice," which they argue is a crucial component of his humor. Because of Keillor's use of statistics, this essay may not lend itself to reading aloud quite so readily as others of his works do. However, some readers might argue that Agee's suggestion for reading aloud needs to be applied to nonfiction in general.

Original publication: *The New Yorker*, March 10, 1975; collected in *Happy To Be Here*. New York: Penguin, 1986.

A couple of us were sitting around in the United States of America one night not long ago when we got this idea for a magazine article. We would call up housewives, farmers, doctors, white-collar workers, black people, students, town officials, teachers, urban planners, airline spokesmen, White House sources, leading economists, cabdrivers, newspaper editors, environmental experts, ministers, controversial writers, moderate Republicans, telephone operators, mediators, welfare recipients, observers, low-income families, grain brokers, country-and-western singers, skilled craftsmen, motorists, steelworkers, rural Americans, alternative life-stylists, bystanders, commuters, historians, gay persons, investors, and small children in California, Louisiana, Toledo, the Apostle Islands, San Jose, Syracuse, Cook County, the Great Plains, Poughkeepsie, New Jersey, North Dakota, Dallas, Duluth, Orlando, Knoxville, New York City, Wichita, Washington, D.C., Winnetka, Kennebunkport, Key Largo, Omaha, Amarillo, Ohio, Oklahoma, Amherst, Tallahassee, Tennessee, and East St. Louis, and ask "How's it going?" Then we would write the article.

All too often, we felt, the media are guilty of reporting the "big" stories and completely overlooking what it's all about—what people are up to and how it looks to them, the constant ebb and flow and pace and rhythm and ceaseless change of our lives, and more or less just what it's like to live in America today and have problems and hopes and fears and dreams and to go to work and come home and watch TV or go to a show or maybe just settle down with a good book or an in-depth magazine article.

Of course, we are all guilty of this to some extent. We tend to think of days as being rather similar to each other, except maybe Christmas, or New Year's or Saturday. However, as the editors of the *Life* Special Report on "One Day in the Life of America" wrote recently, "Days are like fingerprints, no one exactly like another in its whorls and ridges." Or, one might say, like magazine articles, each with its quite different paragraphs and neatly printed but various hundreds of words, many of them verbs.

Some people, in fact, may consider our project rather similar to the *Life* Special Report. But they are as different as two sunrises, or billfolds, or yesterday and tomorrow, or Oakland and Chicago Avenues in Minneapolis.

Hours before the sun, its rays racing westward at the speed of light, its estimated 267 tints dancing on the choppy, oil-streaked waters of the Atlantic, rose, Earth had turned the United States of America, time zone by time zone, into a Tuesday in midwinter. For most Americans, it came in their sleep in the middle of the night, marked by only a barely perceptible change in rapid eye movements, a slight shifting of position in bed. Their attitudes toward Tuesday were yet vague, uncomprehending. Awakened by telephone calls, they tended to feel it was something they could put off until morning.

Even as America slept, West Germany and the Soviet Union had forged ahead in Tuesday production, and Japan was going home to rest up for Wednesday. In a darkened Labor Department, at Fourteenth and Constitution in Washington, figures sheathed in Manila folders spelled out in eight-point type growing unemployment and spiraling inflation.

If there were fears or hopes among friends and foes that America might not get out of bed this morning, however, they were quickly dispelled. Already, the first of 125 million beds, 160 million cigarettes, and 40 million quarts of orange juice were creaking, smoking, and being poured. Four hundred million socks lay in sock drawers waiting to be worn, the holes in them totaling 700,000 square feet, almost as large as the White House grounds.

In the dim light of the Executive Bedroom, the 64-per-cent-approved President was assessing his own sock options. A few minutes before, in keeping with Presidential tradition, he had pulled on his pants one leg at a time, and now, donning a pair of wool sweat socks first worn by former President Eisenhower, he slipped into black hightop shoes from the Hoover Administration and made his way along a darkened corridor toward the Toaster Room.

As daylight spread over the populous, historic East to the fertile Midwest, far-flung Plains, scenic Mountain, and booming Pacific regions, lights came on in millions of homes, apartments, condominiums, town houses, duplexes, mobile homes, hospitals, halfway houses, and correctional institutions. Throats were cleared, toothpaste tubes squeezed, doors slammed, and long strips of bacon arrayed on pans to crackle over low-to-moderate heat. Women sighed, brushed their hair, scolded children, flipped pancakes, tied shoelaces. Men gulped coffee, scanned headlines, put on coats, started cars. Children whimpered, watched TV cartoons, kicked each other, left crusts, wheedled small change. Millions of dogs dozed in breakfast nooks or wandered aimlessly into living rooms.

In Eastport, Maine, the easternmost restaurant owner in the country, Buford Knapp, paused between orders of eggs and hash-browns to raise his prices another nickel. Residents of the Gabriel Nursing Home in Minneapolis were wheeled to their windows for the flag-raising and pledge of allegiance. A bus rumbled along historic Market Street in San Francisco. A flock of bluebirds described graceful arcs over downtown Knoxville.

In the kitchen of a farm commune near Middlebury, Vermont, Norman Lefko slid a pan of blueberry muffins into the ancient wood stove and sat down at a plant table to read the Sunday *New York Times*. In New York, Craig Claiborne arose briefly for a glass of tomato juice. As he did so, Fargo housewife Eula Larpenteur prepared fried eggs, following Claiborne's own recipe ("Break the desired numbers of eggs into a saucer and slip them carefully into the pan. . . . If the eggs are to be cooked on both sides, turn with a pancake turner") and listening to "Don't Give Me a Drink," the new Carson Trucks hit. Meanwhile, Carson Trucks slept fitfully in the Cartesian Suite of the Mambo Motel in Shreveport, having played to an overflow crowd in the Memorial Auditorium the night before. At that moment, "Don't Give Me a Drink" was being heard in St. Louis, Orlando, Wichita, and Philadelphia (where baseballer Pete Rose had just nicked his cheek). It was not being heard in Chicago where columnist Ann Landers was reading her first letter of the day. "Dear Ann," it began. "The woman who said she was tired of her husband's snoring made me sick to my stomach. . . ."

And so the morning began. For several hours, time seemed to pass quickly. Before Americans knew it, it was almost noon Eastern Standard Time. They had worked hard, the more than 77 million employed in mining, construction, manufacturing, transportation, sales, finance, personal services, and government, and now it was time for lunch. They had earned it. Although $1.75 billion of debt had been incurred, 124 persons killed on highways, and $8 million more spent on cigarettes than on education, $2 billion had been added to the gross national product that Tuesday morning. Steel had been rolled, buses driven, beds made, reports typed, tape recorders assembled, Shakespeare taught, windows wiped, washing machines repaired, major policy changes announced. Now the first of 4.6 million cans of soup were opened, the last of 2 million plates of leftovers were brought out of refrigerators. Waxed paper crackled in crowded lunchrooms, waitresses from Miami to Seattle yelled, "One with, skip the pickle," and a gigantic tidal wave of egg salad, tuna, and peanut butter was spread over 89 million slices of bread. Among those who did not eat lunch were Baba Ram Dass, Seiji Ozawa, Francis Tarkenton, and Selby Dale, a stockbroker in San Diego. The Dow-Jones industrial average was down eight points at noon, and his breakfast had come up at eleven.

As the nation slipped into afternoon, it seemed to lose stride and falter. Clocks were watched, wheels spun. From the sequoia-shaded Pacific Coast to the stubbled Kansas wheat fields to rockbound Maine, the national mood shifted to one of boredom, then apathy and resignation, with an occasional moment of outright despair. Many, it is true, maintained momentum. The President, meeting with his economic advisers, pledged continued efforts to curb inflation. The Secretary of State, speaking at the National Press Club, called for continued efforts to establish structures for peace. Hundreds of other efforts continued, or were pledged or called for, as did numerous operations, campaigns, programs, and attempts. Talks on new contracts continued. Searches for lost persons continued, and hopes remained high. Wars against cancer, school dropouts, crime, unemployment, pollution, and discrimination went on, along with planning for the coming biennium, Middle East peace talks, "The Fantasticks," and scores of investigations. Hearings resumed. Many ends, or the beginnings of ends, were sighted.

Nonetheless, interest, for the most part, lagged. Polls showed a twenty-five per cent jump in indecision after lunch: "Don't know" was up almost a third; "Don't care one way or the other" and "Both are just as bad" showed similar increases. In New Haven, sophomore Raymond Doswell took ten minutes to remember the composition of methane. In Albuquerque, New Mexico, Ernest Hollard, a thirty-two-year-old architect, lost the will to live. (Fortunately, nothing was wrong with him, and he soon felt cheerful enough to sharpen several pencils.) In Fargo, Eula Larpenteur called a local radio station and requested anything by the Chenilles. Henny Youngman spoke to a luncheon in Des Moines and made a joke about small businessmen. In hospitals around the country, thousands were treated for self-inflicted cuts suffered in moments of inattention. An estimated 40,000 lost faith in the political process, even though, as of midafternoon, it remained strong and viable. In Shreveport, Carson Trucks abused a bottle of cough syrup.

Many people knew it. Others wondered what it was. Some mistook it for something else. In New York, however, eating sautéed carrots boiled to extinction, Craig Claiborne knew it. John Simon knew it, and knew that he knew it. So did cabdriver Jack Poderhotz. ("People are sheer stark raving crazy nuts. Quote me.") In Colorado, author (Fear and Loathing) Hunter S. Thompson knew it. The big mudslide has started, he thought while writing. This is it. Giant hair balls roll westward, barbiturates float in the reservoirs. Merv smiles on television. The country bleeds from the gums, walks straight into trees.

Of the 6,554 luncheon audiences addressed today, most were told not to sell short. Now, a scant two hours later, the country seemed less sure of itself and its destiny, values, strength, role in the free world, commitment to the arts, and the basic worth of its younger generation, most of whom were in school and, in turn, didn't care for it, if Janice Hoyt of Boise was typical. She thought it reeked.

In Washington, several high-ranking congressional sources felt a sudden wave of intense personal disgust. Journalist Robert Sherrill wadded up a sheet of blank paper and threw it angrily at a potted culp. Eight news conferences were canceled for no reason, including one with a farm spokesman, who had planned to display a hamburger bun and then reveal the few small crumbs of it that are the farmer's portion. Midway through his Chicago radio show, Studs Terkel—talking about the human spirit, the young, Joe Hill, Bach, Lady Day, the life urge, the "little man," Chaplin, the sea, and (his guest on the show) Phil Donahue—faltered, said "But of course that's only my opinion. Others may feel differently," and went to a commercial for patio furniture, causing several Evanston listeners to look out across Lake Michigan for a long time. Eagles were observed diving beak first into the frozen Mississippi north of Brainerd, Minnesota. Strange grinding noises over the horizon were heard by crews of oil tankers in the Gulf of Mexico.

As the sun swept westward toward the Far East, as long shadows fell, from the oyster beds of Maryland to Houston's Astrodome to Seattle's Puget Sound, few Americans took umbrage at the passing of the day, and regret was felt by few of the million who clogged freeways, jostled on trains and subways, jammed buses, piled into taxis, hopped on bicycles, or took off on foot for the 2.6-mile average trip home. At colleges around the country, suggested reading lists of books for further enrichment were stuffed in wastebaskets, and only 86 students remained after class for personal help. The Boston Bruins ended practice early. At the Purity Packing Plant, in Louisville, two workers scrawled obscenities on a hog carcass. In the Oval Office, the President looked at the last item on his schedule ("Call AFL–CIO—ask labor's coop in days, weeks ahead"), said, "The hell with it," and went upstairs to toss quoits. In the garden outside his window, a White House guard spat into a rosebush, chucked a rock at a sparrow. At the State Department, the search for lasting peace slowly wound down, ending officially at 7:40, when the Secretary was logged out of his office, trailed by his bodyguard, Knute. His mind, accustomed to penetrate far beyond the limits of normal men's endurance, had begun to lag shortly after 6. Left behind on his desk were four legal-size papers filled with doodled sketches of horses, slippers, obelisks, holsters, curtains, and peninsulas.

As his limousine sped away from the government curb, Mrs. Buford Knapp was putting on a Polynesian beach dress and coral accessories for a luau at the Eastport V.F.W.; Norman Lefko was carving a hand-made maple-syrup ladle; Eula Larpenteur was telling her husband, Stanley, to take it easy on their oldest son, Craig, sixteen, who was expected home momentarily from a brush with the law. Elsewhere, millions prepared for the evening. Tons of macaroni-and-cheese casseroles baked slowly in moderate heat, hundreds of square miles of tablecloth were smoothed out, and an estimated 45,000 women discovered, to their mild surprise, unsightly spots on glasses and dinnerware. Newspapers were opened, legs were crossed, and alcohol was consumed—enough to carry Bismarck, North Dakota, through the seven-month home-heating season.

At night, America becomes a study in contrasts between light and darkness. This night was no exception. Street lights in cities, villages, townships twinkled in the cold winter air. Neon signs flashed their potpourri of messages. The lights in houses cast bright rectangular shapes onto snowy lawns and sidewalks. Car headlights made fascinating patterns, delicate traceries captured by hundreds of amateur photographers at slow shutter speeds. Traffic lights blinked red and green, as did the lights of aircraft, radio and television towers, police cars and other emergency vehicles, and hundreds of miles of unnoticed Christmas lights remaining on trees or outlining front porches.

At NBC master control in New York, technical difficulties produced a momentary blurring of John Chancellor, prompting 17.5 million persons to lean forward and adjust their sets—an outlay of energy equivalent to 4,000 barrels of crude oil. A majority of Americans would spend at least part of the evening watching television, of which a small minority (28 per cent) would fall asleep while doing so. Others looked forward to movies, plays, ballets, concerts, or intimate dinner parties, for which women sat before mirrors making expressive faces and applying cosmetics, and spent an accumulated national total of almost 400 woman-years, or a lot longer than the Ming Dynasty. Meanwhile, men ran a Niagara of hot water into bathtubs and showers and shaved an area the size of the Pentagon.

Of the 3.5 million Americans who went "out" for the evening, many had a good time, despite the dimly remembered uneasiness of the afternoon, while for countless others it was "O.K." or "not bad." Very few experienced real bummers. Those who did included Buford Knapp, who was publicly berated by his wife for not sending the clams back to the kitchen. She said there was dirt in them. Forty-five cultural events received poor reviews, including three Beethoven Sixth Symphonies ("An exercise in pointlessness," "A leaden sense of rhythm," and "If this is pastoral, then what is sheer tedium?," respectively), and roughly half of the evening's sporting events were lost by one team or the other.

Winning or losing, at home or away, shirts or skins, most Americans found some pleasure before midnight and retired at a reasonable hour to sleep for slightly less than eight hours (Tuesday night is the most restful night in the country—Saturday is the least, leading Sunday afternoon by only two hours—although urban sleepers do slightly better on Wednesday) and to dream, if a test group at U.C.L.A. was indicative, about familiar scenes and faces.

Not that there weren't disturbing signs to upset even the most complacent. In New York, hours after the market had closed, the Dow-Jones industrial average dropped three points unnoticed. In Dallas, a four-year-old child suddenly spoke in her sleep words of dire warning to her parents and to all Americans. And two women sitting in a back yard in Key West, Florida, observed a large, vacuum-cleaner-shaped object with flashing blue lights hover and then land fifty feet away, beside a garage. Two persons in yellow raincoats emerged, exposed themselves briefly, got back in the craft, and flew away. The craft emitted a low hum, like a dial tone. The persons appeared to be from another planet entirely.

If all was not well, it was nevertheless mostly pretty good, on balance. Despite its problems, the nation slipped into a fundamentally sound sleep. Many Americans tossed in their beds, got up to pace the floor, took aspirin, were troubled, pondered complex matters, stared at ceilings, but this was by no means common. And even the restless, for the most part, slept. From the vast bedroom suburbs of New Jersey to sleepy river towns in Minnesota to the long-slumbering natural resources in Alaska, America slept. It slept because it was tired. Soon it was midnight, and another day (and another magazine article) was over.

The Language of Animals

KONRAD Z. LORENZ

Konrad Z. Lorenz got the idea for *King Solomon's Ring*, the collection in which "The Language of Animals" appeared, during the filming of a documentary about animals. When his friend spoke the wrong animal "language," Lorenz thought it was so funny that he wanted to share the story. He decided "to tell it to everybody," making the general public the audience for these scientific essays of "new and important scientific description," as Julian Huxley stated in the foreword of the book. In the preface, Lorenz explains his purpose to his audience: "Why should not the comparative ethologist who makes it his business to know animals more thoroughly than anybody else, tell stories about their private lives? Every scientist should, after all, regard it as his duty to tell the public, in a generally intelligible way, about what he is doing. . . . Thus by modestly keeping to the methods of my own craft, I may hope to convey, to my kindly reader, at least a slight inkling of the infinite beauty of our fellow creatures and their life."

Thus, Lorenz clearly defines his audience and his purpose, hinting at the persuasion that underlines his exposition—he wants readers to appreciate the animals as he does, to recognize their "infinite beauty." But his approach is objective description.

Original publication: *King Solomon's Ring*. New York: Harper & Row, 1952.

Learned of every bird its language,
Learned their names and all their secrets,
Talked with them whene'er he met them.
                                    LONGFELLOW

Animals do not possess a language in the true sense of the word. In the higher vertebrates, as also in insects, particularly in the socially living species of both great groups, every individual has a certain number of innate movements and sounds for expressing feelings. It has also innate ways of reacting to these signals whenever it sees or hears them in a fellow-member of the species. The highly social species of birds such as the jackdaw or the greylag goose, have a complicated code of such signals which are uttered and understood by every bird without any previous experience. The perfect co-ordination of social behaviour which is brought about by these actions and reactions conveys to the human observer the impression that the birds are talking and understanding a language of their own. Of course, this purely innate signal code of an animal species differs fundamentally from human language, every word of which must be learned laboriously by the human child. Moreover, being a genetically fixed character of the species—just as much as any bodily character—this so-called language is, for every individual animal species, ubiquitous in its distribution. Obvious though this fact may seem, it was, nevertheless, with something akin to naïve surprise that I heard the jackdaws in northern Russia "talk" exactly the same, familiar "dialect" as my birds at home in Altenberg. The superficial similarity between these animal utterances and human languages diminishes further as it becomes gradually clear to the observer that the animal, in all these sounds and movements expressing its emotions, has in no way the conscious intention of influencing a fellow-member of its species. This is proved by the fact that even geese or jackdaws reared and kept singly make all these signals as soon as the corresponding mood overtakes them. Under these circumstances the automatic and even mechanical character of these signals becomes strikingly apparent and reveals them as entirely different from human words.

In human behaviour, too, there are mimetic signs which automatically transmit a certain mood and which escape one, without or even contrary to one's intention of thereby influencing anybody else: the commonest example of this is yawning. Now the mimetic sign by which the yawning mood manifests itself is an easily perceived optical and acoustical stimulus whose effect is, therefore, not particularly surprising. But, in general, such crude and patent signals are not always necessary in order to transmit a mood. On the contrary, it is characteristic of this particular effect that it is often brought about by diminutive sign stimuli which are hardly perceptible by conscious observation. The mysterious apparatus for transmitting and receiving the sign stimuli which convey moods is age-old, far older than mankind itself. In our own case, it has doubtless degenerated as our word-language developed. Man has no need of minute intention-displaying movements to announce his momentary mood: he can say it in words. But jackdaws or dogs are obliged to "read in each other's eyes" what they are about to do in the next moment. For this reason, in higher and social animals, the transmitting, as well as the receiving apparatus of "mood-convection" is much better developed and more highly specialized than in us humans. All expressions of animal emotions, for instance, the "Kia" and "Kiaw" note of the jackdaw, are therefore not comparable to our spoken language, but only to those expressions such as yawning, wrinkling the brow and smiling, which are expressed unconsciously as innate actions and also understood by a corresponding inborn mechanism. The "words" of the various animal "languages" are merely interjections.

Though man may also have numerous gradations of unconscious mimicry, no George Robey or Emil Jannings would be able, in this sense, to convey, by mere miming, as the greylag goose can, whether he was going to walk or fly, or to indicate whether he wanted to go home or to venture further afield, as a jackdaw can do quite easily. Just as the transmitting apparatus of animals is considerably more efficient than that of man, so also is their receiving apparatus. This is not only capable of distinguishing a large number of signals, but, to preserve the above simile, it responds to much slighter transmissions than does our own. It is incredible, what minimal signs, completely imperceptible to man, animals will receive and interpret rightly. Should one member of a jackdaw flock that is seeking for food on the ground, fly upwards merely to seat itself on the nearest apple-tree and preen its feathers, then none of the others will cast so much as a glance in its direction; but, if the bird takes to wing with intent to cover a longer distance, then it will be joined, according to its authority as a member of the flock, by its spouse or also a larger group of jackdaws, in spite of the fact that it did not emit a single "Kia".

In this case, a man well versed in the ways and manners of jackdaws might also, by observing the minutest intention-displaying movements of the bird, be able to predict—if with less accuracy than a fellow-jackdaw—how far that particular bird was going to fly. There are instances in which a good observer can equal and even surpass an animal in its faculty of "understanding" and anticipating the intentions of its fellow, but in other cases he cannot hope to emulate it. The dog's "receiving set" far surpasses our own analogous apparatus. Everybody who understands dogs knows with what almost uncanny certitude a faithful dog recognizes in its master whether the latter is leaving the room for some reason uninteresting to his pet, or whether the longed-for daily walk is pending. Many dogs achieve even more in this respect. My Alsatian Tito, the great-great-great-great-great-grandmother of the dog I now possess, knew, by "telepathy", exactly which people got on my nerves, and when. Nothing could prevent her from biting, gently but surely, all such people on their posteriors. It was particularly dangerous for authoritative old gentlemen to adopt towards me, in discussion, the well-known "you are, of course, too young" attitude. No sooner had the stranger thus expostulated, than his hand felt anxiously for the place in which Tito had punctiliously chastised him. I could never understand how it was that this reaction functioned just as reliably when the dog was lying under the table and was therefore precluded from seeing the faces and gestures of the people round it: how did she know who I was speaking to or arguing with?

This fine canine understanding of the prevailing mood of a master is not really telepathy. Many animals are capable of perceiving the smallest movements, withheld from the human eye. And a dog, whose whole powers of concentration are bent on serving his master and who literally "hangs on his every word" makes use of this faculty to the utmost. Horses too have achieved considerable feats in this field. So it will not be out of place to speak here of the tricks which have brought some measure of renown to certain animals. There have been "thinking" horses which could work out square roots, and a wonder-dog Rolf, an Airedale terrier, which went so far as to dictate its last will and testament to its mistress. All these "counting", "talking" and "thinking" animals "speak" by knocking or barking sounds, whose meaning is laid down after the fashion of a morse code. At first sight, their performances are really astounding. You are invited to set the examination yourself and you are put opposite the horse, terrier or whatever animal it is. You ask, how much is twice two; the terrier scrutinizes you intently and barks four times. In a horse, the feat seems still more prodigious for he does not even look at you. In dogs, who watch the examiner closely, it is obvious that their attention is concentrated upon the latter and not by any means, on the problem itself. But the horse has no need to turn his eyes towards the examiner since, even in a direction in which the animal is not directly focusing, it can see, by indirect vision, the minutest movement. And it is you yourself who betray, involuntarily to the "thinking" animal, the right solution. Should one not know the right answer oneself, the poor animal would knock or bark on desperately, waiting in vain for the sign which would tell him to stop. As a rule, this sign is forthcoming, since few people are capable, even with the utmost self-control, of withholding an unconscious and involuntary signal. That it is the human being who finds the solution and communicates it was once proved by one of my colleagues in the case of a dachshund which had become quite famous and which belonged to an elderly spinster. The method was perfidious: it consisted in suggesting a wrong solution of all the problems not the "counting" dog, but to his mistress. To this end, my friend made cards on one side of which a simple problem was printed in fat letters. The cards, however, unknown to the dog's owner, were constructed of several layers of transparent paper on the last of which another problem was inscribed in such a manner as to be visible from behind, when the front side was presented to the animal. The unsuspecting lady, seeing, in looking-glass writing, what she imagined to be the problem to be solved, transmitted involuntarily to the dog a solution which did not correspond to that of the problem on the front of the card, and was intensely surprised when, for the first time in her experience, her pet continued to give wrong answers. Before ending the séance, my friend adopted different tactics and presented mistress and dog with a problem, which, for a change, the dog could answer and the lady could not: He put before the animal a rag impregnated with the smell of a bitch in season. The dog grew excited, wagged his tail and whined—he knew what he was smelling and a really knowledgeable dog owner might have known, too, from observing his behavior. Not so the old lady. When the dog was asked what the rag smelled of, he promptly morsed *her* answer: "Cheese"!

The enormous sensitivity of many animals to certain minute movements of expression, as, for example, the above described capacity of the dog to perceive the friendly or hostile feelings which his master harbours for another person, is a wonderful thing. It is therefore not surprising that the naïve observer, seeking to assign to the animal human qualities, may believe that a being which can guess even such inward unspoken thoughts, must, still more, understand every word that the beloved master utters; now an intelligent dog does understand a considerable number of words, but, on the other hand, it must not be forgotten that the ability to understand the minutest expressional movements is thus acute in animals for the very reason that they lack true speech.

As I have already explained, all the innate expressions of emotion, such as the whole complicated "signal code" of the jackdaw, are far removed from human language. When your dog nuzzles you, whines, runs to the door and scratches it, or puts his paws on the wash basin under the tap, and looks at you imploringly, he does something that comes far nearer to human speech than anything that a jackdaw or goose can ever "say", no matter how clearly "intelligible" and appropriate to the occasion the finely differentiated expressional sounds of these birds may appear. The dog wants to make you open the door or turn on the tap, and what he does has the specific and purposeful motive of influencing you in a certain direction. He would never perform these movements if you were not present. But the jackdaw or goose merely gives unconscious expression to its inward mood and the "Kia" or "Kiaw", or the warning sound escapes the bird involuntarily; when in a certain mood, it must utter the corresponding sound, whether or not there is anybody there to hear it.

The intelligible actions of the dog described above are not innate but are individually learned and governed by true insight. Every individual dog has different methods of making himself understood by his master and will adapt his behaviour according to the situation. My bitch Stasie, the great-grand-mother of the dog I now possess, having once eaten something which disagreed with her, wanted to go out during the night. I was at that time overworked, and slept very soundly, so that she did not succeed in waking me and indicating her requirements, by her usual signs; to her whining and nosing I had evidently only responded by burying myself still deeper in my pillows. This desperate situation finally induced her to forget her normal obedience and to do a thing which was strictly forbidden her: she jumped on my bed and then proceeded literally to dig me out of the blankets and roll me on the floor. Such an adaptability to present needs is totally lacking in the "vocabulary" of birds: they never roll you out of bed.

Parrots and large corvines are endowed with "speech" in still another sense: they can imitate human words. Here, an association of thought between the sounds and certain experiences is sometimes possible. This imitating is nothing other than the so-called mocking found in many song birds. Willow warblers, red-backed shrikes and many others are masters of this art. Mocking consists of sounds, learned by imitation, which are not innate and are uttered only while the bird is singing; they have no "meaning" and bear no relation whatsoever to the inborn "vocabulary" of the species. This also applies to starlings, magpies and jackdaws, who not only "mock" bird's voices but also successfully imitate human words. However, the talking of big corvines and parrots is a somewhat different matter. It still bears that character of playfulness and lack of purpose which is also inherent in the mocking of smaller birds and which is loosely akin to the play of more intelligent animals. But a corvine or a parrot will utter its human words independently of song and it is undeniable that these sounds may occasionally have a definite thought association.

Many grey parrots, as well as others, will say "good morning" only once a day and at the appropriate time. My friend Professor Otto Koehler possessed an ancient grey parrot which, being addicted to the vice of feather-plucking, was nearly bald. This bird answered to the name of "Geier" which in German means vulture. Geier was certainly no beauty but he redeemed himself by his speaking talents. He said "good morning" and "good evening" quite aptly and, when a visitor stood up to depart, he said, in a benevolent bass voice "Na, auf Wiedersehen". But he only said this if the guest really departed. Like a "thinking" dog, he was tuned in to the finest, involuntarily given signs; what these signs were, we never could find out and we never once succeeded in provoking the retort by staging a departure. But when the visitor really left, no matter how inconspicuously he took his leave, promptly and mockingly came the words "Na, auf Wiedersehen"!

The well-known Berlin ornithologist, Colonel von Lukanus, also possessed a grey parrot which became famous through a feat of memory. Von Lukanus kept, among other birds, a tame hoopoe named "Höpfchen". The parrot, which could talk well, soon mastered this word. Hoopoes unfortunately do not live long in captivity, though grey parrots do; so, after a time, "Höpfchen" went the way of all flesh and the parrot appeared to have forgotten his name, at any rate, he did not say it any more. Nine years later, Colonel von Lukanus acquired another hoopoe and, as the parrot set eyes on him for the first time, he said at once, and then repeatedly, "Höpfchen" . . . "Höpfchen". . . .

In general, these birds are just as slow in learning something new as they are tenacious in remembering what they have once learned. Everyone who has tried to drum a new word into the brain of a starling or a parrot knows with what patience one must apply oneself to this end, and how untiringly one must again and again repeat the word. Nevertheless, such birds can, in exceptional cases, learn to imitate a word which they have heard seldom, perhaps only once. However, this apparently only succeeds when a bird is in an exceptional state of excitement; I myself have seen only two such cases. My brother had, for years, a delightfully tame and lively blue-fronted Amazon parrot named Papagallo, which had an extraordinary talent for speech. As long as he lived with us in Altenberg, Papagallo flew just as freely around as most of my other birds. A talking parrot that flies from tree to tree and at the same time says human words, gives a much more comical effect than one that sits in a cage and does the same thing. When Papagallo, with loud cries of "Where's the Doc?" flew about the district, sometimes in a genuine search for his master, it was positively irresistible.

Still funnier, but also remarkable from a scientific point of view, was the following performance of the bird; Papagallo feared nothing and nobody, with the exception of the chimney-sweep. Birds are very apt to fear things which are up above. And this tendency is associated with the innate dread of the bird of prey swooping down from the heights. So everything that appears against the sky, has for them something of the meaning of "bird of prey". As the black man, already sinister in his darkness, stood up on the chimney stack and became outlined against the sky, Papagallo fell into a panic of fear and flew, loudly screaming, so far away that we feared he might not come back. Months later, when the chimney-sweep came again, Papagallo was sitting on the weathercock, squabbling with the jackdaws who wanted to sit there too. All at once, I saw him grow long and thin and peer down anxiously into the village street; then he flew up and away, shrieking in raucous tones, again and again, "the chimney-sweep is coming, the chimney-sweep is coming". The next moment, the black man walked through the doorway of the yard!

Unfortunately, I was unable to find out how often Papagallo had seen the chimney-sweep before and how often he had heard the excited cry of our cook which heralded his approach. It was, without a doubt, the voice and intonation of this lady which the bird reproduced. But he had certainly not heard it more than three times at the most and, each time, only once and at an interval of months.

The second case known to me in which a talking bird learned human words after hearing them only once or very few times, concerns a hooded crow. Again it was a whole sentence which thus impressed itself on the bird's memory. "Hansl", as the bird was called, could compete in speaking talent with the most gifted parrot. The crow had been reared by a railwayman, in the next village, and it flew about freely and had grown into a well-proportioned, healthy fellow, a good advertisement for the rearing ability of its foster-father. Contrary to popular opinion, crows are not easy to rear and, under the inadequate care which they usually receive, mostly develop into those stunted, half-crippled specimens which are so often seen in captivity. One day, some village boys brought me a dirt-encrusted hooded crow whose wings and tail were clipped to small stumps. I was hardly able to recognize, in this pathetic being, the once beautiful Hansl. I bought the bird, as, on principle, I buy all unfortunate animals that the village boys bring me and this I do partly out of pity and partly because amongst these stray animals there might be one of real interest. And this one certainly was! I rang up Hansl's master who told me that the bird had actually been missing some days and begged me to adopt him till the next moult. So, accordingly, I put the crow in the pheasant pen and gave it concentrated food, so that, in the imminent new moult, it would grow good new wing and tail feathers. At this time, when the bird was, of necessity, a prisoner,

I found out that Hansl had a surprising gift of the gab and he gave me the opportunity of hearing plenty! He had, of course, picked up just what you would expect a tame crow to hear that sits on a tree, in the village street, and listens to the "language" of the inhabitants.

I later had the pleasure of seeing this bird recover his full plumage and I freed him as soon as he was fully capable of flight. He returned forthwith to his former master, in Wordern, but continued, a welcome guest, to visit us from time to time. Once he was missing for several weeks and, when he returned, I noticed that he had, on one foot, a broken digit which had healed crooked. And this is the whole point of the history of Hansl, the hooded crow. For we know just how he came by this little defect. And from whom do we know it? Believe it or not, Hansl told us himself! When he suddenly reappeared, after his long absence, he knew a new sentence. With the accent of a true street urchin, he said, in lower Austrian dialect, a short sentence which, translated into broad Lancashire, would sound like "Got 'im in t'blooming trap!" There was no doubt about the truth of his statement. Just as in the case of Papagallo, a sentence which he had certainly not heard often, had stuck in Hansl's memory because he had heard it in a moment of great apprehension that is, immediately after he had been caught. How he got away again, Hansl unfortunately did not tell us.

In such cases, the sentimental animal lover, crediting the creature with human intelligence, will take an oath on it that the bird understands what he says. This, of course, is quite incorrect. Not even the cleverest "talking" birds which, as we have seen, are certainly capable of connecting their sound-expressions with particular occurrences, learn to make practical use of their powers, to achieve purposefully even the simplest object. Professor Koehler, who can boast of the greatest successes in the science of training animals, and who succeeded in teaching pigeons to count up to six, tried to teach the above-mentioned, talented grey parrot "Geier" to say "food" when he was hungry and "water" when he was dry. This attempt did not succeed, nor, so far, has it been achieved by anybody else. In itself, the failure is remarkable. Since, as we have seen, the bird is able to connect his sound utterances with certain occurrences, we should expect him, first of all, to connect them with a purpose; but this, surprisingly, he is unable to do. In all other cases, where an animal learns a new type of behaviour, it does so to achieve some purpose. The most curious types of behaviour may be thus acquired, especially with the object of influencing the human keeper. A most grotesque habit of this kind was learned by a Blumenau's parakeet which belonged to Prof. Karl von Frisch. The scientist only let the bird fly freely when he had just watched it have an evacuation of the bowels, so that, for the next ten minutes, his well-kept furniture was not endangered. The parakeet learned very quickly to associate these facts and, as he was passionately fond of leaving his cage, he would force out a minute dropping with all his might, every time Prof. von Frisch came near the cage. He even squeezed desperately when it was impossible to produce anything, and really threatened to do himself an injury by the violence of his straining. You just had to let the poor thing out, every time you saw him!

Yet the clever "Geier", much cleverer than that little parakeet, could not even learn to say "food" when he was hungry. The whole complicated apparatus of the bird's syrinx and brain that makes imitation and association of thought possible, appears to have no function in connection with the survival of the species. We ask ourselves vainly what it is there for!

I only know one bird that learned to use a human word when he wanted a particular thing and who thus connected a sound-expression with a purpose, and it is certainly no coincidence that it was a bird of that species which I consider to have the highest mental development of all, namely the raven. Ravens have a certain innate call-note which corresponds to the "Kia" of the jackdaw and has the same meaning, that is, the invitation to others to fly with the bird that utters it. In the raven, this note is a sonorous, deep-throated, and, at the same time, sharply metallic "krackrackrack". Should the bird wish to persuade another of the same species which is sitting on the ground to fly with it, he executes the same kind of movements as described in the chapter on jackdaws: he flies, from behind, close above the other bird and, in passing it, wobbles with his closely folded tail, at the same time emitting a particularly sharp "Krackrackrackrack" which sounds almost like a volley of small explosions.

My raven Roah, so named after the call-note of the young raven, was, even as a mature bird, a close friend of mine and accompanied me, when he had nothing better to do, on long walks and even on skiing tours, or on motorboat excursions on the Danube. Particularly in his later years he was not only shy of strange people, but also had a strong aversion to places where he had once been frightened or had had any other unpleasant experience. Not only did he hesitate to come down from the air to join me in such places, but he could not bear to see me linger in what he considered to be a dangerous spot. And, just as my old jackdaws tried to make their truant children leave the ground and fly after them, so Roah bore down upon me from behind, and, flying close over my head, he wobbled with his tail and then swept upwards again, at the same time looking backwards over his shoulder to see if I was following. In accompaniment to this sequence of movements—which, to stress the fact again, is entirely innate— Roah, instead of uttering the above described call-note, said his own name, with human intonation. The most peculiar thing about this was that Roah used the human word for me only. When addressing one of his own species, he employed the normal innate call-note. To suspect that I had unconsciously trained him would obviously be wrong; for this could only have taken place if, by pure chance, I had walked up to Roah at the very moment when he happened to be calling his name, and, at the same time, to be wanting my company. Only if this rather unlikely coincidence of three factors had repeated itself on several occasions, could a corresponding association of thought have been formed by the bird, and that certainly was not the case. The old raven must, then, have possessed a sort of insight that "Roah" was my call-note! Solomon was not the only man who could speak to animals, but Roah is, so far as I know, the only animal that has ever spoken a human word to a man, in its right context—even if it was only a very ordinary call-note.

How I Write

RICHARD MARIUS

For a volume entitled *Writers on Writing*, editor Tom Waldrep asked professional writers who are also writing teachers how they write. Richard Marius, director of expository writing at Harvard University and author of novels, essays, writing textbooks, and biographies, responded with "How I Write." His description stresses communication, revision, the common qualities of fiction and nonfiction, and individuality in the process.

"How I Write" blurs the distinction between autobiography and exposition, but Marius emphasizes the process of writing by describing, in first person, how he writes. He does not, however, move into persuasion by arguing that this is how someone else should write.

Original publication: *Writers on Writing.* Volume II. New York: Random House, 1988.

I am a compulsive writer. I not only love to write; I *must* write. If a day passes when I have written nothing, I am depressed. If I am expecting to write and something interrupts and keeps me from my task, I feel useless and lazy and somehow spent no matter what I have accomplished otherwise or how much good I may have done in another part of my working life. But several hours of writing leaves me in a state of euphoria. It may be lousy stuff. But it is *there*, and I can make it better tomorrow. I have done something worthwhile with my day.

My writing goes through several stages, but it does not pass through a linear progression. It is a stumbling, often disorganized, always difficult business. At times I am not sure when the process begins. It ends only when I am pressed flat against a deadline and someone takes my work away from me.

First seems to come a swirl of ideas that revolve in my head at the oddest moments. Someone has asked me to write something—like this essay or a book review. Or I decide on my own that I want to write something. Sometimes in a conversation someone suggests that I write something, and I take the suggestion to heart and do it.

Once the general topic comes into my mind, the most ordinary daily experiences are filtered through the writing task. Someone will say something to me. Or I will overhear a remark. Or I will try to explain something to a friend. I will read something seemingly utterly unconnected with what I am writing about, and suddenly I will see a connection—a nugget of information, an insight, a comparison, a metaphor. Some of my best thoughts come to me when I am riding my bicycle back and forth between my home and my office four miles away. This is dream time, one of the happiest periods in my day. Sometimes the general shape of what I want to write comes into my mind in the midst of pulling a hill or while pausing at a traffic light. Sometimes a sentence comes to me, or a metaphor, or even a word that I want to use, and I repeat it with the rhythm of the pedals.

I write both fiction and nonfiction. The process is somewhat different for each, but there are probably more similarities in the two than differences. In fiction I find character more compelling than plot. The fiction I like best builds characters who may do surprising things. But on reflection I find continuity between what characters do and what they have already done.

When I am writing fiction, I think about my characters and keep my eyes and ears open for the characters around me. I listen to the way people talk. I watch their gestures, their expressions. Above all, I look at what they do and how they see other people. And I try to incorporate these observations into the characters I am building. No character springs fully formed into my head. But as I write day after day, I see my characters more and more clearly. I hope they become more subtle, more complex, more familiar. I keep notebooks on them, writing comments to myself about them, who they are, what they do, why they do things (though sometimes I do not know).

Nonfiction requires a writer to pay careful attention to the evidence—to the incidents in a nonfictional narrative, to the logic of an analysis, to the details of a factual description. Getting it right in nonfiction is different from getting it right in fiction—though even as I write these words I find that the borderline between the two sorts of writing is more hazy for me than it might seem for others. The most interesting nonfiction that I do is biography. And building a character in a biography has many affinities with building a character in a novel. The evidence for the biography is intractable in a way that the ideas for a character in a novel are not. But descriptions of places, narratives of events, and analyses of causes may appear in both the novel and the biography.

For both fiction and nonfiction, the most important part of the process is the act of writing itself. I am a compulsive writer. I not only love to write; I *must* write. If a day passes when I have written nothing, I am depressed. If I am expecting to write and something interrupts and keeps me from my task, I feel useless and lazy and somehow spent no matter what I have accomplished otherwise or how much good I may have done in another part of my working life. But several hours of writing leaves me in a state of euphoria. It may be lousy stuff. But it is *there*, and I can make it better tomorrow. I have done something worthwhile with my day.

Most of my writing begins in a notebook. I usually carry several notebooks around with me, notebooks stowed in the capacious shoulderbag I carry on my bike commute and onto airplanes and to meetings. You never know when you are going to have some writing time or when an idea is going to strike. (I wrote part of this article during a lecture by a deconstructionist critic who, I decided, had nothing interesting to say. The other day I managed to write a fair chunk of a chapter in my current novel while a Harvard faculty meeting was droning on.)

I devote the notebooks to various subjects. I write both drafts to be reworked and thoughts about my subject that I have no intention of putting into the final draft. When I am writing fiction, I find it valuable to think about characters or purposes by writing out my thoughts about these matters. And when I am writing nonfiction, I find it sometimes helpful to stop and to write myself a few paragraphs to help me think of just what I want to be doing in the piece.

At some point I sit down at a keyboard, prop the relevant notebook in front of me on a stand, and start to pound away at a draft. I used to work at a typewriter, starting with an ancient Royal Standard that my typing teacher in high school sold me for $50 after students had beaten it more than half to death over the years. (I still have it and until the advent of computers wrote all my first drafts on it.) I used an even more ancient Underwood at the little newspaper where I began to work in high school and where I continued working throughout college.

I should pause a moment over my newspaper experience; it was a great way to learn to write. The most important thing about newspaper journalism is that it must communicate. You must find a common level of discourse so that your experience, your thoughts, your story can be quickly picked up by people in a hurry who do not necessarily have college educations. You must be simple. You must tell stories. You must use active verbs and nouns that convey something of sense experience. You must attribute sources. And you must get it all right because if you don't get it right, somebody is going to call you up on the telephone or come in to see you and rip the skin off your bones.

Composition teachers nowadays try to be gentle with students, and I suppose they should be, though I despise the touchy-feely attitude of many composition specialists. But all writers must eventually discover that everybody is not going to like their work, especially if they get something wrong. Newspaper readers make a more demanding audience than most writing students can imagine. And I am glad that early in my life I learned that there was an audience out there and that someone was likely to care deeply about what I said about seemingly the most ordinary things. Report the wrong second prize winner in the Garden Club's contest for the best dry arrangement, and see what happens. You don't get a friendly composition teacher writing in the margins of your paper, "Are you sure?" You get an outraged gardener sometimes weeping on the telephone or, worse, standing over your desk shaking a mean looking trowel in your face.

Newspaper writing also teaches you some things about process. You often have to write fast for a newspaper. Farther along in this essay I will say some things about revision and its pleasures. But every writer should learn to write rapidly, to get the words out on the page, to make thoughts run from one into the other, to fall into the patterns of repetition that make writing flow smoothly from idea to idea. I am glad that I once learned to produce a story in a half-hour if I had to do it.

Newspaper writing also teaches concentration. It pains me to see my academic colleagues demand a perfect environment before they can write. They have to have uninterrupted hours stretching ahead of them and minds free from cares, or they cannot sit down to write. Some of them almost require Proust's cork-lined room or perhaps just the right kind of soft music playing in the background. And of course they must have just the right desk and just the right chair. Many of my colleagues tell me they can write only in the summer when they are not teaching. Or they have to go off to Yaddo or the McDowell Colony or to some other remote place where they are utterly undisturbed for hours at a time and a flunky brings food to their door.

On the little newspaper where I worked, we had to write with the Milhe Vertical press rattling and banging on the other side of a pasteboard wall, with townspeople coming and going in the shabby office, with the telephone ringing, with friends saying interesting things to each other a couple of desks away, and with the reek of ink and newsprint and *foul* coffee and stale tobacco smoke in the air. I have never lost the ability to concentrate no matter what is going on around me. (As I write these lines, my fifteen-year-old son is hammering uncertainly at his piano lesson a short distance away. I am dimly aware that he is repeating the same difficult passage again and again. But I write on without feeling distracted.) If the atom bomb goes off in my neighborhood when I am writing, it is going to have to knock my house down before it interrupts what I am doing.

Having extolled the necessity of now and then writing rapidly, I must say that my favorite part of writing is revision—going over and over a text until it comes out "right." Before my conversion to the computer, I used to type a draft through a page at a time, typing every page over and over before going on to the next. Then I typed a second draft in the same way, running the words through my fingers again and again and again, throwing my discarded papers into the trash, placing the stuff I liked in a "keep" pile next to the typewriter. And almost always there was a third draft, worked through with the same laborious process. As I wrote, I read aloud in a soft mumble, testing the word with my mouth as I produced them with my fingers.

My big biography of Thomas More, published in 1984, came to 1,052 pages of typescript in its final draft. It was the last book that I shall ever write on a typewriter and with that method. While I was working on it, a woman from Ohio flew to Boston to protest a D we had given her sister in our writing program. I shall call the sister Henrietta, though that was not her real name.

She was furious about the grade we had given to Henrietta. She berated me for an hour. Finally she said in final proof of our unfair grade, "Henrietta wrote this paper twice, and you gave her a D for it. It is not fair to give a student a D who has written the paper twice. You have to give *some* credit for hard work."

It was late in the afternoon, and I had been working at a difficult part of my *Thomas More* all day with many interruptions. My trash can was filled with discarded pages. I picked it up off the floor and upended it on my desk. A storm of papers poured out over the desk top and showered onto the floor. I dug out nine different drafts of one page and spread them out before Henrietta and her startled sister. "Look," I said gently, "this is what real writing is. We are not judging your sister on any standard that we do not use for ourselves. We all take pains, and you don't get credit for anything until you get it right."

The woman from Ohio sat back in her chair and looked at her sister. "Well, Henrietta," she said, "maybe he's right."

My discovery of the computer has changed my process. I now edit from the screen most of the time, though sometimes I print out a draft and sit over it with a pen. But usually I sit down at whatever it is I am doing, call up the file onto the screen, read it over quickly from the beginning, then read it over again making insertions and deletions and shifting paragraphs around in the magical way that computers allow. I change sentence forms, play with words, add thoughts, erase failures.

Some things hold constant in my progress from the typewriter to the computer. I still read everything aloud. I have a fundamental conviction that if a sentence cannot be read aloud with sincerity, conviction, and communicable emphasis, it is not a good sentence. Good writing requires good rhythms and good words. You cannot know whether the rhythms and the words are good unless you read them aloud. Reading aloud is also the easiest way to see that prose tracks, that it runs on smoothly from sentence to sentence, idea to idea, section to section within the larger whole. Reading aloud also makes the mind consider connotations of words and perhaps above all their relations to each other.

This long process of revision allows me two benefits. The first is stylistic. I love words. I love dictionaries. I love putting the right words together. What nouns require adjectives? What nouns most adequately convey the meaning I want to express? What metaphors can I design to make my meaning more vivid? What sentence forms make for the greatest efficiency of communication? What words are not necessary? What am I repeating that I have already said? Where am I being overbearing? Where am I not being vigorous enough? The best way to answer these questions is to think about them—and many more—over the time needed for good revision. I read all sorts of things. And if I read something and find a word I like, I may call up some part of my file and insert that word at an appropriate place.

I have already mentioned the newspaper reporter's vivid sense of audience. In my teaching I have always told students that they must write for an audience. Student writers need to learn that they have to interest someone. All too often they come out of high school thinking that the main goals of writing are to fill pages to the required number and to be correct. They can do all these things and be as dull as soap. The trick is to make someone want to read what they have to say and enjoy it and learn from it. Real writers are performers who, like pianists and singers and baseball players and ballet dancers, want their audience to rise to them in a mingling of admiration, pleasure, and something I can only call *participation*. A real writer wants readers to live through an experience the writer has, to identify with it, to *feel* with it in much the same way that a baseball fan thrills to a solid single hammered down the line with the bases loaded or to a great shortstop play that saves a game.

I write especially for my editor and for a few other good friends. I respect them and want them to respect me. I want them to enjoy my work. I often will think of one or the other of them when I am setting something on paper. I want them to think that I am fair, that I am reasonable, that I have worked hard, that I am interesting, that sometimes I am funny without being unkind, that I am confident without being arrogant, that I know how to use the language. Above all, I want them to read my prose with the feeling of participating in it. My editor said that she wept every time she read my account of the death of Thomas More. I wept over the keyboard as I wrote it in each draft of the book. When she told me of her own tears, I felt a marvelous triumph of a sort that made those three drafts worthwhile. We had participated in the same event both intellectually and emotionally through my prose.

But I suppose that in my own high middle age, I now write mostly for myself. I sit here and push and pull my prose into something that seems just right to me. I fall on words that I like, and I resolve to use them. I think of a good metaphor and feel a wonderful satisfaction at being able to incorporate it into something I am doing. I scribble thoughts in my ever-present notebooks and feel tremendous pleasure at shaping those thoughts into good prose.

It is perhaps a bit misleading to speak of writing for myself as though I were the center of the universe. I am a pretty good reader, reading at every opportunity and reading critically. So when I say I write to please myself, I mean that I write to please the sort of reader I am. No one ever pleases everybody. I have read enough to know that important truth. But by this time in my life, I am confident of my ability to please some of the people I am trying to reach, people who share my particular taste, a taste that has been formed by the reading that I have done since childhood. Revision gives me the chance to play with style, to try different things, to look at them, to keep some, and to discard others. The computer allows any writer a facility in that playfulness undreamed of by our spiritual ancestors. And I love it.

The second benefit I get from revision is the demand that I learn more as I write. Most of my students and many of my colleagues believe that research and writing go on in two discrete parts. One does the research; later one writes.

My process is something else. I began my biography of Thomas More after working more than a decade editing More's works as part of the great Yale Complete Edition. I knew much about him when I began. But as I wrote, the narrative form showed me many holes in my knowledge. And I had to fill those holes with substance. More wrote a history of the infamous King Richard III of England. I had read that little book many times before I started writing my biography. I could have summarized what More had to say about the usurper king and the supposed murder of the little princes in the Tower—one of the great mysteries of English history. But then I wanted to know what other people had said about Richard in his own time and then what people thought of children in that time and then of all the people around the king and of the general political and social situation when More wrote the book long after Richard was dead. My touching one part of the story raised other questions that I thought had to be answered. So my writing drove me to other reading.

Much the same thing is true of fiction. I write through one draft to get to know my characters, to think about them, to wonder what they might do to reveal themselves first to me and then to readers. And when I am done with that draft, I love to start all over again, putting my new knowledge to work in the new version. The point is that revising time is thinking time, and that the more thought you can pour into your writing, the better that writing is likely to be as long as you do not inflate the form until it loses its design.

This matter of design is important to the writing process. I am better at it in my nonfiction than I am in my fiction. My novels tend to sprawl all over the place. Sometimes I feel that they are out of control, and I have moments where I must slash and burn. I control my nonfiction more carefully. I can see that one thought leads naturally into the next, that I develop a pattern of repetition of certain nouns and verbs that gives coherence to the whole, that I cut out unnecessary repetition, and that my last paragraph has some relation to my first—one of the surest tests of coherence that I know. Revision allows me to arrive painfully at this coherence, and at the end of one of my essays, I think most people can state fairly clearly in a sentence or two what I have said. This process does not come easily. But it does come. And, as I said, it is much, much harder with a novel.

The design seems to come best after rapid readings that let me check the shape of things. It always helps to spread this process out over time. I think it is always a good idea to write something and then to put it aside for a while, to sleep on it, to think about other things, and then to come back to see it fresh. That fresh new vision will help a writer see the flaws in design that are likely to lurk within the work of anyone who has concentrated long and hard on a piece of prose. Robert Pirsig in his classic *Zen and the Art of Motorcycle Maintenance* speaks of the "*a priori* motorcycle," the motorcycle as it is in itself. We know that motorcycle only as an ideal construct in our minds, since we can never see the motorcycle all at once. Then there is the motorcycle we see from various angles, a motorcycle that we can see only in parts according to our particular view. From that particular point of view, we assume that there is a whole motorcycle, a complete entity. But in fact that assumption may be false.

I like to say that there is an *a priori* book or essay that we have in our minds after we have worked on something for a long time. That is the piece of writing that we think ought to be there. But over against that ideally complete piece is the actual manuscript (or computer file), the thing that we see as a physical presence when we pick it up and read it. We often discover that the ideal manuscript we conceive in our minds is simply not there as we have assumed in the real manuscripts that lie on our desks. Sometimes we have to rest our minds a little while before we can achieve the critical freshness that lets us see our manuscripts as they really are and not as we assume them to be.

Many of my friends write outlines before they start writing, and I often recommend some sort of outline to fledgling writers. But I must confess that I cannot recall ever making a preliminary outline in my life. Sometimes I make lists of points I want to cover, jotting those points down in my notebook. But a list is not the same as the outline I was required to present for papers when I was in college. Then I always wrote the paper and figured out an acceptable outline afterward. My teachers loved outlines, and I thought it best to humor them.

In the end I have to give my manuscripts up. In early 1984 my editor sent back the copyedited version of my final Thomas More manuscript and called me every day for two weeks to see how I was getting along at checking out this final part of the editing process. At a certain point she asked me, "How many pages have you rewritten?" "Only forty-two," I said.

She sighed in disgust and told me that if I did not send the manuscript to her by Express Mail that very afternoon she was going to fly to Boston the next day and take it away from me. "You are going to be embarrassed, and I am going to be furious, and I am going to charge it all off to your royalties account," she said.

She was angry then, and I sent the manuscript off—and passed into a deep depression. When something of mine is in print, I can only rarely bring myself to read it. Once in print, it is unchangeable. To me it is almost dead. And since I cannot revise it any more, I really do not want anything else to do with it. I have never read a book of mine through once it has been published. People often write me letters asking questions about this or that in the book. I can barely make myself open the book to see what they are talking about. I read the reviews somewhat listlessly. I do not believe the good reviews, and the bad reviews make me angry. The only way I can be happy once a book is gone is to start another book.

Then the pleasures of writing begin all anew, and the world itself seems to take on a new form, and a new and glorious light of opportunity shines on every precious moment that I work at the new creation.

The Headmaster

JOHN MCPHEE

William L. Howarth, in his introduction to *The John McPhee Reader*,
uses phrases like "the artistic dimensions of reportage" and "factual
books" to describe McPhee's writing. Certainly McPhee has vividly
captured, in minute detail, such varied subjects as the orange, the
Loch Ness monster, and Bill Bradley's basketball shots. His
immediate audience might be considered the readership of *The New
Yorker*, since that magazine has first option on his works. Many of
his essays have reached a broader readership in textbooks and
anthologies of his essays.

In "The Headmaster," he captures a person for us, demonstrating
some of the same characteristics discussed in the chapter on
autobiography but now applied to biography. In Howarth's words,
"McPhee does not venerate his heroes; he replicates them for our
judgment as fully as he can. His principal aim is to maintain an
artist's distance and catholicity, to bring alive all the possibilities of a
story, not merely a few of its strong points." Howarth might well be
defining exposition.

Original publication: *The Headmaster*. New York; Farrar, Straus & Giroux, 1966;
collected in *The John McPhee Reader*. Editor William L. Howarth. New York, Vintage
Books, 1976.

People seeing the headmaster for the first time often find him different from
what they expected. Those who stay in the Deerfield community for any length
of time quickly become aware that they are living in a monarchy and that the
small man in the golf cart is the king, but visitors who have heard of him and
know what a great man he is seem to insist that he ought to be a tall,
white-haired patriarch. People see him picking up papers and assume it is his
job. Coming upon a group of women outside one of his old houses a few years
ago, he took them in and led them through its ancient rooms. On the way out,
one lady gave him a quarter. People walk right by him sometimes without
seeing him. Someone once stopped, turned around, and said, "I'm sorry, Mr.
Boyden. I didn't notice you."

"That's all right," he said. "No one ever does."

He loves such stories, perhaps in part because they help to fake out the
faculty and the boys. How else, after all, could an inconspicuous man like that
hold an entire community in the palm of his hand? When the stories come back
to him, he lights up with pleasure. He has one way of judging everything: If it's

good for the academy, it's good. He was once walking with an impressive-looking Deerfield faculty member when someone, a stranger, said, "Who was that?"

"That was the headmaster."

"Yes, but who was the little man with him?"

Boyden looked old when he was four, older when he was in college, and older still in the nineteen-twenties, but now he doesn't look particularly old at all. His hair is not white but slate-gray, and his demeanor, which hasn't changed in forty years, still suggests a small, grumpy Labrador. He sometimes dresses in gray trousers, a dark-blue jacket, and brown cordovan shoes—choices that are somewhat collegiate and could be taken as a mild sign of age, because for decades he wore dark-blue worsted suits and maroon ties almost exclusively, winter and summer, hanging on to each successive suit until it fell off him in threads. One of his jacket pockets today has a four-inch rip that has been bound with black thread. He doesn't care. He is an absolutely unself-conscious man. Let one scuff mark appear on a stair riser in his academy and he will quickly find a janitor and report it, but this kind of concern is entirely projected onto the school. He once got up on a cool July morning and put on an old leather coat covered with cracks and lined with sheepskin that was coming loose; he went off to New York in it and obliviously wore it all day in the sweltering city. After eighty-six years, his only impairment is bad hearing. "My ears are gone," he will say, and then he will walk into a roomful of people and pretend that there isn't a syllable he can't catch. He indulges himself in nothing. He will eat anything, and he usually does not notice the components of his meals, unless they happen to be root beer and animal crackers, which he occasionally eats for breakfast. He has been given honorary degrees by Harvard, Yale, Princeton, and seventeen other colleges and universities, but he apparently has not even a trace of a desire to be called Dr. Boyden, and no one calls him that except eraser salesmen and strangers whose sons are applying to the school.

"Never make a decision just to get something done," he says, and no one has ever accused him of being impulsive. His Director of Studies has said, "He has an infinite wisdom, which is as aggravating as hell. But anyone knowing him well who is faced with an important decision would go to him." This is, of course, most true of his students. They call him up in the summertime; they call him up from college; in later life, they call him up to ask if they should run for office. In conversation, he has the ability to give his undivided attention, and the perception to understand the implications of practically anything that is said to him. In this way, he has made several thousand people believe that he especially cares about them, which he does. He rarely loses his temper, but his capacity for absorbing criticism is not large. He is not proud in a narrow, personal sense; his pride is in his school and in his belief that he knows what is best for it. He is lost in the school, and there is nothing of him but the school. On vacation in Florida, he goes around in his blue worsted suit looking for people with money to help keep Deerfield going. He never goes near the water. He was once seen sitting in the lobby of the Breakers in Palm Beach reading a Deerfield yearbook. He is famous for his simplicity, which he cultivates. He is, in the highest sense, a simple man, and he has spent his life building a school according to elemental ideals, but only a complicated man could bring off what he has done, and, on the practical plane, he is full of paradox and politics. Senior members of his faculty, in various conversations, have described him as "a great humanitarian," "ruthless," "loyal," "feudal," "benevolent," "grateful," "humble," "impatient," "restless," "thoughtful," "thoughtless," "selfish," "selfless," "stubborn," "discerning," "intuitive," and "inscrutable"—never once disagreeing with one another. The headmaster's own view of himself, according to one of his two sons, is that he is "indestructible and infallible."

Boyden has the gift of authority. He looks fragile, his voice is uncommanding, but people do what he says. Without this touch, he would have lost the school on the first day he worked there. Of the seven boys who were in the academy when he took over in that fall of 1902, at least four were regarded by the populace with fear, and for a couple of years it had been a habit of people of Deerfield to cross the street before passing the academy. Boyden's problem was complicated by one of the trustees, who was so eager to close the school that he had actually encouraged these boys to destroy the new headmaster as rapidly as they could. The boys were, on the average, a head taller and thirty pounds heavier than the headmaster. The first school day went by without a crisis. Then, as the students were getting ready to leave, Boyden said, "Now we're going to play football." Sports had not previously been a part of the program at the academy. Scrimmaging on the village common, the boys were amused at first, and interested in the novelty, but things suddenly deteriorated in a hail of four-letter words. With a sour look, the headmaster said, "Cut that out!" That was all he said, and—inexplicably—it was all he had to say.

A few days later, a boy asked him if he would like to go outside and have a catch with a baseball. The two of them went out onto the school lawn and stood about fifty feet apart. The boy wound up and threw a smokeball at him, apparently with intent to kill. Boyden caught the ball and fired it back as hard as he could throw it. A kind of match ensued, and the rest of the students collected to watch. The headmaster and the boy kept throwing the baseball at each other with everything they had. Finally, the boy quit. "Of course, I was wearing a glove and he wasn't," says the headmaster, who is a craftsman of the delayed, throwaway line.

He believed in athletics as, among other things, a way of controlling and blending his boys, and he required all of them to participate throughout the school year. This idea was an educational novelty in 1902. He arranged games with other schools, and because there were not enough boys in Deerfield Academy to fill out a football team or a baseball team, he jumped into the action himself. He was the first quarterback Deerfield ever had. He broke his nose and broke it again. Taking the ball in one game, he started around right end, but the other team's defense halfback forced him toward the sideline, picked him up,

and—this was years before the forward-motion rule—carried him all the way
back to the Deerfield end zone and dumped him on the ground. He was a much
better baseball player. Ignoring his height, he played first base. He was a good
hitter, and Greenfield, Springfield, and Northampton newspapers of the time
include items with headlines like "BOYDEN GOES 3 FOR 4 AS DEERFIELD ACADEMY
BEATS ATHOL 2 TO 0." In sports, he captured and held his school, and it may be
in sports that he developed the personal commitment that kept him there. His
teammates were won over by him. Their earlier antagonism became support.
He convinced them that the school would go under without their help, and they
discovered that they wanted to keep it going as much as he did. In one game,
at Arms Academy, he ran after a high pop foul, caught the ball two feet from
a brick wall, crashed into it, and fell to the ground unconscious. The boys told
him to go home and recover and not to worry—there would be no disciplinary
problems at the school during his absence.

A teacher, Miss Minnie Hawks, was hired shortly after the headmaster was,
and she taught German and geometry while he taught algebra and physical
geography. He used to take a rock into class with him, set it on his desk, and
tell his students to write down everything they knew about the rock. But he was
more interested in implications than he was in facts. His mind drifted quickly
from science to behavior. "You're not youngsters anymore," he would say.
"You're going to be the ones who run this town." He read a bit of the Bible to
them every morning. Gradually, he acquired more teachers and spent less time
in the classroom himself. He assembled a sound faculty and gave its members
freedom to teach as they pleased. His own mark was made in moral education
rather than in the academic disciplines. His first-hand relationship with his boys
has always been extraordinary, and Deerfield students for sixty years have been
characterized by the high degree of ethical sensitivity that he has been able to
awaken in them. This is the area within which his greatness lies. From the start,
he assumed responsibility not only for their academic development but also for
their social lives, their recreation, and their religious obligations. He held
dances, supplied dance cards, and, just to be sure that no one lacked interest,
filled in the cards himself. After the dances, he got on the Greenfield-
Northampton trolley car with his boys and girls and rode with them, making
sure that each got off at the correct address. If he happened to be on the trolley's
last run, he walked home—a distance of six miles. He believed in wearing the
boys out. They dug ditches; they also made beehives, incubators, and
wheelbarrows; and, with axes and crosscut saws, they cut lumber for lockers for
their athletic equipment. In his first year, he set up a card table beside a radiator
just inside the front door of the school building. This was his office, not because
there was no room for a headmaster's office anywhere else, but because he
wanted nothing to go on in the school without his being in the middle of it.
Years later, when the present main school building was built, the headmaster
had the architect design a wide place in the first-floor central hallway—the spot
with the heaviest traffic in the school—and that was where his desk was put and
where it still is. While he dictates, telephones, or keeps his appointments, he

watches the boys passing between classes. He has a remarkable eye for trouble. If the mood of the student body at large is poor, he will sense it, and when one boy is disturbed, he will see it in the boy's face, and he will think of some minor matter they need to talk over, so that he can find out what the difficulty is and try to do something about it. He has maintained his familial approach to education despite the spread of bureaucracy into institutions and industries and despite the increased size of his own school. In his early years, he found that he could handle twenty-eight students as easily as fourteen, then fifty-six as easily as twenty-eight, and so on, until, in the late nineteen-forties, he had something over five hundred. The enrollment has remained at that level. "I can handle five hundred," he says. "Another hundred and I'd lose it."

Most schools have detailed lists of printed rules, and boys who violate them either are given penalties or are thrown out. A reasonable percentage of expulsions is a norm of prep-school life. Deerfield has no printed rules and no set penalties, and the headmaster has fired only five boys in sixty-four years. "For one foolish mistake, a boy should not have a stamp put on him that will be with him for the rest of his life," he says. "I could show you a list of rules from one school that is thirty pages long. There is no flexibility in a system like that. I'm willing to try a little longer than some of the other people do, provided there is nothing immoral. You can't have a family of three children without having some problems, so you have problems if you have five hundred. If you make a lot of rules, they never hit the fellow you made them for. Two hours after making a rule, you may want to change it. We have rules here, unwritten ones, but we make exceptions to them more than we enforce them. I always remember what Robert E. Lee said when he was president of Washington College, which is now Washington and Lee. He said, 'A boy is more important than any rule.' Ninety percent of any group of boys will never get out of line. You must have about ninety per cent as a central core. Then the question is: How many of the others can you absorb?"

To say that Deerfield has no set rules is not to say that it is a place where a boy can experiment at will with his impulses. The academy has been described, perhaps fairly, as a gilded cage. The essential underlying difference between Deerfield and schools like Exeter and Andover is that Exeter and Andover make a conscious effort to teach independence and self-reliance by establishing a set of regulations to live by and then setting the boys free to stand or fall accordingly. Exeter and Andover boys can cut classes, within established margins, and they are provided with time they can call their own. Deerfield boys have several free hours each Sunday, but most of their time is programmed for them, and attendance is constantly taken. The headmaster's respect and admiration for Exeter and Andover are considerable, and he likes to quote a conversation he once had with an Andover headmaster, who said, "Maybe you're right. Maybe we're right. There is a need for both schools." Andover and Exeter, looking ahead to the college years, try to prepare their students for the freedom they will have, so that they can enjoy it and not suffer from it. Boyden believes that the timing of a boy's life requires more discipline in the secondary-school years than later, and that there is no point in going to college before you get there. "Boys need a sense of security," he says. "Discipline without persecution adds to that sense of security. People sometimes don't realize this, but boys like a control somewhere. We try to give them what you might call controlled freedom. We're the last bulwark of the old discipline. We're interested in new things, but I'm not going to throw away the fundamentals."

A new boy at Deerfield cannot have been there very long before the idea is impressed upon him that he is a part of something that won't work unless he does his share. The headmaster is able to create this kind of feeling in his boys to a greater degree than most parents are. All boys are given an equal footing from which to develop their own positions. There are no special responsibilities for scholarship boys, such as waiting on table. Everyone does that. In fact, the headmaster insists that scholarship boys not be told that they have scholarships, since that might injure the sense of equality he tries to build. His school, which grew so phenomenally out of almost nothing, has frequently been visited by curious educational theorists. One researcher spent a few days at the academy and finally said, "Well, there isn't any system here, but it works." Such people perplex Frank Boyden almost as much as he perplexes them. "People come here thinking we have some marvelous method," he says. "We just treat the boys as if we expect something of them, and we keep them busy. So many of our things simply exist. They're not theory. They're just living life. I expect most of our boys want to do things the way we want them done. We drive with a light rein, but we can pull it up just like that, if we need to. We just handle the cases as they come up."

His art as a disciplinarian often enables him to prevent things before they happen. He listens to the noise level in a group of boys, and watches the degree of restlessness; he can read these things as if they were a printed page. This is one reason he believes in meetings that involve the entire school. "You must have your boys together as a unit at least once a day, just as you have your family together once a day," he says. Evening Meeting is a Deerfield custom. The boys sit on a vast carpet in the anteroom of the school auditorium and listen to announcements, perhaps an anecdotal story from the headmaster, and reports of athletic contests and other activities. "Junior B Football beat the Holyoke High School Junior Varsity six to nothing this afternoon," says the coach of Junior B Football. "Charlie Hiller scored the touchdown with two minutes left in the game." In the applause that follows, this one low-echelon athlete gains something, and so does the school. On Sunday evenings, there is a vesper service, or Sunday Night Sing, as it is called, in which the boys sing one hymn after another, with a pause for a short talk by a visiting clergyman or educator. The lustre, or lack of it, in their voices is the headmaster's gauge of the climate of the student body for the week to come, and he accordingly chides them or exhorts them or amuses them or blasts them at Evening Meetings on succeeding days, often shaping his remarks around one of several precepts—"keep it on a high level," "be mobile," "finish up strong"—which he uses so repeatedly and effectively that the words continue to ricochet through the minds of Deerfield graduates long after they leave the school. "He has the trick of the wrist with a whole community," one of his teachers has said.

All discipline ultimately becomes a private matter between each boy and the headmaster. Most of the boys feel guilty if they do something that offends his sensibilities. Unlike his great predecessor Arnold of Rugby, he does not believe that schoolboys are his natural enemies; on the contrary, he seems to convince them that although he is infallible, he badly needs their assistance. A local farmer who was in the class of 1919 says, "When you thought of doing something wrong, you would know that you would hurt him deeply, so you wouldn't do it. He had twenty-four-hour control." A 1928 alumnus says, "It didn't matter what you did as long as you told him the truth." And 1940: "Whatever it was, you didn't do it, because you might drop a little in his eyes." He will give a problem boy a second, third, fourth, fifth, and sixth chance, if necessary. The rest of the student body sometimes becomes cynical about the case, but the headmaster refuses to give up. "I would have kicked me out," says one alumnus who had a rather defiant senior year in the early nineteen-fifties. The headmaster had reason enough to expel him, and almost any other school would have dropped him without a thought, but Boyden graduated him, sent him to Princeton, and, today, does not even recall that the fellow was ever a cause of trouble. Boyden is incapable of bearing grudges. He wants to talk things out and forget them. He is sensitive to the potential effect of his forbearance, so he has sometimes taken the risk of calling the student body together and asking for its indulgence. A boy once drank the better part of a fifth of whiskey in a bus returning from another school, reeled in the aisle, fell on his face, and got sick. The headmaster called the school together and said that for the sake of discipline in the academy at large he would have to let the boy go unless they would guarantee him that no episode of the kind would happen again. The headmaster was beyond being thought of as weak, so he got away with it. People often wonder what on earth could make him actually drop a boy, and the five cases in which he has done so are therefore of particular interest. All have a common factor: the offender was unremorseful. One of them was guilty of nineteen different offenses, including arson. Nevertheless, if he had told the headmaster that he was wrong, he could have stayed in school.

A boy of considerable talent once told the headmaster that he could write his English papers only between midnight and dawn. His muse, the boy claimed, refused to appear at any other time of day. The difficulty was that after the boy's inspiration ran out he invariably fell asleep and missed his morning classes. Like all geniuses, this boy was likely to attract imitators. The headmaster addressed the student body. "Are you willing to let Mac Farrell stay up all night writing his English papers?" he said. "Mac Farrell alone?" The boys agreed.

The headmaster has often put himself in an uncomfortable corner for a boy who is different. He once had two students—artistic cousins of Mac Farrell —who liked to paint and particularly liked to go out at night and do nocturnes.

They did the cemetery by moonlight and the old houses in the edge of the glow of street lamps. The headmaster knew that this was going on, but he overlooked it. His own favorites have always been responsible, uncomplicated, outstanding athletes, and he cares even less about art than he knows about it, but, in his way, he was just the right headmaster for these two boys. "With a person as unDeerfield as myself," remembers one of them, who is now Curator of Graphic Arts at Princeton University, "he was sympathetic and understanding. He was patient and—what can I say?—incredibly wise in the way that he handled me."

Certain boys at Deerfield in earlier years would commit long series of petty crimes and believe that all had gone undetected. Then, finally, the headmaster would stop such a boy, pull out a small notebook, and read off to him everything he had done wrong since the first day of school. For years, the headmaster roved the campus late at night, like a watchman. Until the late nineteen-thirties, he made rounds to every room in every dormitory during study hours every night. Since then, he has made spot visits. He never gives a boy bad news at night. He never threatens. He uses shame privately. He more often trades favors than gives them. If a boy asks something of him, he asks something in return. There is no student government, nor are there faculty committees, helping to run Deerfield. The headmaster holds himself distant from that sort of thing. Senior-class presidents are elected on the eve of Commencement. Students who are in the school now say they would not want student government anyway, because they feel that it is a mockery elsewhere.

Boyden's principle of athletics for all has remained one of the main elements of the school's program, and Deerfield is unmatched in this respect today. Where once he did not have enough boys for even one team, he now has teams for all five hundred. When a boy at Deerfield chooses a sport, he automatically makes a team that has a full schedule of games with other schools. For example, Deerfield usually has at least eight basketball teams, each with game uniforms, away games, and all the other incidentals of the sport on the varsity level. This is true in soccer, baseball, football, tennis, lacrosse, hockey, squash, swimming, skiing, track, and cross-country as well. With few exceptions, every boy at Deerfield is required to take part in three sports a year. There is no set number of teams in any sport. According to the boys' choices, there may be a few more football teams one year and a few more soccer teams the next. Deerfield has sent on a share of athletic stars—football players such as Mutt Ray to Dartmouth and Archie Roberts to Columbia, for instance—but Deerfield is not really an atmosphere in which a great athlete is likely to develop. The headmaster's belief in sport is exceeded by his belief that everything has its place and time. Deerfield athletes are given no time for extra practice, nor are they permitted to practice any sport out of season. In the fall and the spring, the basketball courts are locked, and baskets are actually removed from the backboards.

In the early days, having the headmaster as a player produced some disadvantages for Deerfield teams. Once, in a pick-off situation in baseball, when he caught the throw from the pitcher and put his glove down, the opposing player slid safely under him. "Out," said the umpire. Any other baseball player would have congratulated himself on his luck, but the headmaster had to tell the umpire that the fellow had in fact been safe. From the start, he had been preaching sportsmanship to his boys. People who remember those days say that he was the first person in that part of the country to stress courtesy in athletics. "We may wish they were interested in other things," he said at the time, "but we must meet existing conditions, and since they will have athletic sports anyway, let us control them and make them a moral force." No matter how able a Deerfield player was or how close a game had become, if he showed anger he was benched. If a basketball player said anything the least bit antagonistic to the man he was guarding—even something as mild as "Go ahead and shoot"—a substitute would go into the game. Athletics was one of the ways in which Deerfield became known, and from the beginning the headmaster wanted his teams to be smartly dressed and thoroughly equipped. In the early years, he often spent at least a third of his salary on athletic equipment, and when a woman of the town offered a contribution to the school, he asked if he might use it for baseball uniforms. "Something has lifted the spirit of this community," she said to him. "Go and buy the best uniforms you can find, but don't tell anyone I gave the money for it."

The headmaster played on Deerfield teams until he was about thirty-five, and he was head coach of football, basketball, and baseball until he was nearly eighty. "I can't go to a funeral anywhere from Athol to Northampton without an elderly man's coming up and reminding me of a baseball game we once played against one another," he says. His sense of football has always been vague but imaginative. His blocking assignments were not precise. During his years as player-coach, he put straps on the belts of his linemen so that the backs—himself included—could hang on and be pulled forward for short gains. In baseball, he followed a simple strategy. "If you can put your glove on a fast ball, there is no reason you can't put your bat on it," he has said for sixty-four years. "Anyone can learn to bunt." Deerfield teams use the squeeze play as if there were no alternative in the sport. He continued to hit fungoes to his baseball teams until he was seventy-five years old. It was a high point of any Deerfield baseball day to watch him hit precise grounders to his scrambling infield. Toward the end of his coaching years, the headmaster found that he could not hit the ball with quite as much snap as he liked to give it. He complained that the ground was getting softer. His main talent as a coach was that he always seemed to know what a boy could do and then expected no more of him. He knew, somehow, when a pitcher was almost through. If his assistant coaches happened to prevail on him to leave a pitcher in a game, disaster usually followed. What he did not know about football he made up through his knowledge of boys, and he could win a game with the right remark. He once did so—in the early nineteen-twenties—by taking his quarterback aside and saying to him, "You're just like a race horse. Sometimes you're too tense to do your job. Take it easy. You'll run faster."

Visitors today sometimes think that the headmaster is a little theatrical when he walks up and down the sidelines—eighty-six years old, and wearing a player's duffel coat that almost reaches the ground—and acts as if he were on the verge of jumping into the game. Something they may not be able to imagine is what it must mean to him to remember the games against small local schools when he himself was in the backfield and there were fifteen or twenty boys in the academy, and now, more than sixty years later, to be watching his team make one touchdown after another until the final score is Deerfield 28, Exeter 0. As a semi-retired coach, the headmaster still gives the same pre-game talks he has always given. In a way that is desperate, unyielding, and total, he wants to win, but he wants to win with grace. "The consequence of poor sportsmanship is that you lose, somewhere along the line," he says. "Remember, it's better to lose in a sportsmanlike way than to win and gloat over it." And he goes along in that vein for a while, until he has satisfied the requirements of his conscience. Then he says, "Now, boys, let's not let up on them for a minute. Let's win this one, if possible, by forty points."

Money Majors

Each year *U.S. News & World Report* provides a survey of the top colleges and universities in the country. This article has the same purpose, with a more specialized approach—to survey business schools. Despite the designation of the schools covered in this article as "the best professional schools," the emphasis is exposition—descriptions of the top twenty business schools in the nation.

Original publication: *U.S. News & World Report*, November 2, 1987.

Harvard Business School graduates call their alma mater "the West Point of capitalism." That phrase aptly sums up the mission of the top graduate business schools: Molding tomorrow's captains of industry. The same goal probably spawned America's first graduate business school in 1900, the Amos Tuck School at Dartmouth, but today's B schools must prepare leaders for a world several quantum leaps more complex. In a time when the nation's global competitiveness, economic leadership and business ethics are all in question, business schools face a daunting task in training students to steer corporate America past the shoals.

Nonetheless, the allure and the financial reward of a management career have fueled an unexpected boom in business-school applications, up 10 to 20 percent from last year and contrary to the downward trend in most other graduate-degree programs. Last year, nearly 70,000 students took Masters of Business Administration or equivalent degrees. About 600 universities in the U.S. award graduate business degrees. Only about a third, however, are nationally accredited by the American Assembly of Collegiate Schools of Business (AACSB). Most of the others are regionally accredited.

Two words—balance and breadth—encapsulate Stanford's Graduate School of Business, the No. 1 choice in the *U.S. News* survey of deans of nationally recognized business schools. To produce management generals—and generalists—the Stanford curriculum balances the two main approaches to a graduate business education, the historical case-study method made famous at Harvard and the more theoretical or quantitative approach, with heavy emphasis on economics, statistics and accounting. Stanford strives for a diverse student body with real-world experience to stir the intellectual pot. "There are people here who have done amazing things," says second-year student André Hidi, himself a onetime professional hockey player with the Washington Capitals. "You learn at least as much from your classmates as you do from the class." Stanford's faculty draws national praise for the strength of its original research and for infusing students with new ideas.

At Harvard, real-life problems

Harvard's business school, ranked second, has more than twice as many students as Stanford's and dwarfs all others in the number of business leaders who are alumni. First-year grades are largely based on case-study discussions in which 80 or 90 students intensely thrash out analyses of such real-life business problems as United Airlines' choice of a hub airport. The school's central role in U.S. business and the ethics of some of its prestigious professors were questioned in a recent book, *The Empire Builders*, by former Harvard researcher J. Paul Mark, who accused some faculty members of parlaying their jobs into lucrative consulting contracts and directorships in multinational companies. Dean John McArthur dismisses the book as "deeply flawed and apparently unsupported by even minimal research."

Long renowned for its emphasis on finance and production of number-crunching "quant jocks," the third-ranked Wharton School of the University of Pennsylvania is now building a reputation for its international business courses. Nine percent of Wharton's class of 1986 was placed in overseas jobs. "Foreign firms are increasingly looking to the M.B.A. as someone to assist them in their global approach to business," says Wharton placement director James Beirne.

Nearly two thirds of the students at Massachusetts Institute of Technology's Sloan School of Management, in fourth place, have engineering or science degrees. The school is launching a master's-degree program in manufacturing-process technology to capitalize on the shift of interest from high finance to the shop floor. Sloan's technical emphasis also attracts a high share of foreign students, about 30 percent. The University of Chicago, ranked fifth, epitomizes the quantitative approach to business school. It eschews the creation of generalists in favor of "digit heads" well grounded in "the disciplines"— economics, math, statistics and behavioral science. Still, Chicago is reaching out to liberal-arts majors to broaden the classroom perspective.

Unlike most top B schools, Northwestern University's Kellogg School, in sixth place, interviews all applicants—3,800 last year—to get a personal feel for candidates. That concern carries over to the small-group concept for classes. "A lot of what you do in the corporate environment," says graduate Suzanne Blaug, "is consensus management—the only way to get things done is to work with other people." The University of Michigan, ranked seventh, stresses a strong research environment. "Professors are required to be 'knowledge creators,' " says Dean Gilbert Whitaker. "There is a intellectual liveliness found here."

For husband-and-wife chemical engineers Paul and Carol Flack, the deciding factors in choosing eight-ranked Carnegie Mellon were its small size (340 students) and its group-oriented quantitative approach, with an emphasis on computers. Columbia University, in ninth place, takes advantage of its New York City location to attract internationally known professors and a heterogeneous student body. Courses such as the required Conceptual Foundations of Business offer a humanistic perspective on corporate values.

Making money or making products

At the University of California at Berkeley, tied with Columbia for ninth, the Manufacturing Club was created after a campus editorial urged students to "make a contribution to the nation's well-being" by going into the manufacturing sector rather than a higher-paying but less "productive" financial job. Berkeley, says Jean Moe, director of career planning, "has a more altruistic attitude toward the world." Dartmouth College's Amos Tuck School, tied with the University of Texas for 11th, has the fewest students (245) and is in the smallest town (Hanover, N.H.). But it capitalizes on these factors with its residential program, drawing more than 300 executives each year to interact with students who team up in small groups to solve real problems for real clients. Second-year student Dennis Williams once worked at a bank in Yugoslavia. His study group included a Minnesota pig farmer, a New York ad manager and a former auto-making executive. Together, they looked at a financial problem for a nuclear-power company.

Entrepreneurship, a buzzword of 1987, gets its due at both Texas and the 13th-ranked school, the University of California at Los Angeles. Texas's IC^2 Institute—short for innovation, creativity and capital—is cited by one dean for "the most innovative research in the world on entrepreneurship, commercialization of new technology and creative approaches to management." UCLA, says Associate Dean Carol Scott, is imbued with a strong entrepreneurial spirit, perhaps because of its public status. "We get a student body that does its own thing. We get the scrappers of the world."

"Most people see business ethics as an oxymoron," says John Rosenblum, dean of University of Virginia's Colgate Darden School, in 14th place. "But we see it as a redundant expression." The school has had a research center for business ethics since the mid-1960s and is cited for its "extraordinary commitment to teaching," emulating Harvard's case-study approach. The program at the University of Illinois, 15th, is "a well-kept secret," says one administrator. Nearly half of its students come from undergraduate schools at Illinois, but not necessarily right after graduation. They include a deep-sea diver, a radio announcer, a nurse and an architect. Indiana University, 16th, takes only 30 percent of its students from inside the state and stresses an interdisciplinary approach. One joint master's degree in arts and administration trains students for such jobs as managing orchestras or museums.

The University of North Carolina's 17th-ranked B school and the 18th-ranked Fuqua School of Business at Duke are only 8 miles apart, and both are on the move. North Carolina's new Kenan Institute for Private Enterprise tries to bridge the gap between the business world, government and academia. Duke's Fuqua takes 12 percent of its students directly from undergraduate school and is considered a leader in integrating computers into the curriculum. Students are trained to be generalists, explains Dean Thomas Keller. "They learn the basis of decision making."

The Yale difference

Yale, 19th, is the only ranked school not accredited by AACSB—by Yale's own choice. The School of Organization and Management, with a broad focus that encompasses both the private and public sectors, offers not an M.B.A. degree but an M.P.P.M., a Master's of Public and Private Management. Studies in organizational behavior are the keystone for the program. Students must have previous work experience. The school has a high percentage of women, currently 44 percent in the class of 1988.

New York University, No. 20, is one of the biggest national B schools with 2,500 part-time and 1,100 full-time students. Consequently, it has a huge faculty—more than 200 full-time professors and instructors—which tends to be more functionally specialized. The school's size "creates more depth and breadth," says Dean Richard West, who admits that at times "it can be more impersonal."

In each of the three regional categories, the top two schools were named by at least 60 percent of those voting. In the East, Georgetown University's business school, just 6 years old, won top honors for its quality and its international focus. Nearly half of its students have lived, worked or studied abroad and know a foreign language. Its location in Washington, D.C., also gives its students a chance to see how business interacts with government. Second-ranked University of New Hampshire's Whittemore School is tiny—25 to 30 students in each year's class—but runs a weekend residential executive M.B.A. program. The school is praised for an innovative entrepreneurship program.

A few miles from Georgetown, top-rated George Mason University in Fairfax, Va., is accredited in the Southern region. It caters to Washington-area professionals who get degrees by going to class at night for four or five years. A meat-and-potatoes curriculum—accounting, finance, management and marketing—is taught by a continually upgraded faculty. Tied for first in the region is Rice University's Jesse H. Jones School of Administration in Houston, with 78 students in this fall's entering class and with a reputation for high academic standards. A full-time faculty of 24 and an additional 31 part-time professors insure that class sizes are small.

Claremont Graduate School's Peter Drucker Graduate Management Center, first in the combined Midwest-West regions, is named after "the father of modern management," who remains its top professor. The California school embodies its namesake's teachings ("management as a discipline and as a practice deals with human and social values") by encouraging a broad, integrated approach and a balance of theory and practice. Second-place American Graduate School of International Management in Glendale, Ariz., popularly known as Thunderbird, requires graduates to have strong conversational proficiency in a second language. Students can earn a degree in one calendar year with a summer session, taking nine semester hours of world studies and 15 hours of conventional business courses.

Much About Wallace Has Changed As He Campaigns for Nomination

This news release, copyrighted by *The New York Times*, was printed on page two of a Sunday edition of a local paper, in a space normally allocated to news stories. For all the use of verifiable detail, readers must ask what the writer's motive really was. Did he (or she) intend for the reader to ask, "Can I vote for this man to be President of the United States?" The use of loaded adjectives and the juxtaposition of details such as the banner on the "armored lectern" move the news story from pure exposition into a gray area between exposition and persuasion. But the article takes no stand for or against Wallace in its wording; readers raise the question because of what they read.

BOSTON—At first glance, it seems just like the old days.

There he is, George Corley Wallace, once again behind the lectern, running for the presidency for the fourth time preaching the old anti-Washington gospel, tossing off a snappy salute with that stubby right hand, winking at the ladies.

But on closer inspection, much has changed. The 1976 Wallace campaign is like no other the Alabama Governor has conducted.

Arthur Bremmer made sure of that on that May day four years ago in Laurel, Md., when he raised his hand, along with all the others reaching out to touch the candidate, then shot down George Wallace.

For all its burnished mahogany sheen, the 1976 lectern is a bullet-proof enclosure, open only at the back and topped with foot-high sheets of inch-thick protective glass.

The man encased within is not standing but is seated in a chrome wheelchair. He seems to be standing because only his head and a bit of his shoulders are visible through the greenish tinge of the protective glass.

A grim-faced Secret Service agent sits on the dais amid the smiling dignitaries, only an arm's length from the candidate and immediately next to Mrs. Wallace. She starts when a television cable clatters to the floor. The candidate's head swivels sharply toward the noise, eyes searching.

A dozen other agents are positioned elsewhere in the auditorium, including three at the entrance.

No one gets into the auditorium without being searched, not even newsmen long accredited to the Wallace entourage. There have been rumors that anti-Wallace demonstrators might try to cause trouble.

No one gets to approach the lectern and shake the hand of the man who has been known to skip meals to press the flesh.

This is what the Wallace candidacy has come to, the candidacy of the man who professes to represent grass roots America. "Trust the people," says the red, white and blue sign hung on the armored lectern.

Though the spectators are not always searched, though the Secret Service agent does not always sit with the dignitaries, the inescapable fact is that the 1976 Wallace campaign is an armed camp. No other candidate, with the possible exception of President Ford, is so isolated from the voters of the world's greatest democracy.

George Wallace enters and leaves by back doors these days, a fleeting image in that shiny wheelchair, a remote wave and smile from within a squirreling clutch of stone-faced young agents, a moving target.

He spent most of the past week in Massachusetts, campaigning for delegates for the March 2 Democratic primary, and probably shook fewer than 200 hands, mostly those of campaign workers gathered inside rooms.

When he left his hotel for home, he slipped away on a freight elevator.

In the old days, he would have gone out through the lobby, scouring for hands on the way. He was seeking out hands when Arthur Bremmer shot him down and left him paralyzed and near death on the hard pavement of that Laurel shopping center.

He does not like the isolation now imposed on his candidacy. Though he has been drawing some overflow crowds lately, his finely tuned campaign antennae instinctively tell him that isolation is bad politics.

But he is resigned to reality.

"There's no way I can run like I used to," he said.

"It's impossible for a wheelchair man to get out into the crowds."

To counter the armed-camp atmosphere, he has begun scheduling more and more set-piece, controllable, political events—news conferences, small rallies, luncheons.

JFK Slaying "Cut the Heart of a Nation"

A Report From That Time 25 Years Ago

SAUL PETT

Saul Pett describes that November weekend in 1963 in specific detail. His memories raise the question of whether it is possible to recount such an event in our history without the inherent emotion. A basic recording of reactions, however objective the wording, can elicit an emotional response from readers. (Compare Ron Fimrite's account of the San Francisco earthquake.)

Published in *The Montgomery Advertiser and Alabama Journal*, November 22, 1988.

John F. Kennedy was shot and killed on Nov. 22, 1963. There had been other severe shocks in our history before, but somehow, before television, they kept their distance; they did not come into our living rooms. This one did. This probably was the first public event to become a private trauma. Sadly, other profound tremors, other assassinations, a war, riots would come. But this was the first, and here, in words written in that time of pain 25 years ago, was what it was like for four days.

And the word went out from that time and place and cut the heart of a nation. In streets and offices and homes and stores, in lunchrooms and showrooms and schoolrooms and board rooms, on highways and prairies and beaches and mountaintops, in endless places crowded and sparse, near and far, white and black, Republican and Democrat, management and labor, the word went out and cut the heart of a nation.

And husbands called wives and wives called friends and teachers told students and motorists stopped to listen on car radios and stranger told stranger. Oh, no! we cried from hearts stopped by shocks, from minds fighting the word, but the word came roaring back, true, true, true, and disbelief dissolved in tears.

Incredibly, in a time of great numbers, in a time of repeated reminders that millions would die in a nuclear war, in a time when experts feared we were being numbed by numbers and immunized against tragedy, the death of a single man crowded into our souls and flooded our hearts and filled all the paths of our lives. A great shadow fell on the land and the farmer summoned to the house did not find the will to return to the field, nor the secretary to the typewriter, nor the machinist to the lathe.

There was a great slowing down and a great stopping and the big bronze gong sounded and a man shouted the market is closed and the New York Stock Exchange stopped, just stopped. The Boston Symphony Orchestra stopped a Handel concerto and started a Beethoven funeral march and the Canadian House of Commons stopped and a dramatic play in Berlin stopped and the United Nations in New York stopped and Congress and courts and schools and race tracks stopped, just stopped. And football games were canceled and theaters were closed and in Dallas a nightclub called the Carousel was closed by a mourner named Jack Ruby.

In Washington, along Pennsylvania Avenue, they had waited silently all that Friday night outside the iron picket fence, their eyes scarcely leaving the lovely old house.

In the chill darkness before dawn, they were still there, now motionless, standing, staring across the broad lawn and through the bare elms at the house, at the softly lighted windows in the family quarters, at the black crepe lately hung over the door under the north portico.

They saw the blinking red lights of the police cars up Pennsylvania Avenue and they knew this was the moment. The president was coming home. No sirens, no police whistles, no barking of orders that usually accompanied his return. At 4:22 a.m., Saturday, Nov. 23, 1963, there seemed to be no sound on the street or in the land.

The gray Navy ambulance and the six black cars behind it paused at the northwest gate and turned in. And along the fence, men removed their hats and teen-agers removed their hands from the pockets of their jeans and women tightened their fingers around the pickets of the fence. Tears stained their faces, their young and their old faces, their white and their black faces.

At the gate the procession was met by a squad of Marines and led in along the gracefully curving drive between the elms. In two straight lines, glistening bayoneted rifles held across their chests at port arms, they marched oh so slowly up the drive and all that could be heard was the sound of their shoes sliding on the macadam.

Under the portico, under the handsome hanging lantern, they stopped and divided and lined up with the soldiers and sailors and airmen on the sides of the steps, at the stiffest, straightest attention of their lives. Jacqueline Kennedy emerged first from the ambulance, still wearing the same pink suit stained through eternity the afternoon before.

With her husband's brother, the attorney general of the United States, with his other brother, the youngest member of the United States Senate, with his sisters and his friends and aides whom he had led to this house, this far and now no farther, Jacqueline Kennedy waited in motionless silence while the flag-covered casket was removed from the ambulance. Then she and they turned in behind it and walked up the steps and through the glass doors and into the lobby and down the long corridor lined with stiff, silent men in uniform and finally came to a stop in the East Room.

There the casket was laid gently onto the black catafalque that held Mr. Lincoln on another dark incredible night almost 100 years ago.

In the great stillness, under the black-draped chandeliers, one tried not to hear the mocking echoes or see the remembered sights, of Pablo Casals bowing the cello, of ballet dancers pirouetting, of great actors reading Shakespeare and Nobel scientists as excited as children by the house, of the Marine Corps quartet playing while the president and his lady danced and the great and the glamorous of the world danced in a merry swirl of coattails and long gowns.

But now it was 10 o'clock in the morning of a Saturday in another time and Jacqueline Kennedy, still sleepless, returned to the silent East Room. She kissed her husband for the last time and the casket was sealed. A few moments later, she returned with her children and spoke to them quietly, trying to tell them something of the fact and the meaning of death. A fact and a meaning for which millions groped that day.

Radio Moscow played funeral music until sign-off and in London the great tenor bell of Westminster Abbey tolled every minute for an hour. New Ross, Ireland, where they called him "cousin Jack," closed its shops and drew the window shades, and in West Berlin, Germans by the thousands marched in the rain by torchlight, wordlessly. Sihanouk of Cambodia ordered anti-American posters hauled down and in Tokyo Bay flags of the U.S. Seventh Fleet dipped in salute while little Japanese fishing boats, on a condolence call, came close to the great gray warships, their tiny flags at half-mast, too.

Clear, bright sunlight and an arching blue sky promised a serene Sunday in Washington, even a sense of gathering majesty as the procession formed to take John F. Kennedy from the White House to the Capitol.

Soldiers, sailors and airmen stood at ease awaiting the start. Ten army drummers began beating out their muffled tattoo.

"Hey!" shouted a teen-ager with a radio stuck in his ear. "Oswald was just shot!"

Live, on television, before millions, Lee Harvey Oswald was shot in the basement of the Dallas jail by Jack Ruby.

Serenity, dignity, any suggestion of majesty suddenly drained out of the American system. A deep sense of national tragedy was now joined by a deep sense of national disarray. Were we to believe that a sullen little man, for his own twisted reasons, could kill a president and then, while in police custody, himself be killed by another little man with his twisted reasons?

"My God, my God!" cried House Speaker John McCormack. "What are we coming to?"

John Kennedy lay in state in the soaring Rotunda of the Capitol, surrounded by family and friends, by allies and foes in a government now united by shock and shame.

Outside, in the gathering chill, the public had formed itself into a long line to view the bier. Soon the line stretched 20 blocks, a silent, shivering stream of mourners which, by dawn, grew to a great river of sorrow.

Monday, the sun was bright over the White House and the whole panoply of power and grandeur, foreign and domestic, was ready. Under the handsome hanging lantern of the north portico, the caisson and coffin were ready.

He was leaving the noble old house for the last time and one tried to remember what drew John Kennedy here the first time. It was, he used to say, the center of action and the center of action always pulled at him, at home or at college, at war or at peace. And so he went into politics, this man who was not a natural politician, this man whose sense of privacy and dignity rebelled at the Indian feathers to be worn and the babies to be kissed and the whole turning outside of the inside of a man. But there was the center of action pulling at him and there was his favorite proverb from the Greeks, "Happiness is the full use of your powers along lines of excellence in a life affording scope." Here, at this old house, had he reached the peak of his powers?

But now it was time to go.

The muffled drums began and the cadets of the academies moved forward, and across the way, through the elms and over the lawn, the bells of St. John's Episcopal, "the Church of Presidents," began to toll.

There came then striding up the avenue the joint chiefs of staff, heroic in braid, the symbols of the vast power that could not save him. Could not save the man who had survived the war as a Navy lieutenant but not the peace as commander-in-chief. There came then the seven matched grays pulling the caisson and casket and the riderless horse, empty boots reversed, silver sword sheathed in the ancient manner of mourning the fallen warrior.

There came then Jacqueline Kennedy, now the pride of a nation, and she suddenly let go the hand of Robert Kennedy and stepped out on her own, head high, shoulders back, stride firm. Up the avenue she strode, beautiful in black and gallant in purpose, with her husband's brothers and sisters and their wives and their husbands, this remarkable family.

And into the cathedral they all went in such diversity as to include Dwight Eisenhower and Harry Truman and John Glenn and Richard Nixon and Nelson Rockefeller and Barry Goldwater and Billy Graham and Henry Ford II and George Wallace of Alabama and Martin Luther King of Georgia.

And at the end of the Mass, with a sprinkler of holy water in his hand, Cardinal Richard Cushing of Boston circled the coffin, blessing it as he went. "May the angels, dear Jack, lead you into paradise . . ."

And once more they carried the casket out into the bright sunlight and Jacqueline Kennedy paused on the steps of the cathedral with her children. As he watched his father's casket being borne down the steps, little John Kennedy squinted in the sun and saluted.

And the procession reformed in cars, and rolled slowly down the broad boulevard, past the Lincoln Memorial, over the Memorial Bridge and through the high iron gates of Arlington National Cemetery.

And the Marine Corps band played "The Star Spangled Banner" as the body was carried up the grassy slope, the same slope he had visited on a smiling spring day in March. "I could stay up here forever," he had said then. Forever was here and the sun was sinking behind the Virginia hills.

Taps was sounded over the hill and the flag was raised taut and level over the coffin and folded with loving care and passed from hand to hand to the hand of the widow and the eternal flame was lighted and the Lord's Prayer was intoned once more. And at 3:34 o'clock, on the afternoon of the fourth day, John Fitzgerald Kennedy was lowered gently to his grave.

"Cadence of the Heart" and *"The Wolf Inside"*

JOHN STONE

John Stone, M.D., uses his talent as a poet (three published books of poetry) and his knowledge and experience as a cardiologist to make medical subjects accessible to the general public (both of these essays first appeared in *The New York Times Magazine*). He makes extensive use of technical words, but he provides the necessary definitions for readers not versed in medical vocabulary, all within a personal context. Note his use of autobiographical elements as a basic expository tool. His love of literature is fundamental to his discussion of his profession, an approach that provides universality to the discussion of technical subjects in a specialized field.

Original publication: "Cadence of the Heart," *The New York Times Magazine*, April 24, 1988; "The Wolf Inside," *The New York Times Magazine*, April 3, 1988.

"Cadence of the Heart"

My stethoscope, by now, is an old friend. It is, after all, the one I bought in medical school, 28 years ago, though it has been replaced several times over, part by worn-out part, like atoms of the body. The earpieces slip into my ears tightly, the sounds of the world diminish. I enter the cave-dark, tone-dense hollow of the chest and tune in to the mother heart. My patient is a mother, and she's better this morning but still very sick. I bend and listen. As I do, I am aware of the film of sweat over the bridge of her nose and a flaring of her nostrils related to the work of her breathing. Her heart tones remind me of a race horse laboring for the finish line: lup-*dup*-pah, lup-*dup*-pah, and so forth. This triple cadence connotes heart failure: her heart is unable to pump enough and her lungs are congested. Her heart muscle, the pump itself, is sick and unlikely to get better. As I slip the stethoscope back into my pocket, there is no way for me to know that, within two years, she will be dead, suddenly, at the age of 41.

But most of the stethoscope's songs are not as sad. Some are quite happy.

The idea for the stethoscope came to a young man in France as he watched two children at play with a wooden baton; one child scratched his end of the stick while the other, holding the opposite end to his ear, listened expectantly for the scratching to be "telegraphed" to him. The young man's mellifluous name was René Théophile Hyacinthe Laënnec. During his short life (1781–1826), he made many contributions to medicine, but he is best known as the father of the stethoscope.

The ur-stethoscope, in fact, was a rolled-up cylinder of paper improved by Laënnec in 1816 to better examine an obese young woman with heart disease. Laënnec was impressed with his *cornet de papier:* ". . . I was not a little surprised and pleased to find that I could thereby perceive the action of the heart in a manner much more clear and distinct than I had ever been able to do by the immediate application of the ear." Later, the instrument was crafted out of wood, a hole was bored through the baton to facilitate the passage of sound; and it was divided, for portability, into halves that could be screwed together.

Long before Laënnec, doctors listened to hearts by placing the ear on the patient's chest. But the technique was not used often, because of concerns about modesty and hygiene. Laënnec's *cornet* was like the stethoscope of today in one crucial way: there was a human being at each end. To use the stethoscope, as the physician Dickinson Richards said in 1962, requires "the doctor to be within 30 inches of his patient," insuring the "laying on of hands" often said to be lacking in medicine today.

The modern stethoscope—the word derives from the Greek *stethos*, meaning chest—evolved with knowledge of sound transmission. Thus, the tubing between doctor and patient is of a prescribed bore and length; the earpieces must fit snugly. On the other end, the "heads," two or three in number, filter the sound. The flat piece, the diaphragm, picks up high-pitched sounds; the domed piece, the bell, registers low frequencies.

What kinds of music, or noise, arrive at the listening end of the stethoscope? The most common use of the instrument is in the measurement of blood pressure, as the arterial blood column strains to thump under the cuff tightened around the arm. But the stethoscope is useful in decoding all the sounds of the body at work: the tick-tock of the fetal heart tones from the uterus; the rumblings of the stomach under the abdominal wall (sounds that carry the aptly onomatopoeic name borborygmi—from the equally onomatopoeic Greek *borborygmos*, meaning to rumble), the rush of blood in narrowed vessels, notably the carotid arteries leading to the brain. In Laënnec's time, the stethoscope was most frequently employed to monitor the lungs: fully a third of the patients hospitalized in Paris were there because of tuberculosis. But the most dramatic use is in sorting out the cacophony of sound from the heart. Use of the stethoscope to hear the sounds of the body is called *auscultation* (L. *auscultare*, to listen).

The normal heart tones are iambic: a weaker, then a stronger stress—lup-*dup*, lup-*dup*. These sounds, the *lup* and the *dup*, are called the first and second heart sounds, S-1 and S-2. They are due basically to the rhythmic paired closing of the four heart valves (tricuspid and pulmonary on the right side of the heart, mitral and aortic, on the left). They work gracefully, ingeniously, to direct blood flow—from the right heart to the lungs, from the left to the body. The time between the *lup* and the *dup* defines systole (sis-*toll*-ee), the interval of contraction. The interval between the second sound and the subsequent first sound defines diastole (*dye*-as-toll-ee), the interval of relaxation. Flow through the heart is often made turbulent (after exercise, for example, or with structural abnormalities). It is this turbulence that produces cardiac "murmurs," which may occur in systole, diastole, or throughout both intervals.

Most heart murmurs are not pathological at all. An estimated 50 percent of all children, if their hearts are examined often, will have a murmur at some point. The turbulent flow in their active, growing bodies explains such innocent murmurs. These are happy sounds, joys to find. Similarly, many pregnant women develop murmurs as the torrential blood flow to the gravid uterus places an extra workload on the maternal heart. The revved-up circulation that occurs with anemia or an overactive thyroid may also produce such murmurs.

But what of pathological murmurs? Basically, dysfunction takes one of two forms: a narrowing of the valve (stenosis) or a leakage (insufficiency). Stenosis of the aortic valve, situated between the left ventrical and aorta, is a good example. With cardiac contraction, the three pliable leaflets of a normal valve are thrown open, like swinging doors, propelling blood easily into the aorta. If the valve is narrowed by disease and scarring, the squeezing of blood through it may produce enough turbulence to cause a *systolic* murmur.

The loudness of murmurs is graded from 1 to 6 (6 is loud enough to be heard with the stethoscope completely off the chest). Rarely, a murmur is loud enough to be heard several feet away without using a stethoscope. Opening and closing clicks of some artificial-heart valves may be audible to others in a quiet waiting room.

A sense of rhythm is helpful in the interpretation of heart sounds. Generations of students, learning auscultation, have used a rhythmic pronunciation of "Ken-tuck-y, Ken-tuck-y" to help time gallops of the heart. Some conditions produce extra cardiac sounds: a variety of clicks, rubs and murmurs. Inflammation of the sac around the heart—pericarditis—results in a distinctive "scratchy" *rub* (the quality of the rub can be simulated by holding a small pinch of hair near the ear and rubbing the fingers together). One of the most dramatic sounds in medicine is called Hamman's crunch, after the physician who first described its features. After air has been introduced into the chest (after a stab wound, for example), auscultation may reveal a crackling and crunching of the air and fluid around the beating heart, sounds that reminded Hamman (and thousands of clinicians since) of the crunch of snow under heavy boots.

Some murmurs are best heard with the patient lying; in others, the patient's sitting position will tilt the pendulous heart toward the chest wall and facilitate diagnosis. Having the patient stand, or squat, may be useful in special cases.

Despite the long history of the stethoscope, there is much to learn about auscultation. For example, until the 1960's, a click or clicks heard during middle to late systole were thought to be noncardiac. Then J. B. Barlow and co-workers showed that such high-pitched sounds, and sometimes a murmur as well, are caused by minor (occasionally major) dysfunction of the mitral valve, called mitral-valve prolapse. Such sounds occur in at least 5 percent of the population, so proper interpretation is important.

Newer techniques help us understand what we're hearing: phonocardiography (recording heart sounds); echocardiography (viewing with ultrasound); cardiac catheterization/scanning; and magnetic resonance imaging, which gives clear views of cardiac anatomy without injection of dyes. Thus, as the stethoscope keeps the physician near the bedside of the patient, its messages are continually reinterpreted in light of new information.

Physicians and patients are not the only ones interested in the arcane language of the heart. John Ciardi wrote a fine poem called "Lines From the Beating End of the Stethoscope." And Auden, in "Lay your sleeping head, my love," speaks knowingly of the "knocking heart." The very first auscultator, surely, was a lover—head pillowed on the drum of the chest—who heard the murmurs and murmurings of the heart and worried what they might mean long before—as lovers have long since—René Laënnec.

"The Wolf Inside"

Four weeks before she died of a complication of lupus erythematosus, Flannery O'Connor wrote: "The wolf, I'm afraid, is inside tearing up the place. I've been in the hospital 50 days already this year." By the time of her next recorded letter, three days later, she had received the rite of Extreme Unction. I never met Flannery O'Connor, but I never see a patient with lupus now without thinking of those words and of the woman herself.

The word *lupus* was appropriated whole to the medical vocabulary directly from the Latin; it means "wolf." This autoimmune-system disease affects virtually every organ in the body. About 60 percent of patients have a red ("erythematous") rash on the face, over the bridge of the nose and on the cheeks below the eyes, in a more or less "butterfly" pattern, a shape similar to the facial markings of a wolf.

I saw a young woman with lupus today. She doesn't have the rash. She does have extensive kidney disease and, according to an X-ray, a massively enlarged heart. Hers is a dramatic case. In just two months, she has gained 50 pounds, all of it water. I shake her hand. As she tells her story, it's obvious that she is reasonably comfortable. She's breathing easily, her blood pressure and pulse are good. Since I was first asked to see her, I have also learned that, despite the X-ray, her heart is not enlarged. Rather, the pericardial sac around it, designed to hold a scant ounce of fluid, has managed to stretch hugely, accumulating three quarts of fluid—thus the enlarged heart shadow on her X-ray. She is waterlogged, her tissues swimming in excess fluid. The echocardiograph is like a sonar unit, its echo like the sonogram of a fetus: but, instead of a fetus floating within its sac of liquid, there was her heart, normal in size, bobbing and squeezing like a fist.

Her kidney disease is such that she is losing huge amounts of protein in the urine. Normal kidneys filter the total blood volume many times each day, losing into the urine only tiny amounts of protein. Her kidneys are leaking protein like a sieve. Without that protein, there is nothing to hold the plasma within the blood. The kidneys are also leaking water into all her tissues, including the pericardial sac. After talking with her at length about her illness, I examine her. A soft, scratchy noise, synchronous with the heartbeat, confirms her inflamed pericardium. Her legs are grossly swollen. I press my fingers gently into the skin over her shins—the tips of my fingers sink in as though they were poking the soft belly of the puffy little doughboy in the television ad. Several minutes later, as I leave, the deep pits are still there.

Prednisone, a form of cortisone, has been started. The hope is that, in massive doses, it will help seal the protein leaks of her kidneys, and that diuretics will mobilize the 50 pounds of excess fluid. The immediate question is whether to use a needle to draw off the fluid from around her heart. The danger is that the fluid will restrict and restrain the heart's action, like the cellophane wrapper on a box of valentine candy, and jeopardize its all-important pumping. I decide we should not attempt to remove the fluid now, reasoning that it will only reaccumulate: the dike has multiple holes in it—the water would seep back in. The cardiology fellows working with me disagree. They are in favor of the needle. I argue that we should wait for the drugs to work. I worry about her as I go to sleep that night; it is often easier to *do* something, rather than wait, but it's not always best for the patient. We keep a sterile tray, with a long pericardial needle in it, at her bedside, just in case.

Flannery O'Connor had lupus for some 14 years before she imagined the wolf tearing up the place. The disease had begun, in late 1950, with, as she spells it, "awthritus." Arthritis, or joint pain, is present in 90 percent of patients with lupus. Just as common is an overwhelming fatigue, often accompanied by fever, loss of appetite and loss of weight. The exact cause of lupus is uncertain, but it is known that in the course of the disease the body makes antibodies directed against and damaging to its own organs. The process amounts to a kind of immunological betrayal of its owner by the body, an absolute autoimmune revolution. Lupus is primarily a disease of women (90 percent of the cases, with a peak incidence in the childbearing years). Flannery O'Connor's father died of lupus, however, and today, human lymphocyte antigen (HLA) typing, a kind of tissue "matching" that is done for organ transplants, confirms that there may be a genetic predisposition. New drugs to suppress the immune system help slow progression of the disease and also reduce the requirements for steroids, such as cortisone, with their side effects. But lupus is capricious, with both relapses and remissions: statistically, the majority of patients can look forward to a time when they will be relatively free of problems.

But Flannery O'Connor had a severe case: clearly, the wolf *was* inside. Sally Fitzgerald, editor of O'Connor's letters, speaks movingly of the time, late in 1950, when she learned from Flannery's mother "that Flannery was dying of lupus": "The doctor minced no words. We were stunned. We communicated regularly with Mrs. O'Connor while she went through this terrible time and the days of uncertainty that followed, during Dr. Arthur J. Merrill's tremendous effort to save Flannery's life."

Dr. Merrill, Flannery's physician, is a former mentor of mine. About 20 years ago, he told me that Flannery's lupus was diagnosed just as more hopeful therapy became available (e.g., in 1949, P. S. Hench and co-workers reported the efficacy of ACTH and cortisone in arthritis). ACTH, a hormone that causes the body to secrete cortisone, was prescribed for Flannery in the early 1950's. The effect of ACTH (and cortisone, which she took later) is to blunt the body's response to the turncoat antibodies. The drugs worked—at a price. ACTH and cortisone can have significant side effects: thinning of bone (osteoporosis); loss of muscle strength; a "moonlike" shape to the face; exacerbation of duodenal ulcers; altered metabolism; increased susceptibility to infections; mood changes, ranging from a feeling of well-being to depression and even psychosis.

Flannery was well aware of the side effects as she wrote: "My dose of prednisone has been cut in half on Dr. Merrill's orders, because the nitrogen content of the blood has increased by a third. So far as I can see, the medicine and the disease run neck & neck to kill you." But she felt better on the medications. In 1960, after 10 years on steroids, she wrote: ". . . as Dr. Merrill says, it is better to be alive with joint trouble than dead without it. Amen."

Over the next week, as I see my own young lupus patient, I can tell, thank God and prednisone, she is improving. She has lost more than 30 pounds, all of it water. The pericardial fluid has diminished—her echo looks better. She's going to make it. And she gives me a tired, heroic smile.

Heroic is, I think, the word for Flannery O'Connor, too. When the disease struck her, she was 25, a graduate of the Iowa Writers' Workshop, a fledgling writer just beginning to make a name for herself. Despite the wolf, the next 14 years were productive: she won three O. Henry prizes; the National Book Award came posthumously, in 1971. Many of her best short stories were written then: "A Good Man Is Hard to Find," in 1953; "Good Country People," 1955; "Everything That Rises Must Converge," 1961; "Revelation," in 1964, just months before she died.

Flannery O'Connor knew at least two kinds of isolation—that required by her craft, and that imposed by her illness. Listen to her in 1956: "I have never been anywhere but sick. In a sense sickness is a place, more instructive than a long trip to Europe, and it's always a place where there's no company, where nobody can follow." Of course, in a metaphorical sense, Flannery O'Connor never stopped traveling. And the joy of discovery kept her at the typewriter. From one of her earliest of her collected letters (July 21, 1948), there is evidence that the process of writing was, for her, journey enough: ". . . I have to write to discover what I am doing. Like the old lady, I don't know so well what I think until I see what I say. . . ."

Flannery O'Connor *endured*, to use Faulkner's term, despite the lupus. That she weathered the devastating side effect of ACTH and cortisone, continuing to write, slowly, painfully, to find out exactly what she *did* think, makes her a heroine to me. But, then, many of my patients seem heroic to me, especially the ones with chronic illnesses.

Through its Latin root, the word *doctor* means teacher; but very often it is the patient who does the teaching, especially when the lesson is one in courage. It's one thing to have an acute, limited, illness, to pass the bloody agonizing kidney stone and be done with it; it's quite another to go to sleep with pain, to dream that it's gone, then wake back up to the same pain waiting like a wild beast at the foot of your bed. And to persevere despite the pain, feeling it flow like electricity out of your forearms along your sore wrists and out to your stiff fingers to discover precisely how the 26 letters of the alphabet plan to marry *this* time.

Lupus betrayed Flannery O'Connor like a sophisticated Trojan horse, one with a wolf inside. Once within the body's gates, the enemy was everywhere, Still, she prevailed, even if it was only until her 39th year. And her life and words are a study in keeping on keeping on. It is in that spirit that I move to the next patient.

How To Tell a Fine Old Wine

JAMES THURBER

Humorist James Thurber uses process to discuss how to recognize wines—at least, he appears to. By the time readers get to the "mice in the chateau," those who have not been wary just at the appearance of Thurber's name begin to wonder just what he is explaining. His fun with identification of wine blurs the fine line between exposition and persuasion as his readers wonder if they too are objects of his satire.

Original publication: *The New Yorker*, Feb. 24, 1934; collected in *Collecting Himself: James Thurber on Writing and Writers, Humor and Himself.* New York: Harper & Row, 1989.

The great wines of France are divided into only three classifications with which we need to be concerned: the *grands vins*, the *petits vins* and the *vins fins*. And it is with the last that we shall be most particularly concerned. *Vins fins* means, simply enough, "finished wines," that is, wines that did not turn out as well as might have been expected. It is these wines and none others that America is getting today and that America is going to continue to get. Just what causes this I don't exactly know, but something.

In the old days of the great *châteauxiers*, there was never any question about what to do with a *vin* when it turned out to be *fin*. The *châteauxiers* simply referred to it philosophically as "*fin de siècle*" (finished for good) and threw it out. They would have nothing to do with a wine that wasn't noble, distinguished, dignified, courageous, high-souled and austere. Nowadays it is different. The *vins fins* are filtered though to the American public in a thousand different disguises, all spurious—not a genuine disguise among them. It is virtually impossible for the layman, when he picks up a bottle labeled "St.-Julien-Clos Vougeot-Grandes Veuves, 1465A21, *mise du château*, Perdolio, Premier Cru, Marchanderie: Carton et Cie., 1924," to know whether he is getting, as should be the case with this label, a truly noble St.-Estèphe or, as is more likely to be the case, a Bernicarló that has been blended with Heaven only knows what, perhaps even a white Margelaise! Well then, how *is* he to know?

Let us say that a bottle has come into our hands labeled as above. "St.-Julien" is simply the name of the *commune* and "Clos Vougeot" the name of the château around which the grapes are grown. "*Grandes Veuves*" is either an added distinguishing flourish put on the noble old label years and years ago by some *grandes veuves* (large widows) or it is a meaningless addition placed thereon since repeal by those French *flâneurs* who hope to inveigle the American public into buying cheap and tawdry wines under elaborate and impressive-sounding labels. So much for the name of the wine itself.

The number, 1465A21, is nothing to be bewildered by. It is simply the official *estampe française de la douane* and it can be checked against the authentic "serial-running" of the official French revenue stamping machine by applying to somebody in the French Embassy here, or in the French consulate, and asking him to get in touch with the man in charge of the registered files of the French revenue stamping department. If the letter used (in this case "A") proves to be the actual letter employed in 1924 by the revenue stampers, the vintage date on the bottle is authentic, providing, of course, that the identifying letter was, in that year, inserted between the fourth and fifth figures of the serial number and that 146521 fell among the *estampages* allocated to the St.-Julien *commune* in that year.

The phrase *"mise du château"* is extremely simple, and it is astonishing how many Americans are puzzled by it. It means nothing more than "mice in the château," just as it says. The expression goes back to the days, some 20 years ago, when certain French manufacturers of popular "tonic wines" made fortunes almost overnight and in many cases bought up old châteaux, tore them down and built lavish new ones in the rococo manner. These new châteaux were, of course, clean and well kept, but so garish and ugly that a disdainful expression grew up among the French peasantry in regard to them: *"Ils n'ont jamais de mise du château là-bas."* ("They never have any mice in that château over there.") The grand old *châteauxiers* thereupon began to add to their labels *"mise du château"*— in other words. "There are mice in *this* château," a proud if slightly incongruous legend for a bottle of noble old wine.

The label symbol "Perdolio" on our bottle might equally well have been "Manfreda," "Variola," "Muscatel," "Amontillado," "Sauternes," "Katerina" or any one of a couple of hundred others. The idea of this name originated with the old Spanish *vinteriosos*, especially those of Casanovia and Valencia, and indicated simply a desire on the part of a given merchant to place the name of a favorite daughter, son, mistress or wine on the bottles he merchandised.

"Premier Cru," which we come to next in looking back at our St.-Julien label, means "first growth," that is, wine that was grown first. And "Marchanderie: Carton et Cie" is the name of the shipper. In some cases the name of the captain of the ship transporting the wine is also added to the label, some such name as Graves or Médoc, and one need not take alarm at this, but one should be instantly suspicious of any marks, names, numbers or symbols other than those I have gone into here. Bottles that bear such legends as "George H., Kansas City, '24" or "C. M. & Bessie B., '18" or "Mrs. P. P. Bliss, Ashtabula, O., '84" or "I Love My Wife But Oh You Kid (1908)" may be put down as having fallen into the hands of American tourists somewhere between the bottling and the shipping. They are doubtlessly refills containing a colored sugar water, if anything at all.

The vintage year is, of course, always branded into the cork of the bottle and is the only kind of bottle-cork date mark to go by. Dates laid in with mother-of-pearl or anything of the sort are simply impressive and invidious attempts to force high prices from the pockets of gullible Americans. So also are French wine labels bearing the American flag or portraits of Washington or such inscriptions, no matter how beautifully engraved or colored, as "Columbia, the Gem of the Ocean" and "When Lilacs Last in the Dooryard Grew."

In the main, it is safe to go by one's taste. Don't let anybody tell you it is one-tenth as hard to tell the taste of a good wine from the taste of a bad wine or even of a so-so wine as some of the *connaisseurs ecrivants* would have us believe.

•   •   •

Chapter Questions

1. How does your age affect your reading of these expository essays? Can you anticipate how a reader of another generation might react differently? Why and how are there differences?
2. Will geographical location of readers affect their reactions to any of these expository essays? If so, which essay? How?
3. Will the social or economic status of readers make a difference?
4. Various popular magazines are represented by essays in this chapter. Based on the selections here (and not on your knowledge of the magazines in general), how would you characterize the readers of *Sports Illustrated* and *Newsweek*, or the readers of *The New Yorker* and *The New York Times Magazine?*
5. Read the front page of a newspaper, especially the lead news articles. What assumptions do you have about the average readership? Does that audience differ from the newspaper readerships represented by articles in this chapter?
6. Do you note any differences in language between articles written for local newspapers and news stories taken from wire services?
7. Lorenz's and Marius's essays are on specialized subjects collected in books on these subjects. What characteristics do their essays share, not necessarily evident in other expository essays in this chapter? Are there significant differences between these essays and others in the chapter?
8. Is there any essay in this chapter that you would argue is more persuasive or argumentative than expository?
9. Were your expectations for this chapter fulfilled by the selections in it?

Chapter Three
PERSUASION

W̲e all like a good argument. In social settings we will often tear into a controversial subject, raising our voices (based on the assumption that the louder we are the more convincing we are), using loaded words ("abortionist," "murderer," "traitor"), forgetting everything we ever learned about fallacious reasoning, attacking the opposition as "unenlightened" or "stupid"—in other words, arguing emotionally in an effort to persuade our audience. But what do we demand of someone who wants to persuade us? Knowledge of all sides of the argument? Logic? Command of the language? Passion about the issue? Writers of persuasion must, at times, imagine defiant readers, with arms folded, daring someone to convince them.

Some rhetorics make a distinction between argumentation and persuasion: argumentation is the laying out of the various sides of a debate without taking sides, and persuasion is the effort to convince our audience to agree with us, to admit we are right, even to take action based on our stand. With that division between the two, argumentation is simply a form of exposition, informing your audience of the key points in the controversy. Persuasion, therefore, is the emphasis of this chapter. What can writers do to convince their readers to believe the thesis, to agree with it, to take action on it?

Such questions emphasize audience in the writing of persuasion. With this form of writing, perhaps even more than with any other, writers must carefully analyze their audience. How do I organize my ideas to be most persuasive? What evidence do I use? What words can I use to be convincing, perhaps even emotional, without losing my readers?

Writers can approach persuasion in many ways, but most of the approaches can be classified as either emotional arguments or logical arguments. Before using an emotional argument, writers must carefully assess an audience. In a discussion with my advanced writing class, an editorial director gave an example of an editorial he wrote in a fury and aired, essentially in its original form. He was appalled that law enforcement officers had watched a pack of dogs attack and kill deer in a park because a city ordinance forbids shooting firearms in a public park. He used every emotional image he could think of—dogs attacking a helpless child, the eyes of Bambi's mother as she dies—to raise the question of a choice between the letter of the law and the spirit of the law. He considered the listeners and their sympathies and used them in his favor. But that appeal will not always work—especially if readers are coldly rational and demand logical reasoning instead of emotion.

The logical approach to persuasion makes full use of expository skills as the basis of the argument: define the terms, summarize the sides of the argument, compare and contrast the sides, cite authoritative sources for corroboration. The writer must avoid the fallacies learned in earlier composition courses: *argumentum ad hominem* (attack the man), *post hoc ergo* (after this, therefore because of; cause-effect), begging the question, guilt by association, overgeneralization, evasion of the issue, red herring, nonsequitur. Finally, the author must present a sound, logical conclusion that takes a clear, authoritative stand on the subject.

Audience will, in most cases, determine the approach. To which argument will the audience respond more favorably? Can I announce my stance in the title or opening paragraphs without danger of losing readers? Can I use loaded words without offending the intelligence of some of my readers?

The logical approach to argument is the primary one exemplified in this chapter, but even in such an approach, writers may use loaded wording or mention a fallacy they would like to use. Sometimes the thesis appears in the title or opening paragraph; in other cases, readers may be nearly through the essay before they know which way the argument will go. Also, readers of these selections will find autobiography and exposition used as integral parts of persuasion. These varied approaches to content, organization, and diction confirm that there is no one way to approach persuasion.

In his first appearance as editorial director, a local television newsman announced his goals in this new position. Obviously, he wanted to inform his public and, through that information, persuade them to agree with the policies endorsed in his editorial. However, he conceded, if he only made them *think*, he would have accomplished something important with his editorial. There is something to be said for such a goal in persuasive writing, or in all writing, for that matter: make the readers think.

•　　•　　•

America's Medieval Women

PEARL S. BUCK

Pearl Buck, best known for her novels set in China, uses her knowledge of that country and its culture as a basis for this evaluation of the place of women in American society. First published in a 1938 issue of *Harpers*, the essay sounds some early calls for the feminist movement, even though Buck claims to be "an individualist" rather than "a feminist."

She states her thesis—"women are very badly treated in

America"—in the second paragraph and then draws from personal experiences to illustrate and prove the point. We may not agree with her interpretations of these experiences, but because they are from her own life, we cannot discount the details. She is also careful to blame both men and women for this predicament; thus, she does not automatically alienate part of her audience. Of course, it is quite possible that she alienates both males and females.

Original publication: *Harpers*, August 1938.

I am an American woman but I had no opportunity until a few years ago to know women in America. Living as I did in China, it is true that I saw a few American women; but that is not the same thing. One was still not able to draw many conclusions from them about American women. I gathered, however, that they felt that girls in China had a hard time of it, because there every family liked sons better than daughters, and, in the average family, did not give them the same education or treatment. In America, however, they said people welcomed sons and daughters equally and treated them the same. This, after years in a country which defines a woman's limitations very clearly, seemed nothing short of heaven—if true.

When I came to America to live therefore I was interested particularly in her women. And during these immediate past years I have come to know a good many of them—women in business, artists, housewives in city and country, women young and old. I have taken pains to know them. More than that, I have made my own place as a woman in America. And I find that what I anticipated before I came here is quite wrong. It seems to me that women are very badly treated in America. A few of them know it, more of them dimly suspect it, and most of them, though they know they ought to be glad they live in a Christian country where women are given an education, do not feel as happy in their lonely hearts as they wish they did. The reason for this unhappiness is a secret sense of failure, and this sense of failure comes from a feeling of inferiority, and the feeling of inferiority comes from a realization that actually women are not much respected in America.

I know quite well that any American man hearing this will laugh his usual tolerant laughter, though tolerant laughter is the cruelest form of contempt. He always laughs tolerantly when the subject of women is broached, for that is the attitude in which he has been bred. And immaturely, he judges the whole world of women by the only woman he knows at all—his wife. Nor does he want the sort of wife at whom he cannot laugh tolerantly. I was once amazed to see a certain American man, intelligent, learned, and cultivated, prepare to marry for his second wife a woman as silly and unfit for him as the first one had been, whom he had just divorced. I had to exclaim before it was too late, "Why do you do the same thing over again? She's merely younger and prettier than the other one—that's all. And even those differences are only temporary." To which he growled, "I do not want a damned intelligent woman in the house when I come home at night. I want my mind to rest."

What he did not see of course—though he found it out later—was that there could be no rest for him of any kind. He was irritated by a thousand stupidities and follies and beaten in the end by his own cowardice. He died a score of years too soon, exhausted not by work but by nervous worry. His two wives go hardily on, headed for a hundred, since he left them what is called "well provided for." Neither of them has ever done an honest day's work in her life, and he literally sacrificed his valuable life to keep them alive.

And yet, going home that day from his funeral and wondering how it could have been helped, I knew it could not have been helped. He was doomed to the unhappiness, or at least to the mediocre happiness, with which many if not most American men must be satisfied in their relationships with their women. For if he had been married to an intelligent superior woman he would have been yet more unhappy, since, with all his brilliance as a scientist, he belonged to that vast majority of American men who still repeat to-day the cry of traditional male pride, "I don't want *my* wife to work."

That is, he wanted a woman who would contain herself docilely within four walls. And he could not have seen that an intelligent, energetic, educated woman cannot be kept in four walls—even satin-lined, diamond-studded walls—without discovering sooner or later that they are still a prison cell. No home offers scope enough to-day for the trained energies of an intelligent modern woman. Even children are not enough. She may want them, need them and have them, love them and enjoy them, but they are not enough for her, even during the short time they preoccupy her. Nor is her husband, however dear and congenial, enough for her. He may supply all her needs for human companionship, but there is still more to life than that. There is the individual life. She must feel herself growing and becoming more and more complete as an individual, as well as a wife and mother, before she can even be a good wife and mother. I heard a smug little gray-haired woman say last week, "No, I don't know anything about politics. It takes all my time to be a good wife and mother. I haven't time to keep up with other things." Unfortunately, her husband, successful doctor that he is, has time to keep up not only with his business and with being what she calls a "wonderful husband and father," but with another woman as well. But that too is one of the things she knows nothing about. . . . Yet who can blame him? He is clever and full of interest in many things, and his wife is dulled with years of living in the four walls he put round her. It is a little unfair that he so encouraged her to stay in the walls that she came to believe in them completely as her place.

But tradition is very strong in this backward country of ours. We Americans are a backward nation in everything except in the making and using of machines. And we are nowhere more backward than we are in our attitude toward our women. We still, morally, shut the door of her home on a woman. We say to her, "Your home ought to be enough for you if you are a nice woman.

Your husband ought to be enough—and your children." If she says, "But they aren't enough—what shall I do?", we say, "Go and have a good time, that's a nice girl. Get yourself a new hat or something, or go to the matinée or join a bridge club. Don't worry your pretty head about what is not your business."

If she persists in being interested in things beyond her home we insist that she must be neglecting her home. If she still persists and makes a success through incredible dogged persistence we laugh at her. We even sneer at her and sometimes we treat her with unbelievable rudeness. I do not know the Secretary of Labor in our government, but I have seen her. She looks a quiet, serious, unassuming woman. I have taken pains to inquire of people who know, and it seems her home is not neglected. She has done at least as good a job in Washington as a number of men there in leading positions. But the slurs that have been cast upon her, the rudenesses of private and public talk, the injustices that have been done her merely because she is a woman in a place heretofore occupied by a man, have been amazing to a person unaccustomed to the American attitude toward women. It seems nothing short of barbarous.

And yet, vicious circle that it is, I cannot blame Americans for distrusting the ability of their women. For if the intelligent woman obeys the voice of tradition and limits herself to the traditional four walls she joins the vast ranks of the nervous, restless, average American women whose whimsies torture their families, who spoil the good name of all women because they are often flighty, unreliable, without good judgment in affairs, and given to self-pity. In short, she becomes a neurotic, if not all the time, a good deal of the time. Without knowing it or meaning it she falls too often to being a petty dictator in the home, a nag to her husband and children, and a gossip among her women friends. Too often too she takes no interest in any matters of social importance and refuses all responsibility in the community which she can avoid. She may be either a gadabout and extravagant or she may turn into a recluse and pride herself on being a "home woman." Neither of these escapes deceives the discerning. When will American men learn that they cannot expect happiness with a wife who is not her whole self? A restless unfulfilled woman is not going to be a satisfied wife or satisfactory lover. It is not that "women are like that." Anyone would be "like that" if he were put into such circumstances—that is, trained and developed for opportunity later denied.

"Plenty of men like that too nowadays," someone may murmur.

Yes, but the times have done it, and not tradition. There is a difference. And one man has as good a chance as another to win or lose, even in hard times. But no woman has a man's chance in hard times, or in any times.

2

I AM NOT so naïve, however, as to believe that one sex is responsible for this unfortunate plight of the American woman. I am not a feminist, but I am an individualist. I do not believe there is any important difference between men and women—certainly not as much as there may be between one woman and another or one man and another. There are plenty of women—and men, for that matter—who would be completely fulfilled in being allowed to be as lazy as possible. If someone will ensconce them in a pleasant home and pay their bills they ask no more of life. It is quite all right for these men and women to live thus so long as fools can be found who will pay so much for nothing much in return. Gigolos, male and female, are to be found in every class and in the best of homes. But when a man does not want to be a gigolo he has the freedom to go out and work and create as well as he can. But a woman has not. Even if her individual husband lets her, tradition in society is against her.

For another thing we Americans cannot seem to believe or understand is that women—some women, any woman, or as I believe, most women—are able to be good wives, ardent lovers, excellent mothers, and yet be themselves too. This seems strange, for as a nation we have fitted woman to be an individual as well as a woman by giving her a physical and mental education and a training superior to that of women in any other nation. But when she comes eagerly to life, ready to contribute her share, not only to home, but to government, sciences, and arts, we raise the old sickening cry of tradition, "This isn't your business! Woman's place is in the home—" and we shut the door in her face.

I am aware that at this point American men will be swearing and shouting, "You don't know what you're talking about! Why, we give our women more than any women on earth have!" With that I perfectly agree. American women are the most privileged in the world. They have all the privileges—far too many. They have so many privileges that a good many of them are utterly spoiled. They have privileges but they have no equality. "Nobody keeps them back," the American man declares. Ah, nobody, but everybody! For they are kept back by tradition expressed through the prejudices not only of men but of stupid, unthinking, tradition-bound women. Here is what I heard a few days ago.

A young woman wanted a new book to read and her father offered to send it to her. "What do you want?" he asked.

"Anything, only not one by a woman," she said carelessly. "I have a prejudice against books written by women."

Ignoring the rudeness, I asked, "Why?"

"Oh, I dislike women," she said. What she really meant was she despised women so much that she actually disliked women who did anything beyond the traditional jobs that the average women do. There are thousands of women who uphold medieval tradition in America more heartily than do men—just as in China it is the ignorant tradition-bound women who have clung to foot binding for themselves and their daughters. . . . No, women have many enemies among women. It goes back of course to the old jealous sense of general female inferiority. Tradition, if it binds one, should bind all, they feel.

Sometimes, I confess, I do not see how American men can endure some of their women—their imperiousness, their peevishness, their headstrongness, their utter selfishness, their smallness of mind and outlook, their lack of any sense of responsibility toward society, even to be pleasant. And their laziness—look at the motion-picture houses, the theaters, the lecture halls—crowded all day with women! The average house, even with no servant, can be no full-time job or they wouldn't be there in such hordes—they couldn't be there. But children go to school as soon as they stop being babies, and electricity cleans and washes the house and clothing, and husbands are away all day. So what is there for the restless woman to do? She goes to the show—and comes home, if she has any sense, to wonder what life is for, and to think that marriage isn't so much after all, though if she hadn't been married she would have been ashamed of herself. For tradition is there too, and it would have made her seem, if unmarried, unsuccessful as a female.

"But what are we going to do?" the harrassed American man cries. "There aren't enough jobs now to go round. And women are getting into industries more and more."

This is nonsense and a masculine bugaboo, though merely getting a job is not what I mean. The truth is the number of women in industries is increasing at so slow a rate that it is shocking when one considers how long they have had an equal chance with men for education and training. In the past fifty years—that is, half a century, during which education for women has enormously increased—the percentage of women in industry and the professions has increased from fourteen per cent only to twenty-two per cent. That means millions of women have been made ready for work they either had no chance to do or never wanted to do.

As to what men are going to do with women, I do not pretend to know. But I know I have never seen in any country—and I have seen most of the countries of the world—such unsatisfactory personal relationships between men and women as are in America—no, not even in Japan, where women as a class are depressed. For the Japanese are wiser in their treatment of women than we Americans are. They keep them down from the beginning so that they never hope for or expect more than life is to give them. They are not restless or neurotic or despotic, nor are they spoiled children. They have not been trained for equality and they do not expect it. They know they are upper servants, and they fulfil their duties gracefully and ably, and are happier on the whole than women in America. To know what one can have and to do with it, being prepared for no more, is the basis of equilibrium.

3

No, WHAT IS wrong in America is this matter of educating women. Life for the American woman is still controlled by old traditions. Men think of women, if at all, in the old simple traditional ways. Then women ought to be prepared for this sort of life and shaped through childhood and girlhood for what is to come. The root of the discontent in American women is that they are too well educated. What is the use of it? They do not need college educations nor even high school educations. What they ought to have is a simple course in reading, writing, and arithmetic—and advanced courses in cosmetics, bridge, sports, how to conduct a club meeting gracefully, how to be an attractive hostess, with or without servants, and how to deal with very young children in the home. This last course, obviously, should be purely optional.

But all this higher present education is unfortunate. It has led American women into having ideas which they can never realize when they come to maturity. A college education may, for instance, persuade a girl to become interested in biology, which may lead her into wanting to become a doctor. And yet she will never have the chance to become a first-rate doctor, however gifted she is by birth. People will not allow it—not only men, but women will not allow it. They will look at her tentative little shingle and shrug their shoulders and say, "I don't feel I'd *trust* a woman doctor as I would a man." So after a while, since she has to earn something, she takes her shingle down and accepts a secondary position in a hospital or a school or goes into baby-clinic work, supplemented by magazine articles on child care—or she just marries a doctor. But inside herself she knows she still wants to *be* a doctor, only she cannot. Tradition does not allow it.

Or a college education may lead a girl into wanting to be a banker. It is natural for women to be interested in finance since they own about seventy per cent of America's money. But it is unfortunate if a woman thinks she can be a real banker. I have talked with a good many women who work in our American banking system. Not one is where she hoped to be when she began, and a fair percentage are not where they should be with their high executive ability, or where they would be if they were men. As one of the most brilliant of them said to me bitterly, "I know if I were a man I should now, at the age of fifty, and after thirty years of experience, be a bank president. But I'll never be anything but an assistant to a vice-president. I reached the top—for a woman—years ago. I'll never be allowed to go on."

"Why can't you?" I inquired, being then too innocent.

"They say no one would want to put money in a bank run by a woman," she said.

I pondered this. I had then just come from Shanghai, where one of the best modern banks was run and controlled entirely by modern Chinese women. It was a prosperous bank because most people there thought women were probably more honest than men and more practical in the handling of money. So the Chinese women bankers did very well.

A good deal is said too about the profession of teaching for women. There are a great many women teachers in America—many more in proportion to men than in other countries. Men here, it seems, allow women to teach in lower schools because they themselves do not want to teach in anything less than a college. And even the best men do not like to teach in women's colleges nor in coeducational colleges. The finest teaching in America, I am told, is done by men for men.

As for the arts, I know very well that the odds are strongly against the woman. Granted an equally good product, the man is given the favor always. Women artists in any field are not often taken seriously, however serious their work. It is true that they often achieve high popular success. But this counts against them as artists. American men critics may show respect to a foreign woman artist, feeling that perhaps the foreign women are better than their own. But they cannot believe that the fools they see in department stores, in the subways and buses, or running to the movies and lectures, or even in their own homes, can amount to anything in the arts. Indeed they cannot think of a woman at all, but only of "women." And the pathetic efforts of American women to improve their minds by reading and clubs have only heightened the ridicule and contempt in which their men hold them. To educate women, therefore, to think, so that they need the personal fulfillment of activity and participation in all parts of life is acute cruelty, for they are not allowed this fulfillment. They should be educated not to think beyond the demands of simple household affairs or beyond the small arts and graces of pleasing men who seem always to want mental rest. The present method is not only cruel; it is extremely wasteful. Good money is spent teaching women to do things for which there will be no need. Men strain themselves to furnish educations for their daughters which they would be happier without, and not only happier but better women because they would be more contented women.

It is not only wasteful but dangerous. To educate women as we do for our present state of traditionalism is to put new wine into old bottles. A good deal of ferment is going on. And if we keep this up more will come of it. No one knows the effect upon children, for instance, of so many discontented women as mothers. Amiable, ignorant, bovine women make much better mothers than neurotic college graduates. And a woman does not need to complain aloud to let her children know she is unhappy. The atmosphere about her is gray with her secret discontent and children live deprived of that essential gayety in which they thrive as in sunshine. So few American women are really gay. This must have an effect.

4

So, THOUGH I am impressed with the fact that American women do not, as a group, seem happy, privileged as they are, I am not surprised. I know that happiness comes to an individual only as a result of personal fulfillment through complete functioning of all the energies and capabilities with which one is born. I do not for a moment mean that all women must go out and find jobs and "do something" outside the home. That would be as silly and general a mistake as our present general clinging to tradition. I simply mean let us be realistic. Let us face the fact that as a nation we are in a medieval state of mind about the place of women in society. Let each man ask himself—he need not answer aloud—where he really wants his woman. The majority, if they are honest, must acknowledge that they would like contented adoring women who want no more than their homes. I do not quarrel with that. What is, is. All I say is, let us realize facts. Tradition rules the relation of the sexes in America. Women are not welcome outside the home except in subsidiary positions, doing, on the whole, things men do not want to do. The great injustice to women is in not recognizing this frankly and in not preparing them for it.

Of course there is the chimeralike possibility that we might change tradition. But I do not see anyone capable of changing it. Men certainly will not. They do not even want to talk about it. They do not want the woman question stirred up, having as they say, "enough on their hands already." To them, of course, women "stirred up" simply means nervous, illogical, clamoring children who must be placated in one way or another. They cannot conceive of woman as a rational being, equal to themselves and not always fundamentally connected with sex. Emotionally, as it has been truly said, many American men are adolescents—kind, delightful, charming adolescents. "He's just like a boy" seems to be considered a compliment to a man in America. It ought to be an insult. This horrible boyishness lingering in persons who should be adult is as dismaying as mental retardation. It is responsible for our childish tendencies to "jazz things up," to make "whoopee," to think of being drunk, of removing "inhibitions," of playing the clown, as the only way to have a good time, to the complete destruction of adult conversation and real wit and subtler humor. It certainly is responsible for wanting women to be nothing but wives, mothers, or leggy relaxations for tired business men. Even a pretty college girl said despairingly not long ago in my presence, "You can't get anywhere with men if you show any brains. I have to make myself a nit-wit if I want dates. Oh, well, that's the way they are!" There are too many nice and rather sad American women who patiently accept even their middle-aged and old men as perennial "boys." "Men are like that," they say, at least as often as men say, "women are like that."

Nothing could show a greater misunderstanding between the sexes than this frequent fatalistic remark. Neither men nor women are like that if "that" means what they now seem to each other. It is a strange fact that in new America, as in old India or China, the real life of each sex is not with each other but away from each other. Men and women in America meet stiffly for social functions, drink together in an earnest effort to feel less inhibited, play the fool guardedly and feel queer about it afterward. Or they meet for physical sex, in the home or out. And they jog along in family life. Of the delight of exploring each other's differing but equally important personalities and points of view, of the pleasure of real mutual comprehension and appreciation and companionship, there is almost none, inside the home or out. Tradition decrees that after marriage real companionship between persons of opposite sex must cease except between husband and wife. Tradition decrees that all companionship indeed between men and women is tinged with sex. Such an idea as interest in each other as persons, aside from sex, is almost unknown. Women, talking of this among themselves, say, "Men don't want anything else." I am inclined to think they are right. The average American man demands amazingly little from his women—

nothing much except to look as pretty as possible on as little money as possible, to run the home economically with as little trouble as possible to the man when he comes home tired. What educated, intelligent, clever, gifted woman is going to be satisfied with that? What average woman would be satisfied even? Ask the average man if he would change places with a woman—any woman. The idea horrifies him. Yet women are far more like him than he knows or wants to know, and modern times have done everything to make her more so.

No, our men, perennial boys, most of them, will not do anything about changing tradition. They do not know how, absorbed as they are in the game of business, abashed as they are in the presence of sex as anything except simply physical, and afraid as they are of women. They are, naturally, afraid of women or they would not cling so to tradition. They were afraid of their mothers when they were children, their imperious, discontented mothers, and that fear carries over into fear of their wives and fear of all women, in industry as well as at home. It leads to the attitude of petty deception which so many perennially boyish men maintain toward their women.

So, naturally enough, men do not want women "getting too smart." I heard a carpenter working in my home say pontifically to his assistant about to be married, "And why would you want a woman eddicated? Says I, if I want eddication I can go to the public library. A woman should know just so much as when it rains she stands on the sheltered side of the street. It's enough." And after a moment he added solemnly, "You don't want a woman what can talk smart. You want one what can keep quiet smart."

The voice of America's perennial boys, I thought—speaking out in a carpenter, but heard as clearly in the embarrassed reserves of an after-dinner circle in a drawing-room. And yet, I do not blame them. There are so many women who chatter without thought, who stop all attempts at conversation with continual commonplaces uttered with all the petty authority of ignorance. And the fetters of another tradition—that of chivalry—still hang upon American men. Foolish, haughty women, standing in crowded buses, staring at a tired man in a seat, accepting favors as their right; peevish, idle women, wasting their husbands' money; dogmatic women talking ignorantly about practical important matters—men must try to be polite to them all alike. I do not blame American men, except for not seeing that not all women are the same.

We are so clever with machines, we Americans. But we have done a silly thing with our women. We have put modern high-powered engines into old antiquated vehicles. It is no wonder the thing is not working. And there are only two courses to follow if we do want it to work. We must go back to the old simple one-horse-power engine or else we must change the body to suit the engine—one or the other. If the first, then tradition must be held to from the moment a woman is born, not, as it now is, clamped upon her when, after a free and extraordinarily equal childhood and girlhood with boys, she attempts to enter into a free and equal adult life with men and finds it denied her, to discover then that her education has had nothing to do with her life.

Or else we must be willing to let her go on as she began. This means that

American men must cease being "sweet boys" and grow up emotionally as well as physically and face women as adult men. But they, poor things, have not been fitted for that either! Besides of course they are afraid of what women might do. And women, inexperienced and eager, will probably do as many foolish things as men have until they have had as much practice.

Of one thing I am sure, however. There will be no real content among American women unless they are made and kept more ignorant or unless they are given equal opportunity with men to use what they have been taught. And American men will not be really happy until their women are.

The Need for New Myths

GERALD CLARKE

Gerald Clarke uses exposition in defining mythology and explaining its "functions" as the basis for his lament of the loss of myths. Even though the title indicates the "need" for mythology in our modern world, we read about the background and development of myths before we learn exactly the argument that Clarke makes.

Original publication: *Time*, January 17, 1972.

The latest incarnation of Oedipus, the continued romance of Beauty and the Beast, stands this afternoon on the corner of 42nd Street and Fifth Avenue, waiting for the traffic light to change.

—JOSEPH CAMPBELL

That statement, fanciful as it sounds, is simply a shorthand way of saying that everyone is a creature of myth, that the ancient legends and tales of the race are still the master keys to the human psyche. The science-minded Victorians who sneered at myths as superstitious twaddle were guilty of a kind of scientific superstition themselves: the belief that reason could explain all human motives. Aided by psychoanalysis, anthropology and three-quarters of a century of archaeological discovery, modern scholarship has replaced the Victorians' sneers with respect and even awe. Mythology, its partisans are now claiming, tells as much about humanity—its deepest fears, sorrows, joys and hopes—as dreams tell about an individual. "Myths are public dreams," says Joseph Campbell, who is probably the world's leading expert on mythology. "Dreams are private myths. Myths are vehicles of communication between the conscious and the unconscious, just as dreams are."

The trouble is, Campbell asserts, that this communication has broken down in the modern Western world. The old myths are no longer operative, and effective new myths have not arisen to replace them. As a result, he maintains, the West is going through an agony of reorientation matched only by a period during the 4th millennium B.C., when the Sumerians first conceived the concept of a mathematically ordered cosmos and thus changed utterly man's concept of the universe around him.

Campbell's words carry extraordinary weight, not only among scholars but among a wide range of other people who find his search down mythological pathways relevant to their lives today. A professor of literature at Sarah Lawrence College in Bronxville, N.Y., Campbell has written and edited some 20-odd books on mythology. They include a massive four-volume work entitled *The Masks of God: The Flight of the Wild Gander* and the book for which he is most famous, *Hero With a Thousand Faces*, a brilliant examination, through ancient hero myths, of man's eternal struggle for identity. *Hero*, which has had sales of more than 110,000 copies, an impressive figure for a scholarly book, has become a bestseller on campus. After 37 years of teaching in relative obscurity, Campbell, at 67, has now become a well-known and respected figure in academe.

What is a myth? In Campbell's academic jargon, it is a dreamlike "symbol that evokes and directs psychological energy." A vivid story or legend, it is but one part of a larger fabric of myths that, taken together, form a mythology that expresses a culture's attitude toward life, death and the universe around it. The Greek myth of Prometheus, the Titan who stole fire from Olympus and gave it to man, thus symbolizes the race's aspirations, even when they conflict with the powers of nature. The almost contemporary Hebrew myth of the trials of Job, on the other hand, symbolizes man's submission to a power above nature, even when that power seems cruel and unjust. The two myths are, in effect, picture stories that tell the philosophies of two totally divergent cultures. The Greek stresses man's heroic striving for human values and civilization; the Hebrew emphasizes, rather, man's humble spiritual surrender to God's will. Abraham's willingness to sacrifice Isaac is the supreme symbol of this attitude.

Though not true in a literal sense, a myth is not what it is considered to be in everyday speech—a fantasy or a misstatement. It is rather a veiled explanation of the truth. The transformation from fact to myth is endlessly fascinating. The battle of Achilles and Hector, for example, is symbolic, but there was a Trojan War in which great heroes fought. The psychological duel between Faust and the Devil is a philosophical and psychological metaphor, but Georg Faust, a German magician who was born about 1480, did live and did make claims to superhuman power, including the ability to restore the lost works of Plato and Aristotle and to repeat the miracles of Christ. Yet it was not until poets like Christopher Marlowe and Goethe took up the legend that Faust became famous—and mythic. The Faust story appealed to Marlowe and to Goethe because the times in which they lived, eras in which faith and reason were in basic conflict, called for such a symbolic struggle.

What should a mythology do? In Campbell's view a "properly operating" mythology has four important functions:

- To begin with, through its rites and imagery it wakens and maintains in the individual a sense of awe, gratitude and even rapture, rather than fear, in relation to the mystery both of the universe and of man's own existence within it.
- Secondly, a mythology offers man a comprehensive, understandable image of the world around him, roughly in accord with the best scientific knowledge of the time. In symbolic form, it tells him what his universe looks like and where he belongs in it.
- The third function of a living mythology is to support the social order through rites and rituals that will impress and mold the young. In India, for example, the basic myth is that of an impersonal power, Brahma, that embodies the universe. The laws of caste are regarded as inherent features of this universe and are accepted and obeyed from childhood. Cruel as this may seem to Westerners, the myth of caste does give Indian society a stability it might otherwise lack and does make life bearable to the impoverished low castes.
- The fourth and, in Campbell's view, the most important function of mythology, is to guide the individual, stage by stage, through the inevitable psychological crises of a useful life: from the childhood condition of dependency through the traumas of adolescence and the trials of adulthood to, finally, the deathbed.

The churches and synagogues still provide mythological guidance for many, Campbell argues; for many others, however, this guidance fails. The result is that, where once religion served, many have turned to psychoanalysis or encounter groups. "All ages before ours believed in gods in some form or other," wrote Carl Jung, whose theories of the collective unconscious have most profoundly influenced Campbell's thinking. "Heaven has become empty space to us, a fair memory of things that once were. But our heart glows, and secret unrest gnaws at the roots of our being." In search of something that they can hold on to, many people in the West, particularly the young, are either returning to Christian fundamentalism through the Jesus Revolution (TIME, June 21) or turning to the religions of the East, chiefly Buddhism and Hinduism. "The swamis are coming from India, and they're taking away the flock," says Campbell. "They're speaking of religion as dealing with the interior life and not about dogmatic formulae and ritual requirements."

For the vast majority, Campbell believes, the West's general lack of spiritual authority has been a disaster. Forty years in the study of eternal symbols have made Campbell a conservative of a rather dark hue. Though he is optimistic about the long range, he finds the present bleak indeed. "We have seen what has happened to primitive communities unsettled by the white man's civilization," he observes. "With their old taboos discredited, they immediately go to pieces, disintegrate, and become resorts of vice and disease. Today the same thing is happening to us."

Many Oriental and primitive societies even today have working mythologies, and Communist countries have at least the basis of a mythology in Marxism. The Marxist dream of the withering away of the state, after which each man will give according to his abilities and receive according to his needs, echoes numerous religious beliefs of a paradise on earth or a Second Coming. The Chinese Communists have, in addition, the myth of the "Long March" in the '30s and the subsequent sanctuary of Mao Tse-tung and his followers in the caves of Yenan. The events were real enough, but for this generation of Chinese, and probably for generations to come, they will have much the same deep mythological significance that the Trojan War had for the Greeks.

In the West there have been desperate attempts to provide at least fragments of a modern mythology. Churchill brilliantly re-created the myth of St. George and the dragon during World War II: the picture of little Britain, a citadel of justice, besieged by the evil Nazi hordes. The situation, of course, was much as he painted it—Britain was besieged and Hitler was evil—but a Neville Chamberlain would not have been able, as Churchill was, to light up his people with the basic themes of their culture. Charles de Gaulle, both as wartime leader and President of the Fifth Republic, quite consciously resurrected the ghost of Joan of Arc. "To my mind," he wrote, "France cannot be France without greatness." The founders of Israel similarly evoked, and still evoke, mythic images of the Bible's chosen people to enable Israelis to survive in their hostile environment.

Often, such attempts add up merely to rhetoric or incantation. John Kennedy sought to revive the American myth that the U.S. was a country with a messianic mission. "Now the trumpet summons us again," he said in his Inaugural Address, "to a struggle against the common enemies of man: tyranny, poverty, disease and war itself." A post-Viet Nam U.S. can no longer quite believe in such an American mission. And Martin Luther King Jr. worked to provide the nation's blacks with a myth of their own. "I've been to the mountaintop and I've looked over, and I've seen the promised land," King said the night before he was killed, echoing the Bible's story of Moses on Mount Sinai.

For centuries Americans were emboldened by the myth of the endless frontier, the notion that a new life could always be started out West, whether the West was Ohio or California. That version outlasted the frontier itself, but no one believes in it today. Campbell hopes that the landings on the moon will reinvigorate that mythic tradition. Only a handful of people can go to the moon, and no one would want to stake out his 160 acres there, but the excitement of the journey itself is infectious, a re-enactment on the TV screen of Prometheus' stealing fire from the gods. Beyond that, Campbell believes, there is an even more durable myth: the "American Dream." That is the idea, grounded in fact, that a man is judged on his own ability rather than on his family or his place in society. "This pessimistic optimist thinks that the myth still works," he says.

"The fact that Nixon was a poor boy and was yet elected President is a good example."

In the final analysis, however, it is wrong in Campbell's view to ask for one grand mythology that will guide people today. Instead there must be many different mythologies for many different kinds of people. "There is no general mythology today," Campbell says, "nor can there ever be again. Our lives are too greatly various in their backgrounds, aims and possibilities for any single order of symbols to work effectively on us all." The new myths must be internalized and individual, and each man must find them for himself. Some, in fact, are following mythological paths today, unconsciously and without design. The hippie who leaves society and goes off to a commune, for example, is being guided by a mythological map of withdrawal and adventure laid down by Christ in the desert, the Buddha at Bodh-Gaya, and Mohammed in his cave of meditation at Mount Hira.

The man in search of an ideal could at least begin, Campbell thinks, by searching through the myths of antiquity, religion and modern literature. For the elite who can read and understand them, T. S. Eliot, James Joyce, Thomas Mann, among modern writers and poets, and Pablo Picasso and Paul Klee, among modern artists, have updated the ancient mythological motifs. Campbell and the other mythologists are, in a sense, providing the workbooks for the poets—the modern Daedaluses in turtlenecks. "It doesn't matter to me whether my guiding angel is for a time named Vishnu, Shiva, Jesus, or the Buddha," Campbell says. "If you're not distracted by names or the color of hair, the same message is there, variously turned. In the multitude of myths and legends that have been preserved to us—both in our own Western arts and literatures, synagogues and churches, and in the rites and teachings of those Oriental and primitive heritages now becoming known to us—we may still find guidance."

The mythologists are not providing myths, but they are indicating that something is missing without them. They are telling modern man that he has not outgrown mythology and will never outgrow it so long as he has hopes and fears beyond the other animals.

Gatsby at the B School

ROBERT COLES

Though best known for his work in child psychiatry, with emphasis on the study of stress, Robert Coles here considers literature and the education of tomorrow's business leaders. He *describes* his course and *explains* his reasons for using certain authors and works to lead to his quiet but *persuasive* conclusion: "stories . . . can work their magic on the heart—and help one resist the ever-present temptation of the intellect. . . ." Like William Carlos Williams, he has tried to bring readers (and students) "up close."

Original publication: *The New York Times Book Review*, October 25, 1987.

In a reflective moment toward the end of his life, William Carlos Williams brushed aside yet another question about himself and his poems, stories and novels: "The last few years, just when I'm getting ready to kick off, people keep coming at me. They want to know who I am, and what do I mean here and there and everywhere in my writing. I wish they'd take an interest in the readers—not just themselves, but all those people who pick up the books and put in time with them." Later he added, "I know what the professors think of Joe and Gurlie Stecher [central figures in Williams's trilogy 'White Mule,' which describes the rise of a working-class couple to wealth and influence], but not the people who might have plenty of reasons to pay attention to those books— businessmen and their wives. Flossie [Williams's wife] once asked me how many successful Joe Stechers did I think would be reading [the books]. I said, damn few. Maybe I was wrong. I'll never know, though."

A hundred or so businessmen and women have recently been reading Williams's trilogy. They are students in a seminar I began teaching at the Harvard Business School in 1985 entitled The Business World: Moral and Social Inquiry Through Fiction, and I wish Williams had been around to hear them respond to the moral dilemmas he posed. The students were in their middle to late 20's, some older, and had already been out in the worlds of banking and finance, manufacturing, entrepreneurial risktaking. The point of our reading in the seminar was the enjoyment of fiction, of course—but we concentrated on novels and stories that address the 20th-century American business world directly or indirectly. Although that world gets some moments of tough inspection at the hands of each novelist, there is no ideological animus or rancor at work in the reading list. By and large the writers—among them Williams, F. Scott Fitzgerald, Saul Bellow, Walker Percy, John Cheever and Flannery O'Connor—are affectionately interested in their subjects. They work hard with the magic storytellers possess to render faithfully, honestly, fully a way of life familiar to many of us who live and work in what gets called the corporate world.

My students, I think it fair to say, experienced those moments of recognition that novelists have been providing their readers for centuries. Right in class, or certainly in the papers they wrote, or in the exchanges that preceded or followed our weekly meetings, men and women talked of their earlier lives—some not unlike those middle-class suburbanites Cheever portrayed, others in the immigrant tradition Williams evoked. Stories had connected with the memories of those who read them and, too, enlivened their moral imagination.

The recent spate of Wall Street scandals gained notoriety after the first year's seminar. When the following year's class arrived, Ivan Boesky and Dennis Levine had been caught trading stocks on insider information. Suddenly the subject of ethics in the business world was more explicitly on the minds of everyone.

Many students at the Business School were nothing if not ambitious; they saw themselves as future entrepreneurs, as did the hero of Williams's trilogy, Joe Stecher, a worker who becomes an entrepreneur. His wife, Gurlie, is fiercely ambitious for him, not to mention herself. Williams had his wife's family very much in mind as he wrote the trilogy in the 1930's and 1940's—evoking through one family's experience much of what took place in the late 19th century and the early decades of this one, as certain Americans took advantage of any and every opportunity and became rich. But personal costs accompanied the Stechers' achievement; loyalties and once sacred ethical obligations were challenged.

Talking about his trilogy, Williams made the following remarks: "You won't find answers in those novels, but you'll find lots of questions asked—by indirection. How do you balance your business life and your home life? How do you resist the temptation to become callous and selfish? How do you hold to moral and religious values in the face of all sorts of challenges at work? What happens to people, emotionally and spiritually, when they compromise with certain important principles—start down the road of rationalizations and self-justifications? The slope is gradual—sometimes imperceptible—but real. I try to survey the slope carefully—to bring the reader up close, so close that his empathy puts him in the shoes of the characters. You hope when he closes the book his own character is influenced." I thought of putting Williams's words on the reading list, atop the book titles, but decided to forgo the pleasure, maybe the conceit, of a preliminary formulation. "Let the students figure out what they want to do with those novels without an advanced set of instructions," my wife, a teacher, suggested.

We began our reading together with "The Great Gatsby." Fitzgerald's evocations of American wealth and commerce are shrewdly seductive. His celebratory awe of wealth and power only yields gradually to the moralist's judgment. A number of my students found Jay Gatsby's eager and vulgar ambition all too easy to put at arm's length—but, at the end of the novel, had a bit of trouble when the author reveals his hand with his well-known comment, directed through the observer Nick Carraway, at the old established wealth of Daisy and Tom Buchanan: "They were careless people, Tom and Daisy—they smashed up things and creatures and then retreated back into their vast carelessness, or whatever it was that kept them together, and let other people clean up the mess they had made."

Such a remark was meant to be an invitation to the reader to forgo the quick satisfaction of lofty disdain for any particular arriviste (a person, an ethnic group) and instead look hard at certain all too well accepted assumptions and conventions—in Tom's domain of highfalutin banking as well as Gatsby's elusive world of furtive arrangements and deals. For a while many of us snickered about the Boesky-Gatsby pair (their very names a rhyme), but a few students accepted Fitzgerald's invitation—were outspokenly candid about established wealth, the real moral target of the novel.

Saul Bellow's "Seize the Day" offered us another look at New York high finance—this time through the eyes of Tommy Wilhelm, a commodities speculator whose dreams of achievement and glory are constantly undermined by his fears and worries, which he tries to hide from himself, never mind others. The novel is melancholy in obvious ways, but made inviting by the author's wonderful sense of humor. The antic, loony side of Tommy Wilhelm's life (and especially the damage to him as a husband and father) prompted certain students who had worked in commodities markets to remember a certain kind of frenzy—things pushed to the extreme as a kind of gambling fever consumed not only time but any number of souls. One young man summarized two years of such work with these words: "We were on a roller coaster all day. We shouted and screamed. We went wild with joy one minute, and the next you felt the hand of Death on your shoulder. Once, I looked around and said to myself: 'This is all crazy; you are crazy.' One friend of mine jokingly called the room where we worked 'Ward Six.' He'd read a lot of Chekhov in college."

The inherent absurdity not only of the marketplace but much of life figures in Walker Percy's novel "The Moviegoer" as well. Binx Bolling is a 29-year-old New Orleans stockbroker whose wry detachment from the upper-crust world he inhabits enables him to take sharp measure of all kinds of social pretention and cultural rot. He goes through the various motions of a particular life, spotting the absurdities and ambiguities that come his way, calling on his moviegoing habits as a metaphor for so much of what takes place among the late 20th-century bourgeoisie of the West—the passive, ethically neutral esthetics of watching a reel unfold. Such a connection to art is but part of a larger malaise—people anxious to lose themselves in a crowd, to learn their cues from others. Binx is saved from such a fate by his ironic self-consciousness—a problem in itself, however. He makes his money, drives his sports car, has his girlfriend, yet he is morally adrift. He is a victim of his own capacity for aloof self-fulfillment. Only with difficulty can he break through his distance from others, and of course, from himself as well.

Mr. Percy is subtle and knowing in his capacity to remind some of us how mischievously we use our own intellect, along with society's distracting blandishments, to lose our spiritual bearings. Many of the students wanted to go further—some eventually read all of his novels and also his two books of philosophical reflection. I assigned an essay from one of them, "The Message in the Bottle," titled "The Man on the Train," a meditative story, really, based on commuter experiences many of us have: how lost we become, gazing out the window noticing very little that we see, and soon enough, forgetting completely minutes, hours of time—the tuning out that cumulatively can make us resemble automatons.

Mr. Percy's fiction affected a number of those young men and women in important ways—to the point that some of them kept telling me that Binx had become a part of their everyday consciousness: "I smile at some of the hustle-talk I hear and wonder what in hell a lot of this push, push, push is about. I'm going to be in there competing with everyone else, but I don't think I have to trip everyone in sight. It's Percy's humor you can't forget. It's his message to you—and it stays with you, his tough look at a lot of our frantic materialism." Another student, more tersely, told me: "Sometimes Binx's sardonic smile crosses my face, and I have to work hard to look serious, no matter what I'm thinking." Not that Binx was undermining these future executives. Again and again the students insisted that Binx's bemused, if not critical relationship to our culture was not going to undo or unnerve them. What, then, would be the consequence of a reading of "The Moviegoer"? "I think of Binx," a student told me, "when things get wild and absurd; and so I'll hope not to lose my common sense and the kind of larger perspective Percy has—I guess you'd call it a moral perspective."

Several of John Cheever's characters, in his various stories, many of which we read, are Mr. Percy's "man on the train," commuting daily between the thinly disguised suburban paradises that ring Manhattan and their important jobs in the American city of cities. Cheever is forever looking at how life goes for his lawyers and businessmen, who seem to have everything, yet not rarely drink too much, have marital troubles and are at risk of becoming (or already are) smug, arrogant, stupidly full of themselves. One student asked: "Is this our future?" Her neighbor in the class said no, immediately. Others weren't so sure of their answers—but clearly were challenged by the question. A particular favorite story for some students was "The Housebreaker of Shady Hill," whose central figure, Johnny Hake, is an oddly appealing stockbroker in financial distress, who finds himself one day almost unselfconsciously sneaking into a neighbor's house in the middle of the night and taking a wallet full of money from clothes left on a bedroom chair. Johnny Hake knows the house well; he has gone to many a party there. He would be the last person to be suspected of a robbery—and yet, now that he has done such a thing, he becomes (in the tradition of "Crime and Punishment") his own strenuous accuser.

Cheever brilliantly connects this strange moment of petty thievery in Shady Hill to what happens all the time at work in lower Manhattan—the cynicism and hypocrisy that threaten many of us more than we may want to acknowledge. Johnny Hake as thief becomes Johnny Hake suddenly aware of the way he and others try to con customers, begrudge them the smallest amounts of kindness and generosity. The story is at once funny and light, yet on closer inspection, thoroughly disturbing, enough so to prompt intense, spirited discussion and plenty of confessional comment: "I've been like that sometimes." Cheever hits home most when he has Johnny Hake see an apparently well-to-do businessman pocket money left by someone else as a tip, or when Hake himself rakes in the "collect" at an Episcopal church, all too aware, by now, of the deceptions and self-deceptions that so-called respectability can mask.

Self-deception is also at the heart of Flannery O'Connor's cleverly narrated "The Displaced Person"—an account of what happens to a Southern landowner as she tries to run a tighter business operation. In hiring Mr. Guizac, the "displaced person" (a post-World War II refugee from Eastern Europe), Mrs. McIntyre in turn displaces a family that has hitherto worked loyally for her, thereby setting in motion a chain of events that causes her to become "displaced," that is, morally confused. O'Connor's story is not Williams's immigrant chronicle, though in each the same observations are made with respect to covetousness: it can entail loss as well as gain—and diminished self-respect that seeks expression in a person's daily life. Mrs. McIntyre takes to her bed the way some of Cheever's characters take to booze and Binx Bolling to the movies: a manner of dodging the ethical implications of one's life.

When a huge sum of money ($30 million) was given to the Harvard Business School—by a former head of the Securities and Exchange Commission, no less—for the express purpose of encouraging the teaching of ethics, we had extended discussions on what Harvard should do with the money. The suggestions were fascinating: the money should be given outright to "the needy"; some practical, service-oriented relationship with poor youth should be established whereby business students would teach in high schools and encourage students to aim for business careers; the entire curriculum should be shaped differently, so that the fierce competitiveness would be lessened and an end put to the "forced curve" (a provision that in most classes a certain number of students must be designated as the poorest academically). Many students were actually quite cynical about the gift—interpreted it, in the words of one student, as an "expression of guilty hand-washing." He elaborated: "A big-deal financier gives a big-deal gift to a big-deal university on a temporarily big-deal subject, ethics—so we're supposed to relax, because everything goes well, after all!" In a wonderful tribute to Walker Percy and John Cheever, another student came to see me and suggested that Harvard buy thousands of copies of their books and distribute them not only to every Business School student, but to corporate officials across the land. We did agree, however, that the then famous (and maybe, puzzling) $30 million would not thereby be much dented.

For me those two years of teaching "across the river," as it is often put on the occasionally self-important Cambridge side, were both edifying and gratifying. I was not only impressed with, but surprised by the idealism and decency of many of the students I met, with the yearning they had to join with Binx in his moral search, to link arms with Johnny Hake as he shook his world upside down in such a dramatic and unsettling way. I had acquired over the years all sorts of stereotypes about those students—quite wrong-headed notions, I slowly realized. Once, sitting and listening to a wonderfully alert, sensitive discussion of Cheever's stories, I remembered—perhaps to let my patronizing self off the hook—a comment of the cranky Dr. Williams, expressed through a rhetorical question: "Who the hell is without some kind of prejudice, I ask you?"

The first year's class said goodbye during a dinner at which, as one young banker in retrospect put it, "the honorary guests guests were Nick Carraway, Binx Bolling and Johnny Hake." When coupled with continuing practical experiences (such as those the Business School students suggested when they asked for a chance to tutor ghetto children), stories, I believe, can work their magic on the heart—and help one resist the ever present temptation of the intellect to distance anything and everything from itself through endless generalizations. Yes, we used our heads in that course. But mostly we sat back and let those stories get to us, prompt us to remember past times and wonder anew about the future. I can picture us meeting in a board room in a Manhattan skyscraper years from now, some students now in positions of authority, others perhaps having left the business world altogether, but all of us deliberating yet again the whys of human nature in the manner good novelists so often recommend—with an emphasis on life's ironies, paradoxes and complexities.

Abortion Issues Affect Real Women in Real World

SUSAN DUDLEY

Susan Dudley, Ph.D. in biopsychology, uses the standard point-counterpoint approach in her article about abortion published in a local newspaper. She provides some background on the controversy before presenting opposing views and countering them. Even conceding weaknesses in her side of the argument, she builds, point by point, to an authoritative conclusion.

Abortion, like other emotionally charged controversies such as euthanasia, flag-burning, and evolution, raises people's immediate defenses. Thus, Dudley approaches the subject as logically and unemotionally as possible. She strengthens her own stance by introducing the opponents' arguments and refuting or conceding them as appropriate, admitting that this is an imperfect world, with no ideal solutions. This article may not *convince* readers, but it should achieve the goal of making them *think*.

Original publication: *The Montgomery Advertiser and Alabama Journal*, January 22, 1989.

While we still use the ephemism, "debate," to refer to escalating rhetoric about abortion, there is little debating actually taking place. In fact, when the Gallup organization asked Americans four years ago if they ever wondered whether their own positions on abortion were correct, 55 percent said no.

This weekend marks the 16th anniversary of the U.S. Supreme Court decision in the Roe vs. Wade case which held that state laws against abortion violate the 9th Amendment. The lives of countless women have been profoundly affected by this decision. But abortion was not new in 1973.

Abortion has existed for at least 5,000 years, and has occurred in all societies. In common-law nations throughout the world, women were free to obtain abortions, and this right was not abridged until 1803 when England enacted a law which left women liable for prosecution and punishment for aborting a pregnancy. Forty years later the states of the United States began to pass similar laws. Interestingly, debate leading up to these restrictions never centered on the morality of abortion, but on the need to regulate medical treatment and restrict the practice of medicine to licensed physicians. We can only speculate on why the framers of the Constitution did not mention abortion, but scholars generally agree that it was commonly accepted and widespread in America throughout the Colonial period.

Today, rational discussion or political compromise on the issue seems to be impossible, because argument rarely centers on abortion itself, but reverts to questions of ethics, religion, law, or politics. Caught in the middle are women who must deal with unplanned pregnancies and who are faced with the shattering realization that there are no good solutions to their problem.

It has been popular, particularly among those who have a fundamentalist bias, to chastise the unwillingly pregnant woman for the sexuality that led to her pregnancy (though we rarely heap such blame on their partners, whose biological urges we tend to forgive). Inherent in such criticism is the mistaken assumption that the only women who seek abortion are the young and unmarried, who presumably should not be having sex, or those too irresponsible to use birth control. In fact, the U.S. Centers for Disease Control reports that in 1985 approximately 20 percent of all legal abortions were obtained by married women.

In addition, while the effectiveness of various birth control methods varies inversely with the long-term health risk to the woman using the method, up to 3 percent of women using the Pill correctly and conscientiously still become pregnant. When this, our most reliable method of contraception, is contraindicated because of health or age considerations, the failure rate soars to around 20 percent for barrier methods.

A recent study from the Alan Guttmacher Institute indicates that if every woman in America who wanted to postpone childbearing practiced birth control faithfully, there would still be about 500,000 unwanted pregnancies per year—a number equal to 38 percent of reported abortions.

Misinformation about biological facts and birth control, as well as economic and logistical factors limiting the availability of contraception, also contributes to the problem. While studies have shown that fewer than 15 percent of all children get meaningful sex education from their parents, we face enormous resistance to school-based sex education programs and even greater resistance to the suggestion that making birth control available to young people might be the lesser of two evils when we consider the large number of pregnancies among unmarried teen-agers today. Teen-aged women account for one quarter of Americans' abortions annually, and have higher abortion and birth rates than teens from other developed countries. Another study from the Guttmacher Institute has shown that American women have a harder time obtaining birth control than women in most other Western countries, and therefore are more likely to have unplanned pregnancies. Because contraceptives are considered preventive care, they are generally not covered under health insurance policies.

Many assert that women choose abortion when pregnancy is "inconvenient." This patronizing claim suggests that the problems faced by a woman with an unplanned pregnancy are trivial, and that the abortion procedure is undertaken without careful consideration and soul-searching. Consider a few facts about the American family. A quarter of all murders occur within the family. The FBI estimates that one woman is beaten by her husband or boyfriend every 18 seconds, and four women *die* from domestic violence each day. Surveys have shown that one in three girls and one in seven boys have been sexually assaulted by an adult. The vast majority of these assaults are perpetrated by close relatives. The National Committee for Prevention of Child Abuse reports that at least 1 million children are physically abused by their parents each year in non-sexual assaults, and up to 5,000 die. Add those of families rendered dysfunctional due to alcohol or other drug abuse or emotional abuse, and those who live below the poverty level and survive without adequate food, shelter, or medical care.

The point is that as much as we would prefer to cling to the myth of the American family as the warm, supportive source of emotional stability, love and self-esteem, the facts indicate otherwise. These are not trivial concerns, and many pregnant American women are faced with circumstances that will produce unbearable hardship for themselves, their existing children, or the child they are carrying.

Adoption is the alternative most often suggested when a woman cannot support a child for any of these reasons, but again the tendency is to trivialize the impact of such a decision.

Adoption is an option that sometimes puts the child at great risk, and subjects the mother to public condemnation ("What kind of woman could give up a child she has carried for nine months?"). The probability that a perfectly developed Caucasian baby will spend at least some time in foster care before adoption is very high. The probability that a non-white or handicapped child will be permanently placed is very low.

We are arrogant to believe that the choice to have an abortion is an easy one. It is a choice made all the more painful when one must brave the cruel interference of protesters in front of a clinic, who have easy answers to offer to women who are living complicated lives. Studies have shown, however, that while most women are saddened by the necessity of the abortion choices they have made, the vast majority do not regret their decisions when they are weighed against the alternatives. The only women found consistently to have suffered from the much-touted "post-abortion syndrome" are those who faced illegal, back-alley procedures before 1973.

It is estimated that 720,000 illegal abortions were performed each year before the Roe vs. Wade decision, and that at least 17,000 women died each year from complications after these abortions. Untold numbers of additional casualties included serious injury, infection and sterility. For the moral absolutists who claim that no priority overrides the rights of the unborn baby, these facts may arouse no compassion. If our goal is to inflict punishment on the sexual miscreant, our angry rhetoric as we "debate" the issue of abortion and our ultimate denial of the option to start again will be more successful than the Puritans' scarlet letter.

But the sad reality is that as much as we decry a social order that presents us with such problems as unwanted pregnancy, we must deal with the world as it is, and not as we wish it to be. While we debate philosophical questions, while we rail against immorality and godlessness, there are real women out there trying to do the best they can in a sadly imperfect world. The reversal of Roe vs. Wade would not take away the need for abortion, but would drive these desperate individuals back to the back alleys and illegal underworld.

Whose Canon Is It, Anyway?

HENRY LOUIS GATES, JR.

Henry Louis Gates, Jr., is working on *The Norton Anthology of Afro-American Literature*. His work on the anthology and his other scholarly work have led to this argument for the placement of works by Afro-Americans in the canon of American and world literature. Readers can anticipate his answer to the question in the title in his choice of wording in the opening paragraphs. From that point on, he makes a relentless case for his thesis.

In developing his argument, Gates uses expository definitions and classifications, mixing in some autobiography in his discussion of his

childhood and teaching experiences. The diction ranges from
emotionally loaded words to technical terminology in his appeal to
his specific audience of "scholar-critics" who establish literary canon.
But all of us who are affected by this canon need to know and
understand the principles involved in this issue.

Original publication: *The New York Times Book Review*, February 26, 1989.

W illiam Bennett and Allan Bloom, the dynamic duo of the new cultural
right, have become the easy targets of the cultural left, which I am defining here
loosely and generously as that uneasy, shifting set of alliances formed by
feminist critics, critics of so-called minority culture and Marxist and poststruc-
turalist critics generally—in short, the rainbow coalition of contemporary
critical theory. These two men (one a former United States Secretary of
Education and now President Bush's "drug czar," the other a professor at the
University of Chicago and author of "The Closing of the American Mind")
symbolize the nostalgic return to what I think of as the "antebellum esthetic
position," when men were men and men were white, when scholar-critics were
white men and when women and people of color were voiceless, faceless
servants and laborers, pouring tea and filling brandy snifters in the boardrooms
of old boys' clubs. Inevitably, these two men have come to play the roles that
George Wallace and Orville Faubus played for the civil rights movement, or
that Richard Nixon and Henry Kissinger played during Vietnam—the "feel
good" targets who, despite internal differences and contradictions, the cultural
left loves to hate.

And how tempting it is to juxtapose their "civilizing mission" to the racial
violence that has swept through our campuses since 1986—at traditionally
liberal Northern institutions such as the University of Massachusetts at
Amherst, Mount Holyoke College, Smith College, the University of Chicago,
Columbia, the University of Pennsylvania, and at Southern institutions such as
the University of Alabama, the University of Texas and the Citadel. Add to this
the fact that affirmative action programs on campus have become window
dressing operations, necessary "evils" maintained to preserve the fiction of racial
fairness and openness but deprived of the power to enforce their stated
principles. When unemployment among black youth is 40 percent, when 44
percent of black Americans can't read the front page of a newspaper, when less
than 2 percent of the faculty on campuses is black and when only 40 percent of
black students in higher education are men, well, you look for targets close at
hand.

And yet there's a real danger of localizing our grievances; of the easy
personification, assigning celebrated faces to the forces of reaction and so giving
too much credit to a few men who are really symptomatic of a larger political

current. (In a similar vein, our rhetoric sometimes depicts the high canonical as the reading matter of the power elite. You have to imagine James Baker curling up with the "Pisan Cantos," Dan Quayle leafing through "The Princess Casamassima.") Maybe our eagerness to do so reflects a certain vanity that academic cultural critics are prone to. We make dire predictions, and when they come true, we think we've changed the world.

It's a tendency that puts me in mind of my father's favorite story about Father Divine, that historic con man of the cloth. In the 1930's, he was put on trial and convicted for using the mails to defraud. At sentencing, Father Divine stood up and told the judge: I'm warning you, you send me to jail, something terrible is going to happen to you. Father Divine, of course, was sent to prison, and a week later, by sheer coincidence, the judge had a heart attack and died. When the warden and the guards found out about it in the middle of the night, they raced to Father Divine's cell and woke him up. Father Divine, they said, your judge just dropped dead of a heart attack. Without missing a beat, Father Divine lifted his head and told them: "I *hated* to do it."

As writers, teachers or intellectuals, most of us would like to claim greater efficacy for our labors than we're entitled to. These days, literary criticism likes to think of itself as "war by other means." But it should start to wonder: have its victories come too easily? The recent turn toward politics and history in literary studies has turned the analysis of texts into a marionette theater of the political, to which we bring all the passions of our real-world commitments. And that's why it is sometimes necessary to remind ourselves of the distance from the classroom to the streets. Academic critics write essays, "readings" of literature, where the bad guys (you know, racism or patriarchy) lose, where the forces of oppression are subverted by the boundless powers of irony and allegory that no prison can contain, and we glow with hard-won triumph. We pay homage to the marginalized and demonized, and it feels almost as if we've righted an actual injustice. (Academic battles are so fierce—the received wisdom has it—because so little is truly at stake.) I always think of the folk tale about the fellow who killed seven with one blow: flies, not giants.

Ours was the generation that took over buildings in the late 1960's and demanded the creation of black and women's studies programs and now, like the return of the repressed, has come back to challenge the traditional curriculum. And some of us are even attempting to redefine the canon by editing anthologies. Yet it sometimes seems that blacks are doing better in the college curriculum than they are in the streets or even on the campuses.

This is not a defeatist moan, just an acknowledgment that the relation between our critical postures and the social struggles they reflect is far from transparent. That doesn't mean there's no relation, of course, only that it's a highly mediated one. In all events, I do think we should be clear about when we've swatted a fly and when we've toppled a giant. Still, you can't expect people who spend their lives teaching literature to be dispassionate about the texts they teach; no one went into literature out of an interest in literature-in-general.

I suppose the literary canon is, in no very grand sense, the commonplace book of our shared culture, the archive of those texts and titles we wish to remember. And how else did those of us who teach literature fall in love with our subject than through our very own commonplace books, in which we inscribed secretly, as we might in a private diary, those passages of books that named for us what we had deeply felt, but could not say?

I kept mine from the age of 12, turning to it to repeat those marvelous words that named me in some private way. From H. H. Munro to Dickens and Austen, to Hugo and de Maupassant, each resonant sentence would find its way into my book. (There's no point in avoiding the narcissism here: we are always transfixed by those passages that seem to read *us*.) Finding James Baldwin and writing him down at an Episcopal church camp in 1965—I was 15, and the Watts riots were raging—probably determined the direction of my intellectual life more than anything else I could name. I wrote and rewrote verbatim his elegantly framed paragraphs, full of sentences that were somehow both Henry Jamesian and King Jamesian, garbed as they were in the figures and cadences of the spirituals. Of course, we forget the private pleasures that brought us to the subject in the first place once we adopt the alienating strategies of formal analysis; our professional vanity is to insist that the study of literature be both beauty and truth, style and politics and everything in between.

In the swaddling clothes of our academic complacencies, then, few of us are prepared when we bump against something hard, and sooner or later, we do. One of the first talks I ever gave was to a packed audience at a college honors seminar, and it was one of those mistakes you don't make twice. Fresh out of graduate school, immersed in the arcane technicalities of contemporary literary theory, I was going to deliver a crunchy structuralist analysis of a slave narrative by Frederick Douglass, tracing the intricate play of its "binary oppositions." Everything was neatly schematized, formalized, analyzed; this was my Sunday-best structuralism: crisp white shirt and shiny black shoes. And it wasn't playing. If you've seen an audience glaze over, this was double glazing. Bravely, I finished my talk and, of course, asked for questions. "Yeah, brother," said a young man in the very back of the room, breaking the silence that ensued, "all we want to know is, was Booker T. Washington an Uncle Tom or not?"

The funny thing is, this happens to be an interesting question, a lot more interesting than my talk was. It raised all the big issues about the politics of style: about what it means to speak for another, about how you were to distinguish between canny subversion and simple co-optation—who was manipulating whom? And while I didn't exactly appreciate it at the time, the exchange did draw my attention, a little rudely perhaps, to the yawning chasm between our critical discourse and the traditions they discourse upon.

Obviously, some of what I'm saying is by way of *mea culpa*, because I'm speaking here as a participant in a moment of canon formation in a so-called marginal tradition. As it happens, W. W. Norton, the "canonical" anthology publisher, will be publishing "The Norton Anthology of Afro-American

Literature." The editing of this anthology has been a great dream of mine for a long time, and it represents, in the most concrete way, the project of black canon formation. But my pursuit of this project has required me to negotiate a position between those on the cultural right who claim that black literature can have no canon, no masterpieces, and those on the cultural left who wonder why anyone wants to establish the existence of a canon, any canon, in the first place.

We face the outraged reactions of those custodians of Western culture who protest that the canon, that transparent decanter of Western values, may become—breathe the word—*politicized.* That people can maintain a straight face while they protest the irruption of politics into something that has always been political—well, it says something about how remarkably successful official literary histories have been in presenting themselves as natural objects, untainted by worldly interests.

I agree with those conservatives who have raised the alarm about our students' ignorance of history. But part of the history we need to teach has to be the history of the very idea of the "canon," which involves the history both of literary pedagogy and of the very institution of the school. One function of literary history is then to conceal all connections between institutionalized interests and the literature we remember. Pay no attention to the men behind the curtain, booms the Great Oz of literary history.

Cynthia Ozick once chastised feminists by warning that strategies become institutions. But isn't that really another way of warning that their strategies, Heaven forfend, may *succeed?*

Here we approach the scruples of those on the cultural left who worry about, well, the price of success. "Who's co-opting whom?" might be their slogan. To them, the very idea of the canon is hierarchical, patriarchal and otherwise politically suspect. They'd like us to disavow it altogether.

But history and its institutions are not just something we study, they're also something we live, and live through. And how effective and how durable our interventions in contemporary cultural politics will be depends upon our ability to mobilize the institutions that buttress and reproduce that culture. We could seclude ourselves from the real world and keep our hands clean, free from the taint of history. But that is to pay obeisance to the status quo, to the entrenched arsenal of sexual and racial authority, to say that things shouldn't change, become something other and, let's hope, better.

Indeed, this is one case where we've got to borrow a leaf from the right, which is exemplarily aware of the role of education in the reproduction of values. We must engage in this sort of canon reformation precisely because Mr. Bennett is correct: the teaching of literature *is* the teaching of values, not inherently, no, but contingently, yes; it is—it has become—the teaching of an esthetic and political order, in which no person of color, no woman, was ever able to discover the reflection or representation of his or her cultural image or voice. The return of "the" canon, the high canon of Western masterpieces, represents the return of an order in which my people were the subjugated, the voiceless, the invisible, the unpresented and the unrepresentable.

Let me be specific. Those of us working in my own tradition confront the hegemony of the Western tradition, generally, and of the larger American tradition, more locally, as we theorize about our tradition and engage in canon formation. Long after white American literature has been anthologized and canonized, and recanonized, our efforts to define a black American canon are often decried as racist, separatist, nationalist or "essentialist." Attempts to derive theories about our literary tradition from the black tradition—a tradition, I might add, that must include black vernacular forms as well as written literary forms—are often greeted by our colleagues in traditional literature departments as a misguided desire to secede from a union that only recently, and with considerable kicking and screaming, has been forged. What is *wrong* with you people? our friends ask us in genuine passion and concern; after all, aren't we all just citizens of literature here?

Well, yes and no. Every black American text must confess to a complex ancestry, one high and low (that is, literary and vernacular) but also one white and black. There can be no doubt that white texts inform and influence black texts (and vice versa), so that a thoroughly integrated canon of American literature is not only politically sound, it is intellectually sound as well. But the attempts of black scholars to define a black American canon, and to derive indigenous theories of interpretation from within this canon, are not meant to refute the soundness of these gestures of integration. Rather, it is a question of perspective, a question of emphasis. Just as we can and must cite a black text within the larger American tradition, we can and must cite it within its own tradition, a tradition not defined by a pseudoscience of racial biology, or a mystically shared essence called blackness, but by the repetition and revision of shared themes, topoi and tropes, the call and response of voices, their music and cacophony.

And this is our special legacy: what in 1849 Frederick Douglass called the "live, calm, grave, clear, pointed, warm, sweet, melodious and powerful human voice." The presence of the past in the African-American tradition comes to us most powerfully as *voice*, a voice that is never quite our own—or *only* our own—however much we want it to be. One of my earliest childhood memories tells this story clearly.

I remember my first public performance, which I gave at the age of 4 in the all-black Methodist church that my mother attended, and that her mother had attended for 50 years. It was a religious program, at which each of the children of the Sunday school was to deliver a "piece"—as the people in our church referred to a religious recitation. Mine was the couplet "Jesus was a boy like me,/ And like Him I want to be." Not much of a recitation, but then I *was* only 4. So, after weeks of practice in elocution, hair pressed and greased down, shirt starched and pants pressed, I was ready to give my piece. I remember skipping along to the church with all of the other kids, driving everyone crazy, repeating that couplet over and over: "Jesus was a boy like me,/ And like Him I want to be."

Finally we made it to the church, and it was packed—bulging and glistening with black people, eager to hear pieces, despite the fact that they had heard all of the pieces already, year after year, like bits and fragments of a repeated master text. Because I was the youngest child on the program, I was the first to go. Miss Sarah Russell (whom we called Sister Holy Ghost—behind her back, of course) started the program with a prayer, then asked if little Skippy Gates would step forward. I did so.

And then the worst happened: I completely forgot the words of my piece. Standing there, pressed and starched, just as clean as I could be, in front of just about everybody in our part of town, I could not for the life of me remember one word of that piece.

After standing there I don't know how long, struck dumb and captivated by all of those staring eyes, I heard a voice from near the back of the church proclaim, "Jesus was a boy like me,/ And like Him I want to be."

And my mother, having arisen to find my voice, smoothed her dress and sat down again. The congregation's applause lasted as long as its laughter as I crawled back to my seat.

What this moment crystallizes for me is how much of my scholarly and critical work has been an attempt to learn how to speak in the strong, compelling cadences of my mother's voice. As the black feminist scholar Hortense Spillers has recently insisted, in moving words that first occasioned this very recollection, it is "the heritage of the *mother* that the African-American male must regain as an aspect of his own personhood—the power of 'yes' to the 'female' within."

To reform core curriculums, to account for the comparable eloquence of the African, the Asian and the Middle Eastern traditions, is to begin to prepare our students for their roles as citizens of a world culture, educated through a truly human notion of "the humanities," rather than—as Mr. Bennett and Mr. Bloom would have it—as guardians at the last frontier outpost of white male Western culture, the keepers of the master's pieces. And for us as scholar-critics, learning to speak in the voice of the black mother is perhaps the ultimate challenge of producing a discourse of the Other.

What Is Style?

Knowing the Answer Can Make Your Own Life More Exciting, for Style is as Important in Living as in Literature

F. L. LUCAS

F. L. Lucas discusses the elements of style, with a personality all his own. His humor and narration make the subject appealing to an eclectic audience, as he stresses just how important our writing, with style, is in a complex modern world. Because readers stereotype *Holiday* as a travel magazine, many will be surprised to learn this essay was originally published there. But Lucas wrote this essay for a general readership, people with varied tastes and interests. (Compare James Thurber's "Which" for a totally humorous tone applied to at least one of Lucas's principles—"be sparing with relative clauses.")

Original publication: *Holiday*, March 1960.

When it was suggested to Walt Whitman that one of his works should be bound in vellum, he was outraged—"Pshaw!" he snorted, "—hangings, curtains, finger bowls, chinaware, Matthew Arnold!" And he might have been equally irritated by talk of style; for he boasted of "my barbaric yawp"—he would *not* be literary; his readers should touch not a book but a man. Yet Whitman took the pains to rewrite *Leaves of Grass* four times, and his style is unmistakable. Samuel Butler maintained that writers who bothered about their style became unreadable but he bothered about his own. "Style" has got a bad name by growing associated with precious and superior persons who, like Oscar Wilde, spend a morning putting in a comma, and the afternoon (so he said) taking it out again. But such abuse of "style" is misuse of English. For the word means merely "a way of expressing oneself, in language, manner, or appearance"; or, secondly, "a *good* way of so expressing oneself"—as when one says, "Her behavior never lacked style."

Now there is no crime in expressing oneself (though to try to *im*press oneself on others easily grows revolting or ridiculous). Indeed one cannot help expressing oneself, unless one passes one's life in a cupboard. Even the most rigid Communist, or Organization-man, is compelled by Nature to have a unique voice, unique fingerprints, unique handwriting. Even the signatures of the letters on your breakfast table may reveal more than their writers guess. There are blustering signatures that swish across the page like cornstalks bowed before a tempest. There are cryptic signatures, like a scrabble of lightning across a cloud, suggesting that behind is a lofty divinity whom all must know, or an aloof divinity whom none is worthy to know (though, as this might be highly inconvenient, a docile typist sometimes interprets the mystery in a bracket underneath). There are impetuous squiggles implying that the author is a sort of strenuous Sputnik streaking around the globe every eighty minutes. There are florid signatures, all curlicues and danglements and flamboyance, like the youthful Disraeli (though these seem rather out of fashion). There are humble, humdrum signatures. And there are also, sometimes, signatures that are courteously clear, yet mindful of a certain simple grace and artistic economy— in short, of style.

Since, then, not one of us can put pen to paper, or even open his mouth, without giving something of himself away to shrewd observers, it seems mere common sense to give the matter a little thought. Yet it does not seem very common. Ladies may take infinite pains about having style in their clothes, but many of us remain curiously indifferent about having it in our words. How many women would dream of polishing not only their nails but also their tongues? They may play freely on the perilous little organ, but they cannot often be bothered to tune it. And how many men think of improving their talk as well as their golf handicap?

No doubt strong silent men, speaking only in gruff monosyllables, may despise "mere words." No doubt the world does suffer from an endemic plague of verbal dysentery. But that, precisely, is bad style. And consider the amazing power of mere words. Adolf Hitler was a bad artist, bad statesman, bad general, and bad man. But largely because he could tune his rant, with psychological nicety, to the exact wave length of his audiences and make millions quarrelsome-drunk all at the same time by his command of windy nonsense, skilled statesmen, soldiers, scientists were blown away like chaff, and he came near to rule the world. If Sir Winston Churchill had been a mere speechifier, we might well have.lost the war; yet his speeches did quite a lot to win it.

No man was less of a literary aesthete than Benjamin Franklin; yet this tallow-chandler's son, who changed world history, regarded as "a principal means of my advancement" that pungent style which he acquired partly by working in youth over old *Spectators;* but mainly by being Benjamin Franklin. The squinting demagogue, John Wilkes, as ugly as his many sins, had yet a tongue so winning that he asked only half an hour's start (to counteract his face) against any rival for a woman's favor. "'Vote for you!" growled a surly elector in his constituency. "I'd sooner vote for the devil!" "But in case your friend should not stand . . . ?" Cleopatra, that ensnarer of world conquerors, owed less to the shape of her nose than to the charm of her tongue. Shakespeare himself has often poor plots and thin ideas; even his mastery of character has been questioned; what does remain unchallenged is his verbal magic. Men are often taken, like rabbits, by the ears. And though the tongue has no bones, it can sometimes break millions of them.

"But," the reader may grumble, "I am neither Hitler, Cleopatra, nor Shakespeare. What is all this to me?" Yet we all talk—often too much; we all have to write letters—often too many. We live not by bread alone but also by words. And not always with remarkable efficiency. Strikes, lawsuits, divorces, all sorts of public nuisance and private misery, often come just from the gaggling incompetence with which we express ourselves. Americans and British get at cross-purposes because they use the same words with different meanings. Men have been hanged on a comma in a statute. And in the valley of Balaclava a mere verbal ambiguity, about *which* guns were to be captured, sent the whole Light Brigade to futile annihilation.

Words can be more powerful, and more treacherous, than we sometimes suspect; communication more difficult than we may think. We are all serving life sentences of solitary confinement within our own bodies; like prisoners, we have, as it were, to tap in awkward code to our fellow men in their neighboring cells. Further, when A and B converse, there take part in their dialogue not two characters, as they suppose, but six. For there is A's real self—call it A_1; there is also A's picture of himself—A_2; there is also B's picture of A—A_3. And there are three corresponding personalities of B. With six characters involved even in a simple tête-à-tête, no wonder we fall into muddles and misunderstandings.

Perhaps, then, there are five main reasons for trying to gain some mastery of language:

We have no other way of understanding, informing, misinforming, or persuading one another.

Even alone, we think mainly in words; if our language is muddy, so will our thinking be.

By our handling of words we are often revealed and judged. "Has he written anything?" said Napoleon of a candidate for an appointment. "Let me see his *style*."

Without a feeling for language one remains half-blind and deaf to literature.

Our mother tongue is bettered or worsened by the way each generation uses it. Languages evolve like species. They can degenerate; just as oysters and barnacles have lost their heads. Compare ancient Greek with modern. A heavy responsibility, though often forgotten.

Why and how did I become interested in style? The main answer, I suppose, is that I was born that way. Then I was, till ten, an only child running loose in a house packed with books, and in a world (thank goodness) still undistracted by radio and television. So at three I groaned to my mother, "Oh, I *wish* I could read," and at four I read. Now travel among books is the best travel of all, and the easiest, and the cheapest. (Not that I belittle ordinary travel—which I regard as one of the three main pleasures in life.) One learns to write by reading good books, as one learns to talk by hearing good talkers. And if I have learned anything of writing, it is largely from writers like Montaigne, Dorothy Osborne, Horace Walpole, Johnson, Goldsmith, Montesquieu, Voltaire, Flaubert and Anatole France. Again, I was reared on Greek and Latin, and one can learn much from translating Homer or the Greek Anthology, Horace or Tacitus, if one is thrilled by the originals and tries, however vainly, to recapture some of that thrill English.

But at Rugby I could *not* write English essays. I believe it stupid to torment boys to write on topics that they know and care nothing about. I used to rush to the school library and cram the subject, like a python swallowing rabbits; then, still replete as a postprandial python, I would tie myself in clumsy knots to embrace those accursed themes. Bacon was wise in saying that reading makes a full man; talking, a ready one; writing, an exact one. But writing from an empty head is futule anguish.

At Cambridge, my head having grown a little fuller, I suddenly found *I could* write—not with enjoyment (it is always tearing oneself in pieces)—but fairly fluently. Then came the War of 1914–18; and though soldiers have other things than pens to handle, they learn painfully to be clear and brief. Then the late Sir Desmond MacCarthy invited me to review for the *New Statesman;* it was a useful apprenticeship, and he was delightful to work for. But I think it was well after a few years to stop; reviewers remain essential, but there are too many books one *cannot* praise, and only the pugnacious enjoy amassing enemies. By then I was an ink-addict—not because writing is much pleasure, but because not to write is pain; just as some smokers do not so much enjoy tobacco as suffer without it. The positive happiness of writing comes, I think, from work when done—decently, one hopes, and not without use—and from the letters of readers which help to reassure, or delude, one that so it is.

But one of my most vivid lessons came, I think, from service in a war department during the Second War. Then, if the matter one sent out was too wordy, the communication channels might choke; yet if it was not absolutely clear, the results might be serious. So I emerged, after six years of it, with more passion than ever for clarity and brevity, more loathing than ever for the obscure and the verbose.

For forty years at Cambridge I have tried to teach young men to write well, and have come to think it impossible. To write really well is a gift inborn; those who have it teach themselves; one can only try to help and hasten the process. After all, the uneducated sometimes express themselves far better than their "betters." In language, as in life, it is possible to be perfectly correct—and yet perfectly tedious, or odious. The illiterate last letter of the doomed Vanzetti was more moving than most professional orators; 18th Century ladies, who should have been spanked for their spelling, could yet write far better letters than most professors of English; and the talk of Synge's Irish peasants seems to me vastly more vivid than the later style of Henry James. Yet Synge averred that his characters owed far less of their eloquence to what he invented for them than to what he had overheard in the cottages of Wicklow and Kerry:

"*Christy.* 'It's little you'll think if my love's a poacher's, or an earl's itself, when you'll feel my two hands stretched around you, and I squeezing kisses on your puckered lips, till I'd feel a kind of pity for the Lord God is all ages sitting lonesome in His golden chair.'

"*Pegeen.* 'That'll be right fun, Christy Mahon, and any girl would walk her heart out before she'd meet a young man was your like for eloquence, or talk at all.' "

Well she might! It's not like that they talk in universities—more's the pity.

But though one cannot teach people to write well, one can sometimes teach them to write rather better. One can give a certain number of hints, which often seem boringly obvious—only experience shows they are not.

One can say: Beware of pronouns—they are devils. Look at even Addison, describing the type of pedant who chatters of style without having any: "Upon enquiry I found my learned friend had dined that day with Mr. Swan, the famous punster; and desiring *him* to give me some account of Mr. Swan's conversation, *he* told me that *he* generally talked in the Paronomasia, that *he* sometimes gave in to the Ploce, but that in *his* humble opinion *he* shone most in the Antanaclasis." What a sluttish muddle of *he* and *him* and *his!* It all needs rewording. Far better repeat a noun, or a name, than puzzle the reader, even for moment, with ambiguous pronouns. Thou shalt not puzzle thy reader.

Or one can say: Avoid jingles. The B.B.C. news bulletins seem compiled by earless persons, capable of crying round the globe: "The enemy is re*port*ed to have seized this im*port*ant *port*, and reinforcements are hurrying up in sup*port*." Any fool, once told, can hear such things to be insupportable.

Or one can say: Be sparing with relative clauses. Don't string them together like sausages, or jam them inside one another like Chinese boxes or the receptacles of Buddha's tooth. Or one can say: Don't flaunt jargon, like Addison's Mr. Swan, or the type of modern critic who gurgles more technical terms in a page than Johnson used in all his *Lives* or Sainte-Beuve in thirty volumes. But dozens of such snippety precepts, though they may sometimes save people from writing badly, will help them little toward writing well. Are there no general rules of a more positive kind, and of more positive use?

Perhaps. There *are* certain basic principles which seem to me observed by many authors I admire, which I think have served me and which may serve others. I am not talking of geniuses, who are a law to themselves (and do not always write a very good style, either); nor of poetry, which has different laws from prose; nor of poetic prose, like Sir Thomas Browne's or De Quincey's, which is often more akin to poetry; but of the plain prose of ordinary books and documents, letters and talk.

The writer should respect truth and himself: therefore honesty. He should respect his readers: therefore courtesy. These are two of the cornerstones of style. Confucius saw it, twenty-five centuries ago: "The Master said. The gentleman is courteous, but not pliable: common men are pliable, but not courteous."

First, honesty. In literature, as in life, one of the fundamentals is to find, and be, one's true self. One's true self may indeed be unpleasant (though one can try to better it); but a false self, sooner or later, becomes disgusting—just as a nice plain woman, painted to the eyebrows, can become horrid. In writing, in the long run, pretense does not work. As the police put it, anything you say may be used as evidence against you. If handwriting reveals character, writing reveals it still more. You cannot fool *all* your judges *all* the time.

Most style is not honest enough. Easy to say, but hard to practice. A writer may take to long words, as young men to beards—to impress. But long words, like long beards, are often the badge of charlatans. Or a writer may cultivate the obscure, to seem profound. But even carefully muddied puddles are soon fathomed. Or he may cultivate eccentricity, to seem original. But really original people do not have to think about being original—they can no more help it than they can help breathing. They do not need to dye their hair green. The fame of Meredith, Wilde or Bernard Shaw might now shine brighter, had they struggled less to be brilliant; whereas Johnson remains great, not merely because his gifts were formidable but also because, with all his prejudice and passion, he fought no less passionately to "clear his mind of cant."

Secondly, courtesy—respect for the reader. From this follow several other basic principles of style. Clarity is one. For it is boorish to make your reader rack his brains to understand. One should aim at being impossible to misunderstand—though men's capacity for misunderstanding approaches infinity. Hence Molière and Po Chu-i tried their work on their cooks; and Swift his on his menservants—"which, if they did not comprehend, he would alter and amend, until they understood it perfectly." Our bureaucrats and pundits, unfortunately, are less considerate.

Brevity is another basic principle. For it is boorish, also, to waste your reader's time. People who would not dream of stealing a penny of one's money turn not a hair at stealing hours of one's life. But that does not make them less exasperating. Therefore there is no excuse for the sort of writer who takes as long as a marching army corps to pass a given point. Besides, brevity is often more effective; the half can say more than the whole, and to imply things may strike far deeper than to state them at length. And because one is particularly apt to waste words on preambles before coming to the substance, there was sense in the Scots professor who always asked his pupils—"Did ye remember to tear up that fir-r-st page?"

Here are some instances that would only lose by lengthening:

It is useless to go to bed to save the light, if the result is twins.

—CHINESE PROVERB.

My barn is burnt down—
Nothing hides the moon.

—COMPLETE JAPANESE POEM.

Je me regrette.

—DYING WORDS OF THE GAY VICOMTESSE D'HOUDETOT.

I have seen their backs before.

—WELLINGTON, WHEN FRENCH MARSHALS TURNED
THEIR BACKS ON HIM AT A RECEPTION.

Continue until the tanks stop, then get out and walk.

—PATTON TO THE TWELFTH CORPS, HALTED FOR FUEL SUPPLIES
AT ST. DIZIER, 8/30/44.

Or there is the most laconic diplomatic note on record: when Philip of Macedon wrote to the Spartans that, if he came within their borders, he would leave not one stone of their city, they wrote back the one word—"If."

Clarity comes before even brevity. But it is a fallacy that wordiness is necessarily clearer. Metternich when he thought something he had written was obscure would simply go through it crossing out everything irrelevant. What remained, he found, often became clear. Wellington, asked to recommend three names for the post of Commander-in-Chief, India, took a piece of paper and wrote three times—"Napier." Pages could not have been clearer—or as forcible. On the other hand the lectures, and the sentences, of Coleridge became at times bewildering because his mind was often "wiggle-waggle"; just as he could not even walk straight on a path.

But clarity and brevity, though a good beginning, are only a beginning. By themselves, they may remain bare and bleak. When Calvin Coolidge, asked by his wife what the preacher had preached on, replied "Sin," and, asked what the preacher had said, replied, "He was against it," he was brief enough. But one hardly envies Mrs. Coolidge.

An attractive style requires, of course, all kinds of further gifts—such as variety, good humor, good sense, vitality, imagination. Variety means avoiding monotony of rhythm, of language, of mood. One needs to vary one's sentence length (this present article has too many short sentences; but so vast a subject grows here as cramped as a djin in a bottle); to amplify one's vocabulary; to diversify one's tone. There are books that petrify one throughout, with the rigidly pompous solemnity of an owl perched on a leafless tree. But ceaseless facetiousness can be as bad; or perpetual irony. Even the smile of Voltaire can seem at times a fixed grin, a disagreeable wrinkle. Constant peevishness is far worse, as often in Swift; even on the stage too much irritable dialogue may irritate an audience, without its knowing why.

Still more are vitality, energy, imagination gifts that must be inborn before they can be cultivated. But under the head of imagination two common devices may be mentioned that have been the making of many a style—metaphor and simile. Why such magic power should reside in simply saying, or implying, that A is like B remains a little mysterious. But even our unconscious seems to love symbols; again, language often tends to lose itself in clouds of vaporous abstraction, and simile or metaphor can bring it back to concrete solidity; and, again, such imagery can gild the gray flats of prose with sudden sun-glints of poetry.

If a foreigner may for a moment be impertinent. I admire the native gift of Americans for imagery as much as I wince at their fondness for slang. (Slang seems to me a kind of linguistic fungus: as poisonous, and as short-lived, as toadstools.) When Matthew Arnold lectured in the United States, he was likened by one newspaper to "an elderly macaw pecking at a trellis of grapes"; he observed, very justly, "How lively journalistic fancy is among the Americans!" General Grant, again, unable to hear him, remarked: "Well, wife, we've paid to see the British lion, but as we can't hear him roar, we'd better go home." By simile and metaphor, these two quotations bring before us the slightly pompous, fastidious, inaudible Arnold as no direct description could have done.

Or consider how language comes alive in the Chinese saying that lending to the feckless is "like pelting a stray dog with dumplings," or in the Arab proverb: "They came to shoe the pasha's horse, and the beetle stretched forth his leg"; in the Greek phrase for a perilous cape—"stepmother of ships"; or the Hebrew adage that "as the climbing up a sandy way is to the feet of the aged, so is a wife full of words to a quiet man"; in Shakespeare's phrase for a little England lost in the world's vastness—"in a great Poole, a Swan's-nest"; or Fuller's libel on tall men—"Ofttimes such who are built four stories high are observed to have little in their cockloft"; in Chateaubriand's "I go yawning my life"; or in Jules Renard's portrait of a cat, "well buttoned in her fur." Or, to take a modern instance, there is Churchill on dealings with Russia: "Trying to maintain good relations with a Communist is like wooing a crocodile. You do not know whether to tickle it under the chin or beat it over the head. When it opens its mouth, you cannot tell whether it is trying to smile or preparing to eat you up." What a miracle human speech can be, and how dull is most that one hears! Would one hold one's hearers, it is far less help, I suspect, to read manuals on style than to cultivate one's own imagination and imagery.

I will end with two remarks by two wise old women of the civilized 18th Century.

The first is from the blind Mme. du Deffand (the friend of Horace Walpole) to that Mlle. de Lespinasse with whom, alas, she was to quarrel so unwisely: "You must make up your mind, my queen, to live with me in the greatest truth and sincerity. You will be charming so long as you let yourself be natural, and remain without pretension and without artifice." The second is from Mme. de Charrière, the Zélide whom Boswell had once loved at Utrecht in vain, to a Swiss girl friend: "Lucinde, my clever Lucinde, while you wait for the Romeos to arrive, you have nothing better to do than become perfect. Have ideas that are clear, and expressions that are simple." (*"Ayez des idées nettes et des expressions simples."*) More than half the bad writing in the world, I believe, comes from neglecting those two very simple pieces of advice.

In many ways, no doubt, our world grows more and more complex; sputniks cannot be simple; yet how many of our complexities remain futile, how many of our artificialities false. Simplicity too can be subtle—as the straight lines of a Greek temple, like the Parthenon at Athens, are delicately curved, in order to look straighter still.

Let the Dying Die Gracefully

JUDITH H. PATERSON

Judith H. Paterson, Ph.D. in English, journalism professor, Thomas More scholar, and biographer, uses autobiography as the basis for her persuasion. In fact, through the opening narrative about several relatives, readers cannot tell exactly where the argument is going. Her use of symptoms, treatments, and references to a medical authority reinforces the argument based on her personal experiences. Since she was writing the article for distribution to newspapers throughout the country, she had to keep a general readership in mind and make it accessible to all ages, especially members of her generation. (See her review in Chapter 4 for another use of this same background information.)

Publication: *Los Angeles Times*, November 27, 1987, and other newspapers.

My father's mother, who worked as a nurse in a public sanatorium in her youth, called pneumonia "the old man's friend." By the time I was born, Grammy had become a full-time nurturer and provider of housing, food and good company to hordes of relatives and friends, children and grandchildren. The last time I saw her, she was gathering pecans in the grove behind her house and complaining about her inability to carry the heavy load she had picked.

"You know," she said, "I must be an old woman, but I don't feel like an old woman." She died in her sleep a few days later at 92.

My mother's mother suffered a few months with cancer—considered untreatable in the late 1940s—before dying of heart failure at 80. Both my grandfathers died after brief illnesses—one from influenza and the other from peritonitis caused by a ruptured appendix. Though they died young, both died with their savings, as well as their dignity, intact.

Not many people die of pneumonia anymore. In fact, it's getting harder and harder to die of anything. Modern medicine has deprived old men and women of all the friends that used to put a quick and merciful end to terminal suffering.

When my father began dying of lung cancer in 1980, he was a vigorous 68, still working full time in the wholesale florist business that had supported his family for three generations, still driving to the west coast of Mexico every summer for a vacation, still putting in long weekends on the 25 acres he had been landscaping to perfection since the 1940s.

Understanding the slim chance he had of surviving lung cancer—with or without an operation, with or without chemotherapy—he asked to forgo all treatment and live as best he could until he died. My stepmother joined his doctors in "refusing to listen to such talk." The operation that removed a lobe of his right lung brought on a stroke that left him with the shuffle of an old man, broken physically, unable to work or enjoy his family. As his body and his spirits deteriorated, medicine for heart condition, stomach ulcers, high blood pressure and depression kept him going. When the cancer reappeared, he refused a second operation, only to be kept alive for another year by repeated trips to the hospital to have oxygen, drugs and food pumped into his flagging body.

The last time I saw him, he was slumped in a wheelchair, his head too heavy for his decaying body to support. Suffering was the only human thing left to him.

At its most meaningful, death communicates something essential and establishes a final bond between the person who is leaving and those who stay behind. Approval long withheld can sometimes be expressed, sins forgiven, secrets shared, mantles passed. I have come to believe that we imperil a necessary link in the chain of human connection when we keep the body alive in a state that no longer houses the spirit.

I had all this brought home to me again last summer when I went to help my stepmother sell her house in Montgomery and move into a nursing home. She is 78 and terminally ill with emphysema and heart disease. Humiliated by the circumstances of her dying and exhausted from months of unrelenting mental and physical pain, she begs to die.

Every time death approaches, the nursing home ships her off to the hospital to be "rehabilitated" in intensive care. There I see hopeless cases kept alive for no reason. Cancer patients without hope of recovery get chemotherapy, blood transfusions, radiation. The very old lie like corpses in their beds, liquids dripping all day into limbs crisp and yellow as parchment. A social worker calls it the "ritual of prolongation." I ask "What for?" and get no answer.

Medical technology, which taught us that everything could be cured, has hurled two generations—and a whole culture—into a crisis of dying. No one saw the shadow of protracted terminal agony standing behind the bright promise of longevity. Like Tithonus in the Greek myth, we asked for everlasting life and got ever-deteriorating old age instead.

We hear a lot about the quality of living. What worries me now is the quality of dying. My parents' generation could not possibly have foreseen the multitude of health choices that have been thrust upon them. Those of us in our 40s and 50s, a generation that promises to be the longest-lived in history, are going to have to look at those choices and face what they mean. There is no way, either economically or spiritually, that we can afford to die the way our parents are dying.

When people like former Colorado Gov. Richard Lamm and medical ethicist Daniel Callahan suggest that we follow the British in limiting treatment of the old and terminally ill, knee-jerk rhetoric from all sides smothers the soul-searching public debate we need.

Somehow we are going to have to move away from a medical model for dying to a humanitarian one that accepts death as the natural end of life and helps people to die as gracefully and humanely as possible.

As the proverb goes, "God save you from living in interesting times." My generation has lived in interesting times: civil rights, women's rights, sexual liberation, Vietnam. And now this.

The activist generation has another job to do. It's time we got started.

The Heroes of Our Times

REYNOLDS PRICE

Reynolds Price, James B. Duke Professor at Duke University and novelist, states his thesis in the opening sentence: we need heroes. As a basis for his argument, he provides historical background and descriptions and classifies qualities. Ultimately, he argues that we need to re-think our demands on people to be heroes. (See Gerald Clarke's essay in this chapter for a similar thesis.)

Original publication: *Saturday Review*, December 1978.

Our need for heroes is at least as old as our need for enemies. The earliest literary texts of western civilization were propped in powerful compulsion round the names of actual men—large, honorable, and honored in proportion: Gilgamesh, Abraham, Moses, Achilles. The compulsion and its famous results continued, with few interruptions, till a hundred years ago. Tennyson's "Ode on the Death of the Duke of Wellington" and Whitman's poems on the death of Lincoln remain, oddly, the most recent in a line of heroic monuments nearly four millennia long. Where are their successors?

Maybe the pause is not odd and is in fact a break. Where after all are our epics and tragedies?—fragmented into novels and movies, ghosts of their old life-giving forms. Tennyson himself, in contemplating the Iron Duke's corpse, predicted the end—"Mourn, for to us he seems the last." Of later poets writing in English only Auden, in his elegies for Yeats and Freud, succeeded in erecting sizable and apparently durable memorials. Where are the poems on, the distinguished portraits of, the hymns to Marie Curie, Albert Einstein, Douglas MacArthur, Pablo Picasso, Franklin and Eleanor Roosevelt, Claus von Stauffenberg? Where are the odes to the three popular heroes of the recent American past—John and Robert Kennedy and Martin Luther King, Jr.? They are plainly honored in the national imagination—millions of chromos in millions of homes attest to that, and a grotesque hunger for news of their survivors (no gobbet too small or rank) continues to gorge itself. They are of course the subject of numerous memoirs, biographies, films. But is their absence from serious imaginative art only another sign of the disastrous separation of cultured life from common life; or have good writers, painters, sculptors, and composers been sensitive and responsive for years to a rising sound that is only now being widely heard?—*There are no present heroes. Most dead ones were frauds.*

An answer to the first question would lead far afield (though whatever claims are made for a national "arts explosion" can be quickly refuted by any good artist). My answer to the second is a quick yes—artists in droves have turned their backs on their ancient love and preservation of heroes. Why? Because artists of all sorts, as society's most attentive observers, began early in this century to abandon the traditional definitions of heroism and have found no equally fertilizing substitutes. The explanations, again, would be complex; but important among them are the growth of compassion for the poor and powerless (traditional heroes being mostly highborn and powerful), the backwash of revulsion after the Great War at the patent stupidity and savagery of politicians and generals, and—crucial—the steady spread by press, radio, and now television of intimate information.

It's the merciless flood of *information* that has made living heroes apparently so rare, if not invisible, and so perilous on their heights. The classical world decided wisely that any human being accorded the honors and monuments of a hero must be, above all, dead. Even with their primitive apparatus for the dissemination of news, Greeks, Romans, Jews, and early Christians saw that today's still-breathing "hero" may easily be tomorrow's criminal or fool. (The first hero of whom we possess anything approaching a full picture is King David; and if—with his womanizing, his murders and family scandals—he seems more human and interesting than Moses or Elijah, he is also proportionately less inspiring of reverence and emulation.)

By contrast, Americans in the 19th and 20th centuries have often rushed to elevate the living only to discover dark patches of fungus on the idol's face and hands—Henry Ward Beecher, Warren Harding, Richard Nixon, to name only three from a long roll of fallen. All subsequent would-be heroes have suffered from the ensuing disillusion. (It's obvious but accurate to say that President Carter and his family are unavoidably attached by the lingering spores of the Johnson-Nixon blight.) And in the past decade the dead themselves have proved alarmingly vulnerable. Posthumous allegations of sexual adventuring by Franklin Roosevelt, John and Robert Kennedy, and Martin Luther King, Jr.—men who capitalized on the public desire for immaculate family loyalty— have shaken if not toppled their shrines. In short, another human need—for unashamed praise this side idolatry—has been balked; and any parent now searching the walls of his child's room for icons of heroes is likely to find no face older than a rock star's or an athlete's, no person likely to do what he presently does throughout a lifetime.

"Alas. But ho-hum. It was always thus," you may well respond, and I'll partly concur. The cult of living heroes has always been dangerously close to adolescent crush at best and, at worst, to psychopathic craving. At the very word *hero*, a number of our minds automatically run vivid home-movies of Hitler, Mussolini, Stalin on balconies—genuine beasts borne grinning toward us on seas of faces damp with adoration. And nearer to home, most of us endured the daily televised arrival in our homes of the villainous faces of the Vietnam War—just as we continue to endure the efforts of newly skilled electronic artisans to stoke our old hungers to fever-pitch for some man or woman with no greater claim than an out-of-hand ego yearning for worship. In such a dizzying tide, surely we could relish a period of calm, admiring the admirable souls we meet in daily life but sworn off the hunt for national saviors or personal outsized templates for glamour and bravery?

I doubt we can. The need is too old, too ingrained in the kind of creature we are (slow to leave childhood and capable of love). At its purest, the need has always been our strongest lure to education; lives of great men and women *have* always reminded us we can make our lives quite literally sublime—lifted up, raised above the customary trails our nature has cut for itself through eons. And while many of us have had the early good luck to encounter and recognize heroic figures in our own homes, schools, or towns, such encounters have not often permanently satisfied the full need. The need is for figures both grand *and* distant. Why?

Partly because grandeur is best comprehended from a distance—an eye pressed to the floor of the Grand Canyon is seeing only grit. Partly because grandeur seen close often reveals beer cans, chicken bones, immortal plastic.

Mainly, though, because distance itself implies a journey—time and effort, endurance and strengthening. Hometown models have a disconcerting tendency to seem too possible and to shrink as we grow. What we want are models visible on their heights and all-but-inimitable in gifts and achievements. Tennyson at Wellington's bier defined the hope—"On God and Godlike men we build our trust." Provided that our God is merciful and just, we have always profited from real demigods who lure us up. And *up* is the catch. Illusory heroes have frequently lured us *on* if not *down*. Hence the current healthy suspicion and aversion, the falling-off in attendance at old shrines, the consequent awarding of fame and awe to pathetic instant celebrities.

But a lull is a good time to look back and forward, to brace for the next wave—bound to come. What, in an age of nearly total information, can heroes be? Can they exist at all, in any form worth noting? Must we choose them blind as romantic lovers choose—and accept them at our doors like foundlings, bane or blessing? Or may we exercise study and judgment and select what is likely to serve and last? Since I'm proposing a true fool's errand—laying down law for regions where whim has always prevailed—I'll push to a rash end and answer the questions.

Heroes must be figures whom we feel to be unnaturally charged with some force we want but seem to lack—courage, craft, intelligence, stamina, beauty —and by imaginary contact with whom we experience a transfer of the force desired. Since we require that they stand at a distance and since they no longer come to us veiled in impenetrable art, we learn of their triumphs from a press that is equally prone to discover their faults. We're lucky, therefore, when our heroes are chosen for qualities that function more or less independently of our personal sense of morality. If we admire a priest for his charity and self-sacrifice, our admiration will be shattered by news of his intricate involvement with a ring of superior call-girls. If the same revelation includes the name of an idolized professional athlete, the new light may only enhance the athlete's glamour and power (Tennyson was plainly undeterred by Wellington's parallel fame as the sexual hero of a thousand boudoirs).

Hence there's profound unconscious wisdom at work in the present mass cults for athletes, actors, musicians. Since we honor them for what we perceive as *physical* skills, the honor is not so fragile as that we bestow on peacetime rulers, clergy, doctors, lawyers, all kinds of teachers (in wartime, obviously, soldiers are honored for defensive ferocity). Brilliant performing artists *are* the safest heroes. In the current state of moral tolerance, their heroism is seriously threatened only by their health, and maybe by discovery of some involvement in the cruel exploitation of children.

Ideally then, in prevailing conditions of scrutiny, our heroes should be either dead (and judged safe) or alive but revered for strengths that are relatively amoral, though never vicious. Such a caution isn't meant to preclude the finding of large rewarding figures almost anywhere one needs to look—commerce, science, literature, fine arts, law, the military, cookery, labor, even government. It is, however, meant to define again the original core of true heroism, its first and most nearly irresistible base—the human *body* (at its strongest, boldest, most beautiful) and the deeds that flow direct from that body, broad memorable gestures on the waiting air. Few of us are agile, graceful, picturesque, or eloquent enough to be immune to the use of models who stand today in that ancient line. And luckily there's a long line of candidates—from Leontyne Price, John Travolta, and Natalia Makarova to Johnny Weismuller, Bruce Jenner, Martha Graham and on: their recorded perfection preserved from age and failure.

Yet however heroic in their different ways such names seem to me, I cannot hope to convey them intact into your pantheon. For if the recent hawking of celebrities (solid or weightless) has demonstrated their fragility as models, it has simultaneously proved the impossibility of arousing the degree of permanent excitement and admiration that is indispensable for the choice of heroes, by masses or individuals. Lasting and useful heroes *are* objects of love—love of all sorts: altruistic, erotic, passive, potentially destructive—and are chosen by levels of the mind beyond the reach of external persuasion. They may thus be either helpful or damaging, but not premeditated, interviewed, selected by cool personnel procedures. Their suddenness and mystery is precisely their power, their promise and threat. The best we can do, as we scan their dazzling faces and feel their strong pull, is to scan ourselves—to probe our own weaknesses, vacancies, and know which of them need filling and why. Then at least we can wait, informed and prepared, for the unconscious acts of choice and ardor.

It may in fact seem a bad time for heroes. Their old gleam, the old force they promised to lend us, seem genuinely and justly tarnished, worthy of suspicion. It also seems a bad time for love. There can be no question that it's always seemed so (world literature says very little else). Still the world has proved lovable year after year—though in shrinking enclaves of beauty, honesty, excellence, persistence. The chief surviving enclaves, now as always, are single human beings. The list of those whom we—at our own best—can love, serve, honor, and use as anchors in the riptides round us is surely no shorter than it's ever been. To say we lack heroes is to come dangerously close to saying we lack the capacity to love. It is certainly to say that we lack self-knowledge of our own predicament as incomplete creatures, capable of height.

The Money Chase

WILLIAM RASPBERRY

William Raspberry, nationally syndicated columnist, writes on an infinite variety of subjects for the general readership of local newspapers that print his column. Obviously, he must write for the same kind of audience Judith Paterson has in mind for "Let the

Dying Die Gracefully." This essay can also be read in conjunction with Reynolds Price's article about heroes and Susan Dentzer's exposition about M.B.A.'s learning a "human touch." Not only are the three essays on a related subject, but all were written for national newspapers and magazines.

Original publication: *The Washington Post*, June 15, 1987.

A browse of the Sunday papers turns up two texts for a sermon on ethics.

"I want to be rich, I do." That from a high school senior in a Post story on the unabashedly money-oriented goals of many bright teen-agers.

"If the only legitimate goal is maximizing personal income, then there are no ethical principles that must be obeyed." That is Lester C. Thurow, new dean of the business school at MIT, worrying in a New York Times op-ed piece over how to teach ethics to those who will lead corporate America.

Dreams of affluence are nothing new, of course. But this generation of young people, if one can extrapolate from The Post report and personal observation, may be more wealth-oriented than any before it.

Well, one might say, isn't the desire for wealth the engine that drives the capitalist system, the key to America's social and economic progress? Of course it is. But the present-day preoccupation with great wealth has produced criminal excesses, mindless money-grubbing and—Thurow's concern—the money-above-all attitude of so many young lawyers, MBAs and Wall Street operatives.

Why, we demand, aren't the law schools and business schools teaching these bright young people something of ethics? Thurow's answer is correct: graduate school is too late to teach ethics. Indeed, The Post article suggests that high school may be too late. We simply cannot legitimize the maximizing of self-interest as measured by personal income and reasonably hope to produce ethical behavior. Says Thurow:

"Individuals simply face a cost-benefit calculus where there is some probability of being punished if one is caught violating society's ethical principles. A person may obey the law because the costs of getting caught outweigh the benefits of getting away with it, but in doing so he or she is being clever or cautious, not ethical. . . . Choosing to sacrifice one's appetites and self-interest [for the good of the community] is at the heart of ethical action."

No such sacrifice is contemplated by the youngsters who declare openly that they are determined to become not well-compensated contributors to the public but merely rich.

Where do our children get such attitudes to begin with? The answer, I suspect, is: from us. And it is up to us to try to turn things around.

To do so, we must begin, long before they reach college age, to help our children focus on the kind of adults they want to become, not on how much money they hope to accumulate, nor even what fields of endeavor they hope to pursue, but on what sort of people they want to be.

We spend a lot of time talking to young people about their self image—by which we mean that we want them to feel good about themselves. Well, my experience is that an awful lot of rip-off artists and BMW-driving dope dealers feel good about themselves. What we need to do is help young people focus on self concept—the sort of people they would like to become—and help them learn to answer; responsible, respected contributors to general society.

That doesn't mean that Albert Schweitzer and Mother Teresa are the only acceptable role models. When we think of the people we truly admire, we tend to think neither of wealth nor the absence of wealth, but of the qualities that make them worthwhile individuals. Some of the people in that Post piece clearly have adopted such positive role models—for instance, the prospective physical therapist who "would rather help someone than make a lot of money." That sort of attitude, which understands the difference between "Is it legal?" and "Is it right?" is cultivated at home, not in graduate school ethics courses.

Says Thurow, "Ethics will be restored when most individuals come to the realization that they play for a common team and are willing to sacrifice self-interest for the team."

Thurow does not mean we should encourage our young people to take vows of poverty or strive for sainthood. His is the wisdom of a man who would teach our children that it is at once healthier, more worthy, and ultimately more rewarding to think less about doing well and more about doing good.

Euphemism

WILLIAM SAFIRE

William Safire, a syndicated columnist, has for years been writing a "language column" created by and for *The New York Times Magazine.* In "The Great Permitter," printed as the introduction to a collection of his columns, Safire establishes the purposes of the column and describes the "legion of language lovers" who compose his audience: "Who are the Great Permitters? We are the people who care about clarity and precision, who detest fuzziness of expression that reveals sloppiness or laziness of thought. . . . I'm one. If you've read this far and are prepared to go further, you're one. We live the life of the mindful, and we intend each utterance to say a mouthful. We are no fuddy-duddies: If we want to carefully and deliberately split an infinitive, we do so with zest, knowing that the most fun in breaking a rule is in knowing what rule you're breaking." Perhaps he is describing the readers most of us seek.

And he proceeds to prove, through a series of examples that the euphemism is alive and well (the Great Permitter allows the use of an occasional cliché).

Published in *On Language*. New York: Avon, 1981.

T he art of euphemism—refusing to use painful words like "dying"—has not passed away.

At Harvard's Graduate School of Business Administration, Professor Howard Raiffa teaches a course in Competitive Decision Making that realistically faces up to a negotiator's need to lie: Students must realize, instructs Professor Raiffa, that occasions will arise when they will be particularly vulnerable if they honestly reveal information that could be exploited by less scrupulous adversaries. The name he has adopted for one option to be considered when bluffing, or misleading, seems called for is "strategic misrepresentation," which the earliest residents of this continent called "speaking with forked tongue" and which we honestly call "lying."

To some degree, euphemism is strategic misrepresentation. A few years ago, I wrote a column which contained what a State Department spokesman denounced as a "contemptuous lie." (He meant "contemptible," and, when corrected, growled, "That, too.") Henry Kissinger, who was Secretary of State at that time, was more restrained in his public reaction; he called it "a canard." As one who smacks his lips over *canard rôti à l'orange*, I wondered why the French word for duck—*canard*—means lie or great hoax. A nervous man at State's French desk, who kept saying he did not want to get involved, explained that the original expression was *vendre un canard à moitié*, "to half-sell a duck"—that is, to pretend to sell it with intent to cheat. In English, though, "canard" has come to mean "lie"; it carries an overtone of tall story that euphemistically takes much of the sting out of such an accusation.

A Park Ranger in the Grand Canyon has an assignment to kill the wild burros who eat the scrub and cause erosion. Just as C.I.A. operatives used "termination with extreme prejudice" to describe liquidation, itself a euphemism for "assassination," the Park Service calls it necessary intercession with natural ecology "direct reduction." "Are you going to kill the burros?" asked a CBS reporter. "Well, sir, we call it 'direct reduction.' " Calling this to my attention, newsman Michael Winship wonders: "What do you suppose *indirect* reduction of burros constitutes? Birth-control lectures?" (Birth control, by the way, is not a euphemism; it is a more understandable term for contraception.) Another reader, David Silberstein of Connecticut, suggests that the next euphemism for "birth control" will be "evading the issue."

The best new advertising sweetener was sent in by editorial writer Harold Lavine of *The Arizona Republic:* "There is a used-car dealer on Camelback Road in Phoenix who sells 'pre-owned Cadillacs.' " This usage, which eschews "used," can also be heard hawking a previously owned Mercedes in Maryland. Cheap cars become used; expensive cars become previously owned. (Would you buy a previously owned car from this candidate?)

"Sweeten," ironically, is a word advertisers are shying away from in these drying times. An apple-juice manufacturer who adds a sweetener to his product has rejected "sweetened" in favor of a new participle: "sophisticated." Apple juice is less tart when it has been sophisticated by a ton of sugar.

The most significant euphemism of the year was introduced into the field that understands opinion-molding best: public relations. That phrase was coined by Ivy Lee, who burnished John D. Rockefeller's image; it was shaped into "public relations counsel" by Edward L. Bernays, who detested "press agent," and was replaced in the military by "public information," which seemed less manipulative; it has been further euphemized into "public affairs" and "corporate communications."

Comes now the Environmental Protection Agency (populated by what used to be called "conservationists") to comb its flacks in a new and far more other-directed way: the Office of Public Awareness. "There's been a tendency to P.R. the public," explained Joan Nicholson, director and namer of the office, who uses the initials of "public relations" as a pejorative verb, "about how groovy the agency is. I wanted to somehow signal the public that we were wanting to hear from them. . . ." Evidently public awareness is an offshoot of what used to be called "outreach" until it was hooted out of existence, and will one day be followed by an Office of Public Sympathy, headed by a chaplain handing out punchable cards.

Miss Nicholson ought to be made publicly aware that few people use "groovy" anymore. Also, please be aware that calling a flack an awarenik denigrates the pervasive function of public relations, sophisticating a previously owned expression to the point of strategic misrepresentation.

The Decline of Editing

Or Why Are People Asking Whom's Minding the Store?

R. Z. SHEPPARD, reported by
JOHN M. SCOTT and JANICE C. SIMPSON

R. Z. Sheppard, senior writer for *Time*, states the problem in his title and asks about responsibility in his subtitle, with its intentional error. He then proves there is a problem by quoting passages from best-selling writers. About one-third of the way into the article, after commenting on the responsibility of authors (note names of authors that appear elsewhere in this collection), Sheppard answers the question by pointing to the editors. But financial pressures on authors and editors result in some of the sloppy work. Finally, after some exposition about the "top" editors, he urges them to "keep the faith." So how does the readership of *Time* fit into the audience? Are we to add our voices to his in urging the editors—and authors—"to mind the store"?

Original publication: *Time*, September 1, 1980.

The book was No. 1—in everything but prose. *Thy Neighbor's Wife* may appeal to the prurient, the innocent and the curious, but it dismays anyone devoted to English. It hardly corrupts the reader's morals, as some critics have charged, but it may help corrupt his language. The work, eight years in the making, publicized like a space shot, high on the charts, frequently reads as if translated from the Albanian: "This was when Jim Buckley met Al Goldstein, whose spy piece he helped to edit, and whose expressed frustrations he not only identified with but saw as the compatible essence of a viable partnership—or at least some hedge against the probability that neither of them could ever make it alone."

The book is littered with grammatical outrage and wrong usage. "After completing high school in 1949, his sister wrote that she had arranged for him an appointment to Annapolis." It is of course the brother, not the sister, who completed high school in 1949. The same type of mistake sprouts throughout the text; one must finally conclude that the author does not know what a dangling modifier is.

Talese writes that "Bullaro would sometimes peddle alone for fifteen miles." But Bullaro is not selling something; he is a man pedaling a bicycle. The author repeats himself, achieving a sort of tautologous stammer: "What would prove to be decisive in her decision," or the "hearing would not be heard for at least another hour." Plurals and singulars confound him: "Men who noticed that their wives aroused other men became in many cases aroused by her themselves." He confuses *foreboding* with *forbearance*, uses *interfaith* for the opposite, *intrafaith*, and misapplies *who, whom, which* and *that* with abandon.

All this is particularly odd because, unlike many writers who make the talk-show circuit, Talese is an old pro. He earned his reputation with cleanly written magazine articles and *The Kingdom and the Power*, a bestselling dissection of the New York *Times*. His wife Nan Talese, a highly respected senior editor at Simon & Schuster, went over the manuscript before it was sent to Betty Prashker, a top editor at Doubleday, which publishes Talese. Prashker says that Talese was not thin-skinned about taking editorial advice, but adds enigmatically: "Grammar is not etched in marble." Perhaps not; neither should it be polymorphously perverse.

The anything-goes school of writing is exemplified by other recent bestsellers: Judith Krantz's *Princess Daisy*, Robert Ludlum's *The Bourne Identity*, Alvin Toffler's *The Third Wave* or Bob Woodward and Scott Armstrong's *The Brethren*. Like Talese, Woodward and Armstrong are not only verbose but fond of dangling their modifiers and splitting their infinitives. Toffler specializes in hyperbolic jargon: "Vast changes in the techno-sphere and the info-sphere have converged to change the way we make goods. We are moving rapidly beyond traditional mass production to a sophisticated mix of mass and demassified products . . . made with wholistic, continuous-flow processes." Krantz goes for grand howlers: "Thank heaven they'd all be in their staterooms, intently adjusting their resort dinner clothes, caparisoned for the delectation of each other."

Not only the bestsellers offer lessons on how not to write. John Simon, sardonic critic and author of *Paradigms Lost: Reflections on Literacy and Its Decline*, notes that grammatical blunders are showing up more frequently even in the scholarly books of university presses. Most readers are sophisticated enough to know that the best writers suffer lapses. But readers are beginning to wonder why so many mistakes remain, like chiggers, in the texts. Who—definitely not whom—is minding the storehouse of language?

The answer: editors, who are, after authors, the most important figures in the literary world. They are also the most anonymous. Thirty-three years after his death, at 62, the most famous book editor remains Maxwell Perkins, the legendary guide of Hemingway, Fitzgerald and Thomas Wolfe. Today there are a handful of editorial celebrities: Knopf's Robert Gottlieb, an outstanding bookman, put the title *Catch-22* on Joseph Heller's first novel. Today he enjoys a recognition rarely found in publishing. Readers across the country know Michael Korda as the author of *Power* and *Charmed Lives* although few outside the business recognize him as editor in chief of Simon & Schuster. But the vast majority of editors are unknown and not very well paid. Editorial assistants usually start at about $200 a week, and a senior editor earns $30,000 to $40,000 a year.

Bookmen do not entirely agree on the current state of editing, but most concede there has been a decline in standards. Little, Brown's Genevieve Young theorizes: "Something really happened in the 1960s. People forgot how to spell, didn't recognize run-on sentences. I gather it was considered elitist to teach proper English in some places." Agrees Maron Waxman of Macmillan: "You get people coming out of top-rated schools who don't know how to put a sentence together. That's got to affect copy editing." Knopf's Gottlieb takes a more defensive view: "There has always been garbage. There happens to be a spate of it at the moment, but I don't know if you can blame editors in particular."

This cup of responsibility passes over desktops, lunch tables and beach blankets at the Hamptons, literary Manhattan's summer capital. The most frequently mentioned culprit is financial pressure. Business was rosy during the '60s, when the Federal Government poured money into textbooks, which indirectly supported publishers' general lists. The counter-culture, the civil rights and antiwar movements produced dozens of new writers, whose books were eagerly snapped up by affluent armchair guerrillas. Attracted by profit potential, conglomerates bought most of the major publishing houses, giving them much needed capital and managers who could read the bottom line.

Today the bottom line is in danger, and the harsh facts of economic life have become the rude facts of literary life. Inflation pushes up the cost of paper, printing and distribution; recession makes buyers think twice about purchasing a book for $12.95, almost three times the cost ten years ago. Adult trade book orders were down in 1979 to $831.1 million, from $940.5 million in 1978.

Critics of conglomerates argue, without conclusive evidence, that it is now harder to get serious, noncommercial books published. Yet excellent work is still published by conglomerate-owned houses, notably Knopf, a subsidiary of Random House, which in turn is owned by Newhouse Publications; badly written, poorly edited work still pours forth from privately owned houses— Doubleday, for example. A more justified complaint is that the huge bookstore chains, B. Dalton and Waldenbooks, give limited shelf space to titles with less than mass appeal.

The traditional view of publishing as a leisurely life, carried on in mahogany offices and posh resturants, has been replaced by the harrowing vision of a rat race on a roulette table. With the literary agent acting as croupier, editors must frantically get their bets down on potential bestsellers. Says Viking's Alan Williams: "If Maxwell Perkins were around today, he wouldn't have time to be Maxwell Perkins. He would not be able to sit at Scribner's and have wonderful authors turn up in the morning mail. He would be out grubbing with the rest of us, cozening agents and trying to get onto books earlier and wondering how much money to bid." Adds Georges Borchardt, an agent whose clients include John Gardner, Stanley Elkin and Kate Millett: "The facilities offered by publishers to the artists have declined. Editors who would be capable of editing are not allowed to. They have people breathing down their backs, asking,

'Where is the new bestseller?" and 'Why are you spending so much time on this poor-selling author?' even though he may in time become another James Joyce."

There are, of course, various types of editors in the game. At one extreme are the acquisition editors—"belly editors," in trade jargon—who do their most important work at lunch. There the menu and the contract may get a more careful reading than the manuscript. Then there are the creative editors, who see their task as the finding and overall shaping of a manuscript. Finally, there are the pencil editors, who work line by line on messy or complex manuscripts (although that chore is often left to copyreaders).

All these tasks usually overlap. Most acquisition editors must be adept with the pencil as well as the fork. And they must not only coax a blocked author into action, but also negotiate with copyreaders, handle the details of jacket design and flap copy, and send galleys out to well-known writers in the hope they will respond with enthusiastic blurbs. Once such jobs are completed, editors must become in-house cheerleaders, urging their publicity, advertising and sales departments to make an extra effort on behalf of their books. The average editor is doing all this on at least a dozen books at a time. These are busy operatives with a built-in dilemma. Houghton Mifflin's Jonathan Galassi sees the editor as a double agent. "With the writer, he is collaborator, psychiatrist, confessor and amanuensis; in the publishing house, he must be politician, diplomat, mediator."

The pressure on the publishing assembly line is increasing. Trendy books on jogging, herbal medicine and biofeedback must be out by the cash register before the next craze sends them to the remaindered pile. Novels with big advances behind them have to be whizzed through so the publisher can get back his investment. The results are faster production deadlines and more work for fewer people. Says Putnam Editor Faith Sale: "Books on tight schedules are proofread in hunks by different people, and in some cases copy editing is done the same way." This may not affect grammar and spelling, but it can create inconsistencies: a character who enters a room wearing a blue dress and leaves wearing a red one.

In such a frenzied atmosphere, the word *book* may give way in favor of *project, package, hot property* and *blockbuster*. Even editors of noncommercial novels and belles-lettres feel the pressures to score with a Merv missile, a work that will get its author on a TV talk show, the most powerful selling medium of all. Smaller implements, like sharp blue pencils, are often disregarded.

Devotees of Strunk's *Elements of Style* may still keep the faith that good prose is not only clear but also concise. The trouble is that prolixity pays. Publishers can charge more for fat books. Says Journalist John McPhee, whose work has the finish of fine carpentry: "There are a lot of books around that smell of the tape recorder. Writing is so difficult that if a writer is looking at words on paper, say the transcript of a tape recording, it's damn difficult to resist them. So a lot of books go on too long because he recorded too much."

For this sin, as for other literary offenses, writers should bear the most blame. Editors who are criticized for poor books frequently reply, "You should have seen the first draft." Sometimes untold hours are spent just to make the semiliterate printable. Editors may hold back because cutting an author's prose means nicking a famous ego. It is a matter of author awe. Confesses Little, Brown's Young: "There is more hesitation about messing around with prose when you have a writer like Norman Mailer, Gay Talese, Herman Wouk, or a great man in another field like Henry Kissinger. I have a tendency to suggest things mildly, and if he doesn't listen I let it go." TIME asked a sampling of writers, editors and agents to name recent books that needed more editing. High on their lists were William Styron's *Sophie's Choice*, Mailer's *Executioner's Song*, Heller's *Good as Gold*, David Halberstam's *The Powers That Be* and, of course, Talese's book.

Self-regard can be even more rampant among newly successful writers who view their own crudities as an inviolate form of personal expression. But veteran best-selling Novelist Irving Wallace says: "Publishing houses bid now for books at auctions, and they often spend $1 million or $2 million for a book. The result is often unfortunate: words an author has written tend to become frozen on the tablet. I have heard friends say, 'Why should I change anything in my book? Look what they paid for it: it must be good!' "

Despite all these pressures, not every editor is too harried, and not every author is resistant to suggestions and demands. Here are two stories of good editors whose efforts resulted in good books:

Jonathan Coleman, 28, is the youngest senior editor at Simon & Schuster. The newly published *Changing of the Guard* is his project. He arrived at the firm three years ago, after working at Knopf as a $220-a-week publicist. During that time, he had met David Broder, the Washington *Post* journalist.

Coleman's interest began after he read a newspaper series that Broder had written about Congressmen who had been elected for the first time after Watergate. The editor got the columnist to talk about how these new faces in Washington differed in background and interests from their older colleagues. The more Broder talked, the more Coleman was convinced he had the makings of a book.

Simon & Schuster's editorial board thought so too. They gave Broder a $40,000 advance on the basis of an eight-page outline covered by a rousing memo from Coleman. The editor's immediate problems: the book had to be ready for the 1980 presidential elections, and Broder had to meet the deadline while holding his time-consuming job as a journalist. Coleman kept the pressure on with phone calls every week. Chapters and suggestions circulated through the mails, and an entire draft was completed just after Labor Day, 1979. Coleman read it and a few weeks later checked into Washington's Jefferson Hotel, where for a week of 18-hour days he and Broder went over the manuscript line by line. "His fingerprints are on every damn sentence," says the columnist with appreciation. "This book is as much Jonathan Coleman's as it is mine."

The less visible prints on the 884-page manuscript belong to Lynn Chalmers, one of twelve staff copy editors at Simon & Schuster. It normally takes about a month to copyread a book, but Chalmers completed the job in two weeks. She corrected punctuation, broke long segments into paragraphs, and checked facts. Inconsistencies were flagged on strips of pink paper and attached to the offending pages.

Michael di Capua, 42, is among the most respected literary editors in the business. For the past 14 years he has been with Farrar, Straus and Giroux, one of the last major independent houses in New York, where things do not appear to be as rushed as at other firms. Its authors include Isaac Bashevis Singer, Philip Roth, Tom Wolfe and Susan Sontag. Di Capua has edited such acclaimed writers as Larry Woiwode and Michael Arlen. A major project now is the result of one man's highly unusual childhood. *Twelve Years: An American Boyhood in East Germany* is a forthcoming memoir by Joel Agee, son of the late film critic and novelist James Agee. In 1941, Agee and his wife Alma divorced. She took Joel, then a year old, to live in Mexico, where she met and married Bodo Uhse, a Communist novelist and fugitive from Nazism. After the war the family went to East Germany, where Joel lived for twelve years.

Di Capua's acquisition technique was quite different from Coleman's go-go methods. In 1975, the Farrar, Straus editor read Agee's article-length account of his East German childhood in *The New Yorker*. Recalls Di Capua: "I thought, 'I've got to do something about this.' I tore it out and put it in a pile of things to do. But all editors are overworked and I never got to it."

Agent Claire Smith of the Harold Ober agency rekindled Di Capua's interest about a year later. He received a fast O.K. from his editorial board and a $5,000 advance for his new author. Says the editor: "We don't write memos. Who has time? Basically we say to each other, 'I've got this and I think it's great,' or 'I've got this thing by a big name but I think it's awful, and I'm going to turn it down unless someone objects.' "

Agee went off to write at his own pace. When the manuscript arrived last summer, the editor began his real work. He and Agee sat down and went over every paragraph. Explains Di Capua: "My method is to read a book over and over again at every stage until there is nothing that bothers me and I can read it through without stopping." For Agee, the experience marked that point where the craft of editing becomes an art: "Di Capua felt himself into my intentions. At no point did I have the feeling that he was imposing himself into the work."

Examples like these are heartening, but there are still too many books that prompt people like Di Capua to wonder what ever happened to good writing. Literacy continues in its parlous state. Standards decline as the difference between the formalities of written language and the informalities of the spoken word blur. Schools neglect the rigors of grammar, and the last generation that can parse a sentence is dying off.

The world is full of tempting distractions: travel, entertainments, sports, the pervasive din of popular music. People read less decent prose and watch and listen to more TV. When Howard Cosell says *commentation* for *comment*, he is heard by millions of Americans who may not know the difference. The word could become a neologism, like *profitability* and *futurability*, and seep into the language. The fight against the misuse of "hopefully" (for "I hope") is just about lost, and even otherwise literate people keep speaking of the "media" in the singular.

Linguists may argue that English has grown in just this way. Purists grumble about pollution of the mother tongue. The dispute has raged ever since Shakespeare's pedant Holofernes railed against the "rackers of orthography" in *Love's Labour's Lost*. Dr. Johnson's and Mr. Webster's dictionaries have spurred sharp debate. But the disputants have usually known their grammar; they were aware of the necessity for rules. Proper usage matters because writing is thought and clear writing is essential for clear thinking.

Editors must keep this faith even though few will appreciate their efforts. As Critic Dwight Macdonald wrote nearly 20 years ago: "If nine-tenths of the citizens of the United States, including a recent President, were to use *inviduous*, the one-tenth who clung to *invidious* would still be right, and they would be doing a favor to the majority if they continued to maintain the point."

Don't They Know Education Takes Evil Out of Evolution?

DAPHNE SIMPKINS

Daphne Simpkins, freelance writer, writes about the emotional controversy of evolution versus creationism. In a balanced discussion, she denounces both sides as she argues for a meeting, a reconciliation between the two opponents. In the tradition of H. L. Mencken (see his review of Warren G. Harding's inaugural address in Chapter 4), she not only attacks the two sides of this controversy, but also throws a few barbs at other targets—education, science, religion, politics.

Since her audience is a newspaper readership, she realizes the task she faces. Thus, in an effort to educate readers, she provides a history of the theory of evolution before they know where the essay is leading and quit reading, making them *think* even if she cannot *persuade* them.

Original publication: *The Atlanta Journal-Constitution*, August 6, 1989.

F̲ew words in our culture rile people more than the word "evolution." Pronounced by early creationist William Jennings Bryan during the Scopes trial as "evil-ution," the scientific theory that life evolves has been under suspicion for at least the last 64 years.

The theory of evolution gained its negative notoriety by appearing early in its genesis to be unreconcilable with the biblical account of creation. The taint of blasphemy would spark years of legislation.

Perhaps the most famous anti-evolution law was written by John Washington Butler in Tennessee on the occasion of his 49th birthday, after he heard a tale about a girl who had gone off to college and come home with her faith in the Bible severely shaken. Butler wrote the law that made teaching evolution a crime in the state public schools in order to protect the minds of future fledgling saints.

Butler's was an honorable endeavor, written in pure conscience, passed easily by both houses of the Legislature and signed by the governor. Later on, most of the Tennessee lawmakers who had supported the bill claimed they had done so for political reasons—none of them thought that anything drastic would ever come of a goodwill bill like Butler's.

All those good old boys were wrong.

As recently as last March, the state of Texas was still debating whether evolution should be mentioned in its 1991 textbooks. Twenty-one other states that have the right to dictate the editorial content of public school textbooks are still wary of evolution being taught in schools. When it is taught anywhere, it is often presented so sketchily as to be impossible to understand.

To counter this epidemic of scientific illiteracy, the National Center for Science Education was founded in California in the early 1980s. There are chapters in all 50 states. Its goal is to promote the proper teaching of science, particularly evolution. The center's ideological adversary is the National Institute for Creationism, also located in California.

There is some doubt in my mind as to whether both sides of the science-religion debate would actually like to reconcile. After all, this windy conflict has won some politicians a lot of votes, been the fodder for many a crowd-pleasing sermon and sparked a lot of tourism to California, Texas, Tennessee and Arkansas, where, yes, there was a Scopes II trial in 1981. But nothing much new or illuminating has been contributed toward squaring the creation story found in Genesis with the theory of evolution.

The scientists have little patience for anything that can't be measured or seen. (A scientist involved in the textbook debate in Texas told me that he wouldn't dignify the creationist argument by rebutting it!) And the creationists scorn any aspect of science that has a reputation for undermining a literal reading of Scripture. (Only last month, a church in Alabama posted a message: "Evolution is a lie.")

The viewpoints presently being espoused by both sides for public consumption are disappointingly trite, often snide and significantly less enlightening than the original dialogue that took place between two champion orators in the sleepy town of Dayton, Tenn., in July 1925.

Forget for a Moment 'Inherit the Wind'

Put aside what you remember about the Scopes Monkey Trial from the 1960 movie, "Inherit the Wind," which starred Spencer Tracy as a fictionalized Clarence Darrow and Frederic March as William Jennings Bryan, the Bible-thumping fundamentalist.

Picture instead a charming rural village just 30 miles from Chattanooga in the foothills of the Cumberland Mountains and some young, forward-thinking businessmen who were worried about the depressed economy. Sitting in the drugstore across from the Rhea County courthouse, they planned to take advantage of the American Civil Liberties Union's offer to pay for the legal defense of any schoolteacher willing to test Butler's bill, which declared that evolution could not be taught in the Tennessee public schools. They thought that a controversial trial like that would bring in a tourist trade—be good for Dayton's economy.

This time the good old boys were right.

Tourists continue to detour through Dayton, Tenn., and visit the place where Darwin got his courtroom comeuppance. Interest is so keen that the Scopes trial has been staged for the past two years and promises to become an annual tourist draw.

Unlike the newspaper essayist H. L. Mencken, who mercilessly ravaged Bryan's performance at the 1925 trial, I admire Bryan for taking Darrow's challenge in the middle of a July heat wave. But the thrice-defeated presidential aspirant miscalculated the strength of Darrow's argument and failed miserably to answer the now notorious 50 questions designed by Darrow to prove Genesis an inadequate explanation of creation.

"I am more interested in the Rock of Ages than in the age of rocks," Bryan orated over and over again.

There Are Other Chapters, Other Verses

Too bad that in one feeble, worn-out retort, Bryan set a precedent of martyrdom for creationists to follow—implied that rhetoric, if shouted long and loud, could substitute for thought. Bryan's example misled later advocates of creationism into believing that good intentions and state laws written out of pure conscience are an adequate rebuttal to an intelligent cross-examination.

Ironically, I never feel very free in Sunday school. It isn't a comfortable place to ask open-ended questions. No one encourages that heresy called curiosity, and I've never understood why not.

Education could take the evil out of evolution. It would solve the problem of children going off to college and coming home with their faith shaken by new ideas if those new ideas could first be confronted in an environment where the

Bible is consulted. I've never felt that Jesus prohibits the following of one's curiosity. "What do you seek?" is the first sentence attributed to Christ in the Gospel of John. His next sentence is an invitation: "Come and see."

I don't know why we can't do that in Sunday school.

What is so frustrating in this never-ending dialogue is that the traditional defense of using Genesis as the account of the creation of life is not the only choice in the Bible. There are other chapters and verses that deal with the nature of time, and they would have made even the fleet-of-mind Clarence Darrow pause and marvel. But these passages can make obsolete the need to prove evolutionists wrong, a temptation that creationists find unable to resist.

I wonder why Christians, who believe in Christ as the word incarnate, are so often afraid of words like evolution and education. And why isn't the biblical concept of spiritual evolution—known as sanctification—ever considered, compared and contrasted to the nature of evolution?

On the other hand, scientists often shrug off experiences of faith with an insulting ease, agreeing with Darrow that any reported encounter with God is a manifestation of a psychological disorder. That judgment dismisses a lot of people as crazy. One might just as well discount the abstract experiences of many other people: a musician's interpretation of harmony, an artist's rendering of symmetry, a poet's vision of the eternal.

There must be some meeting place besides the courtroom where scientists and creationists can meet. It appears to me that a proper place to discuss evolution would be in Sunday school, where reconciliation is preached and where the truth should ideally set you free.

Which

JAMES THURBER

James Thurber's approach to any subject is humor or satire or both. So he has a good time doing what he is attacking, thus proving his point. What reader can refute a point so cleverly demonstrated?

Original publication: *The New Yorker* May 4, 1929; collected in *The Owl in the Attic*. New York: Blue Ribbon Books, 1936.

The relative pronoun "which" can cause more trouble than any other word, if recklessly used. Foolhardy persons sometimes get lost in which-clauses and are never heard of again. My distinguished contemporary, Fowler, cites several tragic cases, of which the following is one: "It was rumoured that Beaconsfield intended opening the Conference with a speech in French, his pronunciation of which language leaving everything to be desired . . ." That's as much as Mr. Fowler quotes because, at his age, he was afraid to go any farther. The young man who originally got into that sentence was never found. His fate, however, was not as terrible as that of another adventurer who became involved in a remarkable which-mire. Fowler has followed his devious course as far as he safely could on foot: "Surely what applies to games should also apply to racing, the leaders of which being the very people from whom an example might well be looked for . . ." Not even Henry James could have successfully emerged from a sentence with "which," "whom," and "being" in it. The safest way to avoid such things is to follow in the path of the American author, Ernest Hemingway. In his youth he was trapped in a which-clause one time and barely escaped with his mind. He was going along on solid ground until he got into this: "It was the one thing of which, being very much afraid—for whom has not been warned to fear such things—he . . ." Being a young and powerfully built man, Hemingway was able to fight his way back to where he had started, and begin again. This time he skirted the treacherous morass in this way: "He was afraid of one thing. This was the one thing. He had been warned to fear such things. Everybody has been warned to fear such things." Today Hemingway is alive and well, and many happy writers are following along the trail he blazed.

What most people don't realize is that one "which" leads to another. Trying to cross a paragraph by leaping from "which" to "which" is like Eliza crossing the ice. The danger is in missing a "which" and falling in. A case in point is this: "He went up to a pew which was in the gallery, which brought him under a colored window which he loved and always quieted his spirit." The writer, worn out, missed the last "which"—the one that should come just before "always" in that sentence. But supposing he had got it in! We would have: "He went up to a pew which was in the gallery, which brought him under a colored window which he loved and which always quieted his spirit." Your inveterate whicher in this way gives the effect of tweeting like a bird or walking with a crutch, and is not welcome in the best company.

It is well to remember that one "which" leads to two and that two "whiches" multiply like rabbits. You should never start out with the idea that you can get by with one "which." Suddenly they are all around you. Take a sentence like this: "It imposes a problem which we either solve, or perish." On a hot night, or after a hard day's work, a man often lets himself get by with a monstrosity like that, but suppose he dictates that sentence bright and early in the morning. It comes to him typed out by his stenographer and he instantly senses that something is the matter with it. He tries to reconstruct the sentence, still clinging to the "which," and gets something like this: "It imposes a problem which we either solve, or which, failing to solve, we must perish on account of." He goes to the water-cooler, gets a drink, sharpens his pencil, and grimly tries again. "It imposes a problem which we either solve or which we don't solve and . . ." He begins once more: "It imposes a problem which we either solve, or which we do not solve, and from which . . ." The more times he does it the more "whiches" he gets. The way out is simple. "We must either solve this problem, or perish." Never monkey with "which." Nothing except getting tangled up in a typewriter ribbon is worse.

Organic Architecture

FRANK LLOYD WRIGHT

Frank Lloyd Wright is best known for his architectural designs, but he also wrote extensively about his field. Here he makes his case for a blending of the building and its landscape in language that the lay readership of *Common Sense* could understand. He writes authoritatively in the first person, addressing his readers directly in the second person. And he does not hesitate to offend some, specifically the builders, whom he calls "an inebriate lot of criminals." He also criticizes education, capitalism, and even elements of his own field.

Original publication: *Common Sense* [later merged with *American Mercury*], April 1941.

The typical American dwelling of 1893 was crowding in upon itself all over the Chicago prairies as I used to go home from my work with Adler and Sullivan in Chicago to Oak Park, a Chicago suburb. That dwelling had somehow become typical American architecture but by any faith in nature implicit or explicit it did not belong anywhere. I was in my sixth year with Adler and Sullivan then, and they had completed the Wainwright Building in St. Louis, the first expression of the skyscraper as a *tall* building. But after building the great Auditorium the firm did not build residences because they got in the way of larger, more important work. I had taken over dwellings, Mr. Sullivan's own house among them, whenever a client came to them for a house. The Charnley house was done in this way. I longed for a chance to build a sensible house and (1893) soon free to build one, I furnished an office in the Schiller Building and began my own practice of architecture. The first real chance came by way of Herman Winslow for client. I was not the only one then sick of hypocrisy and hungry for reality. Winslow was something of an artist himself, sick of it all.

What was the matter with this typical American house? Well just for an honest beginning it lied about everything. It had no sense of unity at all nor any such sense of space as should belong to a free people. It was stuck up in thoughtless fashion. It had no more sense of earth than a "modernistic" house. And it was stuck up on wherever it happened to be. To take any one of those so-called "homes" away would have improved the landscape and helped to clear the atmosphere. The thing was more a hive than a home just as "modernistic" houses are more boxes than houses. But these "homes" were very like the home Americans were making for themselves elsewhere, all over their new country.

Nor, where the human being was concerned, had this *typical* dwelling any appropriate sense of proportion whatever. It began somewhere way down in the wet and ended as high up as it could get in the high and narrow. All materials looked alike to it or to anything or anybody in it. Essentially, were it wood or brick or stone, this "house" was a bedeviled box with a fussy lid: a complex box that had to be cut up by all kinds of holes made in it to let in light and air, with an especially ugly hole to go in and out of. The holes were all "trimmed"; the doors and windows themselves trimmed; the roofs trimmed; the walls trimmed. Architecture seemed to consist in what was done to these holes. "Joinery" everywhere reigned supreme in the pattern and as the soul of it all. Floors were the only part of the house left plain after "Queen Anne" had swept past. The "joiner" recommended "parquetry" but usually the housewife and the fashionable decorator covered these surfaces down under foot with a tangled rug collection because otherwise the floors would be "bare." They were "bare" only because one could not very well walk on jig-sawing or turned spindles or plaster ornament. This last limitation must have seemed somehow unkind.

The Escapists

It is not too much to say that as a young architect, by inheritance and training a radical, my lot was cast with an inebriate lot of criminals called builders; sinners hardened by habit against every human significance except one, vulgarity. The one touch of nature that makes the whole world kin. And I will venture to say, too, that the aggregation was at the lowest aesthetic level in all history. Steam heat, plumbing, and electric light were the only redeeming features and these new features were hard put to it to function in the circumstances. Bowels, circulation, and nerves were new in buildings. But they had come to stay and a building could no longer remain a mere shell in which life was somehow to make shift as it might.

When I was 11 years old I was sent to a Wisconsin farm to learn how to really work. So all this I saw around me seemed affectation, nonsense, or profane. The first feeling was hunger for reality, for sincerity. A desire for simplicity that would yield a broader, deeper comfort was natural, too, to this first feeling. A growing idea of simplicity as organic, as I had been born into it and trained in it, was new as a quality of thought, able to strengthen and refresh the spirit in any circumstances. Organic simplicity might everywhere be seen producing significant character in the ruthless but harmonious order I was taught to call nature. I was more than familiar with it on the farm. All around me, I, or anyone for that matter, might see beauty in growing things and by a little painstaking, learn how they grew to be "beautiful." None were ever insignificant. I loved the prairie by instinct as itself a great simplicity; the trees, flowers, and sky were thrilling by contrast. And I saw that a little of height on the prairie was enough to look like much more. Notice how every detail as to height becomes intensely significant and how breadths all fall short. Here was a tremendous spaciousness needlessly sacrificed, all cut up crosswise or lengthwise into 50-foot lots, or would you have 25 feet? Reduced to a money-matter, salesmanship kept on parceling out the ground, selling it with no restrictions. Everywhere, in a great new, free country, I could see only this mean tendency to tip everything in the way of a human occupation or habitation up edgewise instead of letting it lie comfortably flatwise with the ground where spaciousness was a virtue. Nor has this changed much since automobilization has made it no genuine economic issue at all but has made it a social crime to crowd in upon one another.

By now I had committed the indiscretion that was eventually to leave me no peace and keep me from ever finding satisfaction in anything superficial. That indiscretion was a determination to search for the *qualities* in all things.

I had an idea (it still seems to be my own) that the planes parallel to the earth in buildings identify themselves with the ground, do most to make the buildings belong to the ground. (Unluckily they defy the photographer.) At any rate, independently I perceived this fact and put it to work. I had an idea that every house in that low region should begin *on* the ground, and not *in* it as they then began, with damp cellars. This feeling became an idea also; eliminate the "basement." I devised one at ground level. And the feeling that the house should *look* as though it began there *at* the ground, put a protecting base course as a visible edge to this foundation where, as a platform, it was evident preparation for the building itself and welded the structure to the ground.

An idea (probably rooted deep in racial instinct) that *shelter* should be the essential look of any dwelling, put the low spreading roof, flat or hipped, or low-gabled, with generously projecting eaves over the whole. I began to see a building primarily not as a cave but as broad shelter in the open, related to vista; vista without and vista within. You may see in these various feelings all taking the same direction that I was born an American child of the ground and of space, welcoming spaciousness as a modern human need as well as learning to see it as the natural human opportunity. The farm had no negligible share in developing this sense of things in me, I am sure.

Before this, by way of innate sense of comfort, had come the idea that the size of the human figure should fix every proportion of a dwelling or anything in it. Human scale was true building scale. Why not, then, the scale fixing the proportion of all buildings whatsoever? What other scale could I use? This was not a canon taught me by anyone. So I accommodated heights in the new buildings to no exaggerated established order nor to impress the beholder (I hated grandomania then as much as I hate it now) but only to comfort the human being. I knew the house dweller could seldom afford enough freedom to move about in built-in or built-over space, so, perceiving the horizontal line as the earth line of human life (the line of repose), this, as an individual sense of the thing, began to bear fruit. I first extended horizontal spacing without enlarging the building by cutting out all the room partitions that did not serve the kitchen or give needed privacy for sleeping apartments or (as in the day of the parlor) serve to prevent some formal intrusion into the intimacy of the family circle. The small social office I set aside as a necessary evil to receive "callers," for instance. Even this one concession soon disappeared as a relic of the barbarism called "fashion": the "parlor."

To get the house down to the horizontal in appropriate proportion and into quiet relationship with the ground and as a more humane consideration anyway, the servants had to come down out of the complicated attic into a unit of their own.

Freedom of floor space and elimination of useless heights worked a miracle in the new dwelling place. A sense of appropriate freedom had changed its whole aspect. The dwelling became more fit for human habitation on modern terms and far more natural to its site. An entirely new sense of space values in architecture began to come home. It now appears that, self-conscious of architectural implications, they first came into the architecture of the modern world. This was about 1893. Certainly something of the kind was due.

A new sense of repose in flat planes and quiet "streamline" effects had thereby and then found its way into building, as we can now see it admirably in steamships, airplanes and motorcars. The age came into its own and the "age" did not know its own. There had been nothing at all from overseas to help in getting this new architecture planted on American soil. From 1893 to 1910 Adler and Sullivan's Wainwright Buildings, the first affirmation of the tall building as *tall*—these prairie houses beginning with the Winslow house which followed the Charnley house, the Larkin Building and Unity Temple had planted it there. No, my dear "Mrs. Gablemore," "Mrs. Platerbilt," and especially, no, "Miss Flattop," nothing from "Japan" had helped at all, except the marvel of Japanese color prints. They were a lesson in elimination of the insignificant and in the beauty of the natural use of materials.

But more important than all, rising to greater dignity as idea, the ideal plasticity was now to be developed and emphasized in the treatment of the building as a whole. Plasticity was a familiar term but something I had seen in no buildings whatsoever. I had seen it in Lieber Meister's ornament only. It had not found its way into his buildings otherwise. It might now be seen creeping into the expressive lines and surfaces of the buildings I was building. You may see the appearance of the thing in the surface of your hand as contrasted with the articulation of the bony skeleton itself. This ideal, profound in its architectural implications, soon took another conscious stride forward in the form of a new aesthetic. I called it *continuity*. (It is easy to see it in the "folded plane.") Continuity in this aesthetic sense appeared to me as the natural means to achieve truly organic architecture by machine technique or by any other natural technique.

Not much yet exists in our country—no, nor in any country outside plans and models—to exemplify steel and glass at its best in the light of the new sense of building. But a new countenance, it is the countenance of principle, has already appeared around the world. A new architectural language is being brokenly, variously, and often falsely spoken by youths, with perspicacity and some breadth of view but with too little depth of knowledge that can only come from continued experience. Unfortunately, academic training and current criticism have no penetration to this inner world. The old academic order is bulging with its own important impotence. Society is cracking under the strain of a sterility education imposes far beyond capacity; exaggerated capitalism has left all this as academic heritage to its own youth. General cultural sterility, the cause of the unrest of this uncreative moment that now stalls the world might be saved and fructified by this ideal of an organic architecture: led from shallow troubled muddy water into deeper clearer pools of thought. Life needs these deeper fresher pools into which youth may plunge to come out refreshed with new creative energy to make the United States for humanity.

Ethics for Greedheads

B.S. At Business School

FAREED ZAKARIA

It is probably safe to say that Fareed Zakaria, in his stinging denunciation of business schools and their goals, loses some of his readership. Those offended may not read the complete essay, but others will. After all, his discussion of business ethics—or the lack of—is also a comment on our age and ethics in general. Thus, the general audience of *The New Republic* has a vested interest in the subject. There is certainly no doubt, from the wording of his title and his opening paragraph, exactly what his feelings on this subject are. And the loaded wording leads right up to his concluding rhetorical question.

Original publication: *The New Republic*, October 19, 1987.

How would you expect a conservative Republican to respond to a problem involving "values"? Throw money at it? Probably not. Yet this is exactly how staunch Reaganite John Shad, former SEC chairman and current ambassador to the Netherlands, has reacted to the uproar over insider trading. "Disturbed" by "the large numbers of graduates of leading business schools who have become convicted felons," Shad has given $30 million to the Harvard Business School—his, and many of the felons', alma mater.

Most large alumni donations pay for the buildings or libraries or laboratories. Shad's pledge is for something intangible—ethical graduates—and it isn't clear what dollars, even 30 million of them, can buy to this end. Was it a failure to take the appropriate course in business school that led Martin Siegel to the Brooklyn Bridge at midnight to receive a cash payoff?

Neither Harvard nor Shad has disclosed in detail how the money will be spent. What little they have mentioned so far is either depressingly familiar ("interdepartmental programs" and "research projects") or just silly (a video archive of "outstanding management practices" and an annual awards ceremony).

While doubts about corporate scruples were rampant in the '60s, more recently such attitudes have become passé. Entrepreneurs are our pop icons, and administration officials wear ties featuring little profiles of Adam Smith. On the Harvard Business School campus, where I lived last year (though not as a business student), I was surprised at how much it resembled not a college but a modern company, with all that implies. The architecture of most buildings runs toward corporate rather than Ivy, slick and antiseptic rather than run-down and tweedy. Every morning the foyer of our building was carpeted with freshly delivered *Wall Street Journals*. Magazines would arrive spanning the gamut from *Forbes* to *Fortune*, with someone's solitary *New York Review of Books* looking quite out of place. Students mill around wearing expensive variants on the preppy uniform, looking and acting like clones of Michael J. Fox. The talk is always of money.

Second-year students discuss their job interviews—in business school an elaborate mating ritual. It starts with a series of formal dinners at posh hotels, and continues with a battery of interviews at corporate headquarters. These are followed by more intimate dinners at fancy restaurants. (Official three-day weekends and three separate spring vacations give second-year students ample time to spend with their corporate suitors.) Each firm repeats this process more than once, and each student interviews with several firms. Even the professors who teach morals—"ethicists"—consult frequently, and for high fees, with these same companies. This, along with the material ambition of the self-selected student body, creates an atmosphere where ideas are not the dominant currency at all. The dominant currency is, well, currency.

This does not mean that schools are not obsessed with their role as the training ground for America's future elite, ethics included. Thomas Piper, associate dean of Harvard Business School, explained that one of the moving forces behind all major business schools' recent efforts is their graduates' need of "a heightened understanding of morals for their exercise of power." Harvard cites, among courses dealing with ethical issues, one on "Power." (You've seen the movie, now take the course.) Students don't read Machiavelli or C. Wright Mills. Instead, they are introduced to the issues with a discussion of David Rockefeller. The "required reading" is a gushing documentary by Bill Moyers. A participant tells how students wonder in hushed tones about the source of Rockefeller's influence (but the word "inheritance" is not mentioned once), while those who have actually met Him describe to their classmates how his handshake radiates pure power. Next week: Tip O'Neill.

Efforts to teach ethics come either packaged in courses labeled as such or as ethical questions integrated into the general curriculum. Stanford Business School advocates the former, and a separate ethics course is now part of its required core. In most special ethics courses, business students consider corporate situations fraught with moral possibilities and are asked how they would conduct themselves. (Hint: giving a bribe is the wrong answer.) Paul MacAvoy, dean of the Rochester Management School, is opposed to the Stanford approach, arguing that "to elevate [ethics] to a separate course is to make it an abstraction." The Wharton School agrees, concluding in a study that students often regard ethics professors as out of touch with the actual business world. Further, "Students wear their ethical hats" in Ethics, only to take it off in say, Finance.

Harvard is moving toward integrating ethics into all its courses. Dean John MacArthur says: "Ethical issues . . . have to permeate all aspects of our work. They have to be imbedded in the very fabric of what we teach at Harvard Business School." The case is strong; adding a few special courses seems the easy solution, integration the difficult but correct one. But integration has its problems as well, first as a cover for doing nothing. Business schools have responded to calls for new ethics courses by claiming that ethics had already *been* imbedded into the fabric. And integration can mean as little as asking the same simpleminded question about bribes for a few minutes in all classes, instead of all the time in one class. What's to say that a professor of, say, Statistics has either the inclination or the expertise to teach moral philosophy?

The case study method, long the pride of business schools, is particularly ill-suited to the teaching of ethics. Almost no books are used, and little history or theory is taught. Course work consists of reading prepared pamphlets on specific problems particular companies once faced, whether or not they stand for any overarching principle.

In fact, it doesn't matter *how* you teach ethics, if what you are teaching is muddled. In business school, ethics is taught as a matter not of morality but of pragmatism. Consider a course that takes off from Shad's belief, in his words, that "crime doesn't pay." This approach tries to convince students that, if they factor in the costs of getting caught, they would see the folly of doing the wrong thing and therefore would not do it. But crimes are committed precisely because the offender thinks he will not be caught (especially if his wrongdoing is buried in a maze of stock transactions). Pragmatism may be the only language MBAs understand, but it misses the point that crime is wrong even though you are not likely to be caught.

Another technique is to make a student calculate the consequences of his actions for other people. Kirk Hanson, who developed Stanford's business ethics program, says, "We must weigh the costs and benefits to all parties affected by our decision." This is generous but unrealistic. Although capitalism is not a zero-sum game, competition does lie at the heart of a free-enterprise system. A firm does not, and should not, consider the potential loss to every competitor as a restraint on its actions. The market as encounter group may be nice, but it wouldn't be very efficient.

The pragmatic approach, aside from abandoning morality altogether, assumes people make rational calculations before doing something unethical, and that behind wrong choices lies misinformation or shoddy thinking. Hanson says, "Unethical behavior occurs mainly because business managers do not understand the situations in which they find themselves." This kind of thinking naturally leads designers of the ethics curriculum to focus on the crime of the moment. In the 1970s, for example, the propriety of bribing foreign officials was the subject of much contention; insider trading was not discussed at all. Who can tell what the moral lapses of the 1990s will be?

There will always be moral gray areas in business, and MBAs are probably better off for having thought about these issues. But it's not the shadings of misleading advertising that Shad and his $30 million are aimed at but cold hard cash changing hands. That a course in ethics could prevent that—by itself, integrated, part of the case study method, or as an adjunct to a course in Power—is a hopeless goal. By the time they arrive at business school, students are a bit old for basic character formation.

Given this limitation, the best approach might be to teach business not simply as an acquisitive trade but as a profession with duties and responsibilities. Law and medical schools create an atmosphere in which students see their fields as noble and themselves as socially useful. (Consider the lawyer's quite sincere belief that he must defend the guilty.) If business schools stood for the proposition that business is an honorable endeavor, and that businessmen are socially useful, students could learn to take pride in their profession and, conversely, feel ashamed to let it down. That is how these schools can marginally influence the behavior of their 26-year-old charges (which is probably the limit of their moral influence).

This does imply a moral defense capitalism, obviously a controversial position for business schools to take. But, as the Critical Legal Studies group has pointed out, the argument that our legal system is a beneficial one is equally tendentious, and yet it may well help to make better-behaved lawyers. Ironically, professional "ethicists" sometimes object to taking any such definitive moral stance at all. In the words of Wharton's Thomas Murfee, "Ethics properly taught is no more value-laden than any other subject . . ." But by shying away from an advocacy of the free market, business schools are refusing to defend themselves. If capitalism is morally neutral, the schools are at best self-interested corporations that identify a need for a product (MBAs) and make a morally neutral decision to produce it. If capitalism is unambiguously good, they are educating an integral part of a prosperous and just society. Which sounds better?

•   •   •

Chapter Questions

1. How significant is the sex of the reader of Pearl Buck's "America's Medieval Women"? Is there any sexism in the article that she might have avoided?
2. Several of these persuasive essays, originally published in popular magazines, make serious demands on their readers. Which selection in this chapter is most demanding or challenging? How?
3. Select any persuasive essay in this chapter with which you *agree*. How would you counter its arguments if you were on the other side? What are its weaknesses?
4. Select an essay in this chapter with which you *disagree*. What are the strengths of the author's argument?
5. Which essay is the most expository in its approach? Explain your selection.
6. After reading Clarke's and Price's essays, can you suggest someone who fulfills their criteria for *hero?* Make an argument for your suggestion.
7. Study Dudley's and Simpkins's logical approaches to arguing controversial and emotional subjects. What are the strengths of their arguments? How would you approach these subjects—or similar ones—in an emotional way?
8. How would you present Zakaria's argument to avoid offending your readers?
9. What did you demand of the selections in this chapter? Were your demands met?

Chapter Four
REVIEW

Many of us lack confidence in our own tastes and judgments. Thus, we want someone in a position of authority, or someone whose opinion we trust, to tell us whether to read a book or see a movie. Ironically, we do not stop to think how often we are reviewers and how much of our time we spend reviewing. "Let's watch *Gone with the Wind* again. It's a *wonderful* movie, and it's been a couple of years since I've seen it." "You really must read Stephen King's latest book. It's *absolutely horrifying*." "Why don't we try that new restaurant in town? I hear they have *superb* French food." And so on we talk, trying to convince someone to do something based on our assessment. And obviously we can review anything—books, movies, plays, recitals, restaurants, speeches, art, pets, cities, vacations, classes and professors, friends and acquaintances.

A review is a careful blend of exposition and persuasion, because readers expect a review to cover (summarize, describe) the subject and provide an opinion, with justification, about it. Regardless of the subject—or object, depending on the tone—of the review, it must provide a summary or a description. The length of the summary (or description) can vary from one sentence to one paragraph or occasionally even several paragraphs, depending on how much readers need to know to understand the discussion in the review. The persuasion appears in the reviewer's analysis and evaluation of the subject. The summary and analysis together should establish the reviewer's credibility and persuade readers that the evaluation is a sound one. Even if they are not convinced by the assessment, they should know the reviewer's reasons for the conclusions. When readers finish a review, they must know what the subject is all about, what the reviewer thinks of it, and why the reviewer has drawn certain conclusions.

The reviews selected for this textbook discuss books (nonfiction and fiction), an art exhibit, architecture, a recital, a speech, and a movie. Through their variety, they exemplify the truism that there is no one way to introduce, to develop, or to conclude a review; there are as many ways to review as there are things to review and writers to review them. But they all must provide readers with the necessary summary, analysis, and evaluation.

The introductions of the reviews included here range from autobiographical or biographical details to descriptions to quotations from the work under consideration. The reviewers' emphases are equally varied: positive raves, gentle denunciation, or vitriolic diatribe. In some we find the reviewer's evaluation in the opening sentence; in others we have to read to the conclusion to learn the reviewer's assessment. Thus, the selections demonstrate that many of the principles of writing persuasion also apply to reviewing.

Just as the author of persuasion may begin thinking and writing without knowing the exact tack of the argument, so the reviewer may begin writing without knowing the direction the review might take. One December at a reunion of graduate school friends, I noticed one of the guests, a book reviewer for a national publication, looking at his watch with some frequency. When I questioned him about this concern with time, he confessed that he had a noon deadline the following day, a confession that led to a discussion of his planned review. Curious about his work, I asked whether he was going to review the book, a novel in which I had some interest, favorably or unfavorably. He answered that he would not know until he finished the review and read what he had written (a professional demonstration that we write to learn what we think). This insight might help novice reviewers: do not agonize over the introduction; write it after you learn what you have to say about the subject.

There is no one pattern of organization to follow, nor is there one level of diction to use. The demands of the audience determine these choices. What do our readers need to know in order to understand the rationale for the evaluation? How much do we need to say, without giving away too much? What level of diction do we use? Are the readers professionals or general public, and isn't there a way to make even a technical review readable to both audiences without insulting either?

Keeping that healthy "respect for the reader" can help reviewers answer these questions, just as the principle guides writers of autobiography, exposition, persuasion, and research.

•　　•　　•

Reviews of
THE PANDA'S THUMB
by Stephen Jay Gould

Books Fit for Rooftop Delivery

Turning Nature's Sprawl into Literature
H. JACK GEIGER

More Variations on a Biological Theme
ASHLEY MONTAGU

The following three reviews of *The Panda's Thumb* by Stephen Jay Gould illustrate the importance of audience—general and professional. Although a medical doctor, H. Jack Geiger has written an informal and detailed review for the general audience of *The New York Times Book Review*, opening with autobiographical narrative and writing without use of technical vocabulary. In the reviews in two more professionally oriented journals, the reviewers' uses of vocabulary are more specialized, more technical—with slight differences between the two. In *Sciquest*, the reviewer defines "craniometrician" (see Stephen Jay Gould's essay in Chapter 5 for more on this subject); in *Nature*, Montagu trusts professional readers to understand wording such as "multicellular creatures," "embryonic growth," "molecular genetics," "hyperselectionism." The most consistent element of the three reviews is the high praise for *The Panda's Thumb*, despite a few weaknesses noted by two of the reviewers.

Careful reading of different reviews of the same work will help potential reviewers understand variety in reviewing at the same time readers are given the basic information needed in a review: summary, analysis, and evaluation.

Original publications:
    "Books Fit for Rooftop Delivery," *Sciquest*, December 1980.

H. Jack Geiger, "Turning Nature's Sprawl into Literature," *The New York Times Book Review*, September 14, 1980.

Ashley Montagu, "More Variations on a Biological Theme," *Nature*, December 4, 1980.

Books Fit for Rooftop Delivery

The Panda's Thumb: More Reflections in Natural History. By Stephen Jay Gould. W. W. Norton & Co., 1980, 343 pages; cloth, $11.95.

This collection of essays on evolutionary biology and a few other topics—wishbones, Mickey Mouse and crazy old Randolph Kirkpatrick—follows "Ever Since Darwin" by Harvard paleontologist Stephen Jay Gould. A charming collection. But you've got to be awake when you read it, or you'll miss the science—and the wit.

Although Gould might dig a little hole with explanations of "On the Various Contrivances by Which British and Foreign Orchids are Fertilized by Insects" (Darwin, 1862) and attempt to tunnel down deep, pulling the reader behind, he rewards us with a wry-humored tidbit just before we begin to squirm.

Anecdotes become statements of not only evolution in a pure sense, but also of culture, attitude and ethics. Take the famous brain debates of the late 1800s between craniometrician, or head measurer, Paul Broca, and fellow anthropologist Louis Pierre Gratiolet over the "great" head of the great anatomist Georges Cuvier. Broca wanted to prove that brain size, through its link with intelligence, could explain why some individuals and groups are more successful than others. Unfortunately, after Cuvier's friends did an autopsy of his wonderful "massive head" they neglected to measure the skull. The inspired Gratiolet remarked: "All brains are not weighed by doctors, but all heads are measured by hatters." And of course, he produced Cuvier's favorite hat. Gould relates, "On the surface, this tale seems ludicrous. The thought of France's finest anthropologists arguing passionately about the meaning of a dead colleague's hat could easily provoke the most misleading and dangerous inference of all about history—a view of the past as a domain of naive half-wits. . . ." But are we so far removed? After all, Gould notes that Einstein's brain rests in a Mason jar in a cardboard box in Wichita, Kan.

One of the main themes throughout the essays is: "Odd arrangements and funny solutions are the proof of evolution—paths that a sensible God would never tread but that a natural process, constrained by history, follows perforce . . . Which brings me to the giant panda and its 'thumb.' "

Turning Nature's Sprawl into Literature

The Panda's Thumb: More Reflections in Natural History. By Stephen Jay Gould. Illustrated. 343 pp. New York: W. W. Norton & Co., $11.95.

The Panda's Thumb reminded me of one happy summer long ago when I worked as a very junior research fellow at a marine biological laboratory, in the company of a lot of other very junior research fellows. We were exploring the kinds of questions that excite biologists because they sense them, however dimly, to be part of a mystery much larger.

Questions like: How do clams tell time? Why does the microscopic, cellular egg of a sea urchin, in a split second, primly slam the door to keep out all but the first triumphantly invading sea urchin sperm? (Well, not a door, exactly, but something complicated called fertilization membrane.) Why does a toadfish—a loathsome creature of truly monumental ugliness, given mostly to lying half submerged in river-bottom muck until the moment is right for a savage convulsive leap at unsuspecting prey—carry a part of its pancreas in its neck?

In that single summer, we didn't get very far. The bivalve study underwent a long metamorphosis, classically following a chance observation, into what became the Great Barnstable County Clam-Jumping Contest. We sacrificed a lot of potential sea urchin babies without getting good answers—without even reflecting on why, in fertilization at least, it makes powerful evolutionary sense that two's company but three's a crowd. We renamed the toadfish the Id-fish. In short, we made little contribution to science, and none at all to literature.

But that is because none of us was Stephen Jay Gould. In "The Panda's Thumb," Mr. Gould—a young Harvard paleontologist and evolutionary theorist and the author of "Ontogeny and Phylogeny"—makes clear that he can take almost any item in nature's great disorderly sprawl and turn it into an elegantly literate essay, a philosophical inquiry, a startling social analogy, or a joyful, rueful reflection on man's history and man's fate. Most of all, he turns it into fun.

The items that he uses are diverse indeed. They include a clam that has elaborated, on what is more or less its rear end, a wonderful anatomical structure that looks deceptively like a small fish and serves as bait—and an angler fish that has done the same thing, only on its nose. There is a male mite that fertilizes all its sisters and then dies before ever experiencing the world outside its mother's body. There are measurements of the changes in Mickey Mouse's features over his 50 years in cartoons. There is a list of the things Darwin really read in the last months before he crystallized his thoughts on natural selection and the origin of species.

And there are, of course, the usually fascinating questions: Were dinosaurs really dumb? Why are some bacteria magnetic? Why did 19th-century biologists weigh brains (and malign women)?

The essays in "The Panda's Thumb," which are drawn from Mr. Gould's column in Natural History magazine, use these items and questions, however, for a serious and coherent purpose. Mr. Gould is not a run-of-the-mill "nature writer" given to tender accounts of wondrous beasties or excited descriptions of biological freaks. Neither is he a popularizer of science, in the worst sense of that term; he is accessible and lucid, but you have to pay attention and you have to think. As he demonstrated in "Ever Since Darwin," his first collection of essays—which established him, several years ago, as the equal of Archie Carr ("The Windward Road") and Lewis Thomas ("The Lives of a Cell"), the two other major biological essayists of our time—Stephen Jay Gould is a serious and gifted interpreter of biological theory, of the history of ideas and of the cultural context of scientific discovery.

First of all, he understands the real nature of the mystery and the excitement in biology, in those odd creatures and odd questions. "It touches all our lives," he says, "for how can we be indifferent to the great questions of genealogy: Where did we come from, and what does it all mean?"

Next, he understands that natural history is "more than the peculiarities of animals—the mysterious ways of the beaver, or how the spider weaves her supple web." Mr. Gould argues: "There is exultation in this and who shall gainsay it? But each organism can mean so much more to us. Each instructs; its form and behavior embodies general messages if only we can learn to read them. The language of this instruction is evolutionary theory. Exultation *and* explanation."

And so the panda's thumb (which is not a true thumb at all, but a wonderfully improvised device made out of an enlarged wristbone, and almost as good as a thumb), the convergent adaptations of the clam and the angler fish, and other messy particularities of diverse creatures are used to illustrate the ways in which natural imperfections and leftovers, more than seeming triumphs of bodily engineering, contribute to the evidence for evolution. The incestuous mite really serves to explore the relationships between evolutionary pressures and sex ratios, the relative proportions of males and females born in any species. The progressive juvenilization of Mickey Mouse (he was drawn to grow younger in appearance, more babylike, as he grew older and more familiar in real time) becomes the framework for explaining the development of human embryos, and for reflecting on human affective response to babies.

Over and over again, Mr. Gould shows us these apparently odd items (wishbones, hermit crabs stuffed uncomfortably into fossil shells, ostriches with calloused knees), examines them through the single prism of evolutionary theory, and explains. And exults. Gradually, we begin to understand what a theory is, and how it ramifies; and how scientists think, sometimes make terrible mistakes and argue.

Indeed, where Mr. Gould is best—I think unique—is not in these biological specifics but in his accounts of the history and development of scientific ideas. It is fascinating to discover that Darwin's thoughts on natural selection were stimulated, in part, by his reading of Adam Smith's laissez-faire economics. We are familiar with the Social Darwinists, who projected their misread version of competition and natural selection onto the social and economic landscape; we can await the day, presumably, when the same misreading causes evolutionary theory to be described as a kind of Biological Capitalism! Mr. Gould would be more amused than horrified by that, I think, precisely because he is so interested in the way scientific ideas fit and are shaped by their times and cultures.

If Mr. Gould's focus on evolutionary theory gives his book coherence, it is also a flaw. The reader may learn rather more about Darwin—and evolution—

than he wants to know at any given moment. There are other, equally magnificent themes in biology, and Mr. Gould has the breadth and range to explore them with eloquence, if only he would.

But that is minor cavil, rather like complaining that a superb piece of music is written in a specific key. "The Panda's Thumb" is fresh and mind-stretching. Above all, it is exultant. So should its readers be.

More Variations on a Biological Theme

The Panda's Thumb. By Stephen Jay Gould. Pp.343. (W. W. Norton: 1980.) $11.95. To be published in the UK in spring 1981, £6.95.

Recently a young student of mine, having ably presented a seminar on Stephen Jay Gould's admirable book, *Ontogeny and Phylogeny* (Harvard University Press, 1977), asked me what Gould's specialty was. Only one answer was possible: versatility. Gould is a professor at Harvard and lectures on geology and palaeontology; he also teaches courses in biology and the history of science, and writes on physical and biological anthropology, growth and development, evolutionary theory, human nature, intelligence testing and sociobiology, to name but a few areas of his competence. In addition he is a highly regarded reviewer in scientific and literary journals and magazines. To cap it all, he writes a monthly column, "This View of Life", in the magazine *Natural History*.

It is from the column that this anthology, lightly edited, has been put together. Gould's earlier collection of essays from the same source, *Ever Since Darwin* (W. W. Norton), appeared in 1977. That volume immediately established him as perhaps the best of our natural history essayists. As a friend remarked the other day, "Whatever he writes is a gift".

In the prologue to the 31 pieces which make up this new volume, Gould expresses the hope that he has avoided that incubus of essay collections: diffuse incoherence. Neither author nor reader need have any qualms on that or any other score: the essays are consistently coherent and follow naturally, one upon the other, as if they were chapters on a single theme. There is a continuity which runs through this eminently readable book like a red thread, giving it a unity behind which an unusual mind is at work trying to figure out, among other things, how multicellular creatures regulate the timing involved in the complex orchestration of their embryonic growth, in the hope that developmental biology might one day unite molecular genetics with natural history to form a unified science of life. In one way or another these essays are mostly directed toward illuminating the routes to be taken to solve that problem.

The book plays variations upon this theme most delightfully, for in addition to being the best-informed of writers, Gould is also one of the most elegant. He is unfailingly interesting, for he has the rare gift of communicating the excitement he feels about whatever his fertile brain encounters. The reader comes away enriched and entertained at the same time. From the first essay, from which the book takes its title, in which the author discusses the manner and the method of evolution, to the last, in which he shows, by way of the chambered nautilus, how the palaeontologist has come to the rescue of the geophysicist and mathematician in arriving at a sound estimate of the rotational slowing of our planet, Gould holds the general principle of evolution steadily in view.

In an essay on Darwin and Wallace, Gould shows how the latter, one of the most remarkable and underestimated of thinkers, ultimately became an intellectual victim of his own hyperselectionism, in arguing that the excessive complexity of the human brain could not have been produced by selection. In another essay, "Darwin's Middle Road", the author writes revealingly of the fibs that the great man told about his insights. Here it is good to see Gould recognizing what few ever do in discussing the historical background of the Wallace-Darwin theory, namely, the role played by sociopolitical ideas, a fact clarified by Patrick Geddes in the late nineteenth century and by Charles Sanders Peirce almost as long ago.

In this essay Gould errs in saying that what was presented at the famous Linnean Society meeting of 1858 was "a joint paper". Though this is often stated, the truth is that what was presented, in the absence of both men, was an extract communicated in 1844 to Lyell and a letter to Asa Gray of 1857 (both by Darwin) and at the same time, but separately, Wallace's 1858 essay "On The Tendency of Variations to Depart from the Original Type". The communications were presented *together*. There was no joint paper as such.

But Gould rarely nods. On the few occasions on which he does he challenges one furiously to think. His book is a treasure.

Reviews of
A TASTE FOR DEATH
by P. D. James

Looking into the Murky and Murderous
JAMES CAMPBELL

Review in
Theology Today
CARL E. ERICSON

Books of *The Times*
CHRISTOPHER LEHMANN-HAUPT

Crime's Le Carré
J. D. REED

These four reviews confirm that not only do writers not write reviews the same way, but they also may not agree in their evaluations of a work. These assessments range from "disappointment" to "best," a considerable range. The approaches also differ, from a concentration on style to a comparison with an American novel (interestingly in the British review) to an analysis of the theological implications of the novel. After all, why is a murder-mystery even being reviewed in "the most widely circulated and influential quarterly journal of theology in the world"? Ericson knows his readers and discusses the work with them in mind.

All four reviewers, out of respect for their audiences, do obey the cardinal rule for writing about mysteries: do not give any hint of "who done it."

Original publications:
  James Campbell, "Looking into the Murky and Murderous," *Times Literary Supplement*, June 27, 1986.
  Carl E. Ericson, review in *Theology Today*, January 1988.
  Christopher Lehmann-Haupt, "Books of *The Times*," *The New York Times*, October 21, 1986.
  J. D. Reed, "Crime's Le Carré," *Time*, October 27, 1986.

Looking into the Murky and Murderous

P. D. James, *A Taste for Death*. 454 pp. (Faber.) £9.95.

"What I like is innocence", says the culprit, once cornered, in *A Taste for Death*—by which we understand, even if he himself doesn't, that he likes to corrupt innocence. It is a characteristic paradox. In P. D. James's novels, it is liable to be the hunger for a life free from responsibility—a kind of innocence, after all—which finally causes guilt; and it is the investigation of this guilt which demands a closer look inside the murky lives of associated "innocent" parties. Murder is a great destroyer of privacy, muses Commander Adam Dalgliesh more than once in the course of his latest inquiry, during which he is bound to uncover quite a range of social vices, including the snobbish, the sexual and the lethal.

The action of *A Taste For Death* takes place, for the most part, around the Notting Hill area—in particular at a desirable fictional address in Campden Hill Square—but at the beginning we are introduced to a Minister of State in the vestry of a Paddington church. His throat has been slit, and beside him lies a similarly mutilated tramp. Sir Paul Berowne had undergone a recent religious conversion and may even have exhibited the stigmata; the priest had granted him permission to sleep in the vestry. Harry Mack was a familiar local bum. Their grotesque partnership, however (and James has a nice line in corpse description: "everything human had drained away from them with their blood . . . they no longer looked like men"), is a mystery.

Dalgliesh rounds up the usual suspects—that is, family, friends, lovers and (the least suspicious by far) enemies. In this case they are Berowne's wife, a beautiful, vain woman of a type James delights in exposing; her lover, a cold-blooded surgeon; Berowne's mistress, plain, sincere, and well-suited to tragedy; the immature brother-in-law, a jealous failure; the daughter and her subversive boyfriend; relatives of two women close to Berowne who died recently in suspicious circumstances; and all the dailies and cleaning women, chauffeurs and church helpers who typically make up the supporting cast. More than one could have had a reason for doing it, all have solid alibis, and most have an air of not quite telling the truth. Moreover, there is an unconvincing desire among the family to have it wrapped up as a case of murder followed by suicide.

Dalgliesh is too much a veteran to be thrown off the trail by such obstinacy. To investigate the death of Sir Paul (not forgetting, as the family principals inevitably do, the tramp) he brings with him Massingham, who has a useful capacity to turn nasty with suspects, plus a new recruit to the squad, Inspector Kate Miskin—too pretty to be entirely resistible, too cold at the heart to fall in love with.

A Taste For Death resembles *Moby Dick* in that if your only interest is in the story you may as well flick from the first chapter to the last and find out who killed whom. The author's main concern is with what happens in between, where the society of the novel's inhabitants is dissected. Indeed, if there is a faint dissatisfaction at the close, it is only because the one thing which does not fit squarely into this comedy of manners is the deed that is the excuse for the making of it.

Admirers of Dalgliesh will be pleased to learn that he is on stronger form than ever. He has not written a poem for four years but he can still quote Crabbe over a corpse, pick up references to Plato in a dead man's letters, distinguish the good and bad in Lawrence and mutter a remark from Sartre. Cold fish though he is, he understands the irony of Berowne's death side by side with a tramp, which the family are incapable of doing. He has an insight into the dead man's spiritual crisis by which Lady Berowne lacks (she, incidentally, gets her kicks by watching her surgeon lover "cut into another woman's body", taking her place in a line of Jamesian female perverts).

Is Dalgliesh a man, or merely a representative of Justice in its ideal form? James avoids making him infallible by presenting him as an inadequate person, but his instincts as a detective are almost perfect. Although he experiences pity and fear, these emotions are subsumed by his desire for the good. His sympathy might be aroused by the plight of the defeated or the desperate, but it is his job to lock them up if they've done wrong.

The antics of Dalgliesh apart, the best thing in *A Taste For Death* is the partnership with which the book opens, between dear, shy, old Miss Wharton, a church helper, and the mischievous, and in many ways unchildlike, ten-year-old Darren: "After the third visit he had, without an invitation, walked home with her and shared her tin of tomato soup and her fish fingers . . . he had become necessary to her." Other writers might have been tempted to build an entire novel around this recognizable pair; P. D. James can afford to spend them on a subplot.

She takes less trouble with those she dislikes. Sir Paul's mother, the dragonish Lady Ursula Berowne, is less a character than a mouthpiece for a set of unlikable attributes of her class. This, like the upstairs-downstairs atmosphere, is a fault of the genre, whose conventions James seems happy to obey, and of which she is one of the best living exponents. In earlier novels, such as *Cover Her Face* (1962), these conventions threatened to squeeze out her other talents, but here she has made room for them all while still writing what is basically a detective story. James often seems less interested in putting forward a convincing explanation of why one person should plot and carry out the killing off another than in dramatizing all the fuss surrounding it. Sometimes she is too fussy in her long descriptions of interiors, the studied backgrounds to minor character's lives, where the background is adequately suggested by the character alone. The alternative view is that the seemingly endless flow of minor characters and subplots—Inspector Miskin's grumbling, dying grandmother, Berowne's daughter's involvement with a revolutionary movement, the affair between a member of the family and one of the staff—makes *A Taste For Death* an even more lavish entertainment than usual, and a more serious entertainment than most.

Review in *Theology Today*

A Taste for Death. by P. D. James. New York, Knopf, 1986. 459 pp. $18.95 ($4.95 pb.)

"He told me he had had an experience of God."

Sir Paul Berowne, Member of Parliament and Minister of the Crown, from time to time furthered an interest in church architecture. At St. Matthew's, Paddington, London—as he told his mistress—he had an experience of God.

He was murdered there.

P. D. James has written ten novels of killing crimes. It may be that her latest has made the best seller lists in 1986–1987 because *A Taste For Death* poses a theological question: "What happened when Paul Berowne had an experience of God?"

Commander Adam Dalgliesh of Scotland Yard successfully pursued the slayer, but none he questioned could imagine what occurred before Berowne took the sacrament at morning mass in the Lady Chapel of St. Matthew's. Perhaps one clue is grasped early on. The story mostly is about people permitting themselves to be church-connected by traditional piety without any real presence of God. There is reason to believe that, for the author, the meaning of such an experience is in knowing intimately the one who has it. No one, it seems knew the real Paul Berowne. As his mother, Lady Ursula, put it, "Until this happened, I would have described him as a conventional Anglican. . . . His experience—his alleged experience—is inexplicable, and, to do him justice, he didn't attempt to explain it, at least not to me. I hope you won't expect me to discuss it."

James, however, depicts a victim whose conventional behavior was a fraud. Beneath the cultural mask, Paul Berowne was unique. It seems that God discovered it so. The priest said he saw the stigmata on Berowne's wrists as he came to receive the sacrament. But Father Barnes did not pursue the matter.

When Dalgliesh asked the lover of Berowne's wife what he made of it, Stephen Lampart, the obstetrician, suggested the victim used his God-encounter as an excuse for "chucking it all"—a suicide. Berowne's estranged daughter, Sarah, a so-so communist, exclaimed: "My God! He couldn't even get converted like an ordinary man. He had to be granted his own personal beatific vision." Conservative party officials were mystified. One said to Dalgliesh: "He wasn't asking for help, was he? Or for advice? He's gone to a higher power for that. It's a pity he ever set foot in that church. Why did he, anyway? D'you know?" Dalgliesh said mildly, "Out of an interest in Victorian architecture, apparently." "Pity he didn't take up fishing or stamp collecting."

The incident aroused a defence of her son by Lady Ursula when Stephen Lampart began making a joke of it. "Whatever happened to my son in that church, and I don't pretend to understand it, in the end he died because of it. When next you're tempted to indulge in a cheap witticism you might remember that."

Another thread is conspicuous in the novel's pattern—P. D. James commenting on the state of religion in our time—like this one sentence: "St.

Matthew's, with its small and aging population, was an uncomfortable reminder of the declining authority of the Established Church in the inner cities."

Was this imputed ecclesiastical weakness mirrored in the upper class life of Paul Berowne? At last, had faith come to be a thing of breaking out, and away from, the life style into which he was born? The mistress, Carole Washburn, told Dalgliesh: "It's such an unlikely thing to have happened, that conversion, divine revelation, whatever it was. . . . He was, well worldly. . . . He wasn't a mystic. He wasn't even particularly religious. He usually went to church on Sundays and on the major feast days because he enjoyed the liturgy. . . . He wouldn't attend if they used the new Bible or Prayer Book. . . . He once said that formal religious observance confirmed identity, reminded him of the limits of behavior."

Dalgliesh asked Carole, "Would you describe him as happy"? "No, not really. . . . What happened to him in that church, whatever it was, I don't think it would have happened if he'd been satisfied with his life, if our love had been enough for him. . . . Nothing was enough for Paul, nothing."

By this, P. D. James must have put her foot in the theological door by design, implying something about suffering and conflict being necessary for faith.

Others associated with Dalgliesh became involved in the question of religion because of the murder. Inspector Kate Miskin and Chief Inspector Massingham decide that Dalgliesh is disturbed about something in the case. Kate begins the conversation by asking:

> "What's bugging him then?"
> "What happened to Berowne in that church, I suppose."
> "Have you tried to talk to him about it?"
> "No, I did try once but all I could get out of him was: 'The real world is difficult enough, John. Let's try to stay in it.' "
> "Do you believe that something really did happen to Berowne in that vestry?"
> "It must have, mustn't it? A man doesn't chuck his job and change the direction of his whole life for nothing."
> "But was it real? . . . Did he really have, well, some kind of supernatural experience?"

A page of talk and reflection on the subject of religion then follows.

Only one of the more than five hundred whodunits on our own shelves has this sort of dialogue. The exception is another by P. D. James, *Innocent Blood*, which concludes with a young woman on her knees in a university chapel after an upbringing and education on the emotionally violent side of atheism.

A bit later in the conversation Kate asks:

> "If you have a kid, will you have him christened?"
> "Yes, why do you ask?"
> "So you believe in it, God, the church, religion."
> "I didn't say so."
> "Then why?"
> "My family have been christened for four hundred years . . . longer, I suppose. Yours, too, I imagine. It doesn't seem to have done us any harm."

Habitual persistence in religious form that "does no harm" may have goaded Berowne to discover something more.

Dalgliesh became bitter after interviewing the grandparents of Theresa Nolan, a nurse employed for Lady Ursula, who committed suicide after an affair with the murdered one that ended in abortion. "He felt himself contaminated by the Nolans' bitterness and pain. He thought: 'And if I tell myself that enough is enough . . . if I resign, what then? Whatever Berowne found in that dingy vestry, it isn't open to me even to look for it.' As the Jaguar bumped gently back onto the road he felt a spurt of irrational envy and anger against Berowne, who had found so easy a way out."

When an angry Dalgliesh mentioned resignation to Gilmartin of government special services, the latter replied: "Oh, I shouldn't do that. . . . I suppose that Berowne was murdered, by the way. There's a rumor that it could have been suicide. After all, he was hardly normal at the time . . . isn't he supposed to have had some kind of divine revelation? Listening to his voices when he should have been listening to the Prime Minister. And such a very curious church to choose. I can understand an enthusiasm for English Perpendicular, but a Romanesque basilica in Paddington surely is an improbable choice for a good night's sleep, let alone one's personal road to Damascus."

Paul Berowne, restless and searching for something better than religion's bifurcation of an eternal heaven and his personal hell on earth, at last met God in a vestry where the church scarcely expected having to defend the unnoticed absence of deity within its precincts. As another party official said: "After that nonsense in the church, no one was going to take him seriously any more."

The body of Paul Berowne was discovered by Miss Emily Wharton, age 65, a spinster who brightened her days by the small duties she was allowed to perform at St. Matthew's, and by Darren Wilkes, age 10, fatherless child of a prostitute, who took a shine to the lonely woman and was befriended by her. "She wants looking after," Darren used to say.

None thought to ask Miss Wharton's opinion of Berowne's religious experience. But at the end, when calmer days prevailed, she came again to see about altar flowers and spent candles. Entering, she is startled to encounter a young woman departing—Carole Washburn, Berowne's mistress. Commander Dalgliesh had told her there was nothing to see, but she had gone anyway, curious about the room where her lover had an "experience," and where he died. Coming onto Miss Wharton, she exclaimed: "He was right. . . . It's just a room, a perfectly ordinary room. There was nothing there, nothing to see."

Surely, it was her use of the word "ordinary" that suddenly made a proper theologian of Emily Wharton, belatedly in her sixty-fifth year. Shaken by the visitor's words, she walked on to the grille at the passage's end. Seeing the red glow of the sanctuary lamp, she thought, "And that, too, is only an ordinary lamp. . . . And the consecrated wafers behind the drawn curtain . . . are . . . only discs of flour and water . . . ready for Father Barnes to say the words over them which will change them into God. But they weren't really changed. God wasn't there in that small recess behind the brass lamp . . . he had gone away."

As this sickening, new doubt possessed her, Miss Wharton recalled the teaching of a former pastor, Father Collins, who advised: "If you find that you no longer believe, act as if you still do. If you feel you can't pray, go on saying the words."

The apostate but still committed Miss Wharton went to her knees and "said the words with which she always began her private prayers: 'Lord, I am not worthy that thou shouldst come under my roof, but speak but the word and my soul shall be healed.' "

It may have been that Paul Berowne, in the vestry, also came to a vision of the transformed ordinary. For him, the mystery and meaning of life may have been joined at last by the paradox of the million dollar house where he resided brought beside this paltry room in the house of God. In one fiery moment, after the manner of Emily Wharton, Sir Paul Berowne, Member of Parliament and Minister of the Crown, may have murmured, "O Lord, I am not worthy. . . ." We are left to wonder whether, by confession, he renounced religion so that he could be visited by God.

Books of *The Times*

A Taste for Death. by P. D. James. 459 pages. Knopf. $18.95.

We find dead bodies, excitingly enough, in the opening sentence of P. D. James's 10th and latest novel, "A Taste for Death"—bodies "discovered at 8:45 on the morning of Wednesday 18 September by Miss Emily Wharton, a 65-year-old spinster of the parish of St. Matthew's in Paddington, London, and Darren Wilkes, aged 10, of no particular parish as far as he knew or cared."

But before we get further details of those bodies, Ms. James begins to circle and digress in a way that provokes uneasiness in the reader. At a too leisurely pace, she portrays "the curious, unspoken, mutual dependence" that binds the woman and the boy. She evokes the smells that bring back to Mrs. Wharton "the lanes of her Shropshire childhood." She describes St. Matthew's—"the green copper cupola of the soaring campanile of Arthur Blomfield's extraordinary Romanesque basilica," built "in 1870 on the bank of this sluggish urban waterway with as much confidence as if he had erected it on the Venetian Grand Canal."

So by the time we arrive at the bloody scene in which woman and boy discover in the church's vestry two corpses with their throats brutally slashed, our curiosity over whom the bodies belong to and how they got that way is nearly overwhelmed by the questions of where Ms. James is headed with her story and how she is going to knit the skein of digressions she has already introduced.

Not that this is necessarily a dismaying dilemma. Except for her previous novel, "The Skull Beneath the Skin," which was a falling off from her other work, P. D. James has grown throughout her career as a writer, demonstrating an increasing grasp of emotions and themes that normally lie beyond the genre of the detective thriller. In her eighth novel, "Innocent Blood"—her most accomplished performance to date despite (or perhaps because of) the absence of the two detective-heroes, Adam Dalgliesh and Cordelia Gray, who have taken turns starring in her previous work—Ms. James created a drama of near Shakespearean complexity and richness.

And indeed, as we plow on into "A Taste for Death," we are increasingly assailed with plot complication, thematic digression, character articulation and details, details, details. The corpses turn out to be those of an alcoholic tramp, one Harry Mack, and a wealthy Member of Parliament, Sir Paul Berowne. What can have brought these two disparate characters to this violent common fate? A deeper, more complex Adam Dalgliesh heads up the team that investigates the murders, including a young assistant named Kate Miskin who keeps puzzling over the role of women in police work. Why is Kate of illegitimate birth, and is there any connection between that fact and the pun in her surname?

Somewhere there may be a key to all the apparent patterning in "A Taste for Death." It may lie in the book's many literary references—to Barbara Pym, Philip Larkin, Anthony Trollope, Edith Wharton and of course William Shakespeare, whose "Love's Labour's Lost" features an attendant lord named Berowne who, as one of Ms. James's characters reminds us, is advised by the woman he loves to go and nurse the sick.

Or the key may lie in the novel's title, which is taken from A. E. Housman ("There's this to say for blood and breath,/they give a man a taste for death.") and whose various shades of meaning are suggested by the brutality of the murderer, by the devotion to their profession of the members of the investigative team, by Kate Miskin's guilty desire to be rid of an overdependent grandmother, and by a gynecologist who has a side practice aborting fetuses of unwanted gender.

Whatever the key to the pattern is, this reader missed it. Or, more precisely, I was never inspired to search for it in the first place. At the beginning, the questions posed by the cut-throat murders of Harry and Sir Paul are not arresting enough to demand one's attention to all the detail that follows. At the end, that welter of detail is insufficiently related to the novel's outcome, which hinges, anticlimactically, on the meaningless behavior of a psychopath. After more than 400 pages of blood imagery and social anatomy, we are entitled to something more symbolically resonant than an erratic madman!

When Adam Dalgliesh first interviews the mother of the murdered Paul Berowne, she indicates, apropos of the inspector's well-known interest in writing poetry, that she has been reading Philip Larkin's "Required Writing." "Mr. Larkin writes," she observes, "that it is always true that the idea for a poem and a snatch or line of it come simultaneously." She adds: "Do you agree, Commander?" Dalgliesh replies that he does. "A poem begins with poetry," he says, "not with an idea for poetry."

Especially since the author makes the point in this context, one would think that the same principle would apply to any written art form, or that form and content should always and inevitably be inseparable, even on the "low" level of a murder mystery. But while "A Taste for Death" begins with a murder, it proceeds by exploring the idea of a murder. To make matters worse, the idea of the murder explored has little artistically to do with the actual murder committed. In short, never does the story explore the particular implications of a throat-slashing. For all its apparent subtlety of thought, Ms. James's novel provokes little more in us than the question, Who done it? This is a disappointment, if only because we've come to expect more from P. D. James.

Crime's Le Carré

A Taste for Death. by P. D. James. Knopf; 459 pages; $18.95.

Just a few decades ago, the whodunit formula demanded by both publishers and readers was compact—and cozy; 180 pages of pure deduction and cardboard characters propped up in a long-gone rural England. Along with a handful of other contemporary crime writers including Dick Francis and Ruth Rendell, P. D. James, 66, has gracefully shattered the rules. In her best and most ambitious tale to date, *A Taste for Death*—her ninth mystery novel in 24 years—James has become a kind of Le Carré of crime, blending the calmer depths of mainstream fiction with the white rapids of the genre, to produce something quite different indeed.

Instead of an old standby, the isolated country house, the setting is a complex, violent and very real London of the '80s. A junior Cabinet Minister is found with his throat slashed in the dingy vestry behind the altar of St. Matthew's Anglican Church in the Paddington section of the city. Across the room, a derelict lies dead, killed in the same grisly manner. In charge of the investigation: the sleuth-protagonist of six previous James novels, brooding Scotland Yard Commander Adam Dalgliesh, a widowed intellectual who loves baroque music. As he did in such previous cases as *The Black Tower* and *Shroud for a Nightingale*, Dalgliesh focuses on himself as much as on the murders; deduction is a voyage of self-discovery. He thinks of himself as the "poet who no longer writes poetry. The lover who substitutes technique for commitment. The policeman disillusioned with policing."

James, however, never lets character overwhelm crime. Dalgliesh and his Scotland Yard colleagues track the killer through the corridors of Whitehall, the hospital of a fashionable abortionist, a painfully trendy suburban restaurant. Among the suspects: the dead politician's vapid second wife, pregnant with his child even though she has had a lover for years; her con-man brother, who has moved into the politician's room; the victim's conniving mother, who mourns the loss of prewar manners more than the loss of her son. The politician himself is a mystery. Why, Dalgliesh wonders, did he suddenly resign his government post, experience a religious conversion during which, it is suggested, stigmata appeared on his body, and come to be killed in a shabby church room?

The tale goes as well with Reeboks and condominiums as Agatha Christie's puzzlers did with spats and country homes. In the '80s, not only the dead are victims: "Was this what murder did to the innocent?" wonders a bystander. "Took away the people they loved, loaded their minds with terror, left them bereft and unfriended under a smouldering sky." Dalgliesh's assistant, Inspector Kate Miskin, provides a counterpoint to the Tory values exemplified by most of the characters on both sides of the law. Miskin has risen from a council-flat childhood to an imitation of chic affluence. A visitor to her sterile, modern apartment notes it is in "dull, orthodox, ghastly, conventional good taste." Like a Renaissance painter, James mischievously slips in a small, sharp portrait of herself as a "buxom grandmother, noted for her detective stories, who gazed mournfully at the camera as if deploring either the bloodiness of her craft or the size of her advance."

Disney's Cinesymphony

THE EDITORS OF *TIME*

The editors of *Time* make their general relationship see the animation in several scenes of Disney's *Fantasia* as they rave about its achievements. The vivid descriptions and the convincing arguments make this review an achievement in its own medium, even if not so well known as its subject.

Original publication: *Time,* November 18, 1940.

Strange and wonderful are the premières (pronounced "premeers") of Hollywood: the trappings of publicity; the lights and decorations painting the gaudy lily of the Carthay Circle Theatre (where the big premières are held); the pushing, star-gazing crowds; the troops of real live stars ("I seen him! Didja see her?"). This week Manhattan sees a première stranger and more wonderful than any of Hollywood's. The celebrities present, the publicity, the lights on the marquee, may be lost in the blare and blaze of Broadway. But strangeness and wonder belong to the show itself. It is Walt Disney's latest, called *Fantasia.*

As the audience enters and the theatre fills with the sweet confusion of an orchestra tuning up, there are no musicians in the pit. As the curtains part, a huge symphony orchestra appears hazily, on the screen. Before it steps a thin, grinning, bald-headed man. He introduces himself as Deems Taylor, welcomes the audience, on behalf of Leopold Stokowski and Walt Disney, to "an entirely new form of entertainment." When he finishes, Leopold Stokowski himself, his back to the audience, steps into the picture, raises his arms, and the great orchestra swirls into Bach's *D Minor Toccata and Fugue*.

The music comes not simply from the screen, but from everywhere; it is as if a hearer were in the midst of the music. As the music sweeps to a climax, it froths over the proscenium arch, boils into the rear of the theatre, all but prances up & down the aisles. The hazy orchestra begins to dissolve, and weird, abstract ripples and filaments begin an unearthly ballet in Technicolor.

This is the beginning of a symphony concert—but what a concert! Illustrated by Walt Disney; written by Bach, Beethoven, Stravinsky, Dukas, Tchaikovsky, Mussorgsky, Schubert; conducted by Stokowski; master-of-ceremonied by Deems Taylor; played by the Philadelphia Orchestra. Mickey and Stokowski together put on a brand-new act.

When Stokowski's orchestra swings into Tchaikovsky's *Nutcracker Suite*, the ballet on the screen turns into flowers, fairies, fish, falling leaves, mushrooms. Mickey Mouse appears in the title role of Paul Dukas' *Sorcerer's Apprentice*, with silent gusto steals the bearded sorcerer's magic cap, commands the broom to fetch water, forgets how to stop it, nearly drowns in the deluge that follows. To Igor Stravinsky's rip-roaring *Rite of Spring*, a primeval world, complete with dinosaurs, bubbles up, parades by, dies down. To Mussorgsky's spooky *Night on Bald Mountain*, hobgoblins and beldams ride their brooms. To Beethoven's *Pastoral Symphony*, centaurs and centaurettes, Pegasus, Mrs. Pegasus and a nestful of little Pegasi gambol and fly; Bacchus and his crew get a good drenching when the storm comes up. The whole cinesymphony concert lasts two hours and a half (intermission included).

Containing everything from the Pierian well water of Johann Sebastian Bach to the violet-bordered stream of Schubert's *Ave Maria*, *Fantasia* is a long succession of very larger orders. Some of these orders (the flower, fish and mushroom dances of the *Nutcracker Suite*, the hulking, saurian epic of Stravinsky's *Rite*, the eerie, fantastic *Night on Bald Mountain*) are so beautifully filled that they may leave callous critics whispering incredulously to themselves. Others (Mickey's *Sorcerer's Apprentice*, the hilarious ostrich and hippopotamus ballets) set a new high in Disney animal muggery. Others (the wave and cloud sequences of Bach's *Fugue*, and a queer series of explosive music visualizations performed by a worried and disembodied sound track, posing diffidently on the screen like a reluctant wire) recall the abstract cinemovies made about five years ago by New Zealand-born Len Lye, show how musical sensation may be transferred to visual images.

It would have taken a Gustave Doré to do justice to the big beauty of Beethoven's *Pastoral Symphony*. No Doré, Disney peoples his classical Olympus with smirking "centaurettes," smirkingly brassiered, with calf-eyed centaurs and kewpie-doll cupids, makes Bacchus' bacchanale look like a nursery lemonade party, leaves his audience wondering whether he is serious, or merely trying to be cute by putting diapers on Olympus.

But, though Disney's toddling cannot keep pace with the giant strides of Ludwig van Beethoven, *Fantasia* as a whole leaves its audience gasping. Critics may deplore Disney's lapses of taste, but he trips, Mickey-like, into an art form that immortals from Aeschylus to Richard Wagner have always dreamed of.

Mickey Began It.   The idea for *Fantasia* had been germinating in Disney's mild-looking head for several years. Even before he did *Snow White* he had a vague notion of some day doing a serious opera in animovie style. As early as 1929 he raided the highbrow symphonic repertory to make Saint-Saëns' bone rattling *Danse Macabre* into a Silly Symphony. But the idea did not really sprout until early in 1938, when Leopold Stokowski, on a visit to Hollywood, begged Disney to let him conduct the music for *The Sorcerer's Apprentice*, a Mickey Mouse short. Disney didn't know what he was letting himself in for.

By the time Stokowski's recordings were done, and the animation half finished, the *Apprentice* began to look too good for a short, too expensive for anything but a feature. Before it was finished, white-haired Maestro Stokowski had come out with so many other bright ideas for symphonic animovies that Disney's ambition near went past itself. Calling ace Musi-commentator Deems Taylor from Manhattan to help with advice, Stoky and Disney decided to build around Mickey Mouse's sorcery act a whole program of cinesymphonies.

Keeping his 1,200 artists, animators, sound engineers and helpers mum, Walt Disney started work, soon got the machinery of his new $3,000,000 Burbank, Calif., studio rolling on *Fantasia*. Deciding to go the whole artistic hog, they picked the highest of high-brow classical music. To do right by this music, the old mouse opera comedy was not enough. The Disney studio went high-brow wholesale, and Disney technicians racked their brains for stuff that would startle and awe rather than tickle the audience.

Dinosaurs and Sound Tracks.   Conductor Stokowski went to work in Philadelphia's mellow and acoustically perfect old Academy of Music, recording his symphonic accompaniments on sound tracks. This time he worked, not with the Hollywood pickup band that had recorded Mickey's *Sorcerer's Apprentice*, but with his own famed, seasoned Philadelphia Orchestra. For this recording job, no ordinary cinema sound equipment would do. So Disney's ace sound engineer, rangy, Brooklyn-born Bill Garity, developed a whole new system of gadgets capable of catching each section of the Philadelphia Orchestra on a separate sound track. By braiding and patching these sound tracks onto a four-ply master track, he could control the faintest breath of every last bassoon. In their recording operations Garity and Stokowski used 430,000 feet of sound track, cut and patched it eventually into 11,953 feet. When the recordings were played back in a specially equipped studio in Hollywood, brother engineers were astounded to hear Soundman Garity's sound follow characters across the screen, roar down from the ceiling, whisper behind their backs. RCA and Disney engineers, having built this equipment at a cost of $85,000, called it "Fantasound," and crowed that it would revolutionize cinema production like nothing since the invention of Technicolor.

Meanwhile the Disney lot rang with the sound of classical music. Patient engineers who had never been to a concert in their lives listened to 35 to 710 performances of each composition, ended up whistling Bach, Beethoven and even Stravinsky at breakfast. Idea men, working on the dulcet strains of Beethoven's *Sixth Symphony*, winced at the bedlam of Stravinsky's *Rite* which other technicians were playing next door. (The *Rite* finally had to be quarantined in a special corner of the lot, where its boom-lay-booms could be studied without disturbing the whole studio.)

Stravinsky's *Rite*, which has caused high-brow audiences to rise, shout and pound on their neighbors' skulls in ecstasy, offered a serious problem. To match its cosmic hullabaloo, nothing less than a planetary cataclysm would do. So Disney men began studying nebulae and comets at California's Mount Wilson Observatory, mugged up on theories of protozoic life, earthquakes and other geologic upheavals, did portraits of every prehistoric monster in Manhattan's American Museum of Natural History.

One of them, studying lightning flashes by reclining on a Los Angeles curbstone in a pouring rain, was rushed to headquarters by suspicious police. Famed paleontologists like Barnum Brown of Manhattan's American Museum of Natural History and Chester Stock of California Institute of Technology were called in for advice. A herd of pet iguanas and a baby alligator wriggled over the Burbank lot, while animators studied their lizardy movements. By the time a complete cast had been rounded up for the *Rite*, the Disney zoo contained eusthenopterons, brachiosaurs, brontosaurs, plesiosaurs, mesosaurs, diplodocuses, triceratopses, pterodactyls, trachodons, struthiomimuses, stegosaurs, archaeopteryxes, pteranodons, tyrannosaurs and enough plain run-of-the-Jurassic dinosaurs to people a planet. Studio cameras groaned under the burden of the whole story of evolution.

For Mussorgsky's halloweenish *Night on Bald Mountain*, Disney went outside his own studio for talent, got famed Fairy-Tale illustrator Kay Nielson (*East of the Sun and West of the Moon*) to design graveyards and ghosts, ended with a Walpurgis nightmare calculated to turn little children's hair white. But Illustrator Nielson's jagged scenes, plus a new high in animation technique, made it by far *Fantasia's* best act. As *Fantasia* took shape, a whole new troupe of Disney comic characters appeared: Hop Low, the self-thwarting little mushroom, who tries to do the Chinese Dance from Tchaikovsky's *Nutcracker Suite*, but can't keep up with the big mushrooms; Ben Ali Gator, premier danseur of an ostrich ballet set to Ponchielli's corny *Dance of the Hours;* Susan, the hippopotamus ballerina whose blimp-like cavortings in a *pas de deux* with Ben Ali Gator literally bring down the house in a wreck of flying plaster; Bacchus and his donkey Jacchus, who trip and roll through the Grant Woodland scape of Beethoven's *Pastoral Symphony*.

Long before *Fantasia* was finished, expenses began to mount, and fellow Hollywoodians began to whisper again about "Disney's Folly." With $200,000 spent on Stokowski's fancy recordings, and a technical bill that overtops *Snow White's*, the total figure for the production amounted to $2,250,000. Because Engineer Garity's new sound mechanism is so complicated and expensive, only twelve theatres at a time will be equipped to show *Fantasia*, and RCA sound-equipment manufacturers figure that it will take several years before small-town cinema houses can get the gadgets to perform it. For the present, *Fantasia* will not be distributed like ordinary films, but will tour the U.S. like twelve road-show companies. But Walt Disney expects *Fantasia* to run for years, "perhaps even after I am gone."

An imposing list of top-flight contemporary composers (Paul Hindemith, Serge Prokofieff, William Grant Still, Deems Taylor, *et al.*) have vowed that they would spend their lives working for Disney if he would given them the chance. Composer Igor Stravinsky himself has signed a contract to do more music with Disney, has blandly averred that Disney's paleontological cataclysm was what he had had in mind all along in his *Rite of Spring*. Musicians and sound engineers who came to hear Soundman Garity's gadgets perform found that such recording had never before been even approached. Music lovers crowed that more ears would be saved for Beethoven by *Fantasia* than by all the symphonic lecture-recitalists in the U.S. The New York Academy of Sciences asked for a private showing of the *Rite of Spring* because they thought its dinosaurs better science than whole museum-loads of fossils and taxidermy.

Meanwhile sharp-faced Cinemartist Disney just crossed his fingers. Said he: "Art is never conscious. Things that have lived were seldom planned that way. If you follow that line, you're on the wrong track. We don't even let the word 'art' be used around the studio. If anyone begins to get arty, we knock them down. What we strive for is entertainment."

A Major Chicago Firm at Its Centennial

ADA LOUISE HUXTABLE

Ada Louise Huxtable, known for her "architecture views," summarizes the achievements of the Chicago architectural firm of Holabird and Root, on its one-hundredth anniversary, with emphasis on the firm's contributions to the development of the skyscraper. Her "reviewing" lies in the assessment of the firm's contributions. With occasional uses of the first-person pronoun, Huxtable demonstrates her knowledge of architectural history, trends, firms, and individuals, lending authority to her tribute to Holabird and Root. She expects the *New York Times* audience who would read an architecture column to know the vocabulary of the field.

Original publication: *The New York Times*, March 2, 1980.

It probably shouldn't, but it still comes as something of a surprise to find American architectural firms celebrating their 100th anniversaries. Last year it was the centennial of the founding of the firm of McKim, Mead and White, which coincided nicely with what might be called the rediscovery of their work. Rediscovery is probably the wrong word, since McKim, Mead, and White buildings have continued to be an important part of the public consciousness— consisting as they do, of a large number of monumental public and institutional structures of the late 19th and early 20th century. What made the occasion special was a kind of McKim, Mead and White revival for a younger generation, a reevaluation that recognized the firm's sophisticated and skillful use of the academic, classical tradition that was consigned to the dust heap by the modernists and remained generally untouchable for the last 50 years. That renewed and generous appreciation made a very nice birthday party.

The most recent centennial celebrant is the Chicago firm of Holabird and Root, which, as Holabird and Roche, was central to the development of the skyscraper in the 30 years from 1880 to 1910, and to what is known, internationally, as the Chicago School.

Probably no single firm reflects more accurately the complete span of American architectural practice over the last 100 years, which includes a varied and quite valid sequence of styles. It has had its esthetic ups and downs. The office began with the pragmatic and innovative emphasis on engineering and esthetic clarity that characterized the early Chicago skyscrapers, which changed to the fashionable and sometimes tortured eclectic conceits with which tall buildings were clothed just before and after World War I. This was followed by the original and elegant "modernistic," or Art Deco, designs of the 1930's, and then a return to something akin to the early structural pragmatism in the "modernism" that followed World War II.

As appreciative as I am of the grand achievements of McKim, Mead and White, give or take a fair number of impressive potboilers, I find myself more interested in the vicissitudes of the Holabird and Root story. It lacks the lordly masterworks of the Eastern establishment firm, but it tells us a good deal more about invention, adaptability, changing taste and the struggle to survive as part of the American architectural mainstream.

I like the kind of tradition in which two and three generations of distinguished architectural names like Holabird (father, son and grandson in the one Chicago firm) and Root (father and son, anchoring two Chicago firms), continued to practice in the same city—particularly a city that has claimed to deal primarily in progress and change. I like it better than the instant, academic tradition in which a firm like McKim, Mead and White wrapped itself so splendidly and successfully for a borrowed style of life and design, that descended into spiritless aridity in the work of its later members.

Holabird and Root produced sound rather than spectacular buildings. Even at its time of greatest strength, from 1880 to 1910, there were other firms and individuals in Chicago, from William Le Baron Jenney to Louis Sullivan, who made the great leaps forward in structure and style. But if other architects build greater buildings, few built consistently better ones. The office's claim to fame is based on that most interesting and important chapter in American architectural history, the development of the skyscraper, a field of design and construction in which it held a leadership position for a surprisingly long time. There were changes in partners and philosophy over the years, but it continued to produce top-rank tall buildings right through the 1920's and 30's.

Chicago's great contributions in the 1880's and 90's were the technological achievements of steel-frame construction and related engineering, and the handsome visual expression of that new technology. The Chicago Style became one of the strongest and handsomest esthetics of modern times. (Revisionists are adding many styles and schools to the Chicago story that have been overlooked in the critical preoccupation with the tall building, but that does not change its significance or supremacy; there is really no point in trying to stand history on its head.)

Holabird and Roche specialized in the careful, logical adaptation of structural means to functional ends—which resulted in the creation of a distinct design formula for the new, large business buildings whose rise skyward was made possible by the metal frame and the elevator.

The historian Carl W. Condit has characterized that formula as "a basic norm or type exactly developed to fit a particular set of conditions." Historian and critic William H. Jordy calls it an architectural type virtually beyond "design," something so well suited to its use that it led inevitably and properly to mass duplication. He makes it clear that it was a "superb type."

The formula became the skyscraper style. To a stroller of Chicago's streets today, these early buildings still have an extraordinary impact. The visible scale and pattern of their structural frames, filled with the generous expanses of bayed or plain glass known as "Chicago windows," have an architectonic clarity and force that is only achieved through a sensuous and rational reference to structure. Architecturally, this is a hard act to follow.

It was exactly suited to the needs of business and builders. Boldly stated in Holabird and Roche's Tacoma Building of 1886-89, the formula was carried further in the Marquette Building of 1894, which definitively established the supremacy of the structural frame. The solution was at its most refined in the Republic Building of 1904–09. (The Tacoma and the Republic were both demolished in the 1960's, and the architectural vandalism is continuing in the 70's. What remains of the Chicago School owes a great deal to the pioneering efforts of the Chicago Heritage Committee, and much of what is gone was beautifully recorded by Richard Nickel who lost his life in the collapse of an Adler and Sullivan building that he was photographing in the process of demolition.)

With a Boston builder named Peter Brooks, Holabird and Roche laid out the fundamental principles of the new commercial construction. They stressed the provision of light and air, and the importance of the quality of public facilities, like lobbies, elevators and corridors. Above all, there was to be no second-class space, because it cost as much to build and operate as first-class space. Proper materials and good details were to simplify operation and maintenance.

Like so many others, Holabird and Roche succumbed to the avalanche of eclecticism after 1910, but the firm never had a sure hand for academic revivalism. In 1928, after a change of partners, the office emerged as Holabird and Root, and in the 1930's it produced a brilliant succession of "modernist" skyscrapers of a radical, streamlined elegance that included the Chicago Board of Trade, the Palmolive, now Playboy Building, and the Chrysler Building at the Chicago World's Fair.

The 1940's brought the war, and the 50's saw a lot of uneven and pedestrian work. In the 70's, some of the senior partners retired; today the principals are Eugene A. Cook, John A. Holabird Jr., Gerrard S. Pook, Gerald Horn and Roy D. Solfisbury III. The firm is now embarked on a search for quality and style that is yet without a name; it reflects the newer, younger partners and the esthetic pluralism of current architectural trends.

Meanwhile, the old Chicago—their old Chicago—is tumbling down around them. The city has been shamefully delinquent in protecting its early skyscraper heritage. Building codes and economics militate against preservation and new projects constantly call for landmark demolition. The British magazine, *The Economist*, in a recent feature on Chicago's historic architecture—which is more admired abroad than at home—deplored "the loss of many of the buildings that have inspired reverence for the city." The second hundred years are the hardest.

A Humid Recital Stirs Bangkok

KENNETH LANGBELL

Kenneth Langbell sets the stage and describes some selections on the program of a piano recital in Bangkok, with appropriate background on the performer. The description of the pianist's attire, complete with boutonniere, hints of writing for a social column. This review demonstrates just how much fun a reviewer can have—and how much entertainment he can provide his readers.

Original publication: *Bangkok Post*, "made available by Martin Bernheimer to the *Los Angeles Times*."

The recital last evening in the chamber music room of the Erawan Hotel by U.S. pianist Myron Kropp, the first appearance of Mr. Kropp in Bangkok, can only be described by this reviewer and those who witnessed Mr. Kropp's performance as one of the most interesting experiences in a very long time.

A hush fell over the room as Mr. Kropp appeared from the right of the stage, attired in black formal evening-wear with a small, white poppy in his lapel. With sparse, sandy hair, a sallow complexion and a deceptively frail looking frame, the man who has repopularized Johann Sebastian Bach approached the Baldwin Concert Grand, bowed to the audience and placed himself upon the stool.

It might be appropriate to insert at this juncture that many pianists, including Mr. Kropp, prefer a bench, maintaining that on a screw-type stool they sometimes find themselves turning sideways during a particularly expressive strain. There was a slight delay, in fact, as Mr. Kropp left the stage briefly, apparently in search of a bench, but returned when informed that there was none.

As I have mentioned on several other occasions, the Baldwin Concert Grand, while basically a fine instrument, needs constant attention, particularly in a climate such as Bangkok. This is even more true when the instrument is as old as the one provided in the chamber music room of the Erawan Hotel. In this humidity the felts which separate the white keys from the black tend to swell, causing an occasional key to stick, which apparently was the case last evening with the D in the second octave.

During the "raging storm" section of the D-minor Toccata and Fugue, Mr. Kropp must be complimented for putting up with the awkward D. However, by the time the "storm" was past and he had gotten into the Prelude and Fugue in D Major, in which the second octave D plays a major role, Mr. Kropp's patience was wearing thin.

Some who attended the performance later questioned whether the awkward key justified some of the language which was heard coming from the stage during softer passages of the fugue. However, one member of the audience, who had sent his children out of the room by the midway point of the fugue, had a valid point when he commented over the music and extemporaneous remarks of Mr. Kropp that the workman who greased the stool might have done better to use some of the grease on the second octave D. Indeed, Mr. Kropp's stool had more than enough grease, and during one passage in which the music and lyrics both were particularly violent Mr. Kropp was turned completely around. Whereas before his remarks had been aimed largely at the piano and were therefore somewhat muted, to his surprise and that of those in the chamber music room he found himself addressing himself directly to the audience.

But such things do happen, and the person who began to laugh deserves to be severely reprimanded for this undignified behavior. Unfortunately, laughter is contagious, and by the time it had subsided and the audience had regained its composure Mr. Kropp appeared to be somewhat shaken. Nevertheless he swiveled himself back into position facing the piano and, leaving the D Major Fugue unfinished, commenced on the Fantasia and Fugue in G Minor.

Why the concert grand piano's G key in the third octave chose that particular time to begin sticking I hesitate to guess. However, it is certainly safe to say that Mr. Kropp himself did nothing to help matters when he began using his feet to kick the lower portion of the piano instead of operating the pedals as is generally done.

Possibly it was this jarring, or the un-Bach-like hammering to which the sticking keyboard was being subjected. Something caused the right front leg of the piano to buckle slightly inward, leaving the entire instrument listing at approximately a 35-degree angle from that which is normal. A gasp went up from the audience, for if the piano had actually fallen several of Mr. Kropp's toes, if not both his feet, would surely have been broken.

It was with a sigh of relief, therefore, that the audience saw Mr. Kropp slowly rise from his stool and leave the stage. A few men in the back of the room began clapping, and when Mr. Kropp reappeared a moment later it seemed he was responding to the ovation. Apparently, however, he had left to get the red-handled fire ax which was hung backstage in case of fire, for that was what he had in his hand.

My first reaction at seeing Mr. Kropp begin to chop at the left leg of the grand piano was that he was attempting to make it tilt at the same angle as the right leg and thereby correct the list. However, when the weakened legs finally collapsed altogether with a great crash and Mr. Kropp continued to chop, it became obvious to all that he had no intention of going on with the concert.

The ushers, who had heard the snapping of piano wires and splintering of sounding board from the dining room, came rushing in and, with the help of the hotel manager, two Indian watchmen, and a passing police corporal, finally succeeded in disarming Mr. Kropp and dragging him off the stage.

Babel Builders

MELVIN MADDOCKS

Melvin Maddocks demonstrates his own linguistic prowess—alliteration, coinages, allusions—in his review of this book about the state of our language, thus expressing his own frustration and indignation with current usage, especially in the field of education. This review is worth reading aloud to appreciate

Maddocks' command of the language, a language he wants his readers to respect and appreciate and enjoy.

Original publication: *Time*, December 7, 1981.

The Graves of Academe by Richard Mitchell. Little, Brown. 229 pages. $11.95.

For almost five years, Richard Mitchell, 51, professor of English at Glassboro (N.J.) State College, has made regular trips to his basement to pump from his ancient, tooth-rattling printing press a broadsheet called *The Underground Grammarian*. With gloriously abusive alliteration he has made it his business to assault deans and department heads for the bureaucratic academese that passes as English. For other professors, the activity might be a mere hobby. For Mitchell, it is a sacred mission. "A mind can be overthrown by words," he says. "Bad language ultimately is *immoral*." These thunderbolts have won the appreciation of such disparate authors as Edwin Newman and Howard Fast. But applause has not mollified him. Gazing at a sea of bad grammarians, he fulminates against "fools and frauds" who spout "mindless and mendacious babble!"

In Mitchellese, that now counts as understatement. For instead of mellowing with time, the stand-up comedian at the pedal press has become a scourging prophet. Woe to a people who have lost their power to read and write passably! Mitchell believes that they have also, verily, lost their power to reason and discriminate.

In *The Graves of Academe* the author, at full boil, arrives at the question behind all his vexations: Why, in spite of more and more education, are Americans less and less educated? Mitchell's finger-pointing answer: the educationists. The very word sends him into a splutter.

Tunneling back into the late 19th century, the Underground Grammarian digs up the father of educationism, Wilhelm Max Wundt, a professor of psychology at the University of Leipzig. Mitchell describes the 70-year process by which Wundt's disciples have nudged American teaching from the "cognitive domain" to the "affective domain." Translation: Feeling comes first, with thinking an also-ran. The skills of reading, writing and arithmetic yield precedence to "values orientation." The classroom turns into a behavior-modification lab, where, in the trade talk, one practices child-centered strategies that optimize the personological variables of interactive relationships, thus producing awareness enhancement.

When these innovations fail, according to the tests devised by the educationists themselves, and the terrible news registers that "Johnny can't read," do the reformers pack up their easy-learner kits and slink off into the night? Not at all. The shameless fellows ask for more money to repair the damage they have done, setting up "Communications Consultancy Centers" to cure illiteracy by means of every audiovisual tool known to the functionally illiterate.

Where will it all end? Mitchell offers no facile solution. The mob is already hard at work on the new Tower of Babel. Only individual men and women can bring it down, stone by misplaced stone. If enough solitaries of the word read and write with loving precision, treating language like a holy and joyous sacrament, well, who knows? "Maybe," the Underground Grammarian whispers in his final sentence.

This is the only qualified statement in a book that makes H. L. Mencken sound like a waffler. But if Mitchell is given to a certain exaggeration, does that mean he is wrong? Only a nattering nitwit would dare think so.

Gamalielese

H. L. MENCKEN

Although his ostensible subject for review is Warren G. Harding's inaugural address, H. L. Mencken uses the occasion to make comments on a number of segments of American society— journalism, education and professors, popular taste, and politics. His characterization of the audience of President Harding's speech (and thus the audience of his review) runs the gamut from "boobery" to "stoneheads" and finally to "jackass," with a few gradations in between. He probably successfully attacked most members of his audience, directly or indirectly. So much for respecting your reader! He did not earn the label of "curmudgeon" for nothing.

Original publication: *Baltimore Sun*, March 7, 1921.

On the question of the logical content of Dr. Harding's harangue of last Friday I do not presume to have views. The matter has been debated at great length by the editorial writers of the Republic, all of them experts in logic; moreover, I confess to being prejudiced. When a man arises publicly to argue that the United States entered the late war because of a "concern for preserved civilization," I can only snicker in a superior way and wonder why he isn't holding down the chair of history in some American university. When he says that the U.S. has "never sought territorial aggrandizement through force," the snicker rises to the virulence of a chuckle, and I turn to the first volume of General Grant's memoirs. And when, gaining momentum, he gravely informs the boobery that "ours is a constitutional freedom where the popular will is supreme, and minorities are sacredly protected," then I abandon myself to a mirth that transcends, perhaps, the seemly, and send picture postcards of A.

Mitchell Palmer, and the Atlanta Penitentiary to all of my enemies who happen to be Socialists.

But when it comes to the style of a great man's discourse, I can speak with a great deal less prejudice, and maybe with somewhat more competence, for I have earned most of my livelihood for twenty years past by translating the bad English of a multitude of authors into measurably better English. Thus qualified professionally, I rise to pay my small tribute to Dr. Harding. Setting aside a college professor or two and a half dozen dipsomaniacal newspaper reporters, he takes the first place in my Valhall of literati. That is to say, he writes the worst English that I have ever encountered. It reminds me of a string of wet sponges; it reminds me of tattered washing on the line; it reminds me of a stale bean-soup, of college yells, of dogs barking idiotically through endless nights. It is so bad that a sort of grandeur creeps into it. It drags itself out of the dark abysm (I was about to write abscess!) of pish, and crawls insanely up the topmost pinnacle of posh. It is rumble and bumble. It is flap and doodle. It is balder and dash.

But I grow lyrical. More scientifically, what is the matter with it? Why does it seem so flabby, so banal, so confused and childish, so stupidly at war with sense? If you first read the inaugural address and then hear it intoned, as I did (at least in part), then you will perhaps arrive at an answer. That answer is very simple. When Dr. Harding prepares a speech he does not think it out in terms of an educated reader locked up in jail, but in terms of a great horde of stoneheads gathered around a stand. That is to say, the thing is always a stump speech; it is conceived as a stump speech and written as a stump speech. More, it is a stump speech addressed primarily to the sort of audience that the speaker has been used to all his life, to wit, an audience of small town yokels, of low political serfs, of morons scarcely able to understand a word of more than two syllables, and wholly unable to pursue a logical idea for more than two centimeters.

Such imbeciles do not want ideas—that is, new ideas, ideas that are unfamiliar, ideas that challenge their attention. What they want is simply a gaudy series of platitudes, of threadbare phrases terrifically repeated, of sonorous nonsense driven home with gestures. As I say, they can't understand many words of more than two syllables, but that is not saying that they do not esteem such words. On the contrary, they like them and demand them. The roll of incomprehensible polysyllables enchants them. They like phrases which thunder like salvos of artillery. Let that thunder sound, and they take all the rest on trust. If a sentence begins furiously and then peters out into fatuity, they are still satisfied. If a phrase has a punch in it, they do not ask that it also have a meaning. If a word slides off the tongue like a ship going down the ways, they are content and applaud it and wait for the next.

Brought up amid such hinds, trained by long practice to engage and delight them, Dr. Harding carries over his stump manner into everything he writes. He is, perhaps, too old to learn a better way. He is, more likely, too discreet to experiment. The stump speech, put into cold type, maketh the judicious to grieve. But roared from an actual stump, with arms flying and eyes flashing and the old flag overhead, it is certainly and brilliantly effective. Read the inaugural address, and it will gag you. But hear it recited through a sound-magnifier, with grand gestures to ram home its periods, and you will begin to understand it.

Let us turn to a specific example. I exhume a sentence from the latter half of the eminent orator's discourse:

"I would like government to do all it can to mitigate; then, in understanding, in mutuality of interest, in concern for the common good, our tasks will be solved."

I assume that you have read it. I also assume that you set it down as idiotic—a series of words without sense. You are quite right; it is. But now imagine it intoned as it was designed to be intoned. Imagine the slow tempo of a public speech. Imagine the stately unrolling of the first clause, the delicate pause upon the word "then"—and then the loud discharge of the phrases "in understanding," "in mutuality of interest," "in concern for the common good," each with its attendant glare and roll of the eyes, each with its sublime heave, each with its gesture of a blacksmith bringing down his sledge upon an egg—imagine all this, and then ask yourself where you have got. You have got, in brief, to a point where you don't know what it is all about. You hear and applaud the phrases, but their connection has already escaped you. And so, when in violation of all sequence and logic, the final phrase "our tasks will be solved," assaults you, you do not notice its disharmony—all you notice is that, if this or that, already forgotten, is done, "our tasks will be solved." Whereupon, glad of the assurance and thrilled by the vast gestures that drive it home, you give a cheer.

That is, if you are the sort of man who goes to political meetings, which is to say, if you are the sort of man that Dr. Harding is used to talking to, which is to say, if you are a jackass.

The whole inaugural address reeked with just such nonsense. The thing started off with an error in English in its very first sentence—the confusion of pronouns in the *one-he* combination, so beloved of bad newspaper reporters. It bristled with words misused: *civic* for *civil*, *luring* for *alluring*, *womanhood* for *women*, *referendum* for *reference*, even *task* for *problem*. "The *task* is to be *solved*"—what could be worse? Yet I find it twice. "The expressed views of world opinion"—what irritating tautology! "The expressed conscience of progress"—what on earth does it mean? "This is not selfishness, it is sanctity"—what intelligible idea do you get out of that? "I know that Congress and the administration will favor every wise government policy to aid the resumption and encourage continued progress"—the resumption of what? "Service is the supreme *commitment* of life—*ach, du heiliger!*"

But is such bosh out of place in a stump speech? Obviously not. It is precisely and thoroughly in place in a stump speech. A tight fabric of ideas would weary and exasperate the audience; what it wants is simply a loud burble of words, a procession of phrases that roar, a series of whoops. This is what it got in the inaugural address of the Hon. Warren Gamaliel Harding. And this is what it will get for four long years—unless God sends a miracle and the corruptible puts on incorruption . . . Almost I long for the sweeter song, the rubber-stamps of more familiar design, the gentler and more seemly bosh of the late Woodrow.

The Modern Way of Dying

JUDITH H. PATERSON

Judith H. Paterson, biographer, Thomas More scholar, and journalism professor, has used personal experience to explain why a person with her background is reviewing a book about a modern medical dilemma. Her personal experiences are the basis for her conclusion that *everyone* must read this book. (See the selection in Chapter 3 for her persuasive essay on this same subject.)

Original publication: *The Texas Observer*, November 20, 1987.

Setting Limits: Medical Goals In An Aging Society by Daniel Callahan. New York: Simon and Schuster. 1987. 256 pages. $18.95.

If Daniel Callahan is right, most Americans don't agree with Shakespeare that death is "a necessary end that will come when it will come."

In *Setting Limits*, his third book on the dilemmas of modern medicine, Callahan asks what it means to grow old and die in a society that attempts to deny death and bases both public policy and personal choice on the illusion of unending youth, everlasting good health, and the hope of perpetually extended life. Callahan's meticulous consideration of the question raises bothersome issues, especially for those of us who have watched the modern drawn-out way of dying.

When my father learned he had lung cancer in 1980, he was 70 years old with too many years of heavy smoking and drinking under his belt to be a good statistic. Understanding the slim chance he had of living for long—with or without an operation, with or without chemotherapy—he asked to forego all treatment and live as best he could until he died. Dissuaded from his decision by his doctors and my mother, he underwent an operation that removed a lobe of his right lung and brought on a stroke that left him with the shuffle of an old man, unable to work or enjoy his family.

As his body and his spirits deteriorated, medicine for heart condition, stomach ulcers, high blood pressure, and depression kept him going. After refusing a second cancer operation, he was kept alive for another year with drugs and repeated trips to the hospital where oxygen, medicine, and food were pumped into his flagging body. By the time he died, an ordeal that might have lasted one year had lasted five. By then my mother's health was broken as well.

Plagued by both emphysema and heart disease, she endured a terminal illness prolonged even more agonizingly than my father's had been.

In the hospital where my mother was taken in her last months, I saw intensive-care rooms filled with bodies kept going for no reason. Cancer patients without hope of recovery got chemotherapy, blood transfusions, radiation. The very old lay barricaded in their beds, liquids dripping all day into limbs deathly still and crisp as parchment.

Agonizing, medically prolonged terminal illness is rapidly becoming the norm in America. As a friend who has practiced internal medicine for 25 years told me, "Hardly anyone dies with dignity anymore. Very few people have grasped the immensity of the problem. Nobody was prepared for this."

Daniel Callahan predicts colossal economic and sociological catastrophe if Americans continue to live longer and longer and medical technology persists in keeping them alive beyond the point where life has meaning. His cautiously stated but troubling conclusions will disturb readers at all points on the political spectrum: from right-to-lifers wanting to preserve life at all costs to egalitarians worried about age discrimination.

Although Callahan opposes both euthanasia and assisted suicide, he calls for radical across-the-board changes in public policy, as well as values and attitudes. His approach includes recommendations such as these:

1. cutting back on research and treatment that benefits mainly the old and seeks to extend life indefinitely;
2. changing Medicare to favor long-term health care for the elderly rather than hospitalization and critical care;
3. encouraging all age groups to work toward an acceptance of the concept of a "natural life span" that ends in old age and death;
4. making age (late 70s or early 80s) the criterion for cutting off government subsidy for life-extending treatment;
5. exchanging life extension for the elderly for health care goals that would improve the quality of life for everyone by instating a "full-blown national health-insurance program, guaranteeing a minimally adequate level of health care for all";
6. reassessing public policy to reduce the danger that the old and terminally ill will deplete resources that should go to medically deprived children, women and minorities.

Callahan addresses the most universal of subjects. Yet his book is so packed with statistics and references and the discussion is so carefully hedged with extenuating arguments that many readers will find it hard to get through. Nevertheless, everyone who can read this book, should read it. Those who can't will probably be influenced by it anyway since it promises to be a benchmark work in a drama soon to be played out in public debate and private lives.

England Rediscovers Its Age of Chivalry

JOHN RUSSELL

This review of an exhibition in the Royal Academy of Arts in London provides lessons in history and culture as well as describing and analyzing the works and displays. In point of view, Russell moves from the perspective of the group "we" to his personal "I do not know. . . ." As basis for his evaluation, he describes funding, the setting, and specific examples of the 748 items in the exhibit. He provides convincing evidence to his readers for the evaluation "that this has to be the best exhibition ever mounted by the R. A. ('Or anywhere,' some will add)." His American readers can plan to see the exhibit in London, or at least they know what they have missed.

Original publication: *The New York Times*, January 31, 1988.

To what extent can an exhibition sum up an entire civilization? Every generation has its own answer to that, but some of the answers haven't worn too well. Once upon a time the huge, baggy, "comprehensive," all-star national survey was in high favor. Governments loved them, and in a time of relative inactivity in the museum world the public often loved them, too.

In the 1980's, the roomy, meandering, panoramic anthology is completely out of step with the times. "Treasures of the Vatican" had some wonderful things in it, but on a deeper level it satisfied nobody. Next year's 200th anniversary of the French Revolution would once have been marked in Paris by an exhibition the size of Central Park in galleries built specially for the purpose. It is a mark of President François Mitterrand's sense of the times that he wouldn't have any of that. We now prefer to get in close to one specific aspect of cultural history and bring to it imaginative energy of a high order.

As to the efficacy of such a sharp-focus exhibition of ideas, we need look no further than the Royal Academy of Arts in London, where people from all over England are now pouring into an exhibition that might not, at first glance, seem slated for top of the charts. "The Age of Chivalry" is essentially a survey of English Gothic as it functioned between the accession of King Henry III in 1216 and the murder of King Richard II in 1399.

This is a period as to which not everyone has a clear idea. It is also a period in which not many of us might care to have lived. Even at the level of privilege, it was often a matter of comfortless castles, sullen and undependable pikemen and rival lords who were forever feuding. For most Englishmen and English women this was a time at which life was what Thomas Hobbes in his "Leviathan" described as "solitary, poor, nasty, brutish and short."

Yet John of Gaunt in "Richard II" still carries an English audience with him when he speaks of England as (among much else) "this other Eden, demi-paradise." As an apostrophe, it rings out more poignantly with every year that passes. But if visitors are deeply moved by "The Age of Chivalry" it may be precisely because the exhibition is so close to John of Gaunt in its general message.

The England that it evokes with such consummate eloquence really *is* another Eden and in many of its aspects a demi-paradise. England here reverts not so much to what it really was—for that, too much has been edited out—as to what English people of every sort and stripe would wish it to have been. In the same way that American Luminism bound up the wounds of the United States after the Civil War, English Gothic in all its manifestations now binds up the wounds of a country that has been much in travail.

That is why visitors to the Royal Academy go in bright of eye and light of step. And when they come out they tell anyone who will listen that this has to be the best exhibition ever mounted by the R. A. ("Or anywhere," some will add). Be that as it may, the show is a triumph of presentation. (Lloyds Bank put up the equivalent of more than half a million dollars toward it, and the J. Paul Getty Junior Charitable Trust also helped with the financing. In its more than 200 years of activity, the Royal Academy has mounted many wonderful shows. But in "The Age of Chivalry" objects of the greatest beauty and rarity are stage-managed with a panache that the academy has never attempted before.

Spotlit or back-lit in darkened rooms, everything in the show looks gorgeous. (Even the runty little fragment of the Black Prince's belt and buckle doesn't look too dreary.) As for the stained-glass windows, the polychrome sculptures in stone, the smooth light-harboring ivories, the translucent alabasters, the wit and finesse of the Dunstable Swan Jewel and the orchestration of gold, silver, sapphires, rubies, pearls and diamonds in the crown that was part of a royal dowry, they are seduction itself.

Neither in the 748 items in the show nor in the 575 pages of the learned and monumental catalogue is there ever so much as a trace of monotony. The exhibition is about kings and queens, but it is also about the charter of 1347 that empowered the mayor, bailiff and citizens of Bristol to build a cage in which evildoers and disturbers of the peace could be locked up and put on public view. (Bakers who sold short-weight bread were pulled through the streets on a hurdle for all to see.)

High deeds and the privileged life play a part in the show, which also includes a section on the 14th-century patrons who spent their money (and they had plenty of it) on building churches, founding great schools and colleges, collecting works of art from all over and in general making England a better place. Yet, there too, the anonymous people of England are not forgotten. The Luttrell Psalter of around 1325, lent by the British Museum, was there to show exactly what it was like for women to work on the harvest and for their men to speed the plough. (In that division of labor, the men won out.)

This show is not, in general, a place for the private or clandestine imagination. But, in that context, everyone who has spent time in English Gothic churches will have learned to head for the sculptured underside of the seats in the choir stalls. These adjustable seats doubled as a kind of shooting stick for people who found them convenient, and the sculptures in question mined a vein of fun and fantasy that was not often encouraged elsewhere. The Royal Academy show has some rich examples of this, as a cat plays the fiddle to the bleating of a goat, another cat sinks its teeth into a mouse, a man and a woman set out on a dance that has its climax in her turning a cartwheel, lewd riddles are proposed and answered and a wodehouse (or wild man) demonstrates that he has a very good seat on a lion.

This is an exhibition about the great English cathedrals, but it also takes in the remote country churches in which later generations of clergymen doubled as antiquarians and came up with many a memorable find. Thanks to one of those moonlighting antiquarians, who held the living of Fersfield in Norfolk from 1729 to 1752, we can see the polychromed recumbent effigy of Sir Robert du Bois, which was carved around 1340 from a single piece of oak and filled with burnt coals to absorb the damp. This effigy might have been outclassed in the final room of the show, where it keeps company with some particularly glorious pieces of stained glass. But is isn't. The plain country gentleman from a plain country church amply holds his own, not only with kings and queens, great soldiers and paragons of learning, but even with Thomas à Becket, saint and martyr.

If the the impact of the show is on the whole both precise and ecstatic, it is not only because of the high quality of the objects. It is because they are taken out of their normal environment and seen in isolation and with every possible help from modern museography. Spotlighting in darkened rooms helps enormously. Placing helps, when we see at eye-level fragments of stained glass, sculptures taken out of context and musical instruments from which we shall not hear so much as a toot. A modicum of make-believe helps, too, when the wraith of a Gothic nave rises before our eyes in the largest and most familiar of the Royal Academy's galleries. In short, we have a one-to-one relationship with objects that might elsewhere be badly lit, hard to find and mixed in with inferior distractions.

It is the greatness of "The Age of Chivalry" that it applies the dictates of chivalry not so much to human beings as to the work that is on view. With hardly an exception, that work is cherished, protected and surrounded with every mark of respect and affection. Chivalry may have had its ups and downs in the world outside, but within the Royal Academy it is alive and very well.

One last aspect of the show should be explored. Gothic was a multinational style, and one to which many countries contributed—France, Germany and Italy among them. In France, England's neighbor across the sea, it flourished enormously. There is hardly a figure in the present show that does not have his counterpart in France. As king, warrior statesman and saint, Louis IX of France (1214-70) had a stature at least equal to that of any of his English contemporaries. The Black Prince, Edward of Woodstock (1330-76), was what the French chronicler Froissart called him—"the flower of chivalry in all the world"—but that formidable French warrior Bertrand du Guesclin (1320-80) was no slouch when it came to routing the enemy.

England had been invaded and beaten by a French army in 1066, and for a long time the French language played a great part in English life. The two countries were constantly linked in matters of marriage, taste and achievement of all kinds. Henry III of England was fascinated by the "Rayonnant'" variant of Gothic architecture that had been taken up by his brother-in-law, the future St. Louis. Both Canterbury Cathedral and Westminster Abbey had strong French elements. And even John of Gaunt—as we can see from a fragment of armorial glass in the present show—had close family attachments with France.

All this being so, it is curious that English Gothic is presented as if in a bell jar, resistant to all foreign influence and striking out sturdily upon its own. English Gothic did indeed have its firmly distinguished characteristics, but I do not know that we need to be told in the introduction to the catalogue that "scholars no longer see English Gothic art as some sort of provincial offshoot under the shadow of French Gothic art." The art can very well speak for itself.

The Beautiful and Damned: Friend Husband's Latest

ZELDA SAYRE [FITZGERALD]

Zelda Sayre Fitzgerald, in her review of F. Scott Fitzgerald's *The Beautiful and Damned*, has a good time with both her husband's "latest" novel and the art of reviewing. Using her maiden name, she makes no effort to deceive her readers as she criticizes the book and its author. At the same time she urges them to buy it, for her own personal reasons. There is no rule that the reviewer has to be objective, but, if not, she should confess biases or prejudices.

Original publication: *New York Tribune*, April 2, 1922.

I note on the table beside my bed this morning a new book with an orange jacket entitled *The Beautiful and Damned*. It is a strange book, which has for me an uncanny fascination. It has been lying on that table for two years. I have been asked to analyze it carefully in the light of my brilliant critical insight, my tremendous erudition and my vast impressive partiality. Here I go!

To begin with, every one must buy this book for the following aesthetic reasons: First, because I know where there is the cutest cloth-of-gold dress for only $300 in a store on Forty-second Street, and also if enough people buy it where there is a platinum ring with a complete circlet, and also if loads of people buy it my husband needs a new winter overcoat, although the one he has has done well enough for the last three years.

Now, as to the other advantages of the book—its value as a manual of etiquette is incalculable. Where could you get a better example how not to behave than from the adventures of Gloria? And as a handy cocktail mixer nothing better has been said or written since John Roach Straton's last sermon.

It is a wonderful book to have around in case of emergency. No one should ever set out in pursuit of unholy excitement without a special vest-pocket edition dangling from a string around his neck.

For this book tells exactly, and with compelling lucidity, just what to do when cast off by a grandfather, or when sitting around a station platform at 4 A.M., or when spilling champagne in a fashionable restaurant, or when told that one is too old for the movies. Any of these things might come into any one's life at any minute.

Just turn the pages of the book slowly at any of the above-mentioned trying times until your own case strikes your eye and proceed according to directions. Then for the ladies of the family there are such helpful lines as: "I like gray because then you have to wear a lot of paint." Also what to do with your husband's old shoes—Gloria takes Anthony's shoes to bed with her and finds it a very satisfactory way of disposing of them. The dietary suggestion, "tomato sandwiches and lemonade for breakfast," will be found an excellent cure for obesity.

Now, let us turn to the interior decorating department of the book. Therein can be observed complete directions for remodeling your bathroom, along modern and more interesting lines, with plans for a bookrack by the tub, and a detailed description of what pictures have been found suitable for bathroom walls after years of careful research by Mr. Fitzgerald.

The book itself, with its plain green back, is admirably constructed for being read in a tub—wetting will not spoil the pages; in fact, if one finds it growing dry simply dip the book briskly in warm water. The bright yellow jacket is particularly adapted to being carried on Fifth Avenue while wearing a blue or henna-colored suit, and the size is adaptable to being read in hotel lobbies while waiting to keep dates for luncheon.

It seems to me that on one page I recognized a portion of an old diary of mine which mysteriously disappeared shortly after my marriage, and also scraps of letters which, though considerably edited, sound to me vaguely familiar. In fact, Mr. Fitzgerald—I believe that is how he spells his name—seems to believe that plagiarism begins at home.

I find myself completely fascinated by the character of the heroine. She is a girl approximately ten years older than I am, for she seems to have been born about 1890—though I regret to remark that on finishing the book I feel no confidence as to her age, since her birthday is in one place given as occurring in February and in another place May and in the third place in September. But there is a certain inconsistency in this quite in accord with the lady's character.

What I was about to remark is that I would like to meet the lady. There seems to have been a certain rouge she used which had a quite remarkable effect. And the strange variations in the color of her hair from cover to cover range entirely through the spectrum—I find myself doubting that all the changes were of human origin; also the name of the unguent used in the last chapter is not given. I find these aesthetic deficiencies very trying. But don't let that deter you from buying the book. In every other way the book is absolutely perfect.

The other things I didn't like in the book—I mean the unimportant things—were the literary references and the attempt to convey a profound air of erudition. It reminds me in its more soggy moments of the essays I used to get up in school at the last minute by looking up strange names in the *Encyclopaedia Britannica.*

I think the heroine is most amusing. I have an intense distaste for the melancholy aroused in the masculine mind by such characters as Jenny Gerhardt, Antonia and Tess (of the D'Urbervilles). Their tragedies, redolent of the soil, leave me unmoved. If they were capable of dramatizing themselves they would no longer be symbolic, and if they weren't—and they aren't—they would be dull, stupid and boring, as they inevitably are in life.

The book ends on a tragic note; in fact a note which will fill any woman with horror, or, for that matter, will fill any furrier with horror, for Gloria, with thirty million to spend, buys a sable coat instead of a kolinsky coat. This is a tragedy unequaled in the entire work of Hardy. Thus the book closes on a note of tremendous depression and Mr. Fitzgerald's subtle manner of having Gloria's deterioration turn on her taste in coats has scarcely been equaled by Henry James.

Book Won't Mystify

DAPHNE SIMPKINS

Daphne Simpkins, a freelance writer, enjoys playing with words and allusions in this review of Harold Robbins's *Spellbinder*, wordplay that she expects her readers to note. She opens the review by putting the novel in the context of Robbins's career. Despite her negative evaluation of this book, she acknowledges Robbins's other successes.

Original publication: *The Montgomery Advertiser and Alabama Journal*, October 10, 1982.

SPELLBINDER. By Harold Robbins. Simon and Schuster. 363 pages. $14.95

Spellbinder, Harold Robbins' newest release, currently holds seventh place on The New York Times' best seller list. Part of this commercial success is due to a band of loyal Robbins readers who remember early books like Never Love A Stranger and have not been discouraged by the latest disappointments The Betsy and Dreams Die First.

Spellbinder falls somewhere in between the two extremes of being a good story in the early Robbins tradition and the kind of book currently associated with Robbins and described as being blasphemous and gratuitously sexual. This latest Robbins book is a fictional tracking of the rise to power of an American religious leader, somewhat Christian.

Robbins doesn't hesitate to equate the hero he has imaginatively named "The Preacher" to modern media-miracle workers like Jerry Falwell, Oral Roberts and Rex Humbard. He does this with the implicit goal of persecuting those who have despised him and said all manner of evil against him for their own sake. In Spellbinder, one may believe that Robbins' interpretation of Christian forgiveness begins with revenge.

Indeed, the novel seems to be a weapon of sorts, leveled against those critics of Robbins who have used their pulpits to boycott his art form. Robbins takes to his own pulpit in a narrative about a holy man who is flawed by being mortal, is betrayed by a Judas and, like Christ, dies for the sinners he loves.

The creation of a Christ-figure as the hero is a predictable theme and reads superficially. The characters move about as if slightly doped, which they often are since they are heavily reliant on marijuana, sometimes cocaine, and their cult-like religion to maintain their own brand of faith. At times, one can almost see Robbins playing God in a long white writer's robe, the strings of his marionette dangling from his sleeves, while he manipulates his puppet people to dance to his tune of revenge against the Moral Majority.

And sex? For those readers who prefer the specifics of erotica, Robbins injects a few choice words upon occasion, designed for shock effect. These moments of love, freed from the trappings of mystery and romance, jar the reader as disjunctively as a sour note in the Wedding March.

Spellbinder may be on the best seller list for some time because of its radical political and religious stance and because of the notoriety of Harold Robbins. However, those readers who do not look to religion or even literature to mesmerize will find the spell of the Spellbinder quite easily broken and Robbins' visionary version of a born-again Messiah an easy guy to forget.

•   •   •

Chapter Questions

1. Which review contains the most effective blend of summary (description), analysis, and evaluation? How does the reviewer achieve this effect?
2. Compare the lengths of the summaries in the various reviews. Which ones are longer? Is the length justified? Do you think any one of the summaries is too long? Why?
3. Is there a summary that you believe is not long enough, or not detailed enough, to provide readers with the background necessary for the review?
4. Are all of the evaluations convincingly established in the analysis?
5. If you are familiar with the primary source of any one of these reviews (that is, you have seen *Fantasia*, read *A Taste for Death* or *The Panda's Thumb*, and so on), do you concur with the reviewer's assessment? Is there any point with which you disagree? Is the evaluation convincing enough?
6. Did the selections in this chapter meet your demands for what reviews should contain?

Chapter Five
RESEARCH

Research makes special demands on writers and readers. Not only must writers achieve their purposes but also they must distinguish between their own words and ideas and those taken from other sources. And readers must read carefully enough to recognize the same distinctions.

For most of us, our first research assignment came in fifth or sixth grade when a social studies teacher sent us to the encyclopedia. We dutifully looked up some topic such as food products of a Central American country, customs in Egypt, the educational system in Scandinavia, or the great rivers of the world. Not knowing any better, we copied several paragraphs and received high praise for an assignment well done—praise that started us on a life of plagiarism. We concluded that copying words and presenting them as our own constituted good research.

Writers must learn the principles of research in order to use, most effectively, the limitless resources available to them—and in order to stay out of court. Correct documentation and careful use of quotation marks are concerns of law as well as concerns of punctuation rules. Writers may not *steal* someone's words or ideas. And readers must be able to identify the "borrowed" words and ideas and the sources from which they were taken.

All writers do research at some time, whether they are writing reviews, exposition, persuasion, or even a diary. They go seeking information that they do not know, evidence to use in some work in progress, or maybe even a subject about which to write. In her diary, Etty Hillesum mentions titles of books and songs as relevant to her personal thoughts, an informal type of research and documentation. Scottie Fitzgerald Smith looks for information—or inspiration—in her attic when she begins to write about her life with her parents. In a more formal use of sources she *quotes* from a letter written by her mother. Reviews naturally use sources; they are written about at least the primary source (a book, a play, a restaurant).

Research becomes indispensible for writing exposition and persuasion. Even though there are essays that use sources in other chapters, for the purposes of this text, I have classified an essay as an example of research when the use of research material is essential or significant to the purpose of the essay, or its reason for being. Regardless of the emphasis on exposition or persuasion, we look up information to use as evidence to help explain a subject or to support an argument. We need statistics, testimony, experiments that we cannot perform, surveys we have not conducted. And to incorporate these materials effectively and correctly, we must quote accurately or paraphrase or summarize. Each one of these three methods of incorporating sources requires documentation and careful handling so that we do not, in any way, misrepresent the original source, use the material incorrectly, or appear to claim it as our own. Respect for readers requires writers to provide their audiences with the necessary information to identify words and sources of material taken from someone else's work.

The forms of documentation are established in style sheets that vary from field to field. The most commonly used style sheets are MLA (published by the Modern Language Association), APA (published by the American Psychological Association), Chicago Manual of Style, the handbook by Kate Turabian (based on the Chicago manual), and some other general forms such as the name-year system and the number system.

No single text can adequately present all styles of documentation. Thus, writers should own the style sheet pertinent to their field and have it accessible, along with a dictionary, an almanac, and a thesaurus, as standard writing tools. These style sheets specify the exact method of citing a source: where to put the author's name, where to put the title and how to punctuate it, how to list publisher and copyright, and how to handle hundreds of other details related to citations. Footnotes, endnotes, or in-text citations may be used, depending on the style sheet. Similarly, bibliographies may appear in alphabetical order, in chronological order, or in numerical order (numbered as the source appears in the essay). Writers need that style sheet as a handy reference book.

Regardless of the style sheet used, certain principles do not vary from one form to another:

- Quote accurately. Do not leave out words without using an ellipsis (. . .). Do not add words without putting them inside brackets—[xxxx]—to indicate they have been added. Do not make careless errors in copying.
- Use quotation marks to open and close a passage taken from a source— unless you are quoting a long passage. In that case, shift to an indented quotation (also called a block quotation). Style sheets specify the form for indenting these long passages.
- When you paraphrase, put the ideas of the original into your own words. Do not let yourself fall into that gray area between quoting and paraphrasing—a few words from the source and a few from you, a few synonyms substituted in the original, a slight change in the order of words from the source. All of these are unacceptable. Either use the words of the original, or use your own.
- Precisely document everything that is not your own—words or ideas.
- Document correctly—every date and page number must be correct. You undercut your credibility with careless errors in documentation.
- Follow the style sheet to the letter of the law. If it abbreviates the state, you abbreviate; if it uses Arabic numerals for the volume number, you must convert Roman numerals to Arabic. Do not be careless—or creative.

• Be sure your reader can identify your words and ideas as opposed to words and ideas taken from another source. And identify that source, formally or informally. The reader should be able to go directly to that source and pursue additional information on the point under discussion.

The styles for writing research may vary as much as writing styles for any other form of writing. The tone may be personal or scientific; the point of view may be first or third; the diction may be formal, informal, or technical. The constants in research writing are the principles for quoting, paraphrasing, and documenting clearly and accurately. And, as always, writers must keep their readers in mind.

• • •

Science Writing
Too Good To Be True?
BOB COLEMAN

Essayist and novelist Bob Coleman surveys the history of scientific writing from the seventeenth century to the present as the basis for his contention that scientists need to write more honestly, more truthfully. On the surface, the members of his audience for such an argument seem to be scientists, but there is a warning to all readers to be wary of being misled by writers of scientific works. In fact, his closing sentence makes all of "us" his audience: "The revival of such discussion might make us all more comfortable with the course and uses of science in the late 20th century." And his language is not so technical that a general reader can not understand it.

The documentation here is informal, with references to authors and titles in the essay itself, not even parenthetical. Despite this informal approach, the emphasis is on use of researched materials— quotations and summaries.

Original publication: *The New York Times Book Review*, September 27, 1987.

In an age when "scientific prose" is a virtual synonym for "literary Novocain," it seems hard to believe that American scientific journals once contained some of the most exciting writing of their era. Two hundred years ago, American scientists publishing their research offered not only sound empirical data but small jokes and vast vistas, the fear of God and the hope of an American paradise. But early scientific papers offered more than stylistic beauties; they included something essential about the nature of scientific endeavor—its difficulties, the prospects for failure and the flexibility necessary to do scientific work.

While a frank discussion of troubles was fundamental to early scientific writing, modern science favors an image of perfection. "Nowadays," a widely published biochemist told me recently, "journals don't even want you to discuss your negative experiments. The very *hint* that you might have erred makes you insufficiently Olympian to be in print." That is a strangely perverse development, since early empiricists prized their difficulties as distinguishing them from the scholastics, who recycled received knowledge. Thus, the chemist Robert Boyle in 1675: "The natural philosophy, wont to be taught in schools, being little other than a system of the opinions of Aristotle, and some few other writers, is not, I confess, . . . very difficult to be learned. . . . But . . . that experimental philosophy, which you will find treated of in the following Essays, is a study, if duly prosecuted, so difficult, so chargeable, and so toilsome, that I think it requisite . . . to convince you, that by endeavouring to addict you to it, I invite you not to misspend your time or trouble on a science unable to merit and requite it."

To be sure, 17th-century British scientific journals only fitfully adopted Boyle's approach. Physicians in particular sometimes used the Royal Society's publication, Philosophical Transactions, for such sweeping claims as Dr. Hans Sloane's promise in February 1698 that, "I will discover . . . an infallible Medicine for curing [dysenteries], how dangerous and inveterate soever the Distemper may be, without fear of any dangerous Accident to follow."

Still, honest confession began at least as early as 1662, when Henry Power told the society he had abandoned a fascinating experiment on gun echoes in mines for fear the noise would collapse the tunnel roof on the miners. By the mid-18th century, frankness prevailed, as in a 1751 study of South American poisons whose author apologetically described having twice almost killed people through carelessness, or in the Abbé Nollet's 1750 remark about an electrical experiment: "When I found my Attempts were fruitless, I without any Difficulty communicated it to all the Philosophers with whom I corresponded."

Early American scientific publications added to the Royal Society's style a good measure of Republican fervor, but they preserved the reverence for a frank account of troubles. Benjamin Franklin's ideal scientist displayed a cross between Yankee ingenuity and Shaftesburyian benevolence; Franklin wanted researchers with ample funds, inquiring minds and charitable souls. In a pamphlet leading to the founding of the American Philosophical Society, our first true scientific society, he called for "men of speculation [who] might produce discoveries . . . to the benefit of mankind in general," and for "experiments that let light into the nature of things, tend to increase the power of man over matter, and multiply the conveniences or pleasures of life." Franklin got the men he wanted (Thomas Jefferson was the society's third president) and they shared their troubles with the freedom of friends and equals.

The first volume of the society's "Transactions" contained mostly reports from various observers of the June 1769 transit of Venus. One typical report reads: "We found on our first landing on the beach, that neither the Light-House, nor any place near the sea-shore, would be suitable for our Observations; as it would be difficult to keep our instruments steady, or defend either the glasses of the Telescopes, or the eyes of the observers, from receiving injury by the sand which is wafted about by the wind."

John Ewing and members of the academy's Venus committee added reports on their many financial and technical trials. David Rittenhouse covered difficulties with workmen, weather, an incomplete observatory, a faulty "equal-altitude instrument," a recalcitrant clock ("the clock was altered several times, once taken down and cleaned, removed back to the Observatory, and regulated anew"), and the "ill state" of Rittenhouse's own health. The cumulative effect for the reader is an understanding of science as an exciting and difficult human venture—along with a very clear notion of how the transit of Venus made it possible to calculate Earth's distance from the sun.

During the society's early years failure, or difficulty, became a fundamental rhetorical device, used both to start and to end reports. Thus, Dr. Benjamin Rush began a 1786 paper: "During my attendance upon the military hospitals of the United States, in the course of the late war, I met with several cases of the Tetanus. I had frequently met with this disorder in private practice, and am sorry to say that I never succeeded with the ordinary remedy. . . . I found it equally ineffectual in the army. Baffled in my expectations from a remedy that had been so much celebrated, I began to investigate more particularly."

The next year, Andrew Ellicott described the collapse of his exploration of Lake Erie: "The same evening the wind began to blow briskly from about two points west of North, and continued to increase till the evening of the 14th, when it was more violent than any thing of the kind I had ever been witness to before, and continued till the evening of the 16th without the least intermission—Our tents were all blown down, and we were under the necessity of fortifying our camp, by driving posts near to each other, firmly into the ground on the windward side, and filling up the vacuities with bushes in form of a hedge." The early volumes of "Transactions" form a sort of joint American epic, in which images of the frontier and of scientific discovery merged, as mathematical tables co-existed with adventure prose outdoing James Fenimore Cooper.

And yet by the mid-1800's this lively, accurate form of narration was rapidly being replaced by what we nowadays think of as scientific writing: a colorless progression of abstracts, protocols, results and interpretation. In the November-December issue of the Philosophical Society's journal for 1841, for example, the potentially exciting account of a geological survey of parts of upper Canada and western Ohio is summarized by the recording secretary, who allots to the hard parts of the venture a single line beginning, "The difficulties of the investigation are then alluded to," before sinking into a discussion of types of limestone, told in the passive voice.

Before the 19th century ended, open discussion of difficulties was apparently obsolete; with some important exceptions (Darwin was one), scientists began writing the way we suppose scientists always have. Several practical concerns may have contributed to this new style of scientific language, including limitations imposed by time and space as science developed more rapidly. Seven years elapsed between the second and third volumes of the American Philosophical Society's "Transactions," each volume running about 350 pages. In 1986, the journal Physical Review printed a total of 20,505 pages—and of course, Physical Review is only one of many journals (albeit a most important one) devoted to a single science, physics.

Early scientific societies used both corresponding and recording secretaries to keep track of reports and papers received. Increasingly over the first half of the 19th century, these overworked functionaries began abbreviating and condensing papers for publication. In the process, they often recast them in the passive voice and discarded any prefatory material, in order to hurry on to what "really mattered": the methods and results of successful experiments. By the latter part of the century, when journals dropped the secretarial format, scientist-authors themselves had internalized these rhetorical habits.

Another factor that contributed to the change in science writing was the shift toward science being done by large institutions and groups. Abraham Pais, in his remarkable history of modern physics, "Inward Bound," notes that Roentgen in the 19th century discovered X-rays alone in his tiny lab; 100 years later, a landmark article in particle physics was signed by the Nobel Prize winner Carlo Rubia and 135 co-authors. Multiple authors mean no author. At the same time, the audience had grown, from a small set of individuals who knew one another to an amorphous mass, including strangers with, presumably, no interest in one another's problems.

The increasing importance of mathematics to science also had an effect on the writing. In 18th-century scientific writing, detailed personal narrative co-existed quite happily with sophisticated mathematics, but later on the narrative disappeared while the mathematics became ever more complex.

But scientific prose was also changing because of the changing economics of science. John C. Green, a historian of science, and others have shown that early American science—for all its proclaimed interest in practical innovation—really produced little of commercial value. Indeed, many early scientists (including Jefferson) opposed even the patenting of scientific inventions, since knowledge belonged to humankind. Franklin's colleagues may have been mostly small businessmen and professional people, but they saw themselves as scientific Squire Allworthys, helping their fellow beings through benevolent curiosity.

That noble, if impractical, ideal was to be revised. For the diamond jubilee of Queen Victoria in 1887, The Times of London ran a retrospective essay that the pre-eminent scientific journal, Nature, reprinted with approval. It left no doubt about the course of 19th-century science: "The keynote of the Victorian era is the development of scientific research, the concomitant growth of practical invention, and the expansion of industry which these have brought about. . . .

An unprecedentedly large army of inquirers has simultaneously pushed the interrogation of nature in a thousand directions, and has attained unprecedented results. But beside them has been working an army larger, and equally keen, of men eagerly seeking to utilize for practical ends every crumb of available information."

That the 19th century integrated science and industrial capitalism is nowadays a commonplace; the phrasing of that article is probably more impressive for its Victorian certainty of tone than for anything else. Yet we might gain a better sense of the impact the integration of science and industry had on working scientists from the letter to the editors that immediately precedes the essay in Nature—an angry, frustrated complaint about an apparent fraud in the sale of some impure chemicals. Science had indeed entered the marketplace, with results both splendid and sad.

The links between American science and the commercial world were, by many accounts, first forged during the 1840's. In "Yankee Science in the Making," Dirk Struik of the Massachusetts Institute of Technology shows New England science in that decade to have been fueled by at least three factors: an upcropping of brilliant "Yankee tinkerers"; a general growth of industry, especially textiles; and the pressure of an agricultural sector suffering from "soil exhaustion, competition with the West, and the drain on labor power by the factory system." Yale and Harvard universities both established their scientific schools in the 1840's, and both went to work soon thereafter seeking financial support from New England capitalists.

Certainly, commerce shaped scientific prose during that decade. In 1847, as part of the groundwork for establishing the Smithsonian Institution, the American Academy of Arts and Sciences reviewed a plan for grants to scientists. The academy, while warning of the dangers of a scientific bureaucracy, approved the plan in language derived as much from industrial capitalism as from public-spiritedness: "Narrow circumstances are too apt to be the lot of genius when devoted to scientific pursuits; and the necessity of providing for personal and domestic wants too often absorbs the time and faculties of those who might, if relieved from cares of this kind, have adorned their age and benefited mankind. . . . The efficacy of market upon production is not limited to the creations of physical labor." That is a long way from the image of the benevolent gentleman-scientist created by Franklin a century earlier.

Equally dramatic were the changes in the way scientific discoveries were reported. The links between American business and science would create not only immense benefits but notable costs. More expensive experiments made researchers ever more dependent on an economic system that favored efficient, and applicable, success. Largely in response, it seems, scientists shifted their attention from their own troubles to those of their colleagues.

Eighteen hundred forty-seven was also the year Harvard installed its "great telescope." The account of its installation in the "Proceedings" of the American Philosophical Society contrasts strikingly with the reports on the transit of Venus 80 years earlier. Now all troubles are either suppressed ("I omit the details of mounting the telescope, as they are of little general interest") or used as gambits for self-congratulation: "The delicate and somewhat difficult task of mounting and adjusting this very large instrument had been performed with great expedition and skill by . . . the Director and Assistant Observer. . . . [The telescope] has, even under the disadvantage of a bad state of the atmosphere, exceeded our expectations." Mostly, the emphasis is on reassuring the academy that it got a square deal from the telescope's German manufacturers.

As scientists became easier on themselves, they became harder on their colleagues. The notion of peer review is at least as old as Boyle's "On the Unsuccessful Experiment," but in the mid-19th century competition brought a certain nastiness to the business. Thus, a single summary of an 1847 proposal for a new Chinese phonology dismisses previous work as (among other things) "erroneous," "badly denominated," "not very clearly stated" and "so utterly fanciful as to justify" the scorn heaped on it by an earlier reviewer.

Ultimately, an efficient and very discreet system of refereeing articles before publication would remove the most caustic disputes from the scientific journals, thereby completely suppressing discussion of research difficulties. Yet a question remains: Did discussion really vanish, or simply migrate elsewhere?

The professionalization of science did spawn writings aimed at nonscientists, but such works nearly always subordinated scientific troubles to other concerns. Once science entered the public arena, its powers were taken for granted (even wildly exaggerated), as polemicists began debating its social role. Increasingly, science was seen as a means for creating wealth (and political power). Controlling its products, and claiming its prestige, became more important than understanding how it worked.

The champions of applied science arose among the middle class. Scientific American ("The Advocate of Industry & Enterprise") was founded by a religious cultist named Rufus Porter in 1845, but it was sold the next year to a group of businessmen. The new owners linked it to a patent preparation service, aimed it at "Every Manufacturer, Mechanic, Inventor and Artisan," and spent the rest of the century gleefully promoting inventions, saluting technological progress and largely ignoring pure research.

In the 1870's, the "pure science" movement began as an upper-class assault on such utilitarian, basically middle-class science. Popular Science Monthly, the new movement's principal organ, worked nobly to promote theoretical science—but always through moral essays dressed up with scientific phrases. Its indifference to experimental fact also made it an outlet for every sort of racist and sexist myth—but that is another, albeit related, topic.

Interestingly, both "pure" and applied scientists spread their belief in omnipotent science during an age in which public scientific experiments became popular entertainment. In 1872 and 1873 the English physicist and "pure science" advocate John Tyndall toured America to thunderous applause. Yet the published version of his lecture-demonstrations made it clear how careful he was to insure that his public experiments were never to fail: "Experiments have two uses—a use in discovery, and a use in tuition. . . . After the discoverer comes the teacher, whose function it is so to exalt and modify the results of the discoverer as to render them fit for public presentation." Subsequent years have brought many new polemics—but, again, all concerned with the uses, not the nature, of science. Despite a few recent histories and biographies attending to difficulties, we have, I believe, faithfully preserved the Victorian view that success, not struggle, is the essence of scientific endeavor.

But what, aside from an epic literary genre, did we lose in accepting this idea of never-failing science? Perhaps the loss has been of two types. The first affects scientists directly. Connie Osborn, a neurophysiologist at the University of Minnesota, has argued convincingly that nowadays even students with undergraduate science degrees seem unaware of the limits of science. Those who choose research careers soon learn better. But all the rest of us, with or without degrees in science, must learn our science and form our judgments about scientific endeavors largely on the basis of essentially flawed texts.

Taken together, modern scientific writing, both the popular and the professional type, makes science look far more precise and reliable than it really is. In an age of immense gambles on the powers of science, it seems crucial to understand accurately scientific fallibility or infallibility. But modern scientific prose (for all its virtues) conceals much more than it reveals. In "Inward Bound," Abraham Pais writes: "Since it is my principal purpose to describe how ideas evolved, I shall need to discuss . . . how false leads, incorrect improvisations, and dead ends are interspersed between one advance and the next. The omission of such episodes would anaesthetize the story." It would also perhaps lead us into considerable dangers. Science is capable of wonderful things—but not always, and rarely as quickly as we would wish. A frank, humane discussion of errors, troubles and limitations was once considered essential to objective scientific writing. The revival of such discussion might make us all more comfortable with the course and uses of science in the late 20th century.

Killing, in Verse and Prose

PAUL FUSSELL

Paul Fussell, professor and writer, has written a number of works illustrating the truism that war is hell. In this essay he has a variation on that theme: war, even in literature, is hell. His research is drawn primarily from poems and short prose (fiction and nonfiction), but he also makes use of interviews. To identify sources he incorporates the authors and titles into his discussion, rather than using formal documentation in notes.

In his foreword to *Thank God for the Atom Bomb and Other Essays*, Fussell warns his audience: ". . . this is not a book to promote tranquillity, and readers in quest of peace of mind should look elsewhere."

Original publication: *Boston Globe*, December 2, 1984; collected in *Thank God for the Atom Bomb and Other Essays*. New York: Summit Books, 1988.

A satire, says Samuel Johnson, is "a poem in which wickedness or folly is censured." This being so, Jon Stallworthy's *The Oxford Book of War Poetry* might just as well be titled *The Oxford Book of Satire*. In "No Man's Land," a poem by Eric Bogle, a skeptical young person sits by the grave of a nineteen-year-old killed in the First World War and addresses him thus:

> Did you really believe that this war would end wars?
> Well, the suffering, the sorrow, the glory, the shame,
> The killing, the dying, it was all done in vain.
> For, William McBride, it all happened again,
> And again, and again, and again, and again.

That suggests the dynamics of Stallworthy's anthology. It provides over and over, piling it very high and very deep, material to gratify the harshest satirist of human nature and of one mad institution people have devised to express themselves. Here a calumniator of humanity would find countless sadistic mass murders and a sufficiency of needless agony and bereavement, not to mention a plethora of stupid blunders, failures of imagination, acts of ignorance, and egregious carelessness with the lives and bodies of others. There's also a lot of fatuous complacency and optimism in the face of avoidable catastrophe, as well as happiness in the misery of others, all the way from the Hebrews' delight at the sufferings of Pharaoh's drowning cavalry and the bloody-mindedness of Achilles to Seamus Heaney's notations of the murderous absurdities in contemporary Ulster and Peter Porter's sardonic, scary take-off on a terminal nuclear civil-defense announcement. For the traducer of human nature, here is God's plenty. Or rather, man's. As Byron puts it in *Don Juan*,

> "Let there be light!" said God, and there was light!
> "Let there be blood!" says man, and there's a sea.

Guiding the strong-stomached through this deplorable scene is the British poet and translator who wrote the excellent standard biography of the Great War poet Wilfred Owen and went on to edit Owen's poems. He offers 259 poems, and considering the difficulties of definition and classification (not the least of which is that "war poetry" turns out to be antiwar poetry, if not outright satire, in effect if not intention), he has done an OK job. He groups the poems chronologically by war (surely a satiric nuance perceptible there?). This has some disadvantages, like Thomas Hardy's appearing in three different places: the Napoleonic Wars (a selection from *The Dynasts*), the Boer War, and the Great War. For this reason dates would be helpful, and there aren't half enough of them, perhaps a reflection of the Oxford Book tradition, going all the way back to Arthur Quiller-Couch's original *Oxford Book of English Verse* (1900), that evidence of precise scholarship is not the mark of a gentleman.

From Stallworthy's selections you can infer the outlines of military as well as literary history. After the obligatory Ancients, he provides a generous helping of the amazing Old English war poems, like "The Battle of Maldon" and "The Battle of Brunanburh," and a bit from Chaucer's "Knight's Tale." He then displays examples of the chivalric swank with which war is conventionally conceived in the Renaissance among such as Spenser, Marvell, and Dryden. (Here some might like a little Shakespeare as a counterweight to all this grandiosity, something like Hotspur's speech from *Henry the Fourth, Part I*, sneering at the staff-officer-like "administrator" unacquainted with the unpleasant facts of the battlefield:

> And as the soldiers bore dead bodies by,
> He call'd them untaught knaves, unmannerly,
> To bring a slovenly unhandsome corse
> Betwixt the wind and his nobility.)

It's only with the onset of bourgeois understanding, in the eighteenth century, that poets begin reaching toward the modern theme that war is a total calamity rather than a welcome or not-too-bad occasion for displaying manliness. Only then does the idea begin to take form that victory is really defeat, as in Johnson's "The Vanity of Human Wishes" on the irony of Swedish Charles XII's "warrior's pride." His humiliation opens the door to an understanding of Napoleon's, Mussolini's, and Idi Amin's.

Coleridge, in "Fears in Solitude," is one of the first to reprehend military euphemisms ("all our dainty terms for fratricide"), which makes him an unexpected forerunner of Sassoon and e e cummings. And with Browning's "Incident of the French Camp" there enters another motif without which the antiwar poetry of the nineteenth and twentieth centuries would be sadly impoverished—tender, quasi-erotic fantasizing about the deaths of boy soldiers, as in Whitman's "Vigil Strange I Kept on the Field One Night," Rimbaud's "The Sleeper in the Valley," the works of Housman and Sir Henry Newbolt, and of course Wilfred Owen. Helping to flesh out Stallworthy's Civil War yield are four poems of Herman Melville's, which occasion the shock one always experiences upon seeing how badly a great writer can write:

> at my window, leaving bed,
> By night I mused, of easeful sleep bereft,
> On those brave boys (Ah War! thy theft) . . .

In this collection Kipling gets a fair shake. Stallworthy selects "Arithmetic on the Frontier," wonderfully "modern" in the irony with which it treats the expense of producing a young officer—all that training, all that costly equipment, all that practice ammunition, all those uniforms and quarters and officers-club amenities—and the inexpensive ease with which he is destroyed:

> The Crammer's boast, the Squadron's pride,
> Shot like a rabbit in a ride!

There's plenty of irony too in Stallworthy's selections from Hardy and Housman on the Boer War, as well, of course, as in the well-known poems of the Great War.

On the other hand, the poems from the Spanish Civil War seem uniformly unsatisfactory. What's the reason? Was their audience too narrow politically, too much a faction? Was it too philistine? Were the poets too self-righteous for irony? Was sophisticated technique conceived to be inappropriate in a "people's war"? That is, was good writing itself thought offensively privileged and suspect, even "Fascist"? Whatever the reason, the Spanish War poems, by John Cornford, Laurie Lee, Auden and Spender and Bernard Spencer, seem to take their places in this collection less because they're good than because the book requires the display of work from each major "conflict" (Stallworthy's euphemism).

In representing poems from the Second World War, Stallworthy has been fair, offering both highminded performances in which remnants of a chivalric understanding may be detected (like some poems by Keith Douglas) and examples of the pissed-off, the demotic, snotty, and nay-saying. Henry Reeds's classic "Lessons of the War" is included, of course, and so is Gavin Ewart's wonderful "When a Beau Goes In" and John Pudney's "To Johnny." I wish Pudney's "Missing" were here too, for in its minimalism, its resolute disinclination to go on and on or to try to interpret the uninterpretable, it is so memorable a registration of the quintessential style of the Second World War. Of the events of that calamity, less said the better:

> MISSING
> Less said the better.
> The bill unpaid, the dead letter,
> No roses at the end
> Of Smith, my friend.
>
> Last words don't matter,
> And there are none to flatter.
> Words will not fill the post
> Of Smith, the ghost.
>
> For Smith, our brother,
> Only son of loving mother,
> The ocean lifted, stirred,
> Leaving no word.

That little twelve-line notation is worth attending to because it is so efficiently emblematic of the verbal culture of the Second World War as contrasted with that of the First.

For participants, the Second War was silent. Not that the explosions made less noise. Rather, no one felt it appropriate to say much, either to try to interpret the war, or to understand it, or even to execrate it. It was simply there, taking place, and there seemed nothing to say. Contrast the troops' flux of talk in the First World War, their constant bringing of language to bear on the war, their unremitting verbalizing, caught nicely in David Jones's long poem *In Parenthesis*. The high-minded loquacity of all those poets of the Great War! Entirely a different scene from the style of the Second War, which is silence—silence ranging from the embarrassed to the sullen. It's as if both the ironic and the elegiac conventions for making some literary sense of modern war had been exhausted earlier. Result: a new laconic style.

In the Civil War, by contrast again, it was appropriate for soldiers on both sides to be noisily enthusiastic. As the officer of an Illinois unit reported of his men, "On the march they make it a point to abuse every man or thing they see." And of an Indiana regiment a survivor remembers:

> Our regiment yelled at everything they saw and heard. When another regiment passed, they yelled at them. . . . As they tumbled out to roll-call in the morning, they yelled. . . . After a hard day's scouting they were never too tired to hail the end of their tasks with a joyous yell. . . . A yell would start at one end of the division, and regiment after regiment and brigade after brigade would take it up and carry it along, and then send it back to the other end; few knowing what it was about, and caring less.

But as the military commentator S. L. A. Marshall has perceived, the Second World War produced "about the mutest army we ever sent to war," an army unwilling to waste its breath on exhortations, noisy encouragements, yelling for the fun of it, or even much conversation. Thus in the Second War a bomber navigator hearkens to the silence that overcomes his aircrew waiting for the start of a mission: "Remember that bit in *Journey's End*," he says, "where the older man engages the younger in a discussion about tea and cocoa as beverages while they talk away the last moments of their lives?" In contrast, he observes, "We usually wait in silence." And virtually in silence too the airmen returned from their missions, most notably when their friends' planes did not. Then, after their interrogation, some of the survivors were likely to assemble in someone's barracks room, open a bottle of whiskey, and sit around wordlessly until one might offer a quiet minimalist toast to the code designation of the missing plane but without specifying anyone's name. He would raise his glass and say very softly, "God bless 'M for Momsie.'" And they would drink and then go about their business. As one airman remembers, "You learned to keep emotion at a very low level."

Pudney's laconic enactment of the bankruptcy of elegy takes place in 55 words only. Compare the 312 words Julian Grenfell needs—or rather uses—to deliver the cheering news of his Great War poem "Into Battle." This assures the reader that, unlike the wordlessness of Pudney's ocean, the elements of nature conspire to say a great deal, speaking to the soldier constant encouraging words:

> The woodland trees that stand together,
>   They stand to him each one a friend;
> They gently speak in the windy weather;
>   They guide to valley and ridge's end.
>
> The kestrel hovering by day,
>   And the little owls that call by night,
> Bid him be swift and keen as they,
>   As keen of ear, as swift of sight.
>
> The blackbird sings to him, etc., etc.

No one and no thing verbalizes so lavishly in the memorable poems of the Second World War. An American counterpart of Pudney's "Missing" is Randall Jarrell's "The Death of the Ball Turret Gunner," which needs only five lines for its understated work. Second World War poetry is so notably an art of litotes that one can almost gauge the merit and staying power of a poem by its brevity. If it's short and small, like Pudney's and Jarrell's, it may be good. If long and large, like, say, Karl Shapiro's "Elegy for a Dead Soldier," probably not. In that war even the voluble, indeed musical, Dylan Thomas feels a certain tug in the direction of silence, registering in one title "A Refusal to Mourn . . ." and declining to expend a load of words memorializing "the Death, by Fire, of a Child in London."

But it is in Jarrell's poem that one sees the Second War poetic action in its essence. The speaker in the poem, the dead gunner, abjures syntax betokening cause and coherence. He is either disinclined or simply unable to do more than specify serially the crazy things that have happened to him. Understanding his experience is as far from his capacity as interpreting it. And he certainly does not object to it. ("I made no comment. / What should I resent?"):

> From my mother's sleep I fell into the State,
> And I hunched in its belly till my wet fur froze.
> Six miles from earth, loosed from its dream of life,
> I woke to black flak and the nightmare fighters.
> When I died they washed me out of the turret with a
>   hose.

If it might be possible to assign a cause to the Second World War, it would not be easy to infer a meaning. When we hear the phrase *war poetry*, we probably think of the poetry of the First, not the Second War. Indeed, at this distance it's not hard to sense behind most of the Allied writing of the Second War the shade of what Susan Sontag will later designate, speaking of Pinter's plays, "The Aesthetics of Silence." The banality I've noted in the writings of the O.W.I. generation is designed to fill a vacuum, the empty space left because there is nothing to say. V. S. Pritchett recalls one of Elizabeth Bowen's characters observing of the London blitz, "It will have no literature." "In that sense," says Pritchett, "it was like a car smash or pile-up."

After silence and failure of understanding, anxiety and shame, as in Howard Nemerov's "Redeployment":

> They say the war is over. But water still
> Comes bloody from the taps, and my pet cat
> In his disorder vomits worms which crawl
> Swiftly away. . . .

That seems to prepare for the next acts: Korea, Vietnam, Lebanon, Northern Ireland, the Falklands, Grenada, and Nicaragua, the last three too recent to have produced their appropriate satirists.

And speaking of Vietnam, how is it that we know ("for certain," it's tempting to add) that no weighty, sustained poems, or even short poems of distinction, are going to come out of it? Why do we expect from it nothing like, say, Herbert Read's "The End of a War," from the Great War, or Louis Simpson's "The Runner," from the Second? Why are we sure that in a back room somewhere no one is writing the equivalent of Isaac Rosenberg's "Break of Day in the Trenches" or Jarrell's "Eighth Air Force"? Is it perhaps that we secretly recognize that real poetry is, as Hazlitt called it, "right royal," aristocratic in essence, and thus unlikely to arise from the untutored or the merely street-smart? (Here, I'm noting how few literary or highly educated people were in that war, how few who had any chance in their high schools to experience real poetry or to gain any sense of how one might write it.) Or is the reason for the paucity of Vietnam war poetry a fact even more unpleasant, namely, that we are now inescapably mired in a postverbal age, where neither writer nor reader possesses the layers of allusion arising from wide literary experience that make significant writing and reading possible? Or is the reason our despair of urging public events toward any "meaning," arising from the suspicions of traditional value that have encouraged "deconstruction" in criticism and "Marxism" in the daydreams of those at once intelligent and powerless? Whatever the reasons, it seems undeniable that no one expects interesting poetry to emerge from that sad war. All we can expect is more of what we have, a few structureless free-verse dribbles of easy irony or easy sentiment or easy political anger. Some samples are in Stallworthy's book, and they are not good, even though written by Denise Levertov and Galway Kinnell.

Indeed, there are many bad poems in his book, perhaps an indication that if you accumulate poems by their themes or subjects, very soon (unless the theme is mortality or evanescence) you're going to be in artistic trouble. It's a sad comment that most of the mediocre poems in Stallworthy's collection come from the twentieth century. I don't mean the readily patronized patriotic Great War pieces by adolescents like Rupert Brooke and Herbert Asquith. Such naïve documents are landmarks in the history of sensibility and one expects to find them in a collection like this. Rather, I mean items like Allen Tate's once-fashionable Eliotic "Ode to the Confederate Dead," which now seems embarrassingly bogus, inert, and unnecessary, as well as poems like Paul Dehn's heartwarming but shallow "St. Aubin d'Aubigné" and Auden's would-be resolute but flaccid "Spain, 1937." The sad fact is that there aren't really enough good "war poems" that succeed as poems to make a book of more than 350 pages. Stallworthy has thus had to pad out with things like Edith Sitwell's preposterous, theologically pretentious "Still Falls the Rain," that implausible theatrical farrago which seems now the very *locus classicus* of 1940s empty portentousness.

That Sitwellian disaster prompts this question: why haven't more women written good "war poems"? From Homer's Andromache to Vera Brittain (and the "Mrs. Smith" of Pudney's "Missing") bereaved women, next to the permanently disabled, are the main victims in war, their dead having been removed beyond suffering and memory to the place where, as Gavin Ewart puts it,

> there falls no rain nor hail nor driven snow—
> Here, there, or anywhere,

and thus

> Do you suppose *they* care?

Yet the elegies are written by men, many of them as "noncombatant" as the women, and poems registering a love of soldiers are written by men, and it's not women who seem the custodians of the subtlest sorts of antiwar irony. This seems odd, and it awaits interpretation.

Any student of antiwar irony must wonder how much and what sort attaches to the quotation marks around Studs Terkel's title *"The Good War."* Even skeptics who think "oral history" better designated "oral fiction" or "oral self-justification" are likely to be impressed by Terkel's book, which exhibits again his talent for eliciting significant emotion from the people he talks to. In essence he is asking his interviewees who were "in" the Second World War in various ways, whether the ironic quotes belong around the title. With rare patience and sympathy he has conversed with more than a hundred "ordinary" people: former servicemen, housewives, businessmen, and girlfriends, and not just those on our side but Germans and Japanese, and such curious Allies as Russians as well. And some of his testifiers are a cut above the ordinary: Mayor Tom Bradley of Los Angeles, Pauline Kael, John Ciardi, John Kenneth Galbraith, Marcel Ophuls, Maxine Andrews (of the harmonic Sisters), Roosevelt's assistant Tommy "The Cork" Corcoran, Averell Harriman, John Houseman, the cartoonist Milton Caniff (*Terry and the Pirates*), Telford Taylor, and Bill Mauldin (can that impudent little GI really now be a bearded sixty-five-year-old?).

"The past is never dead," Faulkner once said. "It's not even past." Many of Terkel's informants broke down in sobs while recalling their war experience forty years back. Of course, war trauma being one of our dirty little secrets, always there beneath the surface, seldom showing except on occasions like this. Terkel has not merely got his people to talk frankly and poignantly. He has edited the results with laudable sense and humanity to produce a striking indictment of American policy in the postwar world, and the popularity of his book suggests widespread approval of an attitude about that war and its aftermath which is powerfully opposed to the official one.

While there are still some who will go to their graves hating the enemy and resolutely not buying Sonys and Volkswagens, a lot of pity for the other side has surfaced after all these years. One former soldier who fought in Europe remembers his shock at discovering that the dead German infantry "were exactly our age. . . . Once the helmet is off, you're looking at a teenager, another kid." A soldier who found himself in Japan just after the surrender recalls a sudden perception after a Japanese father-in-law showed him a picture of a "missing" Japanese soldier: "It dawned on me that they suffered the same as we did. They lost sons and daughters and relatives, and they hurt too."

Others, like the sensitive and honest ex-Marine E. B. Sledge, find the horror unforgettable. He recalls vividly what he wishes more people knew about, the savagery of island fighting in the Pacific, with American lads turning into virtual animals, routinely murdering the Japanese wounded, smashing the faces of corpses to get at the gold teeth. "How could American boys do this?" he asks, and answers, "We *were* savages." Those attentive at once to Golding's *Lord of the Flies* and the data of the Holocaust (as well as the behavior of our troops in Vietnam) will readily understand. In order to "make any sense" at all of the Holocaust, says Marguerite Duras, we must recognize that we could have done all those terrible things ourselves. "We must share the crime." It must be conceived not in German or Nazi but "in world terms" and "understood collectively." *We* did it. "If you give a German and not a collective interpretation to the Nazi horror, you reduce the man in Belsen to regional dimensions. The only possible answer to this crime is to turn it into a crime committed by everyone. To share it." Which means that if you can't imagine yourself an SS officer hustling the Jewish women and children to the gas chamber, you need to be more closely in touch with your buried self.

But if there's guilt here, there's pathos too. Some of Terkel's speakers indicate the war's cost to the unfortunates whose destiny it was to constitute the cutting edge in the now-forgotten ominous places. A former airman in the South Pacific shows Terkel a photograph of a squadron baseball team:

> At first base we had Max and O'Connell; they used to alternate. Both those men died at Cananatuan. . . . At shortstop we had Armando Viselli. . . . Armando died in a reconnaissance flight over Lamon Bay. . . . At third base was Cabbage Clan. . . . He died when his ship was torpedoed off Mindinao . . . by a U.S. Navy submarine. We had two Catchers. We had Beck. He was hit on the first day the Japanese bombed at Clark Field and his leg was badly mangled. . . . The other catcher was Dumas. He was from Massachusetts. Dumas was killed on the first day at Iba. I'm the only one left out of the whole infield, the only one that came back. That's why I treasure that picture.

There is much in Terkel's book about injustice, and not just the inevitable injustice of the unlucky few bearing the awful burden for the many. The notion that the war was a notable moral crusade will hardly survive the testimony about homefront anti-Semitism, much of it found in the Junior-Leaguish Red Cross. "We're supposed to be against Hitler," one woman recalls, "yet we were talking anti-Jew all the time." And the idea that the war was "against Fascism" is embarrassed by the unpleasant facts of rampant racism at home, where it was assumed that blacks were cowards by birth and incompetents by instinct, incapable of flying a plane without an accident or manning a front line without running away. Segregation was rigid, and as one Red Cross worker remembers, "Until we were well into the war, they segregated the blood plasma of the blacks from the whites."

Other memories convey the sense of a period so far back as to be, now, virtually not understandable without great effort. It's not easy to call back a living sense of that pre-pill, pre-porno, pre-abortion world of puritanism and inhibition, when *Esquire* was thought racy, in trouble constantly with the Postmaster General for its sexy drawings, and when a girl could imperil her future by establishing a reputation for being "fast." "There was very little sleeping around," says a girl who was living on the West Coast. "We were still at the tail-end of a moral generation. Openly living together was not condoned."

That girl's name was Dellie Hahne, and she is now only one of many here who register the utmost life-distorting disillusion with the way the postwar world has turned out. The rearming of the Germans and the rapid reversal of the wartime party line toward the Soviet Union were shocks from which many will never recover. The United States government has forfeited the credibility and respect of more people than it knows, and the vein of distrust and cynicism about national purposes runs very deep. Vietnam and Watergate and the Iran-contra perversion are only the latest in a series of debilitating events that date from 1945, when the OSS was transformed into the CIA and the basis established for a secret government on a military model. "When we started to arm Germany," says Dellie Hahne, "I was so shocked. I'd been sold a bill of goods. . . . That was the beginning of distrusting my own government."

Pervasive also is the anti-militarism of these reminiscences. An atomic physicist says, "We can't afford to be weak. That's what the Germans said. And did. . . . Look what happened to them. The same thing will happen to us if we don't cool it." Retired Admiral Gene LaRoque spills beans formerly out of sight but now abundantly visible since the Iran-contra business: "Our military runs our foreign policy. The State Department simply goes around and tidies up the messes the military makes." The United States still tends to see things in terms of the war, LaRoque points out, and the memory of the "Victory"—and subsequent papering over of the agony and the cost—"encourages the men of my generation to be willing, almost eager, to use military force anywhere in the world." An Englishwoman who survived the Blitz says of Americans, "I do wish they wouldn't be so keen to get into wars, because one day it will come back on your territory and God help you."

A former artillery officer, a forward observer at the battle of the Huertgen Forest near the German border, remembers: "I knew another forward observer. He went out with his crew. White phosphorus was thrown at him. Two of the men burned before his eyes. He came running to where I was. . . . I went down the road to meet him. He was sobbing and falling into my arms. He kept saying, 'No more killing, no more killing, no more killing.' " A rational humanity, which is what we have not got, would have no trouble ratifying that resolution.

James Jones and his son, together with Willie Morris and his son (both boys fifteen years old), once visited the battlefield at Antietam. The four of them walked down the Sunken Road, which just after the battle was known as Bloody Lane. Morris recalls the history of the place:

> Here, along a line of a thousand yards, the Confederate center took its stand, thousands of them firing at close quarters against the Federal troops charging across the crest of a ridge. It lasted three hours. And the dead Confederate soldiers lay so thick here that as far as the eye could see a man could walk upon them without once touching ground.

At the end of the Sunken Road is an observation tower. From its top the two men and the two boys surveyed the silent landscape.

> "The way men go to die," Jim said, looking down at the ridge before us. "It's incredibly sad. It breaks my heart. You wonder why it was necessary, why human beings have to do that to each other. . . ."
> Why do men do it, one of the boys wondered. Why did they do it here?

After thinking a while how to answer that question of questions, Jones gave the simple, empirical, irrational answer any ex-soldier would authenticate. They did it, said Jones, "because they didn't want to appear unmanly in front of their friends." Considering the constant fresh supply of young men and the universal young man's need for assurance of his manhood, Jones's answer suggests why reason, decency, and common sense are as unlikely to stop the killing in the future as in the past. Animals and trees and stones cannot be satirized, only human beings, and that's the reason it's all going to happen again, and again, and again, and again.

Women's Brains

STEPHEN JAY GOULD

Stephen Jay Gould's *The Panda's Thumb* (see reviews in Chapter 4) is a collection of essays that are "lightly edited versions" of columns Gould wrote for the magazine *Natural History*. Without

condescending to a general relationship, Gould provides definitions
for some of the technical terminology used in this discussion of
women's brains. For his study he cites literary and scientific sources
in his essay rather than in notes (see the two previous essays), except
for one explanatory passage set off in a note.

Gould thanks the editors of *Natural History*, who "helped in
deconvolution of phrase and thought . . ." in the essays collected in
The Panda's Thumb. He finds "exultation *and* explanation" in the
lessons in nature and hopes to convey these "general messages if only
we can learn to read them," as he states in the prologue. His
audience seems to be a large, indefinite group, one implied in his
epigraph for the collection, taken from Henry Adams: "A teacher
. . . can never tell where his influence stops."

Publication: *The Panda's Thumb: More Reflections in Natural History.* New York: Norton, 1980.

Ⅰn the prelude to *Middlemarch*, George Eliot lamented the unfulfilled lives of
talented women:

> Some have felt that these blundering lives are due to the inconvenient indefiniteness
> with which the Supreme Power has fashioned the natures of women: if there were one
> level of feminine incompetence as strict as the ability to count three and no more, the
> social lot of women might be treated with scientific certitude.

Eliot goes on to discount the idea of innate limitation, but while she wrote in
1872, the leaders of European anthropometry were trying to measure "with
scientific certitude" the inferiority of women. Anthropometry, or measurement
of the human body, is not so fashionable a field these days, but it dominated the
human sciences for much of the nineteenth century and remained popular until
intelligence testing replaced skull measurement as a favored device for making
invidious comparisons among races, classes, and sexes. Craniometry, or
measurement of the skull, commanded the most attention and respect. Its
unquestioned leader, Paul Broca (1824–80), professor of clinical surgery at the
Faculty of Medicine in Paris, gathered a school of disciples and imitators around
himself. Their work, so meticulous and apparently irrefutable, exerted great
influence and won high esteem as a jewel of nineteenth-century science.

Broca's work seemed particularly invulnerable to refutation. Had he not
measured with the most scrupulous care and accuracy? (Indeed, he had. I have
the greatest respect for Broca's meticulous procedure. His numbers are sound.
But science is an inferential exercise, not a catalog of facts. Numbers, by
themselves, specify nothing. All depends upon what you do with them.) Broca
depicted himself as an apostle of objectivity, a man who bowed before facts and
cast aside superstition and sentimentality. He declared that "there is no faith,
however respectable, no interest, however legitimate, which must not accom-

modate itself to the progress of human knowledge and bend before truth."
Women, like it or not, had smaller brains than men and, therefore, could not
equal them in intelligence. This fact, Broca argued, may reinforce a common
prejudice in male society, but it is also a scientific truth. L. Manouvrier, a black
sheep in Broca's fold, rejected the inferiority of women and wrote with feeling
about the burden imposed upon them by Broca's numbers:

> Women displayed their talents and their diplomas. They also invoked philosophical
> authorities. But they were opposed by *numbers* unknown to Condorcet or to John
> Stuart Mill. These numbers fell upon poor women like a sledge hammer, and they
> were accompanied by commentaries and sarcasms more ferocious than the most
> misogynist imprecations of certain church fathers. The theologians had asked if
> women had a soul. Several centuries later, some scientists were ready to refuse them
> a human intelligence.

Broca's argument rested upon two sets of data: the larger brains of men in
modern societies, and a supposed increase in male superiority through time. His
most extensive data came from autopsies performed personally in four Parisian
hospitals. For 292 male brains, he calculated an average weight of 1,325 grams;
140 female brains averaged 1,144 grams for a difference of 181 grams, or 14
percent of the male weight. Broca understood, of course, that part of this
difference could be attributed to the greater height of males. Yet he made no
attempt to measure the effect of size alone and actually stated that it cannot
account for the entire difference because we know, a priori, that women are not
as intelligent as men (a premise that the data were supposed to test, not rest
upon):

> We might ask if the small size of the female brain depends exclusively upon the small
> size of her body. Tiedemann has proposed this explanation. But we must not forget
> that women are, on the average, a little less intelligent than men, a difference which
> we should not exaggerate but which is, nonetheless, real. We are therefore permitted
> to suppose that the relatively small size of the female brain depends in part upon her
> physical inferiority and in part upon her intellectual inferiority.

In 1873, the year after Eliot published *Middlemarch*, Broca measured the
cranial capacities of prehistoric skulls from L'Homme Mort cave. Here he found
a difference of only 99.5 cubic centimeters between males and females, while
modern populations range from 129.5 to 220.7. Topinard, Broca's chief
disciple, explained the increasing discrepancy through time as a result of
differing evolutionary pressures upon dominant men and passive women:

> The man who fights for two or more in the struggle for existence, who has all the
> responsibility and the cares of tomorrow, who is constantly active in combating the
> environment and human rivals, needs more brain than the woman whom he must
> protect and nourish, the sedentary woman, lacking any interior occupations, whose
> role is to raise children, love, and be passive.

In 1879, Gustave Le Bon, chief misogynist of Broca's school, used these data
to publish what must be the most vicious attack upon women in modern

scientific literature (no one can top Aristotle). I do not claim his views were representative of Broca's school, but they were published in France's most respected anthropological journal. Le Bon concluded:

> In the most intelligent races, as among the Parisians, there are a large number of women whose brains are closer to size to those of gorillas than to the most developed male brains. This inferiority is so obvious that no one can contest it for a moment; only its degree is worth discussion. All psychologists who have studied the intelligence of women, as well as poets and novelists, recognize today that they represent the most inferior forms of human evolution and that they are closer to children and savages than to an adult, civilized man. They excel in fickleness, inconstancy, absence of thought and logic, and incapacity to reason. Without doubt there exist some distinguished women, very superior to the average man, but they are as exceptional as the birth of any monstrosity, as, for example, of a gorilla with two heads; consequently, we may neglect them entirely.

Nor did Le Bon shrink from the social implications of his views. He was horrified by the proposal of some American reformers to grant women higher education on the same basis as men:

> A desire to give them the same education, and, as a consequence, to propose the same goals for them, is a dangerous chimera. . . . The day when, misunderstanding the inferior occupations which nature has given her, women leave the home and take part in our battles; on this day a social revolution will begin, and everything that maintains the sacred ties of the family will disappear.

Sound familiar?*

I have reexamined Broca's data, the basis for all this derivative pronouncement, and I find his numbers sound but his interpretation ill-founded, to say the least. The data supporting his claim for increased difference through time can be easily dismissed. Broca based his contention on the samples from L'Homme Mort alone—only seven male and six female skulls in all. Never have so little data yielded such far ranging conclusions.

In 1888, Topinard published Broca's more extensive data on the Parisian hospitals. Since Broca recorded height and age as well as brain size, we may use modern statistics to remove their effect. Brain weight decreases with age, and Broca's women were, on average, considerably older than his men. Brain weight increases with height, and his average man was almost half a foot taller than his average woman. I used multiple regression, a technique that allowed me to assess simultaneously the influence of height and age upon brain size. In an analysis of the data for women, I found that, at average male height and age, a

---

*When I wrote this essay, I assumed that Le Bon was a marginal, if colorful, figure. I have since learned that he was a leading scientist, one of the founders of social psychology, and best known for a seminal study on crowd behavior, still cited today (*La psychologie des foules*, 1895), and for his work on unconscious motivation.

woman's brain would weight 1,212 grams. Correction for height and age reduces Broca's measured difference of 181 grams by more than a third, to 113 grams.

I don't know what to make of this remaining difference because I cannot assess other factors known to influence brain size in a major way. Cause of death has an important effect: degenerative disease often entails a substantial diminution of brain size. (This effect is separate from the decrease attributed to age alone.) Eugene Schreider, also working with Broca's data, found that men killed in accidents had brains weighing, on average, 60 grams more than men dying of infectious diseases. The best modern data I can find (from American hospitals) records a full 100-gram difference between death by degenerative arteriosclerosis and by violence or accident. Since so many of Broca's subjects were very elderly women, we may assume that lengthy degenerative disease was more common among them than among the men.

More importantly, modern students of brain size still have not agreed on a proper measure for eliminating the powerful effect of body size. Height is partly adequate, but men and women of the same height do not share the same body build. Weight is even worse than height, because most of its variation reflects nutrition rather than intrinsic size—fat versus skinny exerts little influence upon the brain. Manouvrier took up this subject in the 1880s and argued that muscular mass and force should be used. He tried to measure this elusive property in various ways and found a marked difference in favor of men, even in men and women of the same height. When he corrected for what he called "sexual mass," women actually came out slightly ahead in brain size.

Thus, the corrected 113-gram difference is surely too large; the true figure is probably close to zero and may as well favor women as men. And 113 grams, by the way, is exactly the average difference between a 5 foot 4 inch and a 6 foot 4 inch male in Broca's data. We would not (especially us short folks) want to ascribe greater intelligence to tall men. In short, who knows what to do with Broca's data? They certainly don't permit any confident claim that men have bigger brains than women.

To appreciate the social role of Broca and his school, we must recognize that his statements about the brains of women do not reflect an isolated prejudice toward a single disadvantaged group. They must be weighed in the context of a general theory that supported contemporary social distinctions as biologically ordained. Women, blacks, and poor people suffered the same disparagement, but women bore the brunt of Broca's argument because he had easier access to data on women's brains. Women were singularly denigrated but they also stood as surrogates for other disenfranchised groups. As one of Broca's disciples wrote in 1881: "Men of the black races have a brain scarcely heavier than that of white women." This juxtaposition extended into many other realms of anthropological argument, particularly to claims that, anatomically and emotionally, both women and blacks were like white children—and that white children, by the theory of recapitulation, represented an ancestral (primitive) adult stage of human evolution. I do not regard as empty rhetoric the claim that women's battles are for all of us.

Maria Montessori did not confine her activities to educational reform for young children. She lectured on anthropology for several years at the University of Rome, and wrote an influential book entitled *Pedagogical Anthropology* (English edition, 1913). Montessori was no egalitarian. She supported most of Broca's work and the theory of innate criminality proposed by her compatriot Cesare Lombroso. She measured the circumference of children's heads in her schools and inferred that the best prospects had bigger brains. But she had no use for Broca's conclusions about women. She discussed Manouvrier's work at length and made much of his tentative claim that women, after proper correction of the data, had slightly larger brains that men. Women, she concluded, were intellectually superior, but men had prevailed heretofore by dint of physical force. Since technology has abolished force as an instrument of power, the era of women may soon be upon us: "In such an epoch there will really be superior human beings, there will really be men strong in morality and in sentiment. Perhaps in this way the reign of women is approaching, when the engima of her anthropological superiority will be deciphered. Woman was always the custodian of human sentiment, morality and honor."

This represents one possible antidote to "scientific" claims for the constitutional inferiority of certain groups. One may affirm the validity of biological distinctions but argue that the data have been misinterpreted by prejudiced men with a stake in the outcome, and that disadvantaged groups are truly superior. In recent years, Elaine Morgan has followed this strategy in her *Descent of Woman*, a speculative reconstruction of human prehistory from the woman's point of view—and as farcical as more famous tall tales by and for men.

I prefer another strategy. Montessori and Morgan followed Broca's philosophy to reach a more congenial conclusion. I would rather label the whole enterprise of setting a biological value upon groups for what it is: irrelevant and highly injurious. George Eliot well appreciated the special tragedy that biological labeling imposed upon members of disadvantaged groups. She expressed it for people like herself—women of extraordinary talent. I would apply it more widely—not only to those whose dreams are flouted but also to those who never realize that they may dream—but I cannot match her prose. In conclusion, then, the rest of Eliot's prelude to *Middlemarch:*

The limits of variation are really much wider than anyone would imagine from the sameness of women's coiffure and the favorite love stories in prose and verse. Here and there a cygnet is reared uneasily among the ducklings in the brown pond, and never finds the living stream in fellowship with its own oary-footed kind. Here and there is born a Saint Theresa, foundress of nothing, whose loving heartbeats and sobs after an unattained goodness tremble off and are dispersed among hindrances instead of centering in some long-recognizable deed.

The Sisters Brontë and the Sisters Collins

A Study in Stunning Literary Parallels

RANDI HACKER AND JACKIE KAUFMAN

This essay has all the earmarks of literary analysis: an argument for certain interpretations of literary works and careers, detailed analysis of lives and texts, precise quoting of texts to prove interpretations— all carefully documented with extensive explanatory endnotes. But the absurdity—thus, the satire—becomes evident in the first comparison: the moors and Rodeo Drive. Hacker and Kaufman have a good time, and entertain their readers, with this satire of literary criticism and the extremes to which critics may go for a thesis. Think of the similar subjects readers with a knowledge of literature and a sense of humor can develop. Or branch out and create similar satire in history or chemistry or biology or . . . . No field has a monopoly on obscure research.

Original publication: *The New York Times Book Review*, August 20, 1989.

"Sometimes . . . the cheap stuff works just as well as the expensive [stuff]."
—JACKIE COLLINS, "LUCKY."

English sisters wrote once. English sisters are writing again. Now that Joan Collins has joined Jackie in the world of books, the inevitable comparisons are being made between the sisters who strolled and laughed on the moors near Haworth, their windswept Yorkshire parsonage, and the sisters who shop and lunch along Rodeo Drive.

Even a casual reader of the Brontës will note that the sisters held a clear looking glass to their era and kept plenty of sharp quills on hand to write down what they saw. While the Collins sisters are much more likely to write with a Cross pen, or even a Montblanc, they too turn a keen, exquisitely made-up observer's eye on life.

As the Brontës transformed their visions of 19th-century social mores and expectations into emotionally gripping Gothic tales of human existence and heather, so the Collinses do for the 1980's and, yes, on into the 90's. Their stories of glitz, greed and sex gone mad in a world of power, Jaguars and St. Tropez tans are no less a social chronicle than "Jane Eyre."

In this book, her first best seller, Charlotte Brontë wrestles with nothing less than the universally eternal topics of survival, death, love and English weather. And by the end of the book, she has pinned them, as it were, to the mat of great British literature.

Plain, small, brave, sometimes hungry, sometimes soaked, Jane Eyre struggles for spiritual integrity through 38 chapters of harsh childhood, modest employment and lots of fires, including one that ignites the man she loves. Starting with her early years, Jane is pummeled by life more than most. Her parents die and she is sent to live with relatives who hate her and pull her hair.

"[John] ran headlong at me: I felt him grasp my hair and my shoulder: he had closed with a desperate thing. I really saw in him a tyrant: a murderer. I felt a drop or two of blood from my head trickle down my neck, and was sensible of somewhat pungent sufferings."

These cruel experiences harden the bedrock of Jane's pluckiness.

In her runaway best seller "Lucky," Jackie Collins also gives us a heroine who must learn to deal with the major themes of human existence: how to live, how to love, how to run a casino. Like Jane, Lucky Santangelo, the pampered, dark-haired, dark-eyed daughter of the Mafia boss Gino (The Ram) Santangelo, starts her reality training young. She wakes up to find her tiny 5-year-old world irrevocably changed just one week after her birthday.

"[T]here were no presents, or kisses or laughter. . . . [T]here was only the pain of her mother's sudden and brutal murder, her naked body left floating on a raft in the center of the swimming pool for Lucky to discover."[1]

An experience like this so early in a character's development can only whet a reader's appetite for the adult Lucky will become.

The same is true for Jane Eyre. We follow her progress with interest as she's packed off to Lowood, a school renowned for its nasty headmaster, frequent punishments and inadequate gruel. On the night Helen, her one beloved friend, dies of consumption, young Jane breaks Lowood's strict rules and climbs into bed with her. It's evident that sweet, cold, thin Helen is dying. The two friends talk about heaven and then fall asleep in each other's arms.

"When I awoke it was day . . . [and] my face [was] against Helen Burns's shoulder, my arms round her neck. I was asleep, and Helen was—dead."

Helen's piety and bad cough influence Jane's own caring, gentle nature, which remains constant in spite of the incredible curveballs life keeps throwing in her direction.

In a stunning literary parallel, Lucky also ends up in bed with a friend while at boarding school. That friend is Olympia Stanislopoulos, the richest girl at L'Evier, a Swiss boarding school full of rich girls. She and Lucky are roommates. When Gino (The Ram) Santangelo calls to tell Lucky he's engaged to Marabelle Blue, "a famous blonde movie star," Lucky crawls into bed sobbing, and Olympia crawls in after her.

"Lucky was sobbing, and Olympia couldn't sleep, so she went to her friend and comforted her, softly at first, but the softness had turned into passion, and before long the two schoolgirls were entwined like lovers."[2]

The comparisons don't stop here. Consider the rest of Jane's life.

Upon leaving Lowood, Jane is hired as governess by Edward Rochester, the proud, leonine, brooding lord of Thornfield. Pretty soon she's in love with him, as is evident in her description of his head.

"He lifted up the sable waves of hair which lay horizontally over his brow, and showed a solid enough mass of intellectual organs, but an abrupt deficiency where the suave sign of benevolence should have risen."

After a tortuous period of doubt, Jane learns Rochester returns her love. He proposes. She accepts. Then some English weather sends them running for shelter. Once inside, they can contain their passion no longer.

"The rain rushed down. . . . We were quite wet before we could pass the threshold. He was taking off my shawl in the hall, and shaking the water out of my loosened hair. . . . He kissed me repeatedly."

After only a few days of happiness, Jane must summon up her pluck reserves yet again. More bad things happen, including the discovery that her beloved is married to a crazy woman he keeps in the attic. Jane packs her bags and leaves. Then she hears through the moors grapevine that Rochester has survived a fire that killed his mad wife and left him blind and one-armed. Jane's heart leaps at the news that Rochester is single at last. She travels an incredible distance in a stagecoach, marries him and finally finds tremendous happiness that lasts for more than a day or two. In Jane's own words:

"I know what it is to live entirely for and with what I love best on earth."

Is this so very different from what happens to Lucky? After her mother's death, Lucky seeks a closer relationship with her father, but Gino (The Ram) Santangelo doesn't have time for a little girl named Lucky. So she finds love in the arms of Marco—but he gets gunned down, so she finds it again in the arms of Lennie Golden, a golden-haired comedian on a collision course with success. While swimming at St. Tropez, they come face to face with their feelings and climb onto a raft to express them.

"He reached out and pulled her to him. She moved into his embrace as naturally as if they had known each other for years. Electricity sparked as they began to kiss, long, lingering kisses, tongues entwined."[3]

On the moors, in love, on privately owned Mediterranean islands, Jane and Lucky stay true to their values. Their stories are gripping, long and ultimately triumphant.

The comparisons between Jackie Collins and Charlotte Brontë aren't merely limited to what they've written. For Charlotte did not grow up alone in that austere, chilly stone house on the moors; neither was Jackie the only little Collins skipping around the English rooms of her parents' London flat at Harley House. Indeed, both homes rang with the sound of siblings. For Charlotte, it was Anne, Emily and brother Branwell. For Jackie, it was Joan[4] and brother Bill.[5] And Anne and Emily each took a pen in one of their hands[6] to write their own stories of moor life, just as Joan Collins tested the waters of authorship.

"Wuthering Heights" is Emily Brontë's portrayal of the all-consuming passion between beautiful, willful Catherine Earnshaw and dark, stormy Heathcliff. Though they have loved each other since childhood, their love is doomed. Cathy marries for status and money. This has a bad effect on Heathcliff. He tortures Cathy with their love, and soon she gets brain fever and dies. That just about rings down the curtain on what's left of Heathcliff's sanity. Years after Cathy's death, he pays someone to dig up her grave. Oddly enough, Heathcliff is not repelled by the contents of that coffin that has lain so long under the English dirt. In fact, he is excited.

"I'll tell you what I did yesterday! I got the sexton to remove the earth off her coffin-lid, and I opened it. . . . I saw her face again—it is hers yet."

A literary passage that cannot but give the willies to all but the most phlegmatic of readers.

Joan Collins is not without her ability to cause a *frisson* of fear to run up and down her readers' spines. In her novel "Prime Time," Calvin Foster is a dangerous guy who harbors a Heathcliff-like obsession—80's style—for the fabulous Emerald Barrymore, survivor, legend, superstar.

When Calvin hears that Emerald is up for the coveted role of Miranda Hamilton, the sexy temptress on "Saga," television's hottest nighttime soap, he decides to eliminate the competition one by one. He too is possessed—indeed deranged—by his love for a woman he cannot have.

"Sometimes Calvin did his [Emerald] doll's hair. He would talk to her as he manipulated the nylon curls with rough hands. 'You *are* Miranda, my lovely girl,' he would croon to the painted face as he turned the curls around his fingers. 'No one but *no one*, can be her except you.' Lovingly he would change her clothes, pausing often to examine and stroke the smooth, sexless body of the doll. . . . He loved this doll. But he loved the real Emerald even more."

Yet these comparisons just scrape the tip of the Brontë/Collins iceberg. Future scholars exploring this literary phenomenon will be at no loss for more things to write about the sisters then and the sisters now. Tantalizing themes such as "Anne Brontë: The Younger Sister the Collinses Never Had" and the Hollywood as moors/moors as Hollywood metaphor are waiting, like ripe snap beans, to be plucked, snapped and tasted.

True: the Brontës never had the opportunity to sign books at B. Dalton's during lunch or host a segment of "Entertainment Tonight," yet is is easy to see that they were the literary superstars of their time. Who can say any less about the Collins sisters?[7]

Notes

[1]For a more detailed description of this pivotal event in Lucky's life, see "Chances," Book Two, "Lucky, 1955," page 496: "Mommy was up and in the swimming pool. Resting on the striped raft that floated lazily in the middle of the pool. . . . [She] was lying

motionless, her long white-blonde hair fanning out in the water, her arms and legs trailing limply from the sides of the raft.

"Two things struck Lucky at once. Mommy was a naughty girl. She was in the nudie rudie.

"And the water in the pool was a different color. It was pink."

[2]For a more detailed description of this pivotal event in Lucky's life, see Changes, Book Two, "Lucky 1965," page 529.

[3]Strong evidence suggests that the raft in this scene is not fictitious. A raft also appears on page 97 of Joan Collins's autobiography "Past Imperfect": "A few days after filming had commenced, we [Richard Burton and the author] took a swim together during the lunch hour to a small diving raft a few hundred yards from shore. . . . I was working on my tan when I felt fingers stroking my wet hair."

[4]While it's true that there were three Brontë sisters and there are only two Collins sisters, the Collins sisters' hair more than makes up for the lack of a third sister. For a critical discussion of the Collins' sisters' writing and their hair, see "Split Ends and Split Infinitives: Copy Editing as Conditioner" by Mr. Rudy, Salon Digest, pages 157–60.

[5]Brontë scholars have demonstrated the significant influence Branwell Brontë had on his sister's writing. Not enough is known about Bill Collins to deduce his influence on such brother characters as Buddy Hudson, the good twin in "Hollywood Wives," or Angelo Bassalino, the youngest of three Mafia brothers in "The Love Killers." We do know that Jackie dedicated "Rock Star" to him: "For my brother, Bill Collins, who has always been there for me." This confirms both his existence and his name.

[6]The authors would appreciate any information on whether the Brontës were left-handed, right-handed or ambidextrous, for a future comparison with the Beat poets.

[7]Who indeed?

The New Age of Schoolbook Protest

EDWARD B. JENKINSON

Edward B. Jenkinson discusses his role in the controversy over textbook censorship as he participated in hearings in an Indiana protest. In his survey of this case, he also provides some commentary on the problems in doing research and drawing questionable conclusions. This essay illustrates the blend of first-person point of view and formal documentation, in which the endnotes are also the bibliography (a variation of the number system).

Jenkinson addresses his audience directly in his conclusion, when he urges them to educate themselves for the coming controversy:

"And I urge educators to find their school systems' materials selection policies, dust them off, examine them carefully, and when challenges arise, be prepared to follow to the letter the procedures for handling complaints." The endnotes, both documentary and explanatory, provide important sources for the educators who may become involved in this fight.

Original publication: *Phi Delta Kappan*, September 1988.

The following assignment comes from a teacher's manual for a thinking-skills program: "Have students focus their attention on some stimulus (e.g., a spot on the wall). Explain to them that you want them to focus all of their energy for about a minute and ask them to be aware of what it is like when they are really trying to attend to something."[1]

That assignment, taken from Robert Marzano's *Tactics for Thinking*, touched off a storm of protest in two school systems in southern Indiana during the spring of 1988. A group of seven determined women and their followers contended that the exercise could cause a student to fall into a self-hypnotic trance. They charged that the technique "is no different from the one used in hypnosis, in mind control, and in New Age meditation."[2] Using an unusual method of reading an author's references, they tied Marzano and his book to the New Age movement and spread fear among members of several communities that their children were being brainwashed into believing in a one-world government and a one-world religion.

When teachers and administrators first hear about such incidents, some dismiss them out of hand and chide the reporter for wasting their time on "nonsense." But even skeptics begin to pay attention when they are reminded of the many schoolbook protests that were—or still are—based on charges that the public schools are teaching the religion of secular humanism. The disbelievers listen more attentively when they learn the fate of *Tactics* in two school systems separated by 2,100 miles. And the doubters demonstrate true concern when they learn that charges accusing schools of teaching tenets of both New Age religion and secular humanism have been aimed at school systems in at least 12 states in the last two years.[3]

New Age is a term applied loosely to individuals and organizations that "have broken with certain key elements of western thought," according to Marilyn Ferguson in *The Aquarian Conspiracy*.[4] She claims that a "leaderless but powerful network is working to bring about radical change in the United States." She says that the loosely connected groups are involved in a "new way of thinking about old problems" that include everything from holistic health to world peace and a new spirituality.

The "Tale of *Tactics*" began in Battle Ground, Washington, when "25 to 30 irate citizens" alleged that the thinking-skills program advances the occult and subjects children to brainwashing. The school board decided that the charges were unfounded. Then two women took the issue to the "Instructional Materials Committee," which voted 24 to 1 to deny the challenge.[5] (One of the two women does not live in the Battle Ground school district. In fact, she heads a school committee in a nearby community. The intense involvement in schoolbook protests of those who do not actually live in a community is increasingly common.)

The overwhelming vote to deny the challenge did not daunt the protesters. The furor over *Tactics* threatened a school bond issue and a mill levy that were not passed until the thinking-skills program was put on hold. The district superintendent told me in a telephone interview in mid-May that *Tactics* is now "in a holding pattern as a result of the backlash from the community." The superintendent said that many of those "who raised objections here were homeschoolers who didn't even have children in school at the time."

A Washington-based publication on home-schooling reported the Battle Ground incident. After an Indiana woman who teachers her own children at home read the report, she sent for more information. Then she organized six other Indiana women (three of whom are teachers in East Gibson) into a group that protested *Tactics* in two Gibson County school corporations. They also prepared a presentation to be used against the thinking-skills program, not only in Gibson County but also in at least three other counties in Indiana.

The seven women not only scrutinized *Tactics*, searching for connections with the New Age movement and globalism, but they also studied Marzano's references. In a 42-page report to the school board,[6] they tied *Tactics* to the New Age by noting that Marzano "references *Megatrends* by John Naisbitt," who received on the back cover of his book "glowing endorsements from Alvin Toffler, author of *The Third Wave*, a New Age book, and from Marilyn Ferguson, one of the world's most infamous new agers and the author of *The Aquarian Conspiracy*."[7] Thus the seven women apparently concluded that Marzano's *Tactics* should be considered a product of the New Age movement since he "references" Naisbitt, who is endorsed by "new agers."

To connect Marzano with globalism, which the seven women denounced as a search for one-world government and one-world religion, they read Alexander Romanovich Luria's *Working Brain*, a standard reference for many psychologists, to which Marzano made reference. Apparently, Luria's involvement in a cross-cultural experiment in Uzbekistan prompted the seven women to tie him to the quest for one-world government.[8] Thus, since Marzano cites a person allegedly interested in one-world government, Marzano himself must also be a globalist, according to the East Gibson protesters.

As they scoured Marzano's references, they searched for any word, phrase, or idea that they could use to tie *Tactics* to the New Age and globalism. In the process, they discovered that Marzano does not always agree with every idea in his reference books. It appears that this is unacceptable to the protesters because a scholar should agree with everything in a book used as a reference.

Early in their document they noted that Marzano does not cite page numbers in his references, which "necessitates a reading of the entire book. Exactly what material he is referencing he does not say." They wrote: "He [Marzano] makes the chore of researching his work as difficult as possible; therefore any rebuttal by Marzano of a critical appraisal of his work would to us have no credibility. Nor would any rebuttal of anyone we would suspect as a supporter of this liberal thinking be acceptable to us."[9]

In intense letters-to-the-editor campaigns in several area newspapers, the seven women denounced *Tactics*, the New Age, and globalism. They did the same in school board meetings in East and North Gibson. But they had a greater impact in East Gibson, since three of the seven are teachers there. And the president of the East Gibson teacher association added his voice to the protest by announcing that the decision to use *Tactics* should be made by the parents and not by teachers, because "students belong to parents, not teachers."[10] He also openly opposed academic freedom for teachers.

In direct contrast, North Gibson's teachers, superintendent, school board, and school administrators stood firmly behind *Tactics*. The thinking-skills program was also endorsed by the Chamber of Commerce, by Partners in Education, by the Community Advisory Council, and by the Ministerial Association. At its meeting in early May 1988, the North Gibson school board voted unanimously to keep *Tactics*.

East Gibson's board concluded a modified debate on *Tactics* at its May 1988 meeting. Ronald Brandt, executive director of *Educational Leadership*, and I were given 35 minutes to present a case for the thinking-skills program and to refute the arguments used by the protesters, who were also given 35 minutes. Then each side was given 15 minutes for rebuttal.

In his opening statement, Brandt noted the purpose of *Tactics*, expressed his faith in the author, refuted the hypnotism charge, and declared that the thinking-skills program "has nothing whatever to do with global education." After complimenting the seven protesters for their thoroughness in reading Marzano's references, he said: "Unfortunately, they have apparently misunderstood the program and misunderstood its intent. There is nothing mysterious or subversive about any of the tactics."

Focusing primarily on the protest leader's arguments to the East Gibson School Board in December, I gave the board and the protesters copies of my commentary on her eight-page presentation.[11] I made 53 notes on her 29 paragraphs, and 14 of my comments were several paragraphs long. Most of my notes challenged the facts and/or the evidence presented in the protest leader's document.

After distributing a two-page definition of global education that was in sharp contrast with the protesters' conception,[12] I compared the attacks on *Tactics* and global education to the strategies used against secular humanism. Then I attempted to refute the protesters' definitions of global education, hypnotism, and pantheism, which the leader designated as the religion of the New Age. I told the board that, in reviewing the documents prepared by the seven women, I had detected the direct influence of five national organizations that attempt to remove materials from public schools: the Eagle Forum, Concerned Women of America, the National Association of Christian Educators, Citizens for Excellence in Education, and Educational Research Analysts. Through further investigation, I found materials that could be traced to the John Birch Society. My findings were not disputed in the protesters' rebuttal.

In their 35-minute presentation, they read from their 42-page document. They used students to act out what they considered to be the similarities between yoga, self-hypnosis, involuntary attention, and semi-trances and three exercises in *Tactics*, which they claimed could cause students to fall into trances without their teachers' realizing it.

A member of the President's Committee on Education, former Indiana State Senator Joan Gubbins, was the major speaker in the protesters' rebuttal. After congratulating the seven women for their fine work and for their concern for the children of the community, she read selected passages from Marzano's own evaluation of the thinking-skills program. She concluded that it is "a little oversold and grossly underinvestigated." Approximately 60% of the audience gave Sen. Gubbins and her companions a standing ovation.

At the end of the modified debate, the president announced that the board would vote on *Tactics* at its June meeting. By votes of 3 to 2, the board passed two resolutions at the June meeting. The first called for the East Gibson school corporation not to use *Tactics* in its staff development program. However, the board stated in its resolution that it "respects the right of individual teachers to use the resources each has in furthering our common goal of educational excellence, and will protect the teachers' right to academic freedom and their commitment to professional responsibility."[13] Thus the board said, in effect, that teachers who had been using *Tactics* in their classrooms could continue doing so.

The second resolution stated that the board "wishes to pursue a thinking-skills program as a part of our School Improvement Process. The first requirement for such a program to be effective is that both the administration and the teaching staff must support that program." The board then resolved to "form a team of teachers and administrators to work together to select materials to formulate a program that will teach our students thinking skills."[14]

Members of the audience jeered, stamped their feet, and sang during that June board meeting. The president of the teacher association admonished the board for "making a landmark decision on academic freedom." He complained that the corporation had "just given teachers complete and unadulterated academic freedom. The teacher will be allowed to use any method he sees fit that would best educate students."[15]

The protesters vowed to continue their fight to remove *Tactics* from the Gibson County schools, to recall board members if necessary, and to elect their own candidates to the board. The leader of the protesters suggested that "if *Tactics* philosophy was carried to its logical end, students would be allowed to experiment with drugs, and nude models in art class would be commonplace." In her pledge to continue the protest, she said: "We won't roll over and play dead. We are not ready to give up our best resource, our children, to education nincompoops."[16]

I believe that it would be a serious mistake for educators to dismiss controversies over *Tactics* in Battle Ground and Gibson County as isolated incidents. The "victory" in Battle Ground has already been reported in the literature read by critics of the public schools; the continuing struggle in Gibson County will surely give courage to unhappy citizens elsewhere as they read about it in the newsletters of protesting organizations. And the seven women have already given their presentation against *Tactics* and global education in at least three other counties. They will undoubtedly receive requests to carry their fight across Indiana's borders into neighboring states.

It is their battle against globalism that will attract the attention of citizens concerned about public education. By interchanging globalism, by which they mean the quest for one-world government, with global education, today's schoolbook protesters may accomplish what their colleagues did when they used the terms *humanism* and *secular humanism* as if they carried a single meaning. By tying *globalism* (and its alleged synonym, *global education*) to the New Age movement, today's protesters can provoke anger in citizens who do not want their children introduced to ideas about one-world government or one-world religion. By attacking the New Age movement as if everything that might be labeled New Age could be seen as part of a single religion, the protesters can attempt to remove from the schools anything they perceive to be New Age because, they charge, it would violate the separation of church and state.

The following best-selling books carry the message of the New Age critics:

- William M. Bowen, Jr., *Globalism: America's Demise* (Shreveport, La.: Huntington House, 1984);
- Constance E. Cumbey, *The Hidden Dangers of the Rainbow* (Shreveport, La.: Huntington House, 1983);
- Douglas R. Groothuis, *Unmasking the New Age* (Downers Grove, Ill.: InterVarsity Press, 1986);
- Dave Hunt, *Peace, Prosperity, and the Coming Holocaust* (Eugene, Ore.: Harvest House, 1983);
- Texe Marr, *Dark Secrets of the New Age* (Westchester, Ill.: Crossway Books, 1987); and
- H. Edward Rowe, *New Age Globalism: Humanist Agenda for Building a New World Without God* (Herndon, Va.: Growth Publishing, 1985).

These books either state directly or imply that New Age (and/or secular humanistic) ideas pervade public school classrooms. And the books make it clear that anything tainted with the New Age can only lead to disaster for American youth. Throughout the books, the message is clear that a single-minded group is attempting to gain control of the world. What is missing is the fact that the

New Age movement has no central headquarters or organization. As one critic of the New Age noted:

> As a working definition, the New Age Movement is a broad coalition of various networking organizations that (a) believe in a new world religion (pantheism), (b) are working for a new world order, and (c) expect a New Age Christ. Of course not all who participate in the New Age movement are necessarily conscious of all these aspects.[17]

Thus, just as people in the schools who are branded as spreaders of the gospel of the New Age do not understand the charge, so it is with so-called "new agers" themselves—not all who are so labeled sing the same song, march to the same tune, or pray similar prayers.

I believe that educators need to become acquainted with the charges leveled by critics of the New Age movement. And I urge educators to find their school systems' materials selection policies, dust them off, examine them carefully, and, when challenges arise, be prepared to follow to the letter the procedures for handling complaints.

Notes

1. Robert J. Marzano and Daisy E. Arredondo, *Tactics for Thinking—Teacher's Manual* (Alexandria, Va.: Association for Supervision and Curriculum Development, 1986), p. 11.

2. Presentation of Jeanne Georges to the school board of the East Gibson (Ind.) School Corporation, 14 December 1987.

3. Individuals or organizations have demanded the banning of global education, the occult, some counseling techniques, and Satanism, all of which they claim can be found in textbooks and library books. The states include: Alabama, California, Colorado, Florida, Georgia, Kentucky, Maryland, Ohio, Oregon, Pennsylvania, Tennessee, and Wisconsin.

4. Marilyn Ferguson, *The Aquarian Conspiracy* (Los Angeles: J. P. Tarcher, 1980), p. 23.

5. Steve Hoskins, co-president, Battle Ground Education Association, letter to the editor, *Oakland City Journal*, 16 December 1987, p. 2.

6. "A Preliminary Report Taken from the Supporting Research of the Tactics for Thinking Manual," 14 March 1988, compiled by Camille Aydt, Patricia Burkhart, Cecile Caldemeyer, Deborah Cochrane, Jeanne Georges, Vicky Georges, and Abby Vukovich.

7. Ibid., p. 5.

8. Ibid., p. 15.

9. Ibid., p. 6.

10. "45 Attend East Gibson Meeting," *Oakland City Journal*, 10 November 1987, p. 1.

11. Edward Jenkinson, "Commentary on the Presentation of Jeanne Georges to the School Board of the East Gibson School Corporation on December 14, 1987," 9 May 1988.

12. James M. Becker, who edited *Schooling for a Global Age* (New York: McGraw-Hill, 1979), prepared a two-page definition of global education for me.

13. Board of School Trustees, East Gibson School Corporation, Resolution 3, passed by a vote of 3 to 2 on 13 June 1988.

14. Board of School Trustees, East Gibson School Corporation, Resolution 4, passed by a vote of 3 to 2 on 13 June 1988.

15. "Board Lets Teachers Decide," *Oakland City Journal*, 14 June 1988, p. 1.

16. "Gibson Parents Vow to Fight 'Tactics' Teaching Program," *Evansville Press*, 14 June 1988, p. 3.

17. Normal L. Geisler, "The New Age Movement," *Bibliotheca Sacra*, January-March 1987, p. 82.

At the College, 1760–1762

DUMAS MALONE

While serving as a history professor at Mr. Jefferson's University, Dumas Malone committed himself to writing a "comprehensive biography" of Thomas Jefferson. Malone wanted to capture Jefferson and his age. This essay on Jefferson's college days at William and Mary (Williamsburg, Virginia) is taken from the first volume of Malone's work. In this chapter he studies the effect of Williamsburg on Jefferson—the teachers, politics, religion, classmates.

The sources for this chapter are primary sources—letters and memoirs. The endnotes are quite detailed, and the bibliography invaluable to a scholar wanting to pursue research into Jefferson's life and times. Readers wanting only the information, not the scholarly documentation, may ignore the notes and read for their own interests and pleasure.

Original publication: *Jefferson the Virginian*. Boston: Little, Brown and Company, 1948.

In the year 1760 Thomas Jefferson emerged from the hills and entered the College of William and Mary in Williamsburg. His future friend and rival John Adams was then five years out of Harvard; but Alexander Hamilton, in the British West Indies, was little beyond the toddling stage. George Washington, whose advanced schooling was gained in Indian warfare, had married Martha Custis and was farming at Mount Vernon, hoping that his days of campaigning were over. Sagacious Benjamin Franklin, who had picked up most of his youthful learning in a printing shop, was in England, high in scientific favor and having the time of his life. In this same year King George III ascended the English throne, unaware that in the village capital of the royal Province of Virginia there was a stripling who would one day denounce him in immortal language.

Up to this time, so far as we know, the future author of the Declaration of Independence had written nothing suggesting the cadences of that historic document or anticipating his later grace, but he had drafted one letter which has survived. This was an eager but stilted note to John Harvie, proposing that he leave the mountains for the College. After talking things over with another executor, Colonel Peter Randolph, he had soberly marshaled his arguments to justify an important step.[1] He could continue his study of the classics at the College, he believed; he could learn something of mathematics, and he could gain "a more universal acquaintance" there. If these reasons were insufficient, others could have been easily adduced. Having outgrown Maury's, this promising boy deserved other opportunities and it seemed highly unlikely that he would waste them. He himself remarked that the coming of company was causing him to lose a fourth of his time at home. He was already impatient with encroachment on his precious hours, and any hindrance to his pursuit of knowledge.

After a while he talked a good deal about going to England, but this possibility seems not to have been considered seriously at first, if it ever was. His advisers were doubtless aware that there was confusion in the College. This was to continue until the Revolution and to cause some of the gentry to question the propriety of sending their sons there for moral improvement and the acquisition of sound learning.[2] On the other hand, there were those who said that education was a good deal worse in England, and with them the mature Jefferson would have heartily agreed. Several Virginians, among them Robert Carter of Nomini Hall (who afterwards fully redeemed himself), had returned "so inconceivably illiterate, and also corrupted and vicious," that Mann Page of Rosewell swore that no son of his should go to school in England. Accordingly, this wealthy planter sent his son John to the grammar school of William and Mary at the age of thirteen and put him to lodge and board with President Thomas Dawson, who was also commissary of the Bishop of London and minister of Bruton Church.[3] Peter Jefferson's son, who entered at a higher level as he was nearing seventeen, likewise escaped foreign contamination, though he gained no high impression of the learning and morals of the clergymen on the faculty during his student days in Williamsburg.

Lodging and eating in the College were not compulsory for "paying scholars," but the surviving records imply that he did not avail himself of the privilege of living in town. He began to pay board on March 25, 1760, and continued to do so for two years and one month. Then, so far as the records show, his college career was over.[4] About this time the faculty were forced to enjoin the housekeeper to serve both fresh and salt meat for dinner, to provide puddings and pies on Sunday and two weekdays, and to see that the suppers were not made up of different sorts of scraps but were the same for every table. The chief complaint came after Jefferson had left the College, but, like the other boys, he probably suffered from the negligence of a housekeeper who was away too often. A year or more after his departure she was away for good.[5]

The main building, then more than sixty years old, was generally termed the College, though there was also the Brafferton, where a handful of Indians stayed. Opposite this stood the President's House. Some twenty years after his student days Jefferson described the College and the hospital in Williamsburg as "rude, mis-shapen piles, which, but that they have roofs, would be taken for brick-kilns."[6] This, however, was after he had fallen under the spell of Palladio; his architectural judgment could hardly have been that severe when he was a youth, fresh from the frame buildings of Albemarle. At a later time he also condemned the educational organization of the College and tried to improve it. The statutes had been revised a couple of years before he entered, but in framework the College was essentially unchanged from 1729 until he became governor of Virginia half a century later.[7] It consisted of the grammar school, which was preparatory; the Indian school, which a few redskins still attended; the philosophy school, in which he himself was enrolled; and the divinity school, which he afterwards helped to abolish. Two professors were assigned to each of the two latter; and each of the former had a single master. With the president, the entire faculty consisted of seven men, and there were probably not more than a hundred scholars and students altogether.

With the single but important exception of William Small, professor of natural philosophy, the members of the William and Mary faculty were Anglican clergymen, and for half a dozen years they had been embroiled in controversy with the local political authorities.[8] Two years before Jefferson enrolled there had been an upheaval, and it was as a result of this that Small had come to the College. Because of their activities against the Two Penny Act, which as we have seen affected the pay of the clergy unfavorably, three of the professors had been dismissed by the local governing body, the Board of Visitors. One of these men died but the two others appealed to England for reinstatement and, after Jefferson had left the College, won their fight. This proved bad for Small. When Jefferson arrived on the scene, however, he was there, teaching physics, metaphysics, and mathematics, and through force of circumstances was soon teaching practically everything else.

Jefferson's other teacher at first was the Reverend Jacob Rowe, professor of moral philosophy, whose field comprised rhetoric, logic, and ethics. In the August of Jefferson's first year (which had begun in late March and was interrupted by no long summer vacation), Rowe and the Master of the grammar school became far too merry and led the college boys in a row with the boys of the town. Consequently, one of these clergymen was summarily dismissed and the other resigned. The immediate results were favorable to Jefferson. Almost a year passed before a successor to the deposed professor of moral philosophy was installed, and in the interim Small added all or many of Rowe's subjects to his own. He was already giving Jefferson his first views of the "expansion of science," and, according to this eminent pupil, he gave the first lectures ever delivered in the College in ethics, rhetoric, and belles-lettres.[9] Either these subjects had been previously sacrificed to logic, or they had been taught more mechanically by men who lacked Small's happy talent of communication. For nearly half of Jefferson's course Small appears to have been the only regular teacher that he had. Whatever may be thought about the organization, administration, and discipline of the College, here was one of those rare personal influences which prove unforgettable and elicit immortal tribute. He afterwards said that Small probably fixed the destinies of his life.

But for Small, the first year must have been deeply disillusioning to him. In the midst of all the woes created by convivial and riotous members of the faculty, President Dawson himself began to drink notoriously, and, when arraigned before the Board of Visitors on the charge of habitual drunkenness, confessed the fact. His friend, Lieutenant Governor Fauquier, defended him, saying that "he had been teased by contrariety of opinions between him and the clergy into the loss of his spirits, and it was no wonder that he should apply for consolation to spirituous liquors."[10] He was granted a pardon on the promise of future sobriety, but the unfortunate man became quite irresponsible. He died in December. Not until spring did the Reverend William Yates, from whose arid teaching John Page had suffered elsewhere, qualify as his successor. He also became minister of Bruton Church, which Jefferson attended, sitting near the pulpit in the half of the south gallery which was assigned to the College.[11]

The scandals and confusion which the youth observed in his first year must have made a deep impression on so sensitive a mind, but at this immature age he was not deeply interested in the continuing struggle between the clerical faculty and the local governing board.[12] The fundamental question was whether the Bishop of London or the gentlemen of Virginia should have final authority over the College and the Church, and the gentry would have given the same answer to this if Thomas Jefferson had never gone to school in Williamsburg. His later distinction among his fellows was owing to his championship, not merely of local self-government, but of complete religious liberty. The seeds of anticlericalism, however, were probably sown in his mind while he was in college or soon afterwards, when he became intimate with Francis Fauquier. He could hardly have failed to learn that the relations between the brilliant Governor and the local representatives of English ecclesiasticism were far from amicable, and on personal grounds his sympathies may have been enlisted against the clergy.[13] It is a highly significant fact, also, that the early teacher who did most to fix the destinies of his life was the only layman in the faculty of the College.

The surviving record of this influential layman is all too brief.[14] He was a Scotchman, designated as "Mr. William Small" when he was appointed in 1758. He remained in Williamsburg six years, returned to England where he is said to have been the friend of James Watt and Erasmus Darwin, and died at

Birmingham in 1775, listed as "William Small, M.D." He had assumed the title after he left Virginia. The circumstances of his going were unpleasant.[15] His predecessor as professor of natural philosophy was successful in his appeal to England and had to be restored. Small had been sent over by the Bishop of London in the first place, but he had less reason than his clerical colleagues to rely on English ecclesiastical authority and during his stay in the Colony he was on more friendly terms than the others with the local political group. It was a sign of the approval of the Board of Visitors that they proceeded to elect him to the chair of moral philosophy, which was again vacant, after he had lost the professorship of natural philosophy. At the same time, however, the Board passed a statute affirming the right to remove any member of the faculty at will. Small balked at agreeing to that, went to England to look into the matter further, and declined to return. There were some other matters of disagreement and in the end he aroused the strong displeasure of the presiding officer of the Board, who wrote him a sarcastic letter.[16] At some time Jefferson probably learned about all this and he may have reflected that local authority itself is likely to become tyrannical. What he learned from his favorite teacher was not obedience to authority but delight in the exercise of his mind.

John Page, in the last year of his own life, referred to this same teacher as "illustrious," and credited to him the beginnings of his own abiding interest in all branches of mathematics.[17] Shortly after Small left the College, Jefferson was probably thinking of him when he described the study of mathematics and natural philosophy as "peculiarly engaging and delightful." He certainly was, when he took up mathematics again long afterwards, in order to guide his grandson's course, and endeavored to rub off the dust of fifty years. It was always his favorite subject, he said: "We have no theories there, no uncertainties remain on the mind; all is demonstration and satisfaction. I have forgotten much, and recover it with more difficulty than when in the vigor of my mind I originally acquired it." But, as he soon wrote to another, "thanks to the good foundation laid at college by my old master and friend Small, I am doing it with a delight and success beyond my expectation."[18]

Jefferson observed that Small pursued an "even and dignified line" of conduct, like others whom he particularly emulated in those crucial days.[19] This layman was not one to be involved in student brawls. On the other hand, in an era of disorder, he alone of the faculty denied the arbitrary power of a master to inflict punishment on an offending scholar. John Page called him his "ever to be beloved professor," and Jefferson said that he gave to his studies enlightened and affectionate guidance and was like a father to him. Actually, this unmarried teacher, whose chief complaint about his position was its loneliness, made a daily companion of young Jefferson, and taught him no less through informal talk than by his memorable lectures. As a mature man Jefferson did not forget him. Just when the Revolution was beginning, and public dissension threatened to divide him from his friend as the ocean had already done, he sent him by a reluctant captain what he described as half of a little present that he had laid by. It consisted of three dozen bottles of Madeira which he had kept for eight years in his own cellar, and he promised to dispatch that many more as soon as possible by another ship. He did not know that his old teacher was in the last year of life.[20]

There is some testimony that Small's influence persisted in the College. It has been said that he, more than any other teacher, was responsible for the liberality of spirit which came to characterize William and Mary.[21] Some people called it "skepticism" and thought it dangerous, but Jefferson and his kindred spirits regarded it as the first step towards true knowledge. Historically, William Small was a minor torchbearer of the Enlightenment, and by any reckoning he was one of those rare men who point the way, who show new paths, who open doors before the mind.

To Jefferson he also opened the door of George Wythe's law office, and he and Wythe ushered this inquiring young man into the Governor's Palace. Thus were the benefits of enlightened conversation increased rather than diminished after Jefferson left the College. He was as intimate with Small for two more years as one of his age could be. His life and associations in Williamsburg before he was admitted to the bar cannot be divided into sharply defined segments; but if his college course can be described separately it is best summed up by saying that he continued to be taught privately, and that his tutor was William Small. The same sort of statement can be made about the five years after that, when he studied law under George Wythe. He gained clear title to fame in later years as a prophet and architect of public education, but his own training was pre-eminently personal and private.

Self-imposed, rather than external, discipline shaped his education from his youth onward. In his last decade he wrote: "I was a hard student until I entered on the business of life, the duties of which leave no idle time to those disposed to fulfill them; and now, retired, and at the age of seventy-six, I am again a hard student."[22] The first period of his amazing life differed in many ways from the important and exacting era of public service which followed, but the habit of study persisted. Drafting state papers brought him no such joy as the free pursuit of knowledge, and he could not approach all public problems with the zeal of the explorer; but in all his tasks he could and did manifest the seriousness and the industry of the scholar.

His characteristic habits of study may have been formed even before he went to Williamsburg. Said one of his young admirers who observed him when he was ripe in years and honors:

> His mind must have been by nature one of uncommon capaciousness and retention, of wonderful clearness and as rapid as is consistent with accurate thoughts. His application from very early youth has not only been intense but unremitted. When young he adopted a system, perhaps an entire plan of life from which neither the exigencies of business nor the allurements of pleasure could drive or seduce him. Much of his success is to be ascribed to methodical industry. Even when at school he used to be seen with his Greek Grammar in his hand while his comrades were enjoying relaxation in the interval of school hours.[23]

The family tradition is that during his college days he studied fifteen hours of twenty-four and habitually until long past midnight, only to rise at dawn. This sounds like too severe a program even for him. In vacations he is said to have devoted almost three fourths of his time to his books. Next only to tyranny he hated indolence, which he regarded as the besetting sin of his hospitable Virginia countrymen, and about which he wrote with appalling frequency to his children in later years. "It is while we are young that the habit of industry is formed," he reflected. "If not then, it never is afterwards." If this is true he himself formed the habit early. "Determine never to be idle," he admonished his growing daughter. "No person will have occasion to complain of the want of time who never loses any." Then he made an observation which aptly sums up his own intellectual history: "It is wonderful how much may be done if we are always doing."[24]

Such a regimen and such a philosophy would impose a strain on any but the strongest physique. He learned to guard his unusual natural gifts by physical regularity and systematic exercise, though we cannot be sure just when he became so wise. He ran and walked when in college, and, if the testimony of his grandson can be accepted, he once swam thirteen times across a millpond that was a quarter of a mile wide.[25] This seems too much for a boy fresh from the little Rivanna, but the physical endurance of Peter Jefferson's heir was remarkable in his youth and prime. It was probably in Williamsburg that he established the habit of bathing his feet in cold water every morning. This practice he continued for upwards of sixty years and to it he attributed his lifelong freedom from colds. At seventy-six, he reported that only two or three times in his life had he had a fever of more than twenty-four hours; and he then could boast that he had been blessed with "organs of digestion which accept and concoct, without ever murmuring, whatever the palate chooses to consign to them," and that he had not lost a tooth by age.[26]

The severe perfection of this portrait is somewhat relieved by his own statement that during his early years in Williamsburg he was extravagant, by occasional remarks of his about youthful temptations, and by other indications of gaiety and frivolity. The most frivolous period probably coincided with the first years that he studied law, when he grumbled about his law books and indulged in much silly chatter about the girls. He participated in the annual battles between town and gown, but there is no suggestion that he was ever disciplined for his part in student scrapes as was his friend John Walker, who was rusticated in the fall of 1763, along with a couple of other boys who afterwards gained considerable renown.[27] He had left the College then and was living in town, but he reported the episode with some zest. He was a member of a student organization known as the Flat Hat Club, which is notable for its primacy as a secret college society but wholly lacked seriousness of purpose. It is not to be confused with Phi Beta Kappa, of which Jefferson knew nothing. It was primarily convivial and its certificates of membership were couched in humorous Latin phraseology. One of its expressed desires was that each member should be "a great ornament and pillar of things general and particular." John Walker was a fellow member and the fact that there were only six altogether may or may not imply that Jefferson was numbered among the socially elite. He continued to attend meetings after he left college and wrote about one of them in frivolous Latin vein.[28]

John Page said that Jefferson "could tear himself away from his dearest friends, to fly to his studies."[29] It seems likely that he did not cultivate the fine art of friendship consciously and assiduously until after he became somewhat discouraged about the girls. But there is no reason to suppose that he flouted the dominant tradition of sociability or that he failed to avail himself of the great opportunities for friendship which this small academic community afforded. Some of his most enduring associations started there.

One of the most distinguishing characteristics of colonial Williamsburg was the seasonal occasion for friendly intercourse which it offered to residents of isolated plantations. In the midst of this sociable village, which teemed periodically, the College was set. Its junior members were drawn from the sons of the gentry and these constituted a close-knit group. There were gradations of rank among them, with the families of the Councillors at the top of the social scale, but there was no such invidious distinction here as John Adams found at Harvard College, where seats in class were assigned according to parental rank or standing. The son of a rugged squire from the Piedmont did not have to take a lower place than John Page of Rosewell. With this particular scion of a highly influential family Jefferson was intimate from the start, and through him became friends with the equally aristocratic Nelsons.

His old schoolmate at Maury's, Dabney Carr, may not have entered until the year after he did. With this single exception, Page was Jefferson's closest college friend. The two were almost exactly the same age and they were to be like brothers for almost half a century. Page had the more impressive economic and social background. Through his grandmother he was a descendant of "King" Carter, and his grandfather, Mann Page, had been a much larger landholder than the second Thomas Jefferson or even Isham Randolph, besides being a member of the Council. It was this Mann Page who had built Rosewell in Gloucester County and left the fabulous house to a son of the same name who spent most of his strength bearing the heavy burden. In this huge, three-storied mansion John had grown up. Jefferson was often to look at its mahogany wainscoting and climb its marble stairways, probably reflecting that his own forebears had been wise in not cultivating magnificence so extravagantly.[30]

To a greater degree than Jefferson's immediate ancestors, the Pages were devoted to the Church and associated with the College, but John may have been removed from the President's House at the time that poor Dawson got into so much trouble and before the Reverend William Yates came in. He appears to have lodged in the College during the second year that his friend from Albemarle was there, and he may have been with him from the first. He had secured a firm grounding in the classics from his revered tutor, William Price; and, like Jefferson, he enjoyed the special attentions of William Small. Both Small and President Dawson commended him to Governor Fauquier. In religious matters he was more conventional than Jefferson, and, being especially sociable, he was more willing to leave his books. There was no touch of genius on him but he was every inch a gentleman. He was a fellow in philosophical inquiry until his boon companion probed more deeply, and he was an intimate confidant in early matters of the heart.

Since Jefferson remained so long in Williamsburg as a student, it may be safely assumed that he knew practically everybody who attended the College from 1760 to 1767. Among his near contemporaries were these: John Walker, who was destined to be a fellow burgess from Albemarle; William Fleming, to whom some of his earliest known letters were directed; Francis Eppes, to whom he was to be closely bound by marriage; a couple of Harrisons, for one of whom he may later have designed Brandon; John Tyler, with whom he was to be associated as a law student; Austin and Bernard Moore, to one of whom he was to address a memorable letter about the study of law; Jacquelin Ambler, who was to win a girl he dreamed of; and Bathurst Skelton, whose widow he was to marry later on.[31] Some of these names are now remembered chiefly because of their association with his. He overtopped his own college generation, but even among its members he met future leaders of the Colony and State. Thomas Nelson, Junior, who was to succeed him as governor in perilous times, had gone to school abroad but was much in Williamsburg in this period. A more noted group came to the College somewhat later: Edmund Randolph, John Taylor of Caroline, and that James Madison who became a bishop; and early in the next decade appeared John Marshall, briefly, and James Monroe. The James Madison who was to succeed Jefferson as President manifested a degree of unconventionality by attending the College of New Jersey at Princeton, but even without him this is an exceedingly distinguished list.

To those who heard of the recurrent disorders among the students at William and Mary, and of the dissensions within the faculty or between the faculty and the Board, the affairs of this historic college may well have seemed chaotic during the period that Jefferson knew it best. The successor to President Dawson as commissary of the Bishop of London, the Reverend William Robinson, thought that it had failed to answer the high ends of its institution and doubted if, under existing conditions, learning and religion would strike deep root in the Colony.[32] He proposed that the College be really put under the care of the ecclesiastical authorities in England, and be entirely divorced from local control. There can be no doubt that the situation was anomalous, but the school was more successful than he realized. The secret of its success lay, not in its organization, not in its identification with the English Church, not even in its faculty, but in its intimate association with the community in which it was placed.

The College could be no mere training school for clergymen, though actually it produced better ministers for the Colony than those who were imported directly from abroad. The gentry had no strong desire that it cultivate learning for its own sake, for their ideal was the well-rounded man. It was pre-eminently a school for statesmen and as such, on the North American continent, its product has never been excelled.[33] The extraordinary distinction of its alumni is chiefly owing to the fact that its students were by birth and station the potential leaders of the Colony, and that their college days were spent at the center of provincial life. The most important fact about it was not that it was relatively old, or that it had considerable resources, but that it was located in Williamsburg.

In this distinctive community Jefferson as a young man met the leading gentlemen of the country, and there before he was grown he saw visitors of quite a different sort. The Indians were in the habit of coming to the capital, often in great numbers, and he reports that he was much with them. One historic visit occurred in the spring of 1762, and with brief mention of it we can end the story of his college days. It was that of a Cherokee chief whom he had seen before, as the guest of his father at Shadwell on previous journeys, and he called him "Ontasseté," though there were other names for the same man—Ostenaco, Oconasta, Judd's Friend, and, best of all perhaps, Outacity.[34]

A party of at least 165 Indians had set out from the Holston country in what is now East Tennessee, and an embarrassingly large number eventually arrived in Williamsburg. The students must have talked about them, and they may have observed Outacity when he was dined at the College. They doubtless heard that he was received by the Governor and Council and granted permission to visit the Great King, his father, in England. They could hardly have anticipated the sensation which the Cherokee created in London, where he was visited by Oliver Goldsmith and painted by Sir Joshua Reynolds; but before his departure he made a profound impression on a youth who was nearing nineteen and who had not yet crossed the sea. Jefferson was in Outacity's camp when he delivered a farewell oration to his people the evening before he sailed, and as an old man he remembered the splendor of the moon. The college student understood no word of the Chief's prayer for his own safety on the voyage and for that of his people until his return; but Outacity's resounding voice and the solemn silence of his followers around their campfires filled him with awe and veneration.

Years afterward, as governor and President, he was to receive visits from Indians, to address them as a Father, and to smoke with them the pipe of peace. He was to observe this race as a philosopher and to inquire into its languages; as a responsible statesman he was to grapple with the problem of depredations and massacres on the frontier. But he was not soon, if ever, to escape from these early emotions. At this time, unquestionably, he was moved not by fear but by curiosity and compassion. Nonetheless, these warriors must have reminded him that the wilderness was not far away from the college halls he was quitting, from the Capitol where decorous statesmen deliberated, from the Palace ballroom where ladies and gentlemen danced the gay reel and the stately minuet. Of such contrasts was provincial life compounded.

Notes

[1]Jan. 14, 1760 (Ford, I, 340).

[2]J. C. Ballagh, ed., *Letters of Richard Henry Lee*, I, 70–71; Fithian, Feb. 12, 1774.

[3]*Va. Hist. Register*, July 1850, p. 146.

[4]"Notes Relating to Some of the Students Who Attended the College of William and Mary," *W. & M.*, 2 ser., I, 27–42; *A Provincial List of Alumni . . . of the College of William and Mary in Virginia, from 1693 to 1888*.

[5]*W. & M.*, 1 ser. III, 196, 262–264. The offending housekeeper, Mrs. Isabella Cocke, was there 1761–1763.

[6]In his *Notes on Virginia* (Ford, III, 258).

[7]Statutes of 1758, *W. & M.*, 1 ser., XVI, 241–256. See also Jefferson's later bill for amending the constitution, Sect. I (Ford, II, 229–232).

[8]The account of the faculty is based largely on "Journal of the Meetings of the President and Masters of William and Mary College," *W. & M.*, 1 ser., III, 60–64, 128–132, 195–197, 262–265; IV, 43–46, 130–132, 187–192; V, 224–229. See also *Ibid.*, 1 ser., IX, 153–154; XIX, 20; R. Goodwin, *A Brief & True Report concerning Williamsburg in Virginia*, pp. 38–43.

[9]"Autobiography," Ford, I, 4; to L. H. Girardin, Jan. 15, 1815 (L. & B., XIV, 231).

[10]W. S. Perry, ed., *Historical Collections Relating to the American Colonial Church* (hereafter cited as Perry, *Hist. Colls.*), I, 517.

[11]W. A. R. Goodwin, *Historical Sketch of Bruton Church*, p. 44.

[12]J. E. Kirkpatrick, "Constitutional Development of the College of William and Mary," *W. & M.*, 2 ser., VI, 95–108.

[13]Perry, *Hist. Colls.*, I, 464, 470–472, 517.

[14]Besides references to faculty meetings, see *W. & M.*, 1 ser., XVI, 164–168; *Va. Mag.*, XVI, 209–210; *Gentleman's Magazine and Historical Chronicle*, XLV, 151 (London, 1775); Burk, *History of Virginia*, III, 399–400. His salary was paid until Sept. 15, 1764, but he probably left earlier.

[15]The most dependable source is a letter from Stephen to Edward Hawtrey, Mar. 26, 1765 (W. & M. Coll. Papers, Folder 12). This is based on a conversation with Small.

[16]MS. copy of letter from the Rector of the College, unsigned and without address but obviously to Small, June 25, 1767, Edgehill Randolph Papers, UVA. This copy was doubtless sent to Jefferson, who was thus familiar with the unpleasant episode.

[17]*Va. Hist. Register*, July 1850, pp. 150–151.

[18]To Benjamin Rush, Aug. 17, 1811 (Ford, IX, 328); to the Reverend James Madison, Dec. 29, 1811 (L. & B., XIX, 183). Earlier comment in Randall, I, 53.

[19]To T. J. Randolph, Nov. 24, 1808 (Ford, IX, 231).

[20]To Small, May 7, 1775, LC, 1:140, partly printed in Ford, I, 453–455.

[21]I. A. Coles to Henry St. George Tucker, July 20, 1799 (*W. & M.*, 1 ser., IV, 105–108).

[22]To Dr. Vine Utley, Mar. 21, 1819 (Ford, X, 126).

[23]F. W. Gilmer, *c.* 1816, in R. B. Davis, *Francis Walker Gilmer* (hereafter cited as Davis, *Gilmer*), p. 350; quoted by courtesy of the author and the Dietz press.

[24]Randall, I, 24; *Domestic Life*, pp. 31, 115, 121. The letters to his daughter Martha were written in 1787.

[25]Memoirs of Thomas Jefferson Randolph, Edgehill Randolph Papers, UVA., p. 3.

[26]To Dr. Vine Utley, Mar. 21, 1819 (Ford, X, 125); to James Maury, June 16, 1815 (L. & B., XIV, 319).

[27]To John Page, Oct. 7, 1763 (Ford, I, 353); to J. C. Cabell, Jan. 24, 1816 (L. & B., XIV, 413); *W. & M.*, 1 ser., IV, 44–45.

[28]G. P. Coleman, ed., *The Flat Hat Club and the Phi Beta Kappa Society*, reproducing letters; Jefferson to John Walker, Sept. 3, 1769, UVA photostat from Yale Univ.; printed in Kimball, *Road to Glory*, p. 141.

[29]*Va. Hist. Register*, July 1850, p. 151.

[30]Incomplete autobiography of Page in *Va. Hist. Register*, July 1850, pp. 142–151; Meade, I, 147–148*n.*, 331–333, especially for Rosewell and churchmanship. The extensive correspondence between him and Jefferson will be cited frequently hereafter.

[31]*Provisional List of Alumni; W. & M.*, 2 ser., I, 27–42.

[32]Robinson to Bishop of London, Oct. 16, 1767, in Perry, *Hist. Collections*, I, 529, and other letters there.

[33]For good comments, see H. B. Adams, *College of William and Mary*, pp. 26–29.

[34]Jefferson to John Adams, June 11, 1812 (L. & B., XIII, 160); S. C. Williams, ed., *Lieut. Henry Timberlake's Memoirs* (Johnson City, Tenn., 1927) esp. pp. 129–131, 170; *Burgesses, Journals*, 1761–1765, pp. xvii–xviii; art. on Outacity by K. E. Crane in *Dictionary of Amer. Biography* (hereafter cited as *D.A.B.*).

Body Ritual Among the Nacirema

HORACE MINER

Horace Miner, an anthropologist, approaches this study of the Nacirema as an anthropologist would. In so doing, he satirizes such sociological studies, complete with their discussions, their language, and their research. He also plays a joke on his readership. Miner uses a standard style sheet of the field, the name-year system.

Original publication: *American Anthropologist*, June 1956.

The anthropologist has become so familiar with the diversity of ways in which different peoples behave in similar situations that he is not apt to be surprised by even the most exotic customs. In fact, if all of the logically possible combinations of behavior have not been found somewhere in the world, he is apt to suspect that they must be present in some yet undescribed tribe. This point has, in fact, been expressed with respect to clan organization by Murdock (1949:71). In this light, the magical beliefs and practices of the Nacirema present such unusual aspects that it seems desirable to describe them as an example of the extremes to which human behavior can go.

Professor Linton first brought the ritual of the Nacirema to the attention of anthropologists twenty years ago (1936:326), but the culture of this people is still very poorly understood. They are a North American group living in the territory between the Canadian Cree, the Yaqui and Tarahumare of Mexico, and the Carib and Arawak of the Antilles. Little is known of their origin, although tradition states that they came from the east. According to Nacirema mythology, their nation was originated by a culture hero, Notgnihsaw, who is otherwise known for two great feats of strength—the throwing of a piece of wampum across the river Pa-To-Mac and the chopping down of a cherry tree in which the Spirit of Truth resided.

Nacirema culture is characterized by a highly developed market economy which has evolved in a rich natural habitat. While much of the people's time is devoted to economic pursuits, a large part of the fruits of these labors and a considerable portion of the day are spent in ritual activity. The focus of this activity is the human body, the appearance and health of which loom as a dominant concern in the ethos of the people. While such a concern is certainly not unusual, its ceremonial aspects and associated philosophy are unique.

The fundamental belief underlying the whole system appears to be that the human body is ugly and that its natural tendency is to debility and disease. Incarcerated in such a body, man's only hope is to avert these characteristics through the use of the powerful influences of ritual and ceremony. Every household has one or more shrines devoted to this purpose. The more powerful individuals in the society have several shrines in their houses and, in fact, the opulence of a house is often referred to in terms of the number of such ritual centers it possesses. Most houses are of wattle and daub construction, but the shrine rooms of the more wealthy are walled with stone. Poorer families imitate the rich by applying pottery plaques to their shrine walls.

While each family has at least one such shrine, the rituals associated with it are not family ceremonies but are private and secret. The rites are normally only discussed with children, and then only during the period when they are being initiated into these mysteries. I was able, however, to establish sufficient rapport with the natives to examine these shrines and to have the rituals described to me.

The focal point of the shrine is a box or chest which is built into the wall. In this chest are kept the many charms and magical potions without which no native believes he could live. These preparations are secured from a variety of specialized practitioners. The most powerful of these are the medicine men, whose assistance must be rewarded with substantial gifts. However, the medicine men do not provide the curative potions for their clients, but decide what the ingredients should be and then write them down in an ancient and secret language. This writing is understood only by the medicine men and by the herbalists who, for another gift, provide the required charm.

The charm is not disposed of after it has served its purpose, but is placed in the charm-box of the household shrine. As these magical materials are specific for certain ills, and the real or imagined maladies of the people are many, the charm-box is usually full to overflowing. The magical packets are so numerous that people forget what their purposes were and and fear to use them again. While the natives are very vague on this point, we can only assume that the idea in retaining all the old magical materials is that their presence in the charm-box, before which the body rituals are conducted, will in some way protect the worshipper.

Beneath the charm-box is a small font. Each day every member of the family, in succession, enters the shrine room, bows his head before the charm-box, mingles different sorts of holy water in the font, and proceeds with a brief rite of ablution. The holy waters are secured from the Water Temple of the community, where the priests conduct elaborate ceremonies to make the liquid ritually pure.

In the hierarchy of magical practitioners, and below the medicine men in prestige, are specialists whose designation is best translated "holy-mouth-men." The Nacirema have an almost pathological horror of and fascination with the mouth, the condition of which is believed to have a supernatural influence on all social relationships. Were it not for the rituals of the mouth, they believe that their teeth would fall out, their gums bleed, their jaws shrink, their friends desert them, and their lovers reject them. They also believe that a strong relationship exists between oral and moral characteristics. For example, there is a ritual ablution of the mouth for children which is supposed to improve their moral fiber.

The daily body ritual performed by everyone includes a mouth-rite. Despite the fact that these people are so punctilious about care of the mouth, this rite involves a practice which strikes the uninitiated stranger as revolting. It was reported to me that the ritual consists of inserting a small bundle of hog hairs into the mouth, along with certain magical powders, and then moving the bundle in a highly formalized series of gestures.

In addition to the private mouth-rite, the people seek out a holy-mouth-man once or twice a year. These practitioners have an impressive set of parapher-nalia, consisting of a variety of augers, awls, probes, and prods. The use of these objects in the exorcism of the evils of the mouth involves almost unbelievable ritual torture of the client. The holy-mouth-man opens the client's mouth and, using the above mentioned tools, enlarges any holes which decay may have created in the teeth. Magical materials are put into these holes. If there are no naturally occurring holes in the teeth, large sections of one or more teeth are gouged out so that the supernatural substance can be applied. In the client's view, the purpose of these ministrations is to arrest decay and to draw friends. The extremely sacred and traditional character of the rite is evident in the fact that the natives return to the holy-mouth-men year after year, despite the fact that their teeth continue to decay.

It is to be hoped that, when a thorough study of the Nacirema is made, there will be careful inquiry into the personality structure of these people. One has but to watch the gleam in the eye of a holy-mouth-man, as he jabs an awl into an exposed nerve, to suspect that a certain amount of sadism is involved. If this can be established, a very interesting pattern emerges, for most of the population shows definite masochistic tendencies. It was to these that Professor Linton referred in discussing a distinctive part of the daily body ritual which is performed only by men. This part of the rite involves scraping and lacerating the surface of the face with a sharp instrument. Special women's rites are performed only four times during each lunar month, but what they lack in frequency is made up in barbarity. As part of this ceremony, women bake their heads in small ovens for about an hour. The theoretically interesting point is that what seems to be a preponderantly masochistic people have developed sadistic specialists.

The medicine men have an imposing temple, or *latipso*, in every community of any size. The more elaborate ceremonies required to treat very sick patients can only be performed at this temple. These ceremonies involve not only the thaumaturge but a permanent group of vestal maidens who move sedately about the temple chambers in distinctive costume and headdress.

The *latipso* ceremonies are so harsh that it is phenomenal that a fair proportion of the really sick natives who enter the temple ever recover. Small children whose indoctrination is still incomplete have been known to resist attempts to take them to the temple because "that is where you go to die." Despite this fact, sick adults are not only willing but eager to undergo the protracted ritual purification, if they can afford to do so. No matter how ill the supplicant or how grave the emergency, the guardians of many temples will not admit a client if he cannot give a rich gift to the custodian. Even after one has gained admission and survived the ceremonies, the guardians will not permit the neophyte to leave until he makes still another gift.

The supplicant entering the temple is first stripped of all his or her clothes. In every-day life the Nacirema avoids exposure of his body and its natural functions. Bathing and excretory acts are performed only in the secrecy of the household shrine, where they are ritualized as part of the body-rites. Psychological shock results from the fact that body secrecy is suddenly lost upon entry into the *latipso*. A man, whose own wife has never seen him in an excretory act, suddenly finds himself naked and assisted by a vestal maiden while he performs his natural functions into a sacred vessel. This sort of ceremonial treatment is necessitated by the fact that the excreta are used by a diviner to ascertain the course and nature of the client's sickness. Female clients, on the other hand, find their naked bodies are subject to the scrutiny, manipulation and prodding of the medicine men.

Few supplicants in the temple are well enough to do anything but lie on their hard beds. Their daily ceremonies, like the rites of the holy-mouth-men, involve discomfort and torture. With ritual precision, the vestals awaken their miserable charges each dawn and roll them about on their beds of pain while performing ablutions, in the formal movements of which the maidens are highly trained. At other times they insert magic wands in the supplicant's mouth or force him to eat substances which are supposed to be healing. From time to time the medicine men come to their clients and jab magically treated needles into their flesh. The fact that these temple ceremonies may not cure, and may even kill the neophyte, in no way decreases the people's faith in the medicine men.

There remains one other kind of practitioner, known as a "listener." This witch-doctor has the power to exorcise the devils that lodge in the heads of people who have been bewitched. The Nacirema believe that parents bewitch their own children. Mothers are particularly suspected of putting a curse on children while teaching them the secret body rituals. The counter-magic of the witch-doctor is unusual in its lack of ritual. The patient simply tells the "listener" all his troubles and fears, beginning with the earliest difficulties he can remember. The memory displayed by the Nacirema in these exorcism sessions is truly remarkable. It is not uncommon for the patient to bemoan the rejection he felt upon being weaned as a babe, and a few individuals even see their troubles going back to the traumatic effects of their own birth.

In conclusion, mention must be made of certain practices which have their base in native esthetics but which depend upon the pervasive aversion to the natural body and its functions. There are ritual fasts to make fat people thin and ceremonial feasts to make thin people fat. Still other rites are used to make women's breasts larger if they are small, and smaller if they are large. General dissatisfaction with breast shape is symbolized in the fact that the ideal form is virtually outside the range of human variation. A few women afflicted with almost inhuman hypermammary development are so idolized that they make a handsome living by simply going from village to village and permitting the natives to stare at them for a fee.

Reference has already been made to the fact that excretory functions are ritualized, routinized, and relegated to secrecy. Natural reproductive functions are similarly distorted. Intercourse is taboo as a topic and scheduled as an act. Efforts are made to avoid pregnancy by the use of magical materials or by limiting intercourse to certain phases of the moon. Conception is actually very infrequent. When pregnant, women dress so as to hide their condition. Parturition takes place in secret, without friends or relatives to assist, and the majority of women do not nurse their infants.

Our review of the ritual life of the Nacirema has certainly shown them to be a magic-ridden people. It is hard to understand how they have managed to exist so long under the burdens which they have imposed upon themselves. But even such exotic customs as these take on real meaning when they are viewed with the insight provided by Malinowski when he wrote (1948:70):

> Looking from far and above, from our high places of safety in the developed civilization, it is easy to see all the crudity and irrelevance of magic. But without its

power and guidance early man could not have mastered his practical difficulties as he
has done, nor could man have advanced to the higher stages of civilization.

References

LINTON, RALPH. 1936. *The Study of Man*. New York, D. Appleton-Century Co.
MALINOWSKI, BRONISLAW. 1948. *Magic, Science, and Religion*. Glencoe. The Free
   Press.
MURDOCK, GEORGE P. 1949. *Social Structure*. New York. The Macmillan Co.

Acting Alone

JAMES L. MUYSKENS

Professor and academic administrator James L. Muyskens poses an
ethical (and potentially a legal) problem for his audience of nurses.
He provides a carefully counterpointed study of the issues involved
in this case study of euthanasia, or "assisted suicide."

   This essay provides some valuable examples of the uses of
research. For one thing, the author makes use of some sources—
Kant, Roman Catholic medical ethics—without citing specific
sources, simply giving a very general summary of common
knowledge from these sources. The two sources he cites are other
works by him, emphasizing the care he is taking to cite things
already in print, even if they are his own. There is the further
emphasis on his own ideas with his specific statements in first
person, taking a stand on the case under discussion.

   Muyskens' conclusion about "reasonable, conscientious people"
defines an audience every writer desires.

Original publication: *American Journal of Nursing*, September 1987.

I had worked for several nights in an intensive care unit with a woman who had
metastatic cancer. At some point, she had refused further chemotherapy and told her
family she wanted to stay home until the end came.

   While she was home, however, it became increasingly difficult for her to breathe.
One evening, a family member took her to the emergency department. The
physician, not knowing the woman had cancer, immediately put her on a ventilator.
With proper oxygenation, she became alert and was furious.

   In the ICU, her arms were restrained. Of course, she couldn't talk, but she begged
with her eyes and hands to have the ventilator discontinued. I had talked with the

family and I knew the physician regretted putting the woman on the ventilator but wouldn't take her off.

I tried to reason with the woman, explaining her lungs wouldn't function without the machine. She understood this but had reached that point where life was unbearable. So, one night I "forgot" to switch on the ventilator alarm, and I didn't secure her arm restraints well. She extubated herself and died that night(1).

Can the actions of this nurse, whom we shall name Nurse Carey, be defended? The patient, Ms. Chance, is restrained to keep her from accidentally or intentionally removing the ventilator. The duty to conserve life appears to require the restraints, so Nurse Carey's failure to secure them seems to violate this duty.

To determine whether Nurse Carey's action is morally defensible, let's first consider whether the duty to save Ms. Chance's life is a sufficient basis for ignoring her wishes.

Justifying The Restraint

Those who support continued use of the restraints may suggest that Ms. Chance's resistance is merely a cry for help or no more than a sign of disorientation, perhaps brought about by oxygen deprivation.

Nurse Carey challenged this, pointing out that Ms. Chance was aware and understood what was going on. In this case, we lack sufficient ground for overriding the strong presumption that a person ought to be taken at his word.

Taking Ms. Chance at her word, we can justify the restraints only if we have compelling ground for maintaining that a duty—for example, our duty to conserve her life—must take priority over respect for Ms. Chance's right of self-determination or autonomy.

As codes of ethics for nurses make evident, a nurse has both the duty to conserve life and the duty to respect the patient's autonomy. Where we may find ourselves in disagreement is on the issue of which duty should take precedence, when (as in this case) acting in accordance with one duty appears to be incompatible with acting in accordance with the other.

Ethical theories are suggestions for ordering our duties. For example, Kantian ethical theories place highest priority on autonomy, as has Nurse Carey in this case.

On the other hand, someone who follows the natural-law tradition (the underlying theory of the Roman Catholic medical ethics tradition) would probably reverse the order of these two duties, placing the saving of Ms. Chance's life ahead of concerns about her rights to determine her own destiny. If the ventilator is seen as an ordinary rather than extraordinary means (a notoriously "slippery" distinction), a natural-law theorist would argue for the restraint.

Many theories supporting each defense could be offered. Suffice it to say that Nurse Carey came down on the side of patient autonomy over conservation of life.

Playing On A Team

A nurse is only one of several members of a health care team, including other nurses, therapists, and physicians. If the members of the team do not coordinate their efforts and act in concert, patient care suffers. We must ask whether this nurse could provide adequate reasons for her failure to act collaboratively.

Clearly, Nurse Carey acted independently, making her own professional judgment. In fact, she saw herself as having a primary allegiance to the patient rather than to the team. She was acting, as she herself would say, as a patient advocate.

The concept of nurse as client advocate is a complex and controversial one(2). Not everyone understands it to entail supporting a patient's autonomy in situations such as this. Here we have grave concern that exercise of such autonomy may not be in Ms. Chance's own best interest.

Yet, if advocacy includes being responsive to a patient's long-standing desires and wishes, the advocate has a special obligation to "come to bat" for the patient. The patient's advocate has not only the general duty to respect patient autonomy but also the special duty to assist the patient in exercising that autonomy.

A defense of Nurse Carey's actions requires a demonstration that this duty to support the patient against the coercion of other members of the team outweighs a nurse's duty to collaborate with the team.

The question we must ask is, in this case, does collaboration or advocacy best meet the underlying objective of quality patient care? From what has been said, we have a good understanding as to why Nurse Carey came down on the side of advocacy.

Those who feel the strong pull toward collaboration and the importance of being a team player will feel uneasy about the form Nurse Carey's advocacy took. Yet, they also may recognize that if Nurse Carey had gone along with the others, the patient would have been maltreated.

The collaborators will search for a compromise position, one that is less drastic than Nurse Carey's. They may suggest that Nurse Carey should have refrained from acting on her own until she had had at least another talk with the physician, hoping to change her mind about the restraints and the ventilator. We would need to know more about this physician to be able to determine whether Nurse Carey gave up too quickly.

If we are inclined to think she gave up too soon, we should keep in mind that if further efforts to convince the physician had failed, she might not have had another chance to help Ms. Chance by leaving the restraints loose. Similar considerations may have kept her from taking up the case with her supervisor or with other physicians. Her challenge, she would likely tell us, would have drawn too much attention to herself and made the action she chose either too risky or impossible.

The hospital in which she worked did not have an ombudsman or an ethics committee to whom she could appeal. She could have looked into securing a court-ordered "objective" outsider. But she did not. Since such action might take weeks, this option probably did not appear to be a promising avenue for an advocate to take.

If, by going through channels rather than by taking unilateral action, Nurse Carey could have had the restraints removed, she has no defense for having taken matters into her own hands. As we have seen, Nurse Carey (whether rightly or wrongly) saw no way to do that. Being forced to choose, she gave higher priority to advocacy than to collaboration.

Even if we accept Nurse Carey's decision, we may feel uncomfortable with the fact that she acted secretively. We may argue that if Nurse Carey is going to engage in an act of "professional disobedience" she must do so openly and be willing to accept the consequences of it.

But she could argue that she is not aiming primarily at changing policy, she is aiming only to serve a particular patient. Although a change in policy would be a happy by-product, since it is not her aim, the action ought not to be faulted if no policy change results.

Moreover, to speak openly of her intention before the act would be self-defeating. To "confess" after the fact would put Nurse Carey in a weak position to work toward change.

Suppose, as Nurse Carey believes, that she has based her action on a morally defensible ordering of all the relevant duties. We would expect to find her at peace with her decision. Yet Nurse Carey harbors grave doubts.

As long as she saw the choice to die as Ms. Chance's and the choice to remove the restraints (in order to restore freedom) as hers, Nurse Carey felt good about her action. But if in restoring the patient's freedom Nurse Carey became an accomplice to suicide, that's a different matter.

Assisted Suicide?

If we give "suicide" the standard meaning, namely, "the intentional termination of one's own life," then surely Ms. Chance committed suicide.

By failing to tightly secure Ms. Chance's arm restraints was Nurse Carey assisting her in suicide? If I load the gun, deliver the bottle of sleeping pills, or hold the cup of poison for a patient, I am assisting that person in suicide. I am providing help with the means to be used to end the life.

If Ms. Chance had asked and Nurse Carey had agreed to "pull the plug," that too would have been assisted suicide. In such a scenario, she would be acting to bring about Ms. Chance's death. That is not what happened.

Nurse Carey did not offer the means to commit suicide. As a way of respecting Ms. Chance's right to self-determination, her right as a competent adult to live her life unencumbered by the intrusions of others (even well-meaning ones), the nurse removed an unwarranted restraint. She restored the patient's freedom.

Ms. Chance chose to exercise her freedom by removing herself from the ventilator. Ms. Chance acted by herself and on her own. *She* ended her life.

If we permit another to exercise autonomy only when we are quite certain that he or she will make the choice we want, that is not respecting another's autonomy. Respect for autonomy cannot be held hostage to second guessing.

Moral Debate

For what it is worth, I agree with Nurse Carey's ranking of duties and I feel that her decision not to securely tighten Ms. Chance's arm restraints, despite the stealth with which she acted, is morally defensible.

Her second thoughts about assisting in suicide are, in my judgment, misguided. My hope is that she will see this and take pride in her courageous action.

Reasonable, conscientious people are likely to disagree about complicated cases. Unanimity in moral matters is out of our grasp. But ethical skepticism— the view that no one moral point of view is any better or worse than any other—does not follow. There is a satisfactory middle position between unanimity and moral chaos.

References

1. Muyskens, James L. *Moral Problems in Nursing: A Philosophical Investigation.* Totowa, New Jersey: Rowman and Littlefield, 1982, p. 135.
2. Muyskens, pp. 32–37, 47–56.

The Elusive Scientific Basis of Creation "Science"

EUGENIE C. SCOTT AND HENRY P. COLE

The instructions for the authors submitting to *The Quarterly Review of Biology* specify that "An article should be written in concise and sufficiently nontechnical language to be intelligible both to specialists in other fields and to general biologists." The authors of this study, both with academic credentials, work to meet that requirement of writing for readers of varied backgrounds and interests. Since their subject is a consideration of the legality of teaching science creationism in the science classroom, their most specific audience is apparently composed of scientists and teachers. However, in the abstract preceding the essay, they identify their audience as "teachers, professors, and lawyers who are striving to maintain high standards of science education in the face of pressures to introduce non-scientific concepts into the public school classroom." But their conclusion broadens the boundary, at least slightly, to "those who directly confront the creationists." Thus, they are addressing a more general audience who must understand some very technical material.

This study centers on the authors' original research, with extensive use of statistics and quotations from the surveys they have conducted. They have also provided a long bibliography to assist readers in their preparation for "confronting" their opponents. One caution: readers must not be misled by some passages that appear to be indented quotations. A close reading reveals that these are summaries simply set off from the text, but not quoted from another source. (See a similar use of this indented format in this chapter: the list of principles of research that do not vary from one style sheet to another.)

The style sheet used here is the name-year system.

Original publication: *The Quarterly Review of Biology*, March 1985.

ABSTRACT

Is there, as claimed, *scientific* support for "scientific creationism"? If so, arguments that scientific creationism is a legitimate scientific discipline deserving "equal time" with evolution in public-school science classes would be strengthened. An early study (Cole and Scott, 1982) revealed that 28 prominent creationists did not publish articles dealing with empirical, experimental or theoretical evidence for the scientific creationist "model" in over 4000 journals covered by the data-retrieval system SCISEARCH. To see if other scientific creationists were publishing proofs of creation, we surveyed editors of 68 journals to which scientific creationists would be likely to submit articles on this subject. Out of over 135,000 submissions from 1980 to 1983, only 18 dealt with empirical, experimental, or theoretical support for scientific creationism, and 12 of these went to one science education journal alone. No creationist articles have been published, although three were still under review at the time of this study. Papers were rejected due to poor scholarship, with editors commenting that the articles appeared to have been written by laymen rather than professional scientists. A number of differences are apparent in comparing the scholarship found in "in house" creation science sources and "mainline" scientific journals. Although scientific creationists complain that "completely scientific papers" would be rejected out of hand by "mainline" journals, it is obvious that none have been submitted. Outside of creationist outlets, then, there is no "scientific" creationism. We have documented this as a service to the teachers, professors, and lawyers who are striving to maintain high standards of science education in the face of pressures to introduce non-scientific concepts into the public school classroom.

At the time of this writing (Summer, 1984), the scientific creationism/ evolution controversy in the United States is viewed by most members of the scientific community as ancient history. Judge Overton's gracefully written decision in *McLean vs. Arkansas* (Anonymous, 1982) appeared to sound the death knell for efforts to require the teaching of scientific creationism in public school science classes. And indeed, that decision depressed *legislative* attempts to promote scientific creationism. In the months following the Overton decision, ten scientific creationism bills died, were killed, or were withdrawn in state legislatures (Weinberg, 1982).

One battle remains in the legislative war: Louisiana, where two lawsuits were at one point proceeding simultaneously, with anti-creationists as plaintiffs in one and as defendants in the other. Evolutionists were disappointed that the Overton decision was not appealed; a favorable decision in an appellate court would have made the Arkansas case a useful precedent for the Louisiana trial and any others. Hopes were raised when the Louisiana State Senate voted in May of 1984 to repeal the law, which would have eliminated a costly trial had the House of Representatives followed suit. Unfortunately, strong lobbying by creationists resulted in a lopsided vote of 41–26 against the repeal (Lewin, 1984b). As part of the Arkansas decision, the plaintiffs (anti-creationists) were awarded close to $400,000, a sum that we assume would make most states cautious about becoming involved in such trials. Creationists, however, are confident they will succeed in Louisiana, where "their" lawyers are arguing the case rather than an outsider, as was the case in Arkansas.

Even if we assume that the eventual Louisiana trial will be another setback to the creationist cause, by no means will this be the end of the controversy. Trial results unfavorable to the creationist cause will probably halt the trickle of bills introduced into state legislatures, but even now the scientific creationism movement is focusing on the local, rather than the state, level. Attempts are being made to convince local school boards to mandate the teaching of creationism. Even more difficult to monitor are the attempts by individual teachers to teach scientific creationism on their own that are already occurring in many parts of the United States (Moyer, 1984).

Scientific creationists are reluctant to have creationism taught in social studies or comparative religion classes, because this would reduce their fundamental Christian world view to merely another of the world views of many religions and cultures. They insist that creationism belongs in the science classroom. Scientific creationism must have scientific backing to be taught in science classes. Arguments that the creationist view is better supported by scientific facts than is evolution is a major thrust of their campaign. In the Institute for Creation Research "Tenets of Creationism" (Morris, 1980), *scientific* creationism is distinguished from *Biblical* creationism as having "no reliance upon Biblical revelation, utilizing *only scientific data* to support and expound the creation model" (italics in original).

What is the nature of this body of scientific data, and where can it be found? There is, of course, a body of *scientific creationist* literature that presents "evidence" for the young earth, Noah's Flood, and Special Creation. Creation Life Publishers (now Masterbooks) has an extensive series of books, pamphlets, tapes, and video cassettes available for purchase, and also publishes the high school biology textbook, *Biology: A Search for Order in Complexity*. This is the publishing wing of the Institute for Creation Research (ICR), a major distributor of information on creation "science" as well as advice for introducing creationism into local schools. The ICR publishes science research articles in the IMPACT series, which accompanies their free monthly newsletter *Acts and Facts*. The oldest journal devoted strictly to the scientific evidence for creationism is the *Creation Research Society Quarterly*, published by the Creation Research Society (CRS). The Bible-Science Association (B-SA) publishes the *Bible Science Newsletter* and *CONTRAST*, which is their equivalent of the ICR *IMPACT* series. The B-SA also has a large list of pamphlets, books, tapes, and other educational materials. The Creation Social Science and Humanities Society publishes the *Creation Social Science and Humanities Quarterly*. The American Scientific Affiliate (ASA), an association of Christian scientists, takes no official stand on scientific creationism, and the *Journal of the American Scientific Affiliate* publishes articles both pro and con. Internationally, Creation Science in Australia publishes *Ex Nihilo*, which also has a U.S. office.

Examination of publication affiliations, content, and editorial guidelines for authors of these journals leads one to question the claim that scientific creationism is independent of religion. Authors who publish in the *Creation Research Society Quarterly* subscribe in writing to the belief that the Bible is the "written word of God and that all of its assertions are historically and *scientifically* true" (emphasis added). The *CRSQ* is not listed in *Science Citation Index*, but it appears in the *Christian Periodical Index*. The ASA also has a statement of belief that supports both religion and science: God is the Creator, but there is no dogma as to how he created (Stipe, 1977).

The major suppositions of creationism are found in a "Summary of the Scientific Evidence for Creationism" by Gish, Bliss, and Bird (1981). This document reveals much about the nature of creationist scholarship. These claims may be summarized as follows:

1. The universe and the solar system were suddenly created. "Evidence" for this comes from the second law of thermodynamics in that "the Universe could not have created itself, but could not have existed forever, or it would have run down long ago. Thus the universe, including matter and energy, apparently must have been created." The "argument from design" is also invoked, an explanation outside of the realm of science.
2. Life was suddenly created. "Evidence" for this is also seen in the second law of thermodynamics, as ". . . simple molecules and complex protein, DNA and RNA molecules seemingly could not have evolved spontaneously and naturalistically into a living cell: such cells apparently were created."
3. Present plants and animals have remained fixed since creation, with only limited genetic variation within the originally created kinds. Gaps in the

fossil record occur between "kinds" such as "single celled organisms and invertebrates, between invertebrates and vertebrates, between fish and amphibians, between amphibians and reptiles, between reptiles and birds or mammals, or between 'lower' mammals and primates. . . ." Later, "kinds" are defined as reproductively isolated, interfertile groups of organisms, corresponding generally to species. The definition of a "kind" therefore extends from phyla to species, making it a most flexible concept.

4. Mutation and natural selection are insufficient to have brought about the emergence of present living kinds from a simple primordial organism. To support this claim, Gish, Bliss, and Bird (1981) state that mutation and selection have an "infinitesimally small" probability of producing more complex living kinds from simpler kinds. They also claim that mutations in the aggregate are "nearly always harmful" and that good ones are too infrequent to account for evolution.

5. Humans and apes have separate ancestry. Quoting the British anthropologist Lord Zuckerman, Gish, Bliss, and Bird (1981) again claim a lack of transitional forms.

6. Catastrophic processes are the main forces shaping Earth's geology. "Geological data reflect catastrophic flooding. Evidence of rapid catastrophic water deposition includes fossilized tree trunks that penetrate numerous sedimentary layers (such as at Joggins, Nova Scotia), widespread pebble and boulder layers (such as at the Shinarump conglomerate of the Southwestern United States), fossilized logs in a single layer covering extensive areas (such as Petrified Forest National Park), and whole closed clams that were buried alive in mass graveyards in extensive sedimentary layers (such as at Glen Rose, Texas.)"

7. The Earth is about 10,000 years old, and no more than 20,000 years old. "Evidence" for this claim is the faultiness of radiometric dating methods, where assumptions such as constancy of decay rate are questionable. Gish, Bliss, and Bird (1981) also claim that alternative methods of measuring the age of the earth, such as use of the earth's magnetic field decay and estimation of cooling times of the earth, support a young earth.

We were curious about whether any creationist science existed outside of their own journals and publishing houses. In 1982, we published an article describing our first attempt to examine creationist claims of positive scientific support (Cole and Scott, 1982.) We searched the scientific literature from January 1978 to October 1981, using SCI-SEARCH, a computerized listing of Science Citation Index plus an additional 1000 journals and proceedings from technical fields. Reasoning that the most prominent creationists would be most likely to publish, we searched both under the names of all editorial board members of the Creation Research Society and research associates and technical advisors of the Institute for Creation Research, and also for keywords such as "creationism", "scientific creationism", "special creation", etc. The keyword search netted only 18 items: 4 articles critical of scientific creationism as pseudoscience, 5 editorials discussing the controversy itself, and 9 letters to editors expressing opinions for or against. Nothing resembling empirical or experimental evidence for scientific creationism was discovered.

A search under the names of 28 prominent scientific creationists revealed a large number of publications. However, it was necessary to check the institutional identification and the specialty field of the author because of common last names and initials. For example, there are two Henry M. Morris's, both in engineering. One had 27 publications, the other had one. The latter was affiliated with the Institute for Creation Research; through a telephone call we discovered the former was a reviewer for the journal *Control Engineering*, and had no affiliation with creationism. Even more confusing was the case of a productive University of Texas-Austin astronomer, T. G. Barnes, with 13 publications. Was he the creationist astronomer Thomas G. Barnes from University of Texas-El Paso, author of the new *Physics of the Future: a Classical Unification of Physics*, "showing that the modern innovations of relativity theory and quantum mechanics are unnecessary and ultimately barren?" He was not. A telephone call to Austin revealed two Texas T. G. Barneses.

After this and similar detective work had been completed, we discovered only six of the 28 prominent creationists had published anything at all during the 45 months covered by our survey. These six had published 52 articles. Two creationist authors had published 75 per cent of the articles, with 17 and 22 publications respectively. All of the articles dealt with the professional or technical field of the author, and included topics such as the chemistry and physics of food processing, simulation studies of loads, vibrations and stresses in aircraft wing structures, the effect of pollutants on aquatic microorganisms, and so forth. None of the articles dealt with theoretical support for the assumptions and concepts upon which scientific creationism is based.

The prominent scientific creationists we surveyed do not appear to be publishing studies supportive of scientific creationism in recognized scientific journals. However, our procedure (keywords and author name searches) could overlook other scientific creationist research. Although it would be impossible to review all scientific literature, we felt a survey of journal editors might accomplish much the same end.

We sought United States journals to which scientific creationists would be likely to submit articles. Criteria for journals were that they:

1. publish scientific articles relevant to the subject matter of scientific creationism (i.e., are non-medical journals in astronomy, anthropology, biology, chemistry, geology, and physics),
2. are refereed,
3. publish volunteered papers rather than solicited articles or symposia,
4. are generalized rather than specialized in focus,
5. have a basic rather than applied research focus,
6. have an empirical rather than philosophical focus,
7. are intended for professional audiences, not popular audiences (i.e., not *Science 84*, *Scientific American*, *Discovery*, *Physics Today*, etc.),

8. draw submissions nationally rather than regionally, and
9. primarily publish articles rather than abstracts.

An exception to rule 9 was *American Zoologist*, which publishes papers and abstracts from the annual meetings of the American Society of Zoologists. Anyone who is a member of the Society can present a 15 minute paper on any topic at the meetings, or can give their "space" to someone else. Abstracts are not refereed and all are published. Such an open procedure would counteract any alleged muzzling of creationist beliefs; thus we retained *American Zoologist* to give creationists all possible chances of getting into our survey. We also retained the *Proceedings of the National Academy of Science*, which accepts articles only from NAS members and individuals sponsored by NAS members. Creationist publications regularly extoll the prominence of their scientists; there is no apparent reason why one of them could not be an Academy member, or alternatively, request a member to submit an article upon his behalf.

Another exception, but one which also increased the opportunity for scientific creationists to publish in relevant outlets, was the addition of science education journals in biology, physics, chemistry, and geology. As will be shown, this inclusion accounted for two-thirds of the creationist submissions.

We compiled a preliminary list of journals after consulting reference sources (Sheehy, 1976; Garfield, 1972, 1976; King, McDonald, and Roderer, 1981; Katz and Katz Sternberger, 1982; Renschler, 1982; Kronik, 1982). We then requested science librarians in geology, astronomy-chemistry-physics, and biology libraries to review our list, and add or delete choices based on their professional experience. As a further check, we consulted colleagues in the various fields. Based on our criteria and selection process, 68 journals were surveyed.

The editors of the following journals were questioned: American Anthropologist, American Journal of Physical Anthropology, Human Biology, Journal of Human Evolution, American Ethnologist, Ethnology, Journal of Anthropological Research, Social Biology, Plains Anthropologist, Anthropological Quarterly, Current Anthropology, Bio-Science, Federation Proceedings, Quarterly Review of Biology, American Naturalist, American Zoologist, Journal of Molecular Biology, Journal of Bacteriology, American Journal of Botany, Botanical Gazette, Plant Physiology, Botanical Review, Evolution, Journal of Paleontology, Paelobiology, Quaternary Research, Journal of Molecular Evolution, Evolutionary Theory, Systematic Zoology, Genetical Research, Life Sciences, American Journal of Physiology, American Journal of Human Genetics, Genetics, Journal of Theoretical Biology, American Biology Teacher, Journal of the American Chemical Society, Journal of Biological Chemistry, Accounts of Chemical Research, Chemical Reviews, Biochemistry, Biochemical and Biophysics Research Communications and Annals of Biochemistry, Inorganic Chemistry, Journal of Chemical Education, Astrophysical Journal, Astronomical Journal, Astronomy Quarterly, Sky and Telescope, Icarus, Physical Review (A, B, C, D), American Journal of Physics, Foundations of Physics, International Journal of Theoretical Physics, Reviews of Modern Physics, Physics Teacher, Physical Review Letters, Annals of Physics, Bulletin of Geological Society of America, Journal of Geology, Geology, Journal of Geological Education, American Journal of Science, Science, Proceedings of the NAS.

After pre-testing our questionnaire on ten journals in the fall of 1982, we made two mailings to editors during 1983. Except for a few telephone call followups in January of 1984, the study was completed during 1983. We requested editors to report on submissions during the previous three years (1980–1983). We sent editors a check sheet asking them to report some basic information about the journal (number of years as editor, number of articles submitted and published) and information about the number of articles dealing with substantive, empirical, or theoretical scientific creationism topics that had been submitted, reviewed, rejected or published during the previous three years.

In case the editor was not familiar with the scientific creationism "model", we included a list of topics commonly found in scientific creationism journals such as the *Creation Research Society Quarterly*. To be sure that the article dealt with substantive creationist ideas, rather than articles *about* creationism, we asked editors to list topics covered in articles submitted on scientific creationism. Any editor reporting submission of creationist articles was contacted by telephone; in some cases the article in question merely concerned the creation/evolution controversy. Journal editors and editorial assistants were all cooperative and helpful.

Some editors were precise about the total number of submissions on all topics (e.g., "1154"); some were general (e.g., "ca. 600"). We took the midpoints of estimates to provide a conservative estimate of over 45,000 submissions to these 68 journals each year (135,000 for the 3 year period). Almost 26,000 articles per year were actually published for a total of approximately 78,000 during the period of our study. Five journals reported the submission of a total of 18 scientific creationism articles during the three-year period of the survey: two science education journals, two anthropology journals, and one biology journal (Table 1). The articles were unevenly distributed; one of the education journals received twelve of the 18 submissions. The biology journal and the other science education journal received one submission each; one anthropology journal

TABLE 1
Results of journal editors survey

		Number of Submissions	Number of Rejections	Number Published
	A	1	1	0
	B	1	1	0
Journal	C	1	1	0
	D	3	3	0
	E	12*	9	0
Total		18	15	0

*3 articles still under review

received one submission, and the other anthropology journal received three. None of the submitted articles has been published, although three of the twelve submitted to the education journal are still under review.

Reviewer comments regarding rejected articles complained about poor presentation ("ramblings . . ."; "no coherent arguments . . ."; "high-school theme quality . . ."; "tendentious essay not suitable for publication anywhere . . ."; "more like a long letter than a referenced article"), and failure to follow accepted scientific canons ("no systematic treatment . . ."; "does not define terms . . ."; "flawed arguments . . ."; "failure to acknowledge and use extensive literature on particular questions . . .").

As indicated above, we included the *American Zoologist* because of its open policy on submission of abstracts. To the best recollection of the editor, no papers had been delivered on empirical evidence for scientific creationism during the time period of the survey.

Our first study showed that some creation scientists perform science well enough to be published in standard scientific journals. A small number of these are quite productive, but apparently only in their non-creationist specialties. Our second study showed that the minuscule number of submitted articles advocating scientific creationism (18 out of 135,000) do not appear to have been written by professional scientists. From the reviewers' comments, it appears as if laymen rather than professional scientists are submitting the few articles that have surfaced during the last three years. Why don't the professional scientists among the creationists publish empirical, experimental, or theoretical evidence for scientific creationism? One answer to this question can be found by comparing the scholarship found in "in house" creationist science sources to that found in "mainline" scientific sources.

Among other differences, there is a difference in the application of logic. Scientific creationists view the creation/evolution controversy as having only two alternatives; evolution or their Biblical literalist view of creation. Oddly, if conveniently, origin stories of all other human cultures are defined as *evolutionary* (Morris, 1975). Given this dichotomy, arguments *against* evolution are arguments *for* creation. Most of the "scientific" evidences "for" creation presented in Gish, Bliss, and Bird (1981) and other scientific creationism sources are of this type: the second law of thermodynamics prohibits evolution, thus creation must have occurred. By their definition, there are no intermediate "kinds." Evolution is impossible; therefore creation must have occurred. If you are wrong, then I am right.

As part of the argument against evolution, much is made of anomalies allegedly "incompatible" with evolution but "compatible" with special creation, ignoring the vast amount of observations compatible with evolution. What Dutch has called the "residue fallacy," a phenomenon that evolution "cannot explain", is used to imply that the whole scientific system is suspect (Dutch, 1982a). One anomaly, of course, does not make a whole theory fall. Probably the best anomaly in the scientific creationists' arsenal is the existence of polonium halos, a "minor mystery" in Judge Overton's words, of which the scientific creationists are quite proud. Gentry (1982a) claims that the existence of Po halos in granite, coalified wood, mica, and other substances indicates that such materials were formed suddenly, under cool conditions, an interpretation supporting special creation. These observations, however, have alternative explanations within normal physical science, and are therefore not unambiguous evidences for Special Creation (Dutch, 1982b; Hashemi-Nezhad, Fremlin, and Durrani, 1979).

Creationist scientists regularly extrapolate from mainline scientific publications to conclusions which support their perspective. All scientists extrapolate to some degree from observation to conclusions, but creationist extrapolations regularly border on the extreme. Many "proofs" of special creation involve extrapolations of rates of change, often taken from evolutionary sources. Thus one source gives a rate of deposition of meteoritic dust on the moon (Peterson, 1960); if one extrapolates from this rate, and if one assumes that the moon and earth are billions of years old, the moon should be covered with hundreds of feet of dust, not just a few inches (Morris, 1974; Kofahl and Segraves, 1975; Barnes, 1982; see Awbrey, 1984, for critique). If one extrapolates the rate of erosion of land masses from the current rate, then all the continents would be washed away if the world were billions of years old (one must ignore well-established principles of isostacy, origenics, and tectonics). In another example, by assuming a constant rate of oil seepage, a young age for the earth's crust was calculated from a *Science* article discussing the relationship between oil seepage and oceanic pollution (Anonymous, 1975; citing Blumer, 1972). Nothing in the *Science* article hinted at this Special Creation application of its results. Readers of scientific creationist literature are familiar with the "living mollusk which was tested by Carbon 14 . . . the reading showed it had been dead for 3000 years" (Chick, 1976, citing Keith and Anderson, 1963). The original article did indeed describe this occurrence, and use it to argue that riverine mollusks (as opposed to lacustrine or marine molluscs) should not be used for Carbon 14 dating. The authors of the original article are not rejecting Carbon 14 dating, but recommending ways in which its use might be improved.

Occasional claims are made for "positive proof" of creation, rather than extrapolations, but not much exists in terms of specifics. The dinosaur tracks of the Paluxy River, Texas, are accompanied by some erosional features claimed to be human tracks (Weber, 1981). If these were true human tracks, then this would be evidence compatible with the creationist model, and most difficult for evolution to accommodate. Some creationists even admit that the better tracks are man-made carvings (Neufeld, 1975; Morris, 1976). Natural erosional processes explain the rest (Cole and Godfrey, in press). The Paluxy River tracks are far from the "silver bullet" terminal refutation that creationists think they are.

We found some cases in which articles written by creationists, with no reference to scientific creationism, were published in mainline journals, but the arguments therein later surfaced elsewhere as "evidence" for the scientific creationist model in in-house publications. These articles present a phenomenon or principle derived through acceptable scientific methodology that, with some stretching, can form the *base* for extrapolations supporting scientific creationism. For example, debates recently took place in scientific journals about the significance of the orientation of petrified wood in Yellowstone National Park (Fritz, 1980; Coffin, 1983; see also Retallack, 1981 and Yuretech, 1981 for comments). The issue concerns in part whether certain formations are composed of trees in situ or trees transported by water from many areas. No mention is made in the scientific journals about the source of water being Noah's Flood, but this is the scientific creationist interpretation (Kofahl, 1977).

Similarly, Robert V. Gentry recently called attention to his polonium halo research which supports a young earth model, although there is little in the original, published sources that would suggest that the articles promote creationism. A letter by Robert V. Gentry in *Physics Today* (1982a) lists articles that discuss his hypothesis. The original articles offer only the vaguest suggestions that his research might be used elsewhere to support scientific creationism. In an article in *Nature* (Gentry, Cristy, McLaughlin, and McHugh, 1974), he asks "Do Po halos imply that unknown processes were operative during the formative period of the earth?" He makes no statement about special creation here, however, and in fact goes on to posit another kind of explanation: "Is it possible that Po halos in Precambrian rocks represent extinct natural radioactivity and are therefore of cosmological significance?" Later in the article (p. 566) another hint is offered: "Just as important as the existence of a new type of lead is the question of whether Po halos which occur in a granite or pegmatic environment . . . can be explained by accepted models of Earth history." In the *Physics Today* letter and in a Bible-Science Newsletter (1982b) he is explicit about this work being "published evidence for Creation." Articles of this sort are likely what creationists refer to as "masked" literature. "Whenever these articles or books (sent to standard scientific journals or secular book publishers) have creationist implications, however, they must be 'masked' in order to get them published in secular outlets. So far, at least, all frankly creationist articles or books are simply rejected out of hand by such publishers" (Morris and Parker, 1982 p. 268).

The phenomena described in this "masked" creationist literature usually fit accepted theory, and can be viewed as evidence for creationism only by going considerably beyond the data. Whether or not water is responsible for particular geological phenomena is a legitimate issue; that this therefore implies a world-wide flood that covered Mt. Everest with 22 feet of water (Whitcomb and Morris, 1961) is a conclusion which any editor would reject as unsupported. Perhaps this is what creationists mean by their inability to publish "frankly creationist" works. If so, it is understandable. We found no evidence for "out of hand" rejections. The articles appeared to have been rejected on their lack of merit. Although we did not survey our editors as to *whether* they would ever publish a "frankly creationist" article, several volunteered that they would, if it met their standards of quality; one editor added, "and [I would] look forward to some interesting letters to the editor."

We think the reason why creationists who are competent scientists in their own fields do not publish empirical, experimental, or theoretical evidence for creation in standard journals has more to do with the difficulty of justifying such a model scientifically than with a conspiracy of editors. Paul A. Bartz, editor of the Bible-Science Newsletter, questions rhetorically in an editorial, "So what future is there for the creation scientist who submits a clearly creationist but completely scientific paper for publication in an evolutionist-dominated publication?" (Bartz, 1983, p. 3). The answer is that if such an article can actually be written, it has as good a chance of getting published as any other "completely scientific paper." The authors will have to avoid "you're wrong, so I'm right" logic, reliance on anomalies for evidence, and unreasonable extrapolations from observations. Mostly, they will have to construct testable (i.e., rejectable) questions, and give up reliance on the occasional miraculous intervention. If creationists can overcome the styles of argument which they utilize, and avoid unreasonable leaps beyond what the data allow, they have no less an opportunity to be published in mainline journals as other scholars. But when only 18 articles are submitted to 68 journals in three years, and those articles are submitted apparently by persons not skilled in established scientific methodology and theory, it is inappropriate to invoke censorship. To be published, one must first submit, and scientific creationists are apparently not submitting manuscripts.

It is difficult to accept "surreptitious" literature as establishing a body of empirical, experimental or theoretical science. Outside of creationist sources, therefore, there is no "scientific" creationism. The reason for this is not a conspiracy against scientific creation or scientific creationists, but the scientific shortcomings of the model itself.

We have two additional points. First, there are many epistemologies; science and religion are two. Science is the best procedure human beings have produced to answer questions about the nature of the physical universe. Science is a powerful tool, but it is not a procedure for answering all the questions people wish to ask. Similarly, religion, revelation, or other ways of knowing may be superior for solving certain other human problems. The "problem" of scientific and religious conflict is resolved by many who appreciate the separate realms in which the different epistemologies are best suited. In this, the scientific creationists err, by attempting to overextend one epistemology into an inappropriate realm. Christian religions not based on Biblical literalism long ago made peace with evolution (Frye, 1983).

Second, even though there is no evidence for scientific creationist claims, the movement has had and continues to have an inordinate influence on science education in the United States (Gould, 1982; Futuyma, 1983; Moyer, 1983). A major focus of this effort concerns textbooks, which in most pre-college classrooms *are* the curricula. The proportion of a biology text devoted to evolutionary ideas and evidences has fluctuated through the years (Skoog, 1979; Gould, 1982; Nelkin, 1982). Pre-Scopes books contained more evolution than post-Scopes books. After Sputnik, and increased concern about science education, federal money was put into NSF for science curriculum and textbook development. The evolution-based BSCS books encouraged publishers to include evolution in their books, and evolution began reappearing in American textbooks in the late 60's. The response was short-lived, however, because in the 70's the coverage of evolution in textbooks declined or the treatments were diluted. This is largely due to pressure from creationists and the religious right wing upon Texas and California, two large states which have state-wide adoption of textbooks (Lewin, 1984a). Because of the size of these markets, publishers tend to cater to their wishes. What sells in Texas, therefore, is published for the rest of the country as well. On March 12, 1984, the Texas Attorney General responded to a request from a legislator and issued an opinion that a controversial Texas Board of Education rule was unconstitutional. The rule required that any textbook which dealt with evolution "shall identify it as only one of several explanations of the origins of humankind . . ." and also that "each textbook must carry a statement on the introductory page that any material on evolution is presented as theory rather than fact." No other scientific theory was singled out for this special treatment; this consideration figured in the Attorney General's decision. Since it was left with the prospect of defending itself against a threatened lawsuit without the assistance of the office of the Attorney General, the Texas Board of Education voted on April 13, 1984 to repeal the rule.

The effect of this repeal is uncertain. Texas will have adopted science textbooks for the next six years in November of 1984, unless a proposed one-year delay was enacted. Publishers will not have had time to revise their books before November (assuming they care to); thus books sold outside Texas as well as inside Texas will continue to include a watered-down coverage of evolution. Future editions of textbooks will bear watching. The recent events in Texas *may* bode well for an improvement in science textbooks. Publishers are no longer *required* to dilute the coverage of evolution, but this does not mean they will therefore *strengthen* it. If evolution is *not* covered in the textbooks, there is a slim chance, indeed, of evolution being covered in the classroom. On the other hand, there continues to be considerable opposition to evolution in many parts of the country, and the easiest strategy for teachers is to simply not teach evolution at all, and avoid the controversy, regardless of what is in the textbook.

Although it is relatively easy for one who is versed in the methods, philosophy, and history of science to dismiss the claims of scientific creationists, many science teachers in secondary schools and community colleges find such dismissal not possible. These science teachers are faced with community campaigns for the teaching of scientific creationism by influential persons, some with scientific credentials, who repeatedly claim there is as much, and equally as good, scientific evidence for scientific creationist concepts as there is for evolution. Teachers, school administrators, and lay persons on school boards are hard pressed to deal effectively with these claims. Support from university-level scholars is often crucial to these disputes, but it is not always offered. Objective documentation of the fallaciousness of the scientific creationist claim that their views are based upon scientific evidence provides "ammunition" for these people. We hope the results of our study will be useful for those who directly confront the creationists.

References

ANONYMOUS. 1982. Creation in schools. The decision in McLean vs. the Arkansas Board of Education. *Science*, 215: 934–943. [This is an easily accessible reprinting of Judge William R. Overton's decision in *McLean vs. Arkansas*.]

ANONYMOUS. 1975. Oil seepage rates indicate young age of earth's crust. *Acts and Facts*, September: 5.

AWBREY, F. T. 1984. Space dust, the moon's surface, and the age of the cosmos. *Creation/Evolution*, XIII: 21–29.

BARNES, T. G. 1982. Young age for the moon and earth. *Acts and Facts Impact Series*, #110 (August).

BARTZ, P. A. 1983. Science and refereed papers. *Bible Science Newsletter*, 21(7): 3.

BLUMER, M. 1972. Submarine seeps: are they a major source of open ocean oil pollution? *Science*, 176: 1257–1258.

CHICK, J. T. 1976. *Primal Man?* Chick Publications, P. O. Box 662, Chico, CA 91710.

COFFIN, H. G. 1983. Erect floating stumps in Spirit Lake, Washington. *Geology*, 11: 298–299.

COLE, H. P., and E. C. SCOTT. 1982. Creation Science and scientific research. *Phi Delta Kappan*, April: 557–558.

COLE, J. R. and C. R. GODFREY. In press. The case of the Texas footprints. *Creation/Evolution*.

CREATION RESEARCH SOCIETY. 1976. Statement of belief. *Creation Research Society Quarterly*, September. Statement is repeated in all issues.

DUTCH, S. I. 1982a. Notes on the nature of fringe science. *J. Geol. Educ.*, 30: 6–13.
_____. 1982b. Letter to the editor. *Physics Today*, April: 12.

FUTUYMA, D. J. 1983. *Science on Trial: The Case for Evolution*. Pantheon, New York.

FRITZ, W. J. 1980. Reinterpretation of the depositional environment of the Yellowstone "fossil forests." *Geology*, 8: 309–313.

FRYE, R. M. 1983. So-called "creation-science" and mainstream Christian rejections. *Proc. Am. Philos. Soc.*, 127: 61–70.

GARFIELD, E. 1972. Citation analysis as a tool in journal evaluation. *Science*, 178: 471–479.
_____. 1976. Significant journals of science. *Nature*, 264: 609–615.

GENTRY, R. V. 1982a. Letter to the editor. *Physics Today*, Oct.: 13.
_____. 1982b. The Creator's signature. *Bible-Science Newsletter*, Jan.: 1.

GENTRY, R. V., S. S. CRISTY, J. F. McLAUGHLIN, and J. A. McHUGH. 1974. Ion microprobe confirmation of Po isotope ratios and search for isomer precursors in polonium radiohalos. *Nature*, 244: 282–283.

GISH, D. T., R. B. BLISS, and W. R. BIRD. 1981. Summary of scientific evidence for creation. *Acts and Facts Impact Series*, #95 (May) and #96 (June).

GOULD, S. J. 1982. Moon, Mann and Otto. *Natural History*, 91(3): 4–6, 8, 10.

HASHEMI-NEZHAD, S. R., J. H. FREMLIN, and S. A. DURRANI. 1979. Polonium halos in mica. *Nature*, 278: 333–335.

KATZ, B., and L. KATZ STERNBERGER. 1982. *Magazines for Libraries*. 4th ed. R. R. Bowker Co., New York.

KEITH, M. L., and G. M. ANDERSON. 1963. Radiocarbon dating: fictitious results with mollucs shells. *Science*, 141: 634–636.

KING, D. M., D. D. McDONALD, and N. K. RODERER. 1981. *Scientific Journals in the United States*. Hutchinson Ross, Stroudsburg.

KOFAHL, R. E. 1977. *Handy Dandy Evolution Refuter*. Beta Books, San Diego.

KOFAHL, R. E., and K. L. SEGRAVES. 1975. *The Creation Explanation: A Scientific Alternative to Evolution*. Harold Shaw Publishers, Wheaton.

KRONIK, D. A. 1982. Scientific journals: a review article. *Library Quarterly*, 52: 265–269.

LEWIN, R. 1984a. Antievolution rules are unconstitutional. *Science*, 223: 1373–1374.

____. 1984b. Creationism survives Louisiana legislature. *Science*, 225: 36.

MORRIS, H. M. 1974. *Scientific Creationism*. Public School ed. Creation Life Publishers, San Diego.

____. 1975. Evolutionary smog. *Acts and Facts*, October: 3.

____. 1980. The tenets of creationism. *Acts and Facts Impact Series*, #85 (July).

MORRIS, H. M., and G. PARKER. 1982. *What is Creation Science?* Creation Life Publishers, San Diego.

MORRIS, J. D. 1976. The Paluxy River tracks. *Acts and Facts Impact Series* #35.

MOYER, W. A. 1983. Evolution and young-earth creationism: a manufactured controversy. *Fed. Proc.*, 42: 3025–3032.

____. 1984. Whatever happened to creationism? A: It's still around. *Education Week*, March 21: 24.

NECKIN, D. 1982. *The Creation Controversy*. Norton, New York.

NEUFELD, B. 1975. Dinosaur tracks and giant men. *Origins*, 2(2): 64–76.

PETERSON, H. 1960. Cosmic Spherules and meteoric dust. *Sci. Am.*, February: 123, 125, 126, 128, 130, 131.

RENSCHLER, C. (ed.). 1982. *Library Literature: An Index to Library and Information Science*. H. W. Wilson, Co., New York.

RETALLACK, G. 1981. Comment and reply on "Reinterpretation of the depositional environment of the Yellowstone 'fossil forests.' " *Geology*, 12: 52–54.

SHEEHY, E. P. 1976. *Guide to Reference Books*. American Library Association, Chicago.

SKOOG, G. 1979. The topic of evolution in high school biology textbooks: 1900–1977. *Sci. Ed.*, 63: 621–640.

STIPE, C. E. 1977. Does the ASA take a "position" on controversial issues? *J. Am. Sci. Affil.*, 29: 1–4.

WEBER, C. G. 1981. Paluxy man—the creationist Piltdown. *Creation/Evolution*, 2(4): 16–22.

WEINBERG, S. 1982. Memo to liaisons for Committees of Correspondence, April, p. 1. A privately circulated newsletter.

WHITCOMB, J. C., JR., and H. M. MORRIS, 1961. *The Genesis Flood: The Biblical Record and Its Scientific Implications*. Baker Book House, Grand Rapids.

YURETICH, R. F. 1981. Comment and reply on "Reinterpretation of the depositional environment of the Yellowstone 'fossil forests' " and 'Stumps transported and deposited upright by Mount St. Helens mud flows.' " *Geology*, 12: 146–147.

Narrowing the Spectrum of Student Expression

PERRY A. ZIRKEL

Perry A. Zirkel, Professor of Education and Law at Lehigh University, surveys a problem facing education today, censorship of school publications. Concentrating on the 1988 U.S. Supreme Court ruling against students at Hazelwood East High School in St. Louis, Missouri, he provides his readers in the field of education with an expository overview of cases relating to this controversy. He does have a hint of persuasion in his closing sentence: ". . . students should fear to tread, but school authorities should not rush in."

His sources, all court cases except for one journal article, are cited according to the number system, endnotes that also serve as a bibliography numbered in the order in which they appear in the text.

Original publication: *Phi Delta Kappan*, April 1988.

U nder the supervision of a faculty advisor, Kathy Kuhlmeier and her fellow students in Journalism II at Hazelwood East High School in St. Louis, Missouri, wrote and edited a newspaper called the *Spectrum*. School board policy specified that "school-sponsored publications are developed within the adopted curriculum and its educational implications in regular classroom activities." The Hazelwood East *Curriculum Guide* described Journalism II as "a laboratory situation in which the students publish the school newspaper applying skills they have learned from Journalism I."

The lessons students were to learn from the journalism courses included "the legal, moral, and ethical restrictions imposed upon journalists within the school community." Students in Journalism II were graded, received academic credit, and produced the paper during regular class hours. In line with the standard practice at Hazelwood High, the teacher reviewed the issue of the *Spectrum* for 13 May 1983 and passed it on to Robert Reynolds, the principal, for his approval.

Reynolds did not approve of two articles: one on student pregnancy and another on the impact of divorce on students. The pregnancy article focused on some girls in the school who were or had been pregnant, and it began with the statement that "all names had been changed to keep the identity of these girls a secret." The story included girls' comments about their sexual histories and their use or nonuse of birth control. However, it did not contain graphic accounts of sexual activity.

The article on divorce quoted a student's remarks that were sharply critical of her father, describing him as an inattentive parent who preferred "playing cards with the guys" to being home with the family. Unbeknownst to Reynolds, the faculty advisor had deleted the student's name from the final version of the article.

Given the other identifying information in the pregnancy article and the small number of students in the school, Reynolds judged that article to be a violation of the students' anonymity. He was also concerned about the privacy interests of the students' boyfriends and parents and about the effect of the frank sexual comments on young readers. As for the article on divorce, he felt that as a matter of journalistic fairness the criticized parent should have been given the opportunity to defend himself in the article.

Reynolds did not consult with the students who wrote and edited the *Spectrum*. Instead, concluding that there was no time to make changes in the articles and that the six-page newspaper had to be printed immediately or not at all, he deleted two of the pages from the proofs, thus removing the two problematic articles, along with four others that happened to be on those pages.

The students who produced the paper did not find out about the deletions until the paper was released. In two subsequent meetings with Reynolds, requested by Kathy Kuhlmeier and six other students, the principal did not give his specific reasons for deleting the pages but responded generally that the two articles were "too sensitive [for] our immature audience of readers" and "inappropriate, personal, sensitive, and unsuitable for the newspaper."

The students filed suit, alleging a violation of their First Amendment right to freedom of expression. The federal district court judge issued a judgment in favor of the school district, relying on the curricular character of the *Spectrum*. The students appealed, and the Seventh Circuit decided in their favor, judging the *Spectrum* to be a public forum based on its record of dealing with controversial issues. The school district appealed to the U.S. Supreme Court, which agreed to hear the case.

By a vote of 5 to 3, the Supreme Court held in an opinion by Justice Byron White that "educators do not offend the First Amendment by exercising editorial control over the style and content of student speech in school-sponsored expressive activities so long as their actions are reasonably related to legitimate pedagogical concerns."[1] These varied educational purposes include, for example, "speech that is ungrammatical, poorly written, inadequately researched, biased or prejudiced, vulgar or profane, or unsuitable for immature audiences." The majority concluded, with more deference than scrutiny, that Reynolds acted reasonably in requiring the deletion of the two pages that contained the articles on pregnancy and divorce.

The majority opinion cited the famous *Tinker* decision (1969), which dealt with students' wearing of black armbands as a protest of the Vietnam War, and the more recent *Fraser* decision (1986), which dealt with sexual innuendo in a nominating speech for student elective office. The Court drew a line between punishing a student for "personal expression that happens to occur on the school premises" and censoring "expressive activities that students, parents, and members of the public might reasonably perceive to bear the imprimatur of the school." The majority also rejected the application of the "public forum" doctrine in this case, concluding that the *Spectrum* had not been opened by policy or practice for the indiscriminate use of its student reporters and editors or of the student body generally.

Justice William Brennan, in a dissenting opinion, was not timid in attacking the rationale and application of the majority's holding. Brennan invoked images of "thought police" and "Orwellian 'guardianship of the public mind,' " suggesting that the majority opinion "denuded high school students of much of the First Amendment protection that *Tinker* itself prescribed."

Rejecting the dissent's strict application of *Tinker*, the majority opinion suggested in a footnote that many public schools would probably eliminate their student newspaper altogether rather than open it to "all student expression that does not threaten 'materia[l] disrupt[ion] of classwork' or 'violation of rights that are protected by law,' . . . regardless of how sexually explicit, racially intemperate, or personally insulting that expression might otherwise be." While this ominous prediction may be no more than a straw man, the majority's decision is nonetheless the law of the land.

How broadly does the majority's decision apply? First, the ruling is not limited to student newspapers that are produced in class, for credit, and for grades. Rather than accept the traditional criterion for what constitutes the curriculum as what takes place within the classroom setting, the Court used the following boundary for activities that are part of the curriculum: "as long as they are supervised by faculty members and designed to impart particular knowledge or skills to student participants and audiences."

Second, the Court did not limit its ruling to curriculum-related student newspapers. It specifically targeted "school-sponsored expressive activity" or, more specifically, "school-sponsored publications, theatrical productions, and other expressive activities that students, parents, and members of the community might reasonably perceive to bear the imprimatur of the school." Thus the relaxed standard of "reasonableness," rather than the strict standard of "substantial disruption," apparently applies to school-sponsored plays, which have been the subject of not completely consistent decisions by lower courts.[2]

However, the effect of the *Kuhlmeier* decision on the wide variety of situations in which the freedom of student speech is at issue in the public schools is not entirely clear. The key criterion appears to be whether the activity in question is "school-sponsored,"[3] as broadly defined by the public perception that it bears the imprimatur of the school.

The two sides of the equation seem relatively uncomplicated: 1) where censorship accompanies sponsorship, the odds clearly favor school authorities, who must have a reasonable justification for their actions; and 2) outside the broad boundary of school sponsorship, the courts will apply strict scrutiny, which will require a compelling justification, such as substantial disruption of the educational process or a threat to the safety of students. However, other variables will cause complications: Do the courts consider the expression to be protected by the First Amendment? Have the school authorities taken disciplinary action against students, or have they merely censored student expression? Have the school authorities created a public forum (according to the strict definition given above)?

Consider, for example, a sampling of situations that have arisen in cases considered by lower courts within the past two years. In light of the Supreme Court's line of decisions running from *Tinker* to *Fraser* to *Kuhlmeier*, how would these cases be decided today?

- a school district policy providing for prior review of unofficial (i.e., not school-sponsored) written material on school premises;[4]
- a school newspaper's refusal of an ad from an anti-draft group despite its previous publication of ads from military recruiters;[5]
- a junior high school's restriction of students' distribution of a religious newspaper to an area outside the school building, although the school had a relatively open activities period;[6]
- a suspension of a high school student for wearing a T-shirt depicting the school administrators in an alcoholic stupor;[7] and
- enforcement of dress regulations that resulted in two high school students not being allowed to attend the prom in clothes of the opposite sex.[8]

Of the five cases listed above, the students won the first three, and the administrators won the next two. How would these cases be decided today? The current direction of the line of cases from *Tinker* to *Kuhlmeier* is clear, but its exact breadth and ultimate length must await future decisions. In the meantime, students should fear to tread, but school authorities should not rush in.

Notes

1. *Hazelwood School Dist. v. Kuhlmeier*, 56 U.S.L.W. 4079, 4082 (12 January 1988).

2. *Seyfried v. Walton*, 668 F. 2d 214 (3d Cir. 1981); *Bowman v. Bethel-Tate Bd. of Educ.*, 610 F. Supp. 577 (S.D. Ohio 1985), *vacated*, 798 F. 2d 468 (6th Cir. 1986); and *Bell v. U-32 Bds. of Educ.*, 630 F. Supp. 939 (D. Vt. 1986).

3. Although the lower courts have been split concerning the constitutional protection of student publications, school sponsorship has generally been treated as one distinguishing factor. See Kay Avery and Robert Simpson, "The Constitution and Student Publications: A Comprehensive Approach," *Journal of Law and Education*, vol. 16. 1987, pp. 1–61.

4. *Burch v. Barker*, 651 F. Supp. 1149 (W.D. Wash. 1987); *cf. Bystrom v. Friday*, 822 F. 2d 747 (8th Cir. 1987).

5. *San Diego Comm. Against Registration for the Draft v. Governing Bd. of Groosmont High School*, 790 F. 2d 1471, (9th Cir. 1986).

6. *Thompson v. Waynesboro Area School Dist.*, 673 F. Supp. 1379 (M.D. Pa. 1987).

7. *Gano v. School Dist. No. 411*, 674 F. Supp. 796 (D. Idaho 1987).

8. *Harper v. Edgewood Bd. of Educ.*, 655 F. Supp. 1353 (S.D. Ohio 1987).

•   •   •

Chapter Questions

1. Obviously, subject matter influences a reader's interest. Can you identify anything else the writers of these essays did to attract—and hold—your attention in their research?
2. Which form of documentation illustrated by essays in this chapter is most useful to you? Why?
3. Is there a form of documentation used in this chapter that is distracting from the essay itself?
4. Ignoring the demands of your specific field of study, which method of documentation would you prefer to read?
5. Which method would you prefer to use in your writing?
6. Which style sheet best fulfills the demands of your field (regardless of whether it is currently used)?
7. Which author has most effectively incorporated research material into the essay?
8. Study the examples of satire in this chapter (and those in previous chapters). What special demands does satire make of readers?
9. Did the authors of these selections meet your expectations and demands as a reader of research? Did you learn anything new about using research in your own writing?

AUTHOR INDEX

Agee, James, 61
Angelou, Maya, 3
Baker, Russell, 14
Baldwin, James, 20
Broyard, Anatole, 24
Buck, Pearl S., 127
Campbell, James, 206
Clarke, Gerald, 137
Coleman, Bob, 241
Coles, Robert, 141
Dentzer, Susan with Maggie Malone, 65
Dudley, Susan, 147
Dyson, Freeman, 29
Ericson, Carl E., 208
Fimrite, Ron, 69
Fussell, Paul, 247
Gates, Henry Louis, Jr., 150
Geiger, H. Jack, 200
Gould, Stephen Jay, 199, 257
Hacker, Randi and Jackie Kaufman, 263
Hillesum, Etty, 38
Huxtable, Ada Louise, 218
James, P. D., 205
Jenkinson, Edward B., 267
Keillor, Garrison, 73
Langbell, Kenneth, 221
Lehmann-Haupt, Christopher, 211
Lorenz, Konrad Z., 79

Lucas, F. L., 157
Maddocks, Melvin, 223
Malone, Dumas, 274
Marius, Richard, 41, 88
McPhee, John, 96
Mencken, H. L., 225
Miner, Horace, 285
Montagu, Ashley, 203
Muyskens, James L., 290
Paterson, Judith H., 165, 228
Paulk, Tom, 50
Pett, Saul, 111
Price, Reynolds, 167
Raspberry, William, 171
Reed, J. D., 213
Russell, John, 230
Safire, William, 173
Sayre, Zelda [Fitzgerald], 233
Scott, Eugenie C. and Henry P. Cole, 294
Sheppard, R. Z., 176
Simpkins, Daphne, 236
Smith, Scottie Fitzgerald, 51
Stone, John, 115, 115
Thurber, James, 121, 185
Time, 214
Wideman, John Edgar, 55
Wright, Frank Lloyd, 187
Zakaria, Fareed, 191
Zirkel, Perry A., 309

SELECTION INDEX

A Humid Recital Stirs Bangkok,   221

A Major Chicago Firm at Its Centennial, 218

A Scientific Apprenticeship,   29

A Taste for Death,   205

Abortion Issues Affect Real Women in Real World,   147

Acting Alone,   290

America's Medieval Women,   127

An Interrupted Life,   38

At the College, 1760–1762,   274

At the Forks,   61

Babel Builders,   223

The Beautiful and Damned: *Friend Husband's Latest*,   233

Body Ritual Among the Nacirema,   285

Book Won't Mystify,   236

Books Fit for Rooftop Delivery,   200

Books of the Times,   211

Cadence of the Heart,   115

Crime's LeCarre,   213

The Decline of Editing,   176

Disney's Cinesymphony,   214

Don't They Know Education Takes Evil Out of Evolution?,   182

The Elusive Scientific Basis of Creation Science,   294

England Rediscovers Its Age of Chivalry, 230

Ethics for Greedheads,   191

Euphemism,   173

Foreward,   51

Gamalielese,   225

Gatsby at the B School,   141

Growing Up,   14

The Headmaster,   96

The Heros of Our Times,   167

The Home That Lies Always in Memory, 41

How I Write,   88

How It Was in America a Week Ago Tuesday   73

How To Tell A Fine Old Wine,   121

I Know Why the Caged Bird Sings,   3

JFK Slaying "Cut the Heart of a Nation", 111

Killing, in Verse and Prose,   247

The Language of Animals,   79

Let the Dying Die Gracefully,   165

Looking into the Murky and Murderous, 206

The Modern Way of Dying,   228

The Money Chase,   171

Money Majors,   105

More Variations on a Biological Theme, 203

Moving Day,   24

Much About Wallace Has Changed As He Campaigns for Nomination,   109

M.B.A.'s Learn a Human Touch,   65

Narrowing the Spectrum of Student Expression,   309

The Need for New Myths,   137

The New Age of Schoolbook Protest,   267

Notes of a Native Son,   20

Organic Architecture,   187

The Panda's Thumb,   199

Science Writing,   241

The Sisters Brontë and The Sisters Collins, 263

Theology Today,   208

Thoughts on Myself That I'm Willing to Share,   50

To Robby,   55

Turning Nature's Sprawl Into Literature, 200

What Is Style?   157

When the World Series Became "A Modest Little Sporting Event",   69

Which,   185

Whose Canon Is It, Anyway?   150

The Wolf Inside,   115

Women's Brains,   257

Acknowledgments

Maya Angelou. "I Know Why the Caged Bird Sings," from *I Know Why the Caged Bird Sings* by Maya Angelou. Copyright © 1969 by Maya Angelou. Reprinted by permission of Random House, Inc.

Russell Baker. "Growing Up," from *Growing Up* by Russell Baker. Copyright © 1982 by Russell Baker. Reprinted by permission of Congdon & Weed, Chicago.

James Baldwin. Excerpted from *Notes of a Native Son.* Copyright © 1955, renewed 1983, by James Baldwin. Reprinted by permission of Beacon Press.

Anatole Broyard. "Moving Day: The Books I Left Behind," from *The New York Times Book Review.* Copyright © 1989 by and reprinted by permission of Anatole Broyard.

Freeman Dyson. "A Scientific Apprenticeship," from *Disturbing the Universe* by Freeman Dyson. Copyright © 1979 by Freeman Dyson. Reprinted by permission of HarperCollins Publishers.

Etty Hillesum. Excerpted from *An Interrupted Life: The Diaries of Etty Hillesum 1941–43.* Copyright © 1983 by and reprinted by permission of Uiteverij Balans and Jonathan Cape Ltd.

Richard Marius. "The Home That Lies Always in Memory," by Richard Marius from *Touchstone.* Copyright © by and reprinted by permission of Richard Marius.

Tom Paulk. "Thoughts on Myself That I'm Willing to Share," by Thomas Paulk. Copyright © by Thomas Paulk.

Scottie Fitzgerald Smith. Foreword by Scottie Fitzgerald Smith to *Bits of Paradise: 21 Uncollected Stories by F. Scott and Zelda Fitzgerald,* selected by Matthew J. Bruccoli. Copyright © 1973 by Mrs. F. Scott Fitzgerald Smith. Reprinted with permission of Charles Scribner's Sons, an imprint of Macmillan Publishing Company.

John Edgar Wideman. "To Robby," by John Edgar Wideman. Copyright © 1981 by John Edgar Wideman. Reprinted by permission of Wylie, Aitken & Stone, Inc.

James Agee. "At the Forks," from *Let Us Now Praise Famous Men* by James Agee and Walker Evans. Copyright 1939 and 1940 by James Agee. Copyright 1941 by James Agee and Walker Evans. Copyright © renewed 1969 by Mia Fritsch Agee and Walker Evans. Reprinted by permission of Houghton Mifflin Company.

Susan Dentzer. "MBA's Learn a Human Touch," from *Newsweek.* Copyright © 1986 by Susan Dentzer. Reprinted by permission of Newsweek, Inc.

Ron Fimrite. "When the World Series Became 'A Modest Little Sporting Event'," by Ron Fimrite, from *Sports Illustrated* October 30, 1989. Copyright © by and reprinted by permission of The Time Inc. Magazine Company. All rights reserved.

Garrison Keillor. "How it Was in America a Week Ago Tuesday," from *Happy To Be Here,* by Garrison Keillor. Copyright © 1986 by Garrison Keillor. Reprinted by permission of Penguin USA.

Konrad Z. Lorenz. "The Language of Animals," from *King Solomon's Ring,* by Konrad Z. Lorenz. Copyright © 1952 by Konrad Z. Lorenz. Reprinted by permission of HarperCollins Publishers.

Richard Marius. "How I Write," from *Writers on Writing,* Vol. II, by Tom Waldrep. Copyright © 1988 by Richard Marius. Reprinted by permission of Richard Marius and Tom Waldrep.

John McPhee. "The Headmaster," from *Headmaster,* by John McPhee. Collected in *The John McPhee Reader,* by John McPhee. Copyright © 1966 by John McPhee. Reprinted by permission of Vintage Books, an imprint of Random House.

Editors of *U.S. News & World Report.* "Money Majors." Copyright © 1987 by and reprinted with permission of U.S. News & World Report.

Editors of *The New York Times.* "Much About Wallace Has Changed As He Campaigns for Nomination," from *The Montgomery Advertiser and Alabama Journal.* Copyright © 1976 by and reprinted by permission of The New York Times Company.

Saul Pett. "JFK Slaying 'Cut the Heart of a Nation'," by Saul Pett. From *The Montgomery Advertiser and Alabama Journal*. Copyright © 1988 by and reprinted by permission of The Montgomery Advertiser and Alabama Journal.

John Stone. "Cadence of the Heart," by John Stone. Copyright © 1988 by The New York Times Company. Reprinted by permission.

John Stone. "The Wolf Within," by John Stone. Copyright © 1988 by The New York Times Company. Reprinted by permission.

James Thurber. "How to Tell a Fine Old Wine," by James Thurber, from *Collecting Himself*, ed. M. Rosen, published by Harper & Row. Copyright © 1989 by and reprinted by permission of Rosemary A. Thurber.

Pearl S. Buck. "America's Medieval Women," by Pearl S. Buck, from *Harper's*. Copyright © 1938 Pearl S. Buck. Reprinted by permission of Harper's.

Gerald Clarke. "The Need for New Myths," by Gerald Clarke. Copyright © 1972 by and reprinted by permission of Time Inc.

Robert Coles. "Gatsby at the B School," by Robert Coles, from *The New York Times Book Review*. Copyright © 1987 by and reprinted by permission of The New York Times Company.

Susan Dudley. "Abortion Issues Affect Women in Real World," by Susan Dudley, from *The Montgomery Advertiser and Alabama Journal*. Copyright © 1989 by Susan Dudley. Reprinted by permission of The Montgomery Advertiser and Alabama Journal.

Henry L. Gates. "Whose Canon Is It, Anyway?" by Henry L. Gates, from *The New York Times Book Review*. Copyright © 1989 by and reprinted by permission of The New York Times Company.

F. L. Lucas. "What is Style?" by F. L. Lucas, from *Holiday*. Copyright © 1960 by F. L. Lucas. Reprinted by permission of Holiday/Curtiss.

Judith H. Paterson. "Let the Dying Die Gracefully," by Judith H. Paterson, from *The Los Angeles Times*. Copyright © 1987 by and reprinted by permission of Judith H. Paterson.

Reynolds Price. "The Heroes of Our Time," by Reynolds Price, from *Saturday Review*. Copyright © by and reprinted by permission of Reynolds Price.

William Raspberry. "The Money Chase," by William Raspberry, from *The Washington Post*. Copyright © 1987 by and reprinted by permission of The Washington Post Writers Group.

William Safire. "Euphemism," by William Safire, from *On Language*. Copyright © 1981 by William Safire. Reprinted by permission of Morton L. Janklow Assoc., Inc.

R. Z. Sheppard. "The Decline of Editing," by R. Z. Sheppard, from *Time*, as reported by John M. Scott and Janice C. Simpson. Copyright © 1980 by and reprinted by permission of Time Inc.

Daphne Simpkins. "Don't They Know Education Takes Evil Out of Education?" by Daphne Simpkins, appeared in "Perspective," from *The Atlanta Journal-Constitution*. Copyright © 1989 by and reprinted by permission of Daphne Simpkins.

James Thurber. "Which," by James Thurber, from *The New Yorker*, collected in *The Owl in the Attic*, published by Harper & Row. Copyright © 1931, 1959 James Thurber. Reprinted by permission of Rosemary Thurber.

Frank Lloyd Wright. "Organic Architecture," by Frank Lloyd Wright, from *Common Sense*. Copyright 1941 by Frank Lloyd Wright. Reprinted by permission of the Estate of Frank Lloyd Wright.

Fareed Zakaria. "Ethics for Greedheads," by Fareed Zakaria, from *The New Republic*. Copyright © 1987 by and reprinted by permission of The New Republic, Inc.

Editors of *Sciquest*. "Books Fit for Rooftop Delivery." Copyright © 1980 by and reprinted by permission of Sciquest.

H. Jack Geiger. "Turning Nature's Sprawl into Literature," by H. Jack Geiger, from *The New York Times Book Review*. Copyright © 1980 by and reprinted by permission of The New York Times Company.

Ashley Montagu. "More Variations on a Biological Theme," by Ashley Montagu, from *Nature*, December 4, 1980. Copyright © 1980 by and reprinted by permission of Nature, a subsidiary of Macmillan Magazines Ltd.

James Campbell. "Looking into the Murky and Murderous," by James Campbell, from *The Times Literary Supplement*. Copyright © 1986 by and reprinted by permission of The Times Literary Supplement.

Carl E. Ericson. Review in *Theology Today* by Carl E. Ericson. Copyright © 1988 by and reprinted by permission of Theology Today.

Christopher Lehmann-Haupt. "Books of The Times," by Christopher Lehmann-Haupt, from *The New York Times Book Review*. Copyright © 1986 by and reprinted by permission of The New York Times Company.